JAMES H. SOLTOW

# THE STRUGGLE FOR NEUTRALITY

ALBERT HALL BOWMAN

# THE STRUGGLE FOR NEUTRALITY

Franco-American Diplomacy During the Federalist Era

*The University of Tennessee Press: Knoxville*

*Library of Congress Cataloging in Publication Data*

Bowman, Albert Hall, 1921—
  The struggle for neutrality: Franco-American
diplomacy during the federalist era.

  Bibliography: p.
  1. United States—Foreign relations—France.
2. France—Foreign relations—United States.
3. United States—Foreign relations—Constitutional
period, 1789–1809.  I. Title.
E183.8.F8B65        327.73′044        73–21917
ISBN 0–87049–152–0

*Publication of this book was assisted by the American Council of Learned Societies under a grant from the Andrew W. Mellon Foundation.*

*To Vicki, Betsy, and Cathy,*
who grew up with it.

# Preface

No period in American history save our own has been so dominated by foreign concerns as that covered in this book. It was the ironic American fate that a new, weak, and isolated republic, groping for identity and a place in a largely hostile world of traditional monarchies, was caught between the two superpowers of that day in their titanic struggle to determine, not only which power would dominate Europe, but which political ideology would dominate the future. It was not enough that Americans had to organize and establish a new system of government, create and confirm the institutions of a free society, rationalize relations between social and economic groups and interests and between states and nation in the new federal system. Americans and their government had to meet and respond to the demands of great powers, Great Britain and France in particular, which tended to think of small powers as pawns. The resulting pressures produced sudden shifts in American foreign policies; passionate political conflict, with alarming assaults on individual freedoms; and, eventually, war with each of the European giants—an undeclared war with France in the first phase, and a declared one with Britain in the second.

In the first phase, 1793–1801, relations between the United States and France illustrate dramatically the effect of these stresses and strains. Although the United States owed its independence to the Anglo-French competition for supremacy, the French Revolution, which converted France into a republic, complicated the great-power struggle by adding an ideological element. Since most Americans saw the French Revolution in its early stages as an extension of American ideals, this great convulsion intensified the American problem by reviving issues and passions related to liberty at home. The "struggle for neutrality," therefore, was waged on both foreign and domestic fronts, against the efforts of both Britain and France to use the United States against each other, and against the efforts of American enthusiasts for one or the other to abet their aims.

It is in this context that the experiment in unpartisan government collapsed at the end of 1793, with the retirement of Thomas Jefferson as secretary of state. Thereafter, American policy tended more and more, under the leadership of Alexander Hamilton and his followers, to favor Britain against France. Those who followed the leads of Jefferson and of James Madison, the earliest opponent of Hamiltonian programs, resisted as much as they could; but within the government, dissidents were expelled as quickly, and as harshly, as circumstances permitted. The consequence of Federalist policy was the undeclared war with France which President Adams belatedly stopped by negotiating peace, thereby splitting his party and paving the way for its defeat in the election of 1800.

Given the centrality of relations with France during this period, it is remarkable that the French archival sources have never before been systematically exploited. Some diplomatic historians —notably Samuel F. Bemis and Alexander DeConde—have used them, as have biographers—such as Dumas Malone, Peter Hill, and, especially, Irving Brant—but their principal focus was elsewhere. One of my purposes has been to give equal attention to the French side of the French-American equation and to balance traditional American views with French ones. I have also tried to unravel events which have usually been treated ambiguously and have sometimes dissented sharply from traditional explanations.

The Jay Treaty was the central event of the Federalist period. I concur with the most recent historian of that treaty—that both Federalists and Republicans in their conflicting approaches to it "balanced goals with the power available." (Jerald Combs, *The Jay Treaty*.) I agree also that Federalist ideas sprang from a consciousness of American weakness, while Republicans saw American strengths. Both earlier and later historians of Jay's treaty,

Samuel F. Bemis and Combs, present accounts which lean to the side of American strength, yet both conclude that the Federalists were right. Combs points out this contradiction in Bemis and then repeats it in his own work. The power of tradition and the weight of repetitive, one-sided argument have long been formidable obstacles to independent judgment.

My conviction is that the struggle of the decade involved contrasting ideas of American power primarily as a practical, immediate consideration. More important and basically controlling were competing visions of the American future. Federalists agreed in varying degrees on the creation of a traditional society, one dominated by an aristocracy of wealth and learning—the wise, the rich, and the good, as Federalists were fond of saying—although probably few shared Hamilton's dream of a glorious, powerful, and martial empire second to none. Despite wide differences in Federalist attitudes and motives, however, it was Hamilton who dominated Federalist foreign policy from 1794 until the break with Adams in 1799.

Hamiltonian policy tended inevitably to involvement in international affairs, but Republicans generally, despite the enthusiasm of many for the French experiment with liberty, were isolationists, wanting to shun Old World contagion and keep America pure, to grow and prosper in liberty and tranquillity. Republicans fought Federalist foreign policy not only because it was inimical to the preservation of liberty in France, but also because they feared its suppression at home.

French policy toward the United States ran the gamut as revolutionary governments succeeded each other too fast for Americans to follow. Girondist expectations of American participation in a common crusade for "liberty, equality, and fraternity" gave way to more sober considerations of mutual self-interest under the Jacobins; but after the Jay Treaty, French policy under the Directory became punitive toward America. The rejection of Charles Cotesworth Pinckney and the "XYZ affair" almost led to formal hostilities between the two countries, and the French side of those stories has not been told before. It was during these episodes that Talleyrand was converted into an apostle of peace; French records show to my satisfaction that Talleyrand, having failed to bring the Directory to agree to negotiations with the Pinckney-Marshall-Gerry mission, was mainly responsible for bringing peace in 1800. Perhaps not surprisingly, French historians have given as little attention to American attitudes and responses to all of this as American historians have given to those of France. It is the aim of this book to repair omissions on both sides.

Over the years I have incurred obligations to many institutions and individuals. The Library of Congress provided much more than the indispensable manuscript collections on which this study is based, but I am particularly grateful to two librarians of the Manuscripts Division, Dr. Percy Powell and Mr. John de-Porry. I began my work long ago at the Butler Library of Columbia University and the New-York Historical Society, and since then I have been cheerfully welcomed at the Massachusetts Historical Society, at the archives of the French Foreign Office on the Quai D'Orsay, and at the Knoxville and Chattanooga libraries of the University of Tennessee. I am indebted for financial assistance on different occasions to the Southern Fellowships Fund and to the University of Chattanooga Foundation.

The assistance and, especially, encouragement and friendship for many years, of Dumas Malone of Columbia University and the University of Virginia have been invaluable to me. Lawrence S. Kaplan of Kent State University has been an unfailing source of inspiration and encouragement, as was Irving Brant years ago. I would also like to express my gratitude to Stephen G. Kurtz and James H. Hutson, both formerly of the Institute of Early American History and Culture, both for their good-humored criticisms and for their friendly encouragement.

ALBERT HALL BOWMAN

*Chattanooga, Tennessee*
*January, 1973*

# Contents

# Abbreviated Titles

AECPE-U Archives des Affaires Étrangères, Correspondance Politique, États-Unis. (The first number after the source is the volume number; volumes cited, as in F. O., include 35–52.)

*Works of Adams* Charles F. Adams, ed., *The Works of John Adams.*

*ASP, Commerce and Navigation* Walter Lowrie and Matthew St. Clair Clarke, eds., *American State Papers, Class IV. Commerce and Navigation.*

*ASP, FR* *American State Papers. Class I. Foreign Relations.*

C. F. M. Frederick J. Turner, ed., "Correspondence of French Ministers to the United States 1791–1797."

*DAB* Allen Johnson and Dumas Malone, eds., *Dictionary of American Biography.*

F. O. Great Britain, Public Records Office, Foreign Office. (The first number is the volume number; volumes cited include 4–29.)

*Hamilton Papers*     Harold Syrett and Jacob E. Cooke, eds., *The Papers of Alexander Hamilton.*

*Works of Hamilton*     Henry Cabot Lodge, ed., *The Works of Alexander Hamilton.*

I. B. M.     Bernard Mayo, ed., "Instructions to the British Ministers to the United States, 1791–1812."

*Jefferson Papers*     Julian P. Boyd, ed., *The Papers of Thomas Jefferson.*

FORD, *Jefferson's Writings*     Paul L. Ford, ed., *The Writings of Thomas Jefferson.*

L & B, *Writings of Jefferson*     Andrew A. Lipscomb and Albert E. Bergh, eds., *The Writings of Thomas Jefferson.*

*Writings of Madison*     Gaillard Hunt, ed., *The Writings of James Madison.*

*Writings of Monroe*     Stanislaus M. Hamilton, ed., *The Writings of James Monroe.*

Otto, "Considérations"     Louis-Guillaume Otto, "Considérations sur la conduite du gouvernement Américain envers la France, depuis le commencement de la Révolution jusqu'en 1797."

*Writings of Washington*     John C. Fitzpatrick, ed., *The Writings of George Washington.*

*Oliver Wolcott*    George Gibbs, ed., *Memoirs of the Administrations of Washington and John Adams, edited from the Papers of Oliver Wolcott, Secretary of the Treasury.*

*W & M Quarterly*    *William and Mary Quarterly.*

# THE STRUGGLE FOR NEUTRALITY

## CHAPTER I

The New Nation

Hail Glorious Spirit of the Times!
Before thee Tyrants sink, and crimes;
Truth, at thy Torch, her Lamp illumes,
Before its flames pale Vice consumes,
While, from this conflagrating earth,
The Phenix Virtue springs to birth.

> NEW YEAR'S GREETING FROM THE
> CARRIER OF THE *American*
> *Mercury*, JANUARY 1, 1793.

LOOKING back over the generation before Thomas Jefferson's inauguration as president of the United States in 1801, John Adams's friend Christopher Gadsden had reason to complain: "Long have I been led to think our planet a mere bedlam, and the uncommonly extravagant ravings of our own time . . . have greatly increased and confirmed that opinion."[1] Adams, who at this time must have felt that he was bedlam's chief lunatic, probably agreed.[2]

Gadsden had shared the American "bedlam" since its beginnings more than three decades earlier in the aftermath of the French and Indian War. A South Carolina delegate to the Stamp Act Congress of 1765, he was distinguished for his extravagant ravings against Parliament's right to tax the American colonies. He served in the First and Second Continental Congresses, leaving to join South Carolina's forces opposing the British, and he was instrumental in securing the disestablishment of the church

---

[1] Gadsden to Adams, Mar. 11, 1801, *Works of Adams* 10 vols. (Boston, 1856), IX, 579.

[2] "To the Printers of the Boston Patriot," 1809, *ibid.*, IX, 310.

and the popular election of senators in the South Carolina Constitution of 1778. As "A Steady and Open Republican," Gadsden supported the federal Constitution in the up-hill struggle for ratification in South Carolina in 1788, but he was also a leader of the opposition in his state to the Jay Treaty with Great Britain in 1795.[3]

In 1800, Gadsden had emerged briefly from a retirement of several years to support his old friend for the last time, and he sympathized deeply with Adams's hurt and frustration at being rejected by his countrymen so soon after performing what Adams thereafter regarded as the greatest of his public services: the re-establishment of peace with France. One of the major causes of the bedlam Gadsden deplored was the noise accompanying the progress of American relations with France from the alliance of 1778 and its initial fulfillment in the establishment of American independence, through the desuetude of the Confederation years and its revival with the outbreak of a new Anglo-French war, to the undeclared Franco-American war and its settlement in 1800. John Adams had been in the thick of events from the beginning; at the end, he was the central figure, if not the principal victim.

French aid was decisive in winning American independence, and in the years following the Peace of 1783 virtually all Americans continued to entertain fraternal sentiments toward France. The alliance between the two countries was the cornerstone of American foreign policy as the new federal government took office in 1789, notwithstanding the view of some Americans that it had expired with the successful conclusion of the War of the American Revolution.[4] The opening scenes of France's revolution rekindled American enthusiasm for the great ally now ex-

3Allen Johnson and Dumas Malone, eds., *DAB* VII, 82–83; Gordon S. Wood, *The Creation of the American Republic* (Chapel Hill, 1969), 560, 560n.; Marvin R. Zahniser, *Charles Cotesworth Pinckney: Founding Father* (Chapel Hill, 1967), 125.

4Alexander DeConde, "Washington's Farewell, the French Alliance, and the Election of 1796," *Mississippi Valley Historical Review* 43 (Mar. 1957), 641; Alexander DeConde, *Entangling Alliance* (Durham, N. C., 1958), viii, 4–5, 9–15. Speaking in the Federal Convention of 1787, James Madison said that he believed that it was to the rivalry between England and France that "we owe perhaps our liberty." Felix Gilbert, *To the Farewell Address* (Princeton, 1961), 89.

perimenting with the American example of liberty. Furthermore, experience had shown Americans that their country was weak and alone in a hostile world, and they tended to look again to France for protection and support.

A sentimental attachment for France was comfortable and harmless during the decade after the establishment of peace. The resumption of war between France and Great Britain in February 1793, however, posed most serious problems for the new nation. There were the treaties of 1778: the alliance which, although defensive, committed the United States in perpetuity to the guarantee to France of her West Indian islands; and the treaty of commerce, by which the two countries had granted each other reciprocal advantages and obligated themselves to deny other rights to the enemies of either party in time of war. Although the denial of rights to the enemies of one party or the other was ambiguous and later caused trouble—for example, the prohibitions against the issuance of commissions or letters of marque (ARTICLE 21) and against outfitting and receiving enemy privateers (ART. 22) and were susceptible to conflicting interpretations—the most important provision of the treaty was the unambiguous declaration that

> free Ships shall also give a freedom to Goods, and that everything shall be deemed free and exempt, which shall be found on board the Ships belonging to the Subjects of either of the Confederates, although the whole lading or any Part thereof should appertain to the Enemies of either, contraband Goods being always excepted.[5]

If any single principle of foreign policy rested at the center of United States foreign embroilments during the era of the French Revolution, it was the principle that "free ships make free goods." How that principle became American doctrine tells much about the American attitude toward the world outside.

---

[5] These treaties may most conveniently be found in Hunter Miller, ed., *Treaties and Other International Acts of the United States of America, 1776–1863* (Washington, D. C., 1931), II, 3–34, 35–44. For the guarantee of the French islands, ART. 11 of the Treaty of Alliance, see 39–40; for the "free ships, free goods" stipulation of the commercial treaty, ART. 23, see 20–21.

On June 11, 1776, the Continental Congress adopted three great resolutions and appointed committees to implement them: one, to declare independence of Great Britain; a second, to propose a treaty to France; and a third, to prepare articles of confederation to be proposed to the states. The committee to draft a model of a treaty to be proposed to France consisted of John Adams, Benjamin Franklin, John Dickinson, Benjamin Harrison, and Robert Morris. To Adams was delegated the actual drafting of the Model Treaty, which he accomplished with the benefit of "a printed volume of treaties" in which Franklin had marked some articles for his particular notice.[6]

Evidently, Adams relied principally upon two Anglo-French commercial treaties, those of 1686 and the still-born one of 1713, which was signed on the same day as the Peace of Utrecht. The latter treaty was especially liberal: it contained a precise and extremely limited list of goods designated contraband in wartime; the principle that neutrals should have the right to trade with belligerents; and a provision that free ships gave enemy goods immunity to seizure. These principles were incorporated in the Model Treaty, which the Continental Congress adopted. They went a long way toward the complete freedom and equality of commerce which Adams and his colleagues ardently desired.[7]

It was a cardinal principle of enlightened eighteenth-century thought that commercial rivalries and conflicts were fundamental causes of war, and that commercial treaties had generally perpetuated the causes of conflict. Since they were usually incorporated in treaties of alliance, commerce itself was an instrument

[6] *Works of Adams* II, 510–17; Gilbert, 48–50.

[7] Gilbert, 50–52; Samuel F. Bemis, *The Diplomacy of the American Revolution* (New York, 1935), 46; Arthur M. Wilson, *French Foreign Policy During the Administration of Cardinal Fleury* (Cambridge, Mass., 1936), 46–47; Charles Petrie, *Earlier Diplomatic History* (London, 1949), 234. Wilson notes that the proposed Anglo-French commercial treaty of 1713 "would probably have been of great value to France, and which the House of Commons, suspecting such to be the case, refused to ratify." Petrie, however, remarks of Bolingbroke, who negotiated the treaty for England: "In this respect he was too far in advance of his age." For a concise history of the development of the "free ships, free goods" concept, see J. Holland Rose, A. P. Newton, and E. A. Benians, eds., *The Cambridge History of the British Empire* I (Cambridge, England, 1929), 548–53.

of power politics. Separating commercial from political arrangements, therefore, was the first step toward neutralizing commerce in the political struggle. A second step was to avoid political arrangements altogether. Thus the United States, abjuring the traditional accommodations of European politics and trading on free and equal terms with all, could avoid embroilment in Europe's constant wars. Furthermore, the new nation would be contributing to the creation of a new era in international relations.[8]

The millennium of free trade had not arrived, although France was happy to promote it as a weapon against England. France did accept the separation of commercial arrangements from the political alliance which, as Congress had feared, the exigencies of war required. The principles of the Model Treaty—free ships make free goods, a narrow definition of articles to be declared contraband, and a limitation of the concept of blockade to cases where it was actually effective—became the provisions of the commercial treaty with France and the *sine qua non* of treaties the Confederation Congress sought to conclude with other powers after the peace. Some successes were achieved; but Britain, the most important trading empire, refused to be convinced.

Foreign commerce was a principal impetus behind the movement for a new constitution.[9] In No. 45 of *The Federalist*, James Madison asserted that the proposed new system of government merely "invigorated" powers of the old Confederation, except for one feature: the power to regulate commerce. "But that seems to be an addition which few oppose, and from which no apprehensions are entertained."[10] Commerce had in fact long been for Madison, as for many other thoughtful leaders, the Achilles' heel of American sovereignty. In 1786, Madison lamented "the present anarchy of our commerce" to his friend Thomas Jefferson,

8Gilbert, ch. 3, analyzes Enlightenment ideas on foreign relations as pointing toward a "Novus Ordo Seculorum."

9Vernon G. Setser, *The Commercial Reciprocity Policy of the United States, 1774–1829* (Philadelphia, 1937), 58, dates the origin of the movement resulting in the Constitutional Convention of 1787 at Sept. 29, 1783, when Congress adopted a committee report embodying a program to aid commerce.

10Jacob E. Cooke, ed., *The Federalist* (Middletown, Conn., 1961), 314.

then American minister at Paris. "In fact, most of our political evils may be traced up to our commercial one, and most of our moral may to our political."[11]

Contemporary writers agreed. Timothy Pitkin reminded his readers: "this unfortunate state of American commerce, it is well known, was one of the principal causes of the adoption of the present Constitution." And about the same time, Adam Seybert stated the case even more emphatically: ". . . it was absolutely necessary, that the power to regulate and control our intercourse with foreign nations, should be confided to Congress alone; and it was that conviction, which, principally, induced the people of the United States to call the Convention to revise the articles of the Confederation."[12]

The reasons for the "anarchy of our commerce" are fairly clear. Before the Revolution, membership in the British mercantilist empire conferred upon colonial commerce valuable privileges and protection and, most important, a place in the commercial order of the European world. With a predominantly extractive economy, Britain's colonies in America fulfilled the requirements of mercantilism, exporting raw materials to England and importing manufactured goods. The factoring and credit operations of this trade, and therefore most of the profit, accrued to British merchants.

In the Treaty of Commerce of 1778, France had granted the United States a limited entry into its mercantilist system, primarily to encourage American independence of Great Britain, but also in the hope of permanently diverting a large share of the American trade from her powerful rival. John Adams persuaded the Dutch to sign a commercial treaty with the United States in 1782, and Benjamin Franklin signed one with Sweden in 1783, but both the United Netherlands and Sweden were members of

11Madison to Jefferson, Mar. 18, 1786, in *Letters and Other Writings of James Madison, published under the direction of the Congress of the United States* (Philadelphia, 1865), I, 226–27. Dumas Malone, *Jefferson and the Rights of Man* (Boston, 1951), 21–22.

12Timothy Pitkin, *A Statistical View of the Commerce of the United States* 2d ed. (Hartford, 1817); Adam Seybert, *Statistical Annals* (Philadelphia, 1818).

the Armed Neutrality of 1780 and thus at war with Britain. Neither power, of course, was the equal of the British or French imperial systems in commercial importance to the United States, although Dutch bankers provided invaluable financial assistance during and after the Revolution.

France, however, reverted to protectionism after the peace because she could not compete successfully with Britain; and Spain, next of the imperial powers in commercial importance to the United States, remained oblivious to liberal commercial principles until after its empire was gone, partly owing to more than a century of British commercial encroachment. Despite American dreams of a new liberal commercial order which had received persuasive support with the publication in 1776 of Adam Smith's *An Inquiry into the Nature and Causes of the Wealth of Nations*, the United States was born into a mercantilist world of closed imperial economic systems.[13]

In accordance with the spirit of the generous Treaty of Peace with the United States and the free-trade ideas of his friend Adam Smith, the Earl of Shelburne proposed to complete an Anglo-American rapprochement by offering full commercial reciprocity. By the time Parliament took up his American Intercourse Bill in 1783, however, Shelburne's ministry had fallen; his interim successor, the younger William Pitt, was lukewarm; and the Fox-North coalition, which came to power in the midst of the debates, was hostile. While Shelburne would have restored the old complementary commercial relationship between the two countries—Britain the manufacturer and carrier, the United States the customer and producer of raw materials—confirmed mercantilists feared that reciprocity would encourage an ultimately successful American challenge to the British carrying trade, particularly that of the West Indies, which produced the trained seamen who constituted the vital foundation of naval predominance.[14]

---

13Setser, *Commercial Reciprocity*, 2–3. See Merrill Jensen, *The New Nation* (New York, 1950), ch. 7.

14Richard B. Morris, *The Peacemakers: The Great Powers and American Inde-*

No doubt, the defenders of the navigation system were supported by vengeful Tories determined to punish the former colonies for their impertinence of rebellion. Both motives were served by the famous pamphlet of that uncompromising champion of mercantilism, Lord Sheffield—*Observations on the Commerce of the United States*, published in 1783 in London. Lord Sheffield argued that letting Americans carry their own produce to British West Indian colonies would lead to the loss of the carrying trade and, ultimately, maritime supremacy. Furthermore, the United States deserved no special consideration and its trade would soon be forced back into its traditional British channels anyway. His Lordship proved to be right in the short run, and for practical purposes the United States remained economically an English colony, but without the advantages formerly enjoyed.[15]

Parliament through temporizing had slipped into a policy of economic nationalism directed against the United States. Rather than treat the substance of the issue, it gave the King-in-Council temporary authority to regulate Anglo-American trade. Lord Sheffield's victory over Shelburne was fixed by the Order-in-Council of July 2, 1783, prohibiting trade in American vessels between the West Indies and the United States. Until this event, John Jay and the other peace commissioners had clung to a hope that England would agree to favorable commercial arrangements. But now Jay sailed for home, convinced that only by establishing its own navigation system in retaliation could the United States induce Britain to respect American commercial interests.[16]

Jay became secretary for foreign affairs to Congress, which soon sent John Adams to London as minister to continue the effort to

*pendence* (New York, 1965), 429; Charles R. Ritcheson, *Aftermath of Revolution: British Policy Toward the United States, 1783–1795* (Dallas, 1969), 5–6.

15Ritcheson, *Aftermath*, 6; Samuel Flagg Bemis, ed., *The American Secretaries of State and Their Diplomacy* I (New York, 1927), 222–24; Setser, *Commercial Reciprocity*, 80. See also Curtis P. Nettels, *The Emergence of a National Economy, 1775–1815* (New York, 1962), ch. 3.

16Bemis, ed., *American Secretaries of State* I, 225–26; Ritcheson, *Aftermath*, 16, 6.

establish commerce on a reciprocal, free-trade basis. But after three trying years, Adams was so disgusted by his contemptuous treatment by British officialdom that he gave up and quit Europe, never to return. Like Lord Sheffield, Adams recognized the basic weakness of the American position and he agreed with Jay on the means of remedying it:

> I see no resource for us but in a navigation act, and this will not relieve us soon. Our merchants have enslaved themselves to this country by the debts they have contracted. They are afraid to explore new channels of commerce, lest they should offend the British merchants and be sued. But there is no choice left us. Our country must not be ruined, in tenderness to those who have run imprudently too far into debt.[17]

Contemplating the scene from Paris, Jefferson was encouraged by news from home. "I am well informed," he wrote to Madison,

> that the late proceedings in America have produced a wonderful sensation in England in our favour. I mean the disposition which seems to be becoming general to invest Congress with the regulation of our commerce, and in the mean time the measures taken to defeat the avidity of the British government, grasping at our carrying business. I can add with truth that it was not till these symptoms appeared in America that I have been able to discover the smallest token of respect towards the United States in any part of Europe. . . . The late proceedings seem to be producing a decisive vibration in our favour. I think it possible that England may ply before them. It is a nation which nothing but views of interest can govern. If it produces good there, it will here also.[18]

The Congress of the Articles of Confederation could not enact an effective navigation act because control of commerce rested with the states. This glaring weakness of Congress gave plausibility to the arguments of the British mercantilists. Under their influence, the British government not only refused to establish

17Adams to Arthur Lee, Sept. 6, 1785, in *Works of Adams* IX, 536. See Ritcheson, *Aftermath*, 21–45.

18Jefferson to Madison, Sept. 1, 1785, *Jefferson Papers* VIII (Princeton, 1953), 460–61; Malone, *Jefferson and Rights of Man*, 23–26. Jefferson's long campaign to construct an independent American commercial policy is recounted in Merrill D. Peterson, "Thomas Jefferson and Commercial Policy, 1783–1793," *W & M Quarterly* 3d ser., XXII (Oct. 1965), 584–610.

commercial relations with the United States through treaty negotiations, but it would not even sanction official diplomatic intercourse through sending and receiving ministers. In effect, it
waged economic war on its former colonies, while many British
Tories looked for the collapse of American independence in a
world organized economically to exclude it. As Jefferson complained, a substantial part of the English press kept busy encouraging expectations of the return of the prodigal to Britain's
protection.[19]

To meet these difficulties, Congress attempted to make treaties
of commerce with foreign powers and thus automatically to transfer power over commerce from the states to the national government. As Jefferson told James Monroe, a Virginia delegate to
Congress, the "primary object in the formation of treaties is to
take the commerce of the States out of the hands of the States, and
to place it under the superintendence of Congress, so far as the
imperfect provisions of our constitutions will admit, and until
the States shall, by new compact, make them more perfect."[20]

Jefferson shared the almost unanimous American belief in
freedom of trade as part of the philosophy of natural rights, and
he opposed the artificial shackles of mercantilism on principle.
Indeed, the circumstances of international economics seemed to
give the United States no real choice of commercial philosophy:
either battle commercial monopoly under the free-trade banner,[21] or accept economic dependence on one of the imperial

19DeConde, *Entangling Alliance*, 12; *Jefferson Papers* VIII, 461. Prime Minister
Pitt himself apparently was a contributor to the campaign of belittlement against
the U. S. In the spring of 1792, Gouverneur Morris reported to Alexander Hamilton a conversation with the Russian minister in London in which the latter confessed "that when he came to this country believing [sic] as he did in Mr. Pitts
Integrity he readily adopted the State given to him of our Country which was as
poor and despicable as need be." The Russian added that Pitt was at one time disposed to make a commercial treaty with the U. S., but Lord Sheffield and some
ministerial colleagues had caused him to change his mind. Morris to Hamilton,
Apr. 10, 1792, *Hamilton Papers* (New York, 1961– ), XI, 260–61; Beatrix C. Davenport, ed., *A Diary of the French Revolution* 2 vols. (Boston, 1939), II, 409–10.

20Jefferson to James Monroe, June 17, 1785, *Jefferson Papers* VIII, 231. Peterson,
"Jefferson and Commercial Policy," 593–94.

21See Setser, *Commercial Reciprocity*, 2–3.

mercantilist systems, almost inevitably Great Britain. While Jefferson therefore would have preferred that the United States make treaties on the basis of completely free trade (assuming that the constitutional difficulties could be surmounted), he recognized that mercantilist restrictions were too deeply imbedded in the commercial policies of European nations and "interwoven with the body of their laws and the organization of their government" to be got rid of. The only course available, he concluded, was to make treaties on the basis of the treatment accorded the most favored nation, as Congress, in instructions proposed by James Madison, had already decided. American commerce was valuable to Britain and France; it should be "the price of an admission into their West Indies, and to those who refuse the admission, we must refuse our commerce, or load theirs by odious discriminations in our ports." This suggestion of commercial warfare, or in the case of Britain commercial counter-warfare, was based on the hard realities of the situation and seemed the only means of establishing American commercial independence in the long run. Jefferson was not particularly hopeful in 1785, but he was not squeamish either. He had already told Monroe: "We ought to begin a naval power, if we mean to carry on our own commerce."[22]

The failure of Congress during 1784–86 to negotiate treaties of commerce according to liberal principles naturally strengthened the constitutional movement. Perhaps no grant of power by the federal Constitution was less controversial than that over commerce, and it was popularly believed that the new government possessed a mandate to pursue a commercial policy that would punish those countries refusing concessions to American commerce and reward those that extended reciprocal benefits.[23]

No one expressed this view more clearly or forcefully than did Alexander Hamilton in *The Federalist*, No. 11. Hamilton said that the maritime powers of Europe, fearful of "the adventurous

---

[22]Jefferson to Monroe, Nov. 11, 1785, *Jefferson Papers* VII, 511–12. Malone, *Jefferson and Rights of Man*, 25–27; Setser, *Commercial Reciprocity*, 74.

[23]Setser, *Commercial Reciprocity*, 74, 102–103, 119.

spirit, which distinguishes the commercial character of America," pursued policies harmful to the United States, with "the three-fold purpose of preventing our interference in their navigation, of monopolizing the profits of our trade, and of clipping the wings by which we might soar to a dangerous greatness." Through a more perfect Union, continued Hamilton, "we may counteract a policy so unfriendly to our prosperity in a variety of ways." The enactment of prohibitory regulations and the creation of a federal navy occurred at once; these events would force foreign countries to bid against each other for the American market and give the United States a balancing influence, especially in the vital West Indies, between the competing powers. Hamilton even suggested that the exclusion of Great Britain from American ports "would produce a relaxation in her present system, and would let us into the enjoyment of privileges in the markets of those islands and elsewhere, from which our trade would derive the most sub-stantial benefits."[24]

Hamilton thus articulated the general American view regard-ing United States foreign commerce, particularly that with Great Britain. But Lord Sheffield's opposite view, widely held in Eng-land, promised some difficulty. In 1791, the American political economist Tench Coxe published a pamphlet refuting Lord Sheffield. Pointing out that the United States was the principal customer for British manufactured goods, Coxe noted that for the years 1784 and 1785, Britain had sold one-third of her total exports of manufactured goods in the United States. By 1790, Britain's total exports had increased to about eighteen million pounds sterling annually, of which about thirteen million pounds represented her own manufactures and the rest, re-exports. Of this total, the United States took three million pounds sterling; but much of the British re-export trade was in American prod-ucts, tobacco, rice, and indigo. In addition, stated Coxe, exports to Britain from the United States ". . . consist principally of the essential elements of her manufactures, shipping, and navy." These items included lumber, bark, cotton, flax, iron, wax, in-

24Cooke, ed., *The Federalist*, 66–67.

14

digo, potash, tar, pitch, turpentine, skins, furs—commodities which, according to Coxe, were "more precious than gold to her."[25] Together, American imports from Britain and far greater exports to Britain and her colonies amounted to almost two-thirds of the total commerce of the United States.[26]

Lord Sheffield's view that American trade would naturally seek the familiar channels again after the peace proved generally correct, although the commercial regulations discriminating against Great Britain, passed by some of the states, caused hardship to some British merchants. But as Lord Sheffield knew, long-established custom is a powerful influence; and safe, old ways are generally preferred to new, uncertain ones even when the greater risks promise much greater rewards. British merchants had long ago adapted their products and methods to American tastes and customs, and this advantage in the American market was firmly buttressed by an elaborate credit and marketing structure.[27]

Despite the hostile commercial policy of Great Britain and the real but limited French efforts to expand trade with the United States, American commerce for the most part shunned France. The United States took an annual average for the years 1787–89 of 1,800,000 livres' worth of goods from France, while selling to France an annual average for that period of 9,600,000 livres' worth; for the French West Indies, the corresponding figures were 6,400,000 livres and 11,100,000 livres.[28] Although American merchants were accumulating huge credits in the commerce with

[25]Tench Coxe, *A Brief Examination of Lord Sheffield's Observations on the Commerce of the United States* (Philadelphia, 1791), 60–61.

[26]Samuel Flagg Bemis, *Jay's Treaty* (New York, 1924), 33–35.

[27]Setser, *Commercial Reciprocity*, 65, 52; Jensen, *New Nation*, 175. Defending the Pitt government's failure to offer a commercial treaty to the Americans, its friends in Parliament referred to old prejudices and animosities which made negotiation difficult and to "the silent operation of convenience" which made negotiation unnecessary. Ritcheson, *Aftermath*, 31.

[28]Setser, *Commercial Reciprocity*, 91. At the same time, American trade with Britain showed a balance favorable to Britain of more than £1,080,000: imports amounting to £2,106,000 and exports, £1,024,000. Four years earlier, however, the respective figures were £4,250,000 and £700,000. Britain's staggering favorable balance had evidently declined to one which was merely comfortable. Ritcheson, *Aftermath*, 31–32, 368 (app. D).

15

France and her colonies, they were, at the same time, repeating the old colonial pattern with the former mother country and getting ever deeper in debt to British merchants. The adventurous American commercial spirit which Hamilton perceived had not made its presence felt in any significant way.

In view of the primacy of commercial problems from the beginning of the movement leading to formation of the new government, it was appropriate that James Madison, the "Father of the Constitution," should open the business of the first federal Congress with a bill to impose import and tonnage duties. Madison had two objects in mind, the regulation of commerce and the raising of a revenue to support the government, but the former clearly had priority. Confessing his own bias in favor of free trade, he nevertheless proposed a system of graduated duties, with American ships paying the lowest rates, ships of nations having commercial treaties with the United States paying higher duties, and ships of other countries paying the highest rates. This was the initiation of the generally anticipated program of commercial discrimination against Great Britain in defense of American shipping, but probably few expected it would be so short lived. Although fear of British reprisals was expressed, the principle survived and the bill went to the Senate, but there concern over Britain's reaction was strong enough to defeat it and to establish only two categories of duties: one for American vessels, the other for all foreigners.[29]

Uniform commercial regulations for the Union had been enacted and a federal revenue provided for; but the practical effect was that the American government would collect the duties, while the profits of the commerce went as before to Britain. Soon thereafter, George Washington was inaugurated as first president of the United States; the executive departments of the government were established, foreign affairs first, then treasury and

---

[29]Apr. 14, 1789. *Annals of the Congress of the United States* (Washington, D. C., 1834–56), III, 210–11. Ritcheson, *Aftermath*, 92–94; Jerald A. Combs, *The Jay Treaty* (Berkeley, 1970), 31–33; DeConde, *Entangling Alliance*, 40; Irving Brant, *James Madison: Father of the Constitution, 1787–1800* (Indianapolis, 1950), 246–54.

war; and the two giants of the formative years, Alexander Hamilton and, later, Thomas Jefferson, assumed their offices.

One of the least noted circumstances which attended the establishment of the new government under the Constitution has been the subordination of foreign affairs to finance in both executive and legislative actions. A principal reason for this situation lies in the exceptional abilities and energies of Alexander Hamilton who, having led the successful fight for ratification of the Constitution in New York, was now preparing himself for a leading role in implementing it. Owing largely to his efforts, the New York legislature had sent to the United States Senate his father-in-law, General Philip Schuyler, and his friend Rufus King, a New Yorker since his unsuccessful candidacy in Massachusetts for the United States Senate. In the spring and summer of 1789, Hamilton was also running a successful law practice; prosecuting his political war against the governor of New York, George Clinton, defeated leader of the anti-Constitution forces, through a pseudonymous series of letters to the press; consulting on fundamental questions of Anglo-American relations with the unofficial British agent in the United States, Major George Beckwith; and corresponding with a large number of men of influence regarding plans for launching the new government. In September, after the prominent Philadelphia financier and Revolutionary War superintendent of finance, Robert Morris, had declined the President's offer of the secretaryship of the treasury, Hamilton, on Morris' recommendation, was appointed to the post. Interestingly enough, James Madison had also urged on Washington the appointment of Hamilton, doubtless unaware that his *Federalist* collaborator had already denounced his plan for commercial discrimination against Britain to Major Beckwith. Hamilton thus not only had reversed the commercial views he espoused in *The Federalist*; he had also rejected his principal ally: Madison, he told Beckwith, "is a clever man, [but] he is very little acquainted with the world."[30]

[30]*Report on Canadian Archives, 1890* (Ottawa, 1891), 121–22. "H. G. Letters," *Hamilton Papers* V, 262–332. Brant, *Madison: Father of Constitution*, 245; John C.

Only thirty-four years old, Hamilton was short, handsome, and charming. He was particularly attractive to women, who presumably admired his dominating manner, but unfriendly males might have considered him foppish. No one, however, could fail to appreciate the driving energy which powered his vaulting ambition. Hamilton had come to America from the West Indies in 1773 to attend King's College (now Columbia University) and ultimately to study medicine. Lacking ties of ancestry or attachment to any continental colony or region, he presumably intended to return to St. Croix, in the Danish islands, where he had been a clerk in a mercantile house for some years before coming to New York, or to his native Nevis, British West Indies. But the deepening American quarrel with the mother country soon offered far greater scope for his talents and energy. Throwing himself into the struggle for American independence, his services during and after the Revolution brought him to the attention of many of the new nation's leaders, including General Washington and Robert Morris. Almost as important, in 1780 Hamilton had married Elizabeth Schuyler, second daughter of one of the wealthiest and most influential members of the old New York landed aristocracy, thereby acquiring the social acceptability which he hitherto conspicuously lacked, as well as the sponsorship of a wealthy and powerful clan.[31]

Hamilton illustrates the truism that genius is nine-tenths hard work; his inexhaustible energy was constantly the despair of

---

Miller, *Alexander Hamilton: Portrait in Paradox* (New York, 1959), 223–25. For Hamilton's confidential relationship with British agent Beckwith, see Julian P. Boyd, *Number 7: Alexander Hamilton's Secret Attempts to Control American Foreign Policy* (Princeton, 1964), ch. 1. Boyd's charges of deceit and treachery against Hamilton are vigorously challenged in Ritcheson, *Aftermath*, 112–19, and in Gilbert L. Lycan, *Alexander Hamilton & American Foreign Policy* (Norman, Okla., 1970), 122–27.

31Hamilton's background is discussed in Harold Larson, "Alexander Hamilton: The Fact and Fiction of His Early Years," *W & M Quarterly*, 3d ser., IX (Apr. 1952), 139–51. A recent discussion of Hamilton's marriage connection is John C. Miller, *Hamilton*, 62–66. Hamilton's military service is thoroughly discussed in Broadus Mitchell, *Alexander Hamilton: The Revolutionary Years* (New York, 1970). Joseph Dorfman, *The Economic Mind in American Civilization* 2 vols. (New York, 1946–49), I, 404, refers to Hamilton as "one of those great minds thrown up by wars and their aftermath."

his opponents. He had a tremendous additional advantage over them, however, because he never had to concern himself with formulating aims but only with devising means by which to reach his established goals. As Vernon L. Parrington has noted, "his mind hardened early as it matured early, and he never saw cause to challenge the principles which he first espoused."[32]

During his counting-house years at St. Croix and between campaigns during the Revolution, Hamilton read widely in the High Tory English philosophers of the recent past, particularly Hume and Hobbes. From these works he gained his conviction that men were naturally turbulent and governed by their passions; that avarice was the surest mover of men; and that the creation of a rich and powerful state could be achieved by harnessing avarice to that goal.

Hamilton's reading of history had shown him the means. As he told the Federal Convention of 1787: "All communities divide themselves into the few and the many. The first are the rich and well-born, the other the mass of the people . . . . The people are turbulent and changing; they seldom judge or determine right. Give, therefore to the first class a distinct, permanent share in the government. . . . as they cannot receive any advantage by a change, they therefore will ever maintain good government." Hamilton offered the convention a model, the British government, "the best model the world ever produced." Jefferson relates that Hamilton, in the spring of 1791, repelled John Adams's suggestion that the English government would be the most perfect ever devised if purged of corruption and made more representative. "Purge it of its corruption," said Hamilton, "and give to its popular branch equality of representation, and it would become an *impracticable* government: as it stands at present, with all its supposed defects, it is the most perfect government which ever existed."[33]

---

[32]Parrington, *Main Currents in American Thought* I (New York, 1927), 297.

[33]"Robert Yates's Version," *Hamilton Papers* IV, 200; L & B, *Writings of Jefferson* 20 vols. (Washington, D. C., 1905), I, 279. See Miller, *Hamilton*, 46–51, and Clinton Rossiter, *Alexander Hamilton and the Constitution* (New York, 1964), 113–49.

Like his interlocutors, Jefferson and Adams, Hamilton was not thinking in merely theoretical terms. He was acutely conscious of the nation-building opportunities history had provided for his generation of Americans, and he was determined to play a major—perhaps *the* major—role in the building. Such a destiny had been forming in his dreams since adolescence, when his idol was General James Wolfe, who died gloriously while securing a continental empire for Great Britain, and when he wrote to a boyhood friend in his first letter of record: "I wish there was a war."[34]

Years (and wars) later, Jefferson reported an exchange with Hamilton in the spring of 1791 on the subject of the greatest men who had ever lived. Jefferson's dining room was hung with portraits of remarkable men, among whom he identified Bacon, Newton, and Locke as his trinity of immortals. Hamilton demurred: " 'The greatest man,' he said, 'that ever lived, was Julius Caesar.' " The name of Caesar suggests the thirst for military glory which ran from beginning to end in Hamilton's career, and Jefferson doubtless had reason to impute to him dictatorial tendencies. But the eighteenth century and earlier ones not obsessed with wealth and power saw more in Caesar, and Gerald Stourzh and Douglass Adair are probably right in arguing that, to Hamilton, Caesar was one of "the most illustrious and important" of men: "the founder of an empire."[35]

Stourzh called attention more than a dozen years ago to a little-noticed early pamphlet of Hamilton's which revealed the youthful aide to General Washington as a close student not only of Plutarch but of Jefferson's hero, Sir Francis Bacon. At the beginning of the seventeenth century, Bacon offered a scale of greatness which placed first "founders of States and commonwealths." Hamilton wrote in 1778:

34Douglass Adair, "Fame and the Founding Fathers," in Edmund P. Willis, ed., *Fame and the Founding Fathers* (Bethlehem, Pa., 1967), 30; Mitchell, *Hamilton: The Revolutionary Years*, 1.

35Jefferson to Benjamin Rush, Jan. 16, 1811, L & B, *Writings of Jefferson* XIII, 4. Adair, "Fame and the Founding Fathers," 37–41; Gerald Stourzh, *Alexander Hamilton and the Idea of Republican Government* (Stanford, 1970), 174–75; Malone, *Jefferson and Rights of Man*, 287.

The station of a member of C[ongre]ss is the most illustrious and important of any I am able to conceive. He is to be regarded not only as a legislator, but as the founder of an empire. A man of virtue and ability, dignified with so precious a trust, would rejoice that fortune had given him birth at a time, and placed him in circumstances so favourable for promoting human happiness. He would esteem it not more the duty, than the privilege and ornament of his office, to do good to mankind; from this commanding eminence, he would look down with contempt upon every mean or interested pursuit.[36]

Caesar was one of Bacon's examples of "founders of States and commonwealths," but Hamilton may also have had in mind Plutarch's estimate of the great Roman:

Caesar was born to do great things, and had a passion after honor, and the many noble exploits he had done did not now serve as an inducement to him to sit still and reap the fruit of his past labors, but were incentives and encouragements to go on, and raised in him ideas of still greater actions, and a desire of new glory, as if the present were all spent.

Grandiose and breathtaking scarcely describe such an ambition as Hamilton's; his whole being was consumed with what Adair calls "the lust for the psychic reward of fame, honor, glory." In short, Hamilton aspired to immortality![37]

Hamilton's ambitions for himself and for his adopted country were inextricably united, and his own immortal fame depended on the new nation's fulfilling the destiny he perceived. Europe, he told his countrymen in *The Federalist*, No. 11, was tempted "to plume herself as the Mistress of the World, and to consider the rest of mankind as created for her benefit." He concluded with a summons:

It belongs to us to vindicate the honor of the human race, and to teach that assuming brother moderation. Union will enable us to do it. Disunion will add another victim to his triumphs. Let Americans disdain to be the instruments of European greatness!

[36]*Hamilton Papers* I, 580–81; Stourzh, *Hamilton*, 174–75; Adair, "Fame and the Founding Fathers," 40.

[37]Adair, "Fame and the Founding Fathers," 31; Stourzh, *Hamilton*, 179, 261n.

21

> Let the thirteen States, bound together in a strict and indis-
> soluble union, concur in erecting one great American system,
> superior to the controul of all trans-atlantic force or influence,
> and able to dictate the terms of the connection between the old
> and the new world![38]

Agreeing with Hume and Hobbes that the power and glory of
the state, rather than the tranquillity and happiness of its subjects, were the noblest objects of statesmanship, Hamilton had
little use for the Lockean idealism of the Declaration of Independence. However much lip service he paid to Locke's justification of revolution, his rejection of Locke in favor of Caesar
at Jefferson's dinner reflected a consistent judgment. Hamilton
recognized that the masses of men were generally shortsighted in
seeking their own interests, hence their turbulence and change-
ableness, and also the meanness and selfishness of their individual
goals. Convinced that limitations of mind and spirit prevented
all but an exceptionally virtuous and able few from compre-
hending his own glorious vision, he easily accepted the English
jurist Blackstone's view of the absolute authority of the state.
Yet the subjects of the state had absolute rights, which the ruler
was bound to protect. Hamilton really favored monarchy, but
on the medieval principle of reciprocal absolute rights and
obligations.[39]

As Hamilton rejected the modern political science of John
Locke, so he also excluded the modern free-trade economics of
Adam Smith. He might accept the free-trade argument, he implied in his great Report on Manufactures, "If the system of perfect liberty to industry and commerce were the prevailing system
of Nations." The opposite, however, was the case, and he did not
need to rehearse the defeat a few years earlier of free trade in the
British Parliament. Even if Europe had abandoned mercantilism,

---

[38]Cooke, ed., *The Federalist*, 72–73; Stourzh, *Hamilton*, 196–98.

[39]Stourzh, *Hamilton*, 6, 17–30, 107. Brant, *Madison: Father of Constitution*,
156, refers to "the veiled monarchism of Hamilton." Thomas P. Govan points out
that Hamilton advocated monarchy because the rich and well-born, if possessed of
all power, "will oppress the many." "The Rich, the Well-born, and Alexander
Hamilton," *Mississippi Valley Historical Review* 36 (1950), 675–80.

however, it is doubtful that he would have advocated free trade, for "it is the interest of nations to diversify the industrious pursuits of the individuals who compose them." Manufacturing was indispensable to the balanced economy which Hamilton believed was necessary to a powerful and independent nation able to command respect abroad. His aim was the mercantilistic one of self-sufficiency and, because of "the strong influence of habit and the spirit of imitation—the fear of want of success in untried enterprises—the intrinsic difficulties incident to first essays toward a competition with those who have previously attained to perfection in the business to be attempted . . . ," self-sufficiency must be pursued under government "incitement and patronage." Thus the absolute authority of the state was to be used to establish an economic autarchy—in Stourzh's phrase, "to guide the United States through her period of present infancy to future strength and greatness."[40]

If the mistress of the world was Europe, the mistress of Europe was England. Hamilton saw that England's wealth and power depended on her trade, particularly in manufactured goods, and it was ultimately England that he hoped the United States would surpass. Meanwhile, however, his elaborate fiscal system depended on the revenue from British trade, and the development of a balanced economy would depend substantially on British capital. There is a brilliant irony in the Hamiltonian conception: Britain was the model which would be the agency for the creation of a powerful American rival. Hamilton "favored establishing an aristocratic society at home and rejoining the British Empire as a contractual partner," as a recent commentator remarks, but only on a temporary and contingent basis.[41]

[40]Jacob E. Cooke, ed., *The Reports of Alexander Hamilton* (New York, 1964), xxii, 137–38, 141; Stourzh, *Hamilton*, 167–98. See also Edward M. Earle, "Adam Smith, Alexander Hamilton, Friedrich List: The Economic Foundations of Military Power," in Edward M. Earle, ed., *Makers of Modern Strategy* (Princeton, 1944), 128–39. Earle concludes that Hamilton was "an American Colbert or Pitt or Bismarck."

[41]Stourzh, *Hamilton*, 170; John C. Miller, *Hamilton*, 47, 290; Broadus Mitchell, *Alexander Hamilton: Youth to Maturity* (New York, 1957), x; Rexford G. Tugwell and Joseph Dorfman, "Alexander Hamilton: Nation Maker," *Columbia University*

As Hamilton selected bits and pieces from the philosophical systems and theories current, so he practiced a pragmatism bordering on opportunism in executing policy: "utility," he asserted "is the prime end of all laws." So dominating were his purpose and his vision that "utility" extended to his relations with his closest colleagues. At the beginning of 1791, Jefferson had recommended that French ships be granted an exemption from the tonnage duty. Rejecting the secretary of state's appeal, Hamilton replied:

> My commercial system turns very much on giving a free course to Trade and cultivating good humour with all the world. And I feel a particular reluctance to hazard any thing in the present state of affairs which may lead to commercial warfare with any power.[42]

A few days after this grandly impartial policy statement, however, Hamilton assured the British secret agent Beckwith that "Upon the subject of commerce and navigation, which I mentioned to you yesterday, I think, I can assure you that nothing will take place during the present Session [of Congress], to the injury of your trade." This was the same Beckwith to whom Hamilton had confided fifteen months earlier:

> I have always preferred a Connexion with you, to that of any other country. . . . [American power] may become considerable in half a Century or less . . . connected with you, by strong ties of Commercial, perhaps of political, friendships, our naval Exertions, in future wars, may in your scale be greatly important; and decisive. These are my opinions, they are the sentiments, which I have long Entertained, on which I have acted, and I think them suited to the future welfare of both Countries.[43]

*Quarterly* 29 (Dec. 1937), 209–26; Dorfman, *Economic Mind* I, 410; William A. Williams, "The Age of Mercantilism," *W & M Quarterly* 3d ser., XV (Oct. 1958), 423, is the source of the quotation.

42"The Farmer Refuted"; Hamilton to Jefferson, Jan. 13, 1791, *Hamilton Papers*, I, 126; VII, 425–26.

43Conversations with George Beckwith, Jan. 19–20, 1791; Oct. 1789, *ibid.*, VII, 440–42; V, 482–90. Boyd, *Number 7*, 24–25. Combs, *Jay Treaty*, 46, concludes that Hamilton's reasoning "would leave America forced to follow a foreign policy of appeasement for the rest of Hamilton's life. Where would be the glory and greatness he so desperately sought for himself?"

The issue here is not Hamilton's "unconstitutional and trea-sonous role in his dealings with Major Beckwith," as Stourzh, following Boyd's *Number 7*, labels it, but the evidence that Hamilton was determined, on the one hand, to yield no com-mercial concession to France, whether justified or not, and on the other hand, to permit no injury to British trade, regardless of the provocation. Hamilton had already repudiated in prac-tice the course he had urged in *Federalist*, No. 11, that of com-mercial retaliation against Britain. Madison, supported by the secretary of state, contended for Hamilton's theory against Ham-ilton's policy.[44]

The secretary of state, who was to become the symbol of oppo-sition to the Hamiltonian philosophy and program, in most ways was Hamilton's antithesis. In the circumstances as well as the geography of his birth, in the assured ease and honor of his in-herited position in society, in the openness and inquisitiveness of his mind, in the capacity to doubt which made him appear on occasion indecisive, even in his personal appearance the author of the Declaration of Independence seems to have been designed by Nature to counterbalance Hamilton.

Jefferson was forty-three years old in 1789, tall, loose-jointed, and, while unprepossessing in appearance, quiet and serious of

[44]Stourzh, *Hamilton*, 203. Stourzh explains Hamilton's conduct thus: "because the purpose of steering the new nation in the right direction prevailed, for a self-appointed founder of an empire, over the strict adherence to constitutional rules." The sharp objections to the Boyd-Stourzh interpretation of Hamilton's dealings with Beckwith of Lycan, *Hamilton & American Foreign Policy*, 122–23, 178–79, amount for the most part to semantic quibbles and to the assertion that Hamilton brilliantly and purposefully used Beckwith for his own ends. Ritcheson's criticisms, in his review of *Number 7* in *Journal of Southern History* 31 (May 1965), 202–203, fault Boyd for focusing his work too narrowly and for, at least inferentially, dis-approving Hamilton's purposes which, according to Ritcheson, "the question of their moral character aside, receive a considerable measure of justification from *salus populi suprema lex*." John C. Miller, *Hamilton*, 368, states flatly: "In effect, Hamilton was proposing to aid the representatives of a foreign power in counter-acting the policies of the Secretary of State." Mitchell, however, in his two-volumed Hamilton biography, evidently preferred to pass over the entire question in silence. See also Cecilia M. Kenyon, "Alexander Hamilton: Rousseau of the Right," *Po-litical Science Quarterly* 73 (June 1958), 161–78; and Albert H. Bowman, "Jefferson, Hamilton and American Foreign Policy," *Political Science Quarterly* 71 (Mar. 1956), 18–41.

manner. He was related by blood and marriage to the first families of Virginia, and he accepted public service as an obligation deriving from his place in society rather than as a means to personal fame and glory. He had acquired a classical education and regular habits of study before graduating from the College of William and Mary, where Professor William Small stimulated his eclectic intelligence and later was responsible for George Wythe's agreeing to accept him as a student of law. Wythe was not only one of the leaders of the Virginia bar; he was the most learned of that fraternity and was distinguished for the breadth and liberality of his mind. The student became thoroughly versed in the history as well as the practice of the law, but he abandoned a promising legal career on the eve of the Revolution and never resumed it.[45]

After his signal contribution to American independence as a member of the Second Continental Congress, Jefferson returned to Virginia, where he became the leader of the progressive group in the House of Delegates which aimed at the "reformation" of what Jefferson liked to call his "country." There followed two terms as governor of Virginia; the first showed some accomplishment but more frustration, while the second came to an unheroic end following General Cornwallis' invasion of Virginia in 1781. An investigation of his conduct as governor resulted in his vindication, but years later his Federalist enemies disseminated allegations of personal cowardice against him. Whether Governor Jefferson was insufficiently zealous in mobilizing Virginia's resources to thwart General Benedict Arnold's unexpected foray against Richmond, the new Virginian capital, and whether he was too dilatory in summoning militiamen from their homes for uncertain military service are matters that are still debated; his personal courage in defending his country, despite his deep-seated aversion to military occupations, is not.[46]

45 *DAB* X, 15–16. The best account of Jefferson's early life is Dumas Malone, *Jefferson the Virginian* (Boston, 1948); especially 51–64.

46 *DAB* X, 20–21; Malone, *Jefferson the Virginian*, 314–44. Merrill D. Peterson, *Thomas Jefferson and the New Nation* (New York, 1970), 239, notes that Jefferson "knew, and frankly conceded, how far character and training unsuited him to the

Though Jefferson was devoted to the common cause and was determined that Virginia should contribute her just share and play a loyal part in the new nation, he was first and last a Virginian. He was deeply attached to his native soil as well as to the interests of its people. More than once he said that all his hopes ended where he hoped his life would end, on his beloved Virginia hilltop. As with most Americans of his time, his profound identification with his native state gave him a particularistic outlook and a highly subjective vision of his own and his country's destiny—one filtered, as it were, through a Virginia prism.

Jefferson's perspective contrasts sharply with that of Hamilton, whose foreign birth deprived him of a strong attachment to any particular state and powerfully shaped a wholly nationalist frame of reference. Unlike Jefferson, Hamilton could look at the United States as, at least potentially, the grand sum of its parts, a nation instead of a congeries of disparate sovereignties with some mutual traditions and interests. He was never a New Yorker in the sense that Jefferson was a Virginian: "the eccentric West Indian," as one historian recently dubbed him, saw a nation, and his own role in its future, objectively, from the outside.[47]

Jefferson's political principles and moral attitudes remained fixed throughout his life. His dedication to the ideals of individual liberty and human dignity which he enshrined in the Declaration of Independence was total, and he never forgot that "the first principle of republicanism" is majority rule, which he labored unceasingly to make effective and enlightened. But he was never doctrinaire, and his intellectual versatility enabled him to adapt his methods to existing situations. There was always an *ad hoc* quality to the positions he was forced to take during a long life of public service. In contrast to his great antagonist, he had never systematically worked out an elaborate

---

role of a war-time governor, and he endorsed the assembly's choice of a military commander, General Nelson, to succeed him."

[47]David H. Fischer, *Historians' Fallacies* (New York, 1970), 109.

political philosophy on which to found his own ambition, nor boldly developed plans and programs for its realization.[48]

The "little engine of ambition" that William H. Herndon saw in Lincoln was doubtless present also in Jefferson; but it was not the mighty machine which drove Hamilton. What moved Jefferson were the related ideals of the eighteenth-century Enlightenment: that Man could improve the conditions of his earthly existence—the pursuit of happiness—and his own human nature as well; and that the means to these ends is the free exercise of human reason. The means and the ends, therefore, combined in a love of liberty. The sage of Monticello, "whose sensitized mind picked up and transmitted every novel vibration in the intellectual air," in Carl Becker's phrase, also shared a basic premise of the French *philosophes* of the Enlightenment: that the primacy of foreign affairs in the existing system of politics was wrong and evil, and that foreign policy should serve the domestic needs of the people rather than the other way around. He thus was committed to a fundamental revolution in the traditional function of government, what two centuries later would be called a massive re-ordering of priorities. He wanted a government strong enough to serve the people, but not strong enough to serve ends of its own. Rejecting the theories of Hume and Hobbes, he probably would have agreed with the acerb comment of the *philosophe* Condillac: "True fame consists not in the glory which the stupidity of the people connects with conquests and which the still more stupid historians love to praise to the point of boring the reader."[49]

Like many other Americans of his day, Jefferson thought of international relations as mutually beneficial commercial links which, because they should be equal and reciprocal in their advantages, would minimize if not eliminate causes of conflict and

[48]Bernard Mayo, *Myths and Men* (Athens, Ga., 1959), 67; Dumas Malone, *Jefferson the President: First Term* (Boston, 1970), 434–45; Marshall Smelser, *The Democratic Republic* (New York, 1968), 10–15.

[49]Carl Becker, *The Heavenly City of the Eighteenth-Century Philosophers* (New Haven, 1932), 33–34; Étienne Bonnot de Condillac, *Oeuvres Complètes* IV (Paris, 1921), 278, quoted in Gilbert, 59–60.

reinforce independence. He was therefore devoted to the expansion of American trade with France as the means of establishing his country's economic independence of Great Britain. Succeeding the celebrated Dr. Franklin as minister at Paris in 1785, in the next five years he was able to persuade the French court to relax some of its mercantilist duties in favor of the United States, but this was done merely by royal decree and could be easily reversed. He achieved scant success in loosening the grip of the monopolistic French Farmers-General over the tobacco trade, the most important American commodity in the French market, but he was instrumental in getting France to break the monopoly Robert Morris enjoyed for the exclusive supply of tobacco. He was unable to expand significantly the market in France for unaccustomed American products, but he succeeded in negotiating with France in 1788 the first United States Consular Convention. Although Jefferson was far from despairing of greater Franco-American commercial intercourse, that convention removed some of the extraterritorial features of the commercial treaty of 1778 and thus represented the first formal step in the long American disengagement from the close ties to France of the Revolutionary period.[50]

Jefferson left Europe for rest and consultation in the United States in October 1789, expecting to return to Paris in the spring. Winds of change were blowing hard in France and he needed "to take the sense of government on some subjects which require viva voce explanations." His own country had just adopted a new system of government, one which at last had the power to regulate commerce, which Jefferson of course approved, but without

---

[50]Malone, *Jefferson and Rights of Man*, 200–202; W. K. Woolery, "The Relation of Thomas Jefferson to American Foreign Policy, 1783–1793," *Johns Hopkins University Studies in Historical and Political Science* 45 (Baltimore, 1927), 456. Ritcheson, *Aftermath*, 23–26, summarizes some of the reasons for the failure of France to capitalize on opportunities to become the American entrepôt for Europe, and Peterson, "Jefferson and Commercial Policy," 597–98, notes that the efforts of Jefferson, supported by Lafayette and other Frenchmen, "presaged a virtual revolution in the French commercial system." Frederick L. Nussbaum has analyzed "American Tobacco and French Politics" in *Political Science Quarterly* 40 (Dec. 1925), 497–516, and in his *Commercial Policy in the French Revolution* (Washington, D.C., 1915), 47–49.

the guarantees of individual liberty which he thought essential. Probably with the hope of influencing the new government to some degree on these matters, and also to permit it to make its own arrangements regarding foreign missions without embarrassment, Jefferson planned to go to Virginia to see to his estates and then to the new federal capital at New York. On landing at Norfolk late in November, however, he learned of his nomination by President Washington as secretary of state. The French consul at New York, Louis-Guillaume Otto, probably did not exaggerate much when he reported that Jefferson had been welcomed home by his countrymen with the same honors previously bestowed upon Franklin and that Jefferson was "in importance indubitably first after the dignity of the President."[51]

The Tonnage Act of 1789 had already been enacted by Congress before either Jefferson or Hamilton took office. Jefferson could not have approved the defeat of Madison's effort to discriminate against Britain and in favor of France, for this was the most obvious weapon by which Britain might be forced into a commercial treaty on the basis of reciprocity and American trade with France encouraged. But Hamilton did approve, as his assurances to Major Beckwith showed, and he had undoubtedly exercised his influence to that end in the Senate, where Madison had noted particular tenderness for British sensibilities from "New York City's Anglicism."[52]

The Tonnage Act may therefore be viewed as the first of a series of measures tending to tear away the bonds linking the United States with France and to orient it toward closer relations with Great Britain. Although it has never received the attention accorded the measures originating in Hamilton's great Reports on Public Credit, on Manufactures, and on the National Bank, it provided the essential foundation for his later fiscal program. Foreign trade was the obvious source of a revenue to support the

[51]Jefferson to William Short, Oct. 17 and 23, 1789; Short to Richard O'Bryen, Oct. 22, 1789; Jefferson to John Jay, Nov. 23, 1789; Otto to Montmorin, Dec. 1789, *Jefferson Papers* XV, 524-25, 527, 537-38, 553, 557n.
[52]Brant, *Madison: Father of Constitution*, 253; Combs, *Jay Treaty*, 33.

national government, and it remained the principal one for a century. As the first year's operation of the act demonstrated, British shipping accounted for more than three-fourths of the revenue received, and thus the financial support of the government depended on undisturbed commercial relations with England. This fact dominated Hamilton's attitude toward political as well as economic policy.[53]

The Tonnage Act imposed duties on all foreign vessels equally, and France was quick to resent the absence of an exemption in her favor. On January 3, 1790, the French minister of marine demanded that Comte Armand-Marc de Montmorin, the foreign minister, obtain such an exemption. The following July, Otto, now French chargé in the United States, was instructed to protest the tonnage duty as contrary to ARTICLE 5 of the Treaty of Amity and Commerce of 1778. This article specifically exempted American vessels from the French duty of 100 sols per ton on all foreign vessels, except when carrying French goods from one port of France to another. The same article expressly gave the United States the right to levy "a Duty equivalent in the same case," thus inferentially prohibiting the United States from imposing any other duty on French vessels.[54]

In answer to the formal protest Otto handed him on December 13, 1790, after the Act had been renewed for a second year, Jefferson drew up a report and sent it to Hamilton for comment. Pointing out that France "takes one third of our tobacco, more than half our fish oil and two thirds of our fish, say one half of the amount of these great staples and a great deal of rice, and from whom we take nothing in return but hard money to carry over and pour into the coffers of their enemies . . . ," he proposed granting the exemption as a gesture of good will. However, he

[53]*Annals of Congress* II, 2186. "Duties arising on Tonnage, for the year ending September 30, 1790." Communicated to the House of Representatives, Jan. 6, 1790. *ASP, Commerce and Navigation* (Washington, D. C., 1832), I, 7. Total receipts from the tonnage duty, Oct. 1, 1789, to Oct. 1, 1790, amounted to $165,456, of which English vessels paid $111,117, and French, $6,602.
[54]AECPE-U, vol. 35, folios 5, 128vo; Hunter Miller, ed., *Treaties* II, 7.

rejected the French interpretation of the treaty, as he told James Madison, on account of the consequences to which it could lead, though Madison maintained that the French were right.[55]

Hamilton also rejected the French interpretation of the treaty. He opposed granting the exemption because that would tend to weaken the force of the argument on the treaty's stipulations, "and inconvenient precedents are always embarrassing." He pointed out that tonnage receipts were by law required to be applied to the discharge of the national debt, and from this he concluded that an elimination of this revenue should be accompanied by the provision of its equivalent. But his strongest objection arose from another consideration: an exemption in France's favor might offend other powers, an obvious reference to Great Britain.[56]

If Jefferson's argument against the French claim regarding the treaty of 1778 was labored, at least his caution concerning France demonstrates that he was no tool of the Paris government. Having had experience of the ease with which commercial concessions could be granted and then withdrawn by royal decree, he was understandably reluctant to place his own government under any necessity to match favors with the French king. His solution would have given the French their due, without committing the United States to go further in the future.

Probably neither Jefferson nor Hamilton realized how seriously the French regarded the matter, though in Paris Gouverneur Morris knew. The Count de Moustier, the French minister who was about to be recalled to France, was shocked to discover that Congress should thus violate its treaty with France. He concluded that, far from combatting the monopolistic system of Britain, the United States was copying it: "The tonnage act is so

---

[55]*ASP, FR* (Washington, D. C., 1832), I, 109–10, 112; *Annals of Congress*, II, 2300–2301; Paul L. Ford, ed., *The Writings of Thomas Jefferson* 10 vols. (New York, 1892–99), VI, 175n., 175–76. Jefferson's report was dated Jan. 18, 1791, and the President sent it to the Senate the following day. Brant, *Madison: Father of Constitution*, 348–49; Malone, *Jefferson and Rights of Man*, 328–29.
[56]Hamilton to Jefferson, Jan. 11 and 13, 1791, *Hamilton Papers* VII, 423–24, 425–26.

rigorous in respect to foreigners that it amounts to almost a prohibition against our navigation to the United States."[57]

Otto, a much abler and more experienced analyst of commercial affairs than Moustier, explained the situation to Foreign Minister Montmorin in broader terms:

> As commerce will be actually the common measure of attachment of the United States for different countries with which they have relations, these can be classed at present in the following order: Great Britain, France, Spain, the United Provinces, Portugal, Germany, Denmark and Sweden. It must be remarked, however, that the commerce with France, although apparently inferior to that of Britain is really more profitable for the United States than any other. It is this which leaves them a large money balance. Jefferson is the only one among his compatriots who acknowledges it; the merchants, entirely devoted to England which gives them long credit, stand forth vainly against this doctrine.[58]

His skirmish with Hamilton over the tonnage duty doubtless convinced Jefferson that his imperious colleague could not be persuaded by friendly discussion. Hamilton was not one to change his mind, and his already dominant influence over Congress was reflected in the brusqueness with which he rejected the views of the secretary of state. But Washington, not Hamilton, was president, and Jefferson persevered.[59]

Toward the end of 1791, Jefferson presented a report on United States foreign commerce directly to the President. He had prepared a chart which demonstrated that England was the best customer of the United States, while France was second. But in terms of actual consumption, France was the best customer, since England re-exported at least five-eighths of her imports from the United States. In addition, almost one-fourth of the American merchant marine was engaged in the carrying trade to France and her possessions, and the American tonnage em-

[57]Morris to Montmorin, July 23, 1789; to Washington, July 31, 1789, Anne Cary Morris, ed., *The Diary and Letters of Gouverneur Morris* 2 vols. (New York, 1888), I, 160–61, 170. Moustier to Montmorin, July 24, 1790, AECPE-U, 35, 142.

[58]AECPE-U, 35, 356–56vo.

[59]See Malone, *Jefferson and Rights of Man*, 305.

ployed in trade with the French West Indies alone was far greater than that carrying goods to any single nation.[60]

To Jefferson, it was plain that the interest of the United States lay in the diversion of part of America's trade with Britain to France, thus bringing a greater share of the profit to the producer and also stimulating the expansion of the American merchant marine. But Jefferson and his allies in Congress, led by Madison, were repeatedly overborne. When Madison again introduced in the House of Representatives a measure designed to establish reciprocity of treatment with the nations with which the United States had commercial relations, Hamilton's supporters raised the cry that Madison was trying to put the United States under French domination. Jefferson commented bitterly that the subject was "banished in a reference . . . to me to report on our commerce and navigation generally, to the next session of Congress. I have little hope that the result will be anything more than to turn the left cheek to him who was smitten the right." He apparently was unaware that the mere threat of American commercial retaliation against Britain had already so alarmed Colonel Beckwith that, despite his confidence in Hamilton's influence, he had succeeded in persuading Lord William Wyndham Grenville that the presence of an accredited minister at Philadelphia was essential.[61]

In the summer of 1790, Britain and Spain reached the verge of war over possession of a remote harbor on the northwest coast of North America. This Nootka Sound dispute fused two principal problems of American diplomacy: Spanish denial of the navigation of the Mississippi River to Americans; and British retention of the posts in the United States' Northwest Territory in violation of the treaty of peace of 1783. Jefferson immediately perceived an opportunity to extract American advantage from

60Jefferson to Washington, Dec. 23, 1791, L & B, *Writings of Jefferson* VIII, 281. "Tonnage for the year ending 30th September 1790, communicated to the Senate November 28, 1791," *ASP, Commerce and Navigation* I, 45.

61Jefferson to Edward Rutledge, Aug. 25, 1791, Ford, *Jefferson's Writings* VIII, 232. Boyd, *Number 7*, 76–85; Ritcheson, *Aftermath*, 116–19; Edward Channing, *A History of the United States* 6 vols. (New York, 1905–25), IV, 120.

the expected conflict, in which the attitude of the United States would inevitably be of importance to both antagonists. If the United States should guarantee not to support Spain, Britain might be induced to evacuate the posts; conversely, Spain might be persuaded to yield the navigation of the Mississippi. The United States might thus escape involvement and also resolve its most pressing problems.[62]

So spectacular a diplomatic triumph would surely have united Americans in grateful support of their new federal government, but its failure to materialize was not Jefferson's fault. He moved at once to exert pressure on Spain through France, her partner in the Family Compact. William Short, chargé d'affaires at Paris, was instructed to solicit French intervention at Madrid. Jefferson correctly assumed that France had an interest in reducing the number of her ally's potential enemies: "She cannot doubt that we will be of that number if she does not yield our right to the common use of the Mississippi, and the means of using and securing it."[63]

This was diplomatic bluster, for neither Jefferson nor any other responsible American had any idea of war with Spain. Jefferson believed, on the contrary, that the only possible danger to the United States from Nootka Sound was war with Britain. This possibility so concerned President Washington that he asked his advisers how he should answer in case Britain demanded the passage of its troops through American territory from Canada to attack Spanish Louisiana. Blunt John Adams, the vice-president, recommended an outright refusal of such a demand, but his views were never taken seriously during Washington's administrations. The significant opinions were those of Jefferson and Hamilton.[64]

[62]Jefferson to Gouverneur Morris, Aug. 12, 1790; to William Carmichael, Aug. 2, 1790, Ford, *Jefferson's Writings* V, 224–25, 216–18.

[63]Aug. 10, 1790, *ibid.*, V, 218–21.

[64]Aug. 27, 1790, John C. Fitzpatrick, ed., *Writings of Washington* 39 vols. (Washington, D. C., 1931–41), XXXI, 102–103. The British ministry was also concerned: the foreign secretary suddenly shed his coolness toward President Washington's unofficial emissary, Gouverneur Morris, and after apologizing for the British impressment of several American sailors and assuring him of British willingness to negotiate a treaty of commerce, invited Morris to meet Prime Minister

Jefferson thought the best answer would be none at all, because evasion was most likely to guarantee the neutrality which was America's real interest and retain the freedom to act as subsequent developments required. At this stage, Jefferson's aim was to gain time, if possible by prolonging the crisis, so that his diplomatic offensive could produce results. For Hamilton, there was a devil's choice: to refuse Britain, risking the loss of the regular commerce on which his financial system, the national credit, and therefore the stability of the government and the nation itself depended; or to accept the demand and a corroding humiliation. After balancing the awful alternatives, he painfully concluded that submission would pose the least danger.[65]

How Washington would have chosen is not in doubt, but he was spared the necessity when the threatened storm suddenly dissipated. Lacking firm French support, Spain gave way before a British ultimatum and no summons was forthcoming. Neither the diplomatic opportunities prepared for by Jefferson nor the mortal perils feared by Hamilton materialized, but each man had been required to take a stand. When war clouds reappeared in 1793, their opposing attitudes had become harder and more sharply focused by the progress of the French Revolution, in which Britain soon intervened. From then until the advent to power of Napoleon, American foreign policy was hammered out on the anvil of European war. The connections of the United States with the two powerful antagonists guaranteed that its progress would be turbulent.

Hamilton's approach to the Nootka Sound crisis suggested what the course of events in the next ten years was to demonstrate conclusively. Although urged on fiscal and economic grounds, and long explained in those terms, his policies were framed primarily by political considerations. In the words of one of his re-

---

Pitt himself. As Ritcheson concludes, albeit parenthetically: "(Evidently the cabinet had had time to reflect on the value of American benevolence in an Anglo-Spanish war.)" *Aftermath,* 99.

[65]Aug. 28, 1790, Ford, *Jefferson's Writings* V, 238–39. Sept. 15, 1790, *Hamilton Papers* VII, 37–57. See Malone, *Jefferson and Rights of Man,* 308–15.

cent biographers: "In the Treasury his economic devices drew breath from and in turn animated his political purposes."[66]

It can be argued that Hamilton's economic competence is open to question, considering the American context in which he worked. There is no doubt that he was "an innovator of economic expedients" designed to establish a "traditional" society, meaning "an aristocracy of wealth and learning and a great respect for the accumulation of money, both by the individual and the nation, as the source of power and prosperity."[67] But Hamilton was little interested in economic theory and his mind was too hard and impatient, too unoriginal, to evolve elaborate new economic systems. Hence the "devices" and "expedients" which he borrowed to build in the shortest possible time and with whatever means came to hand the foundations for his dream of a glorious and powerful empire.[68]

Jefferson exaggerated when he insisted that Hamilton was devoted to "monarchy bottomed on corruption," because Jefferson could not conceive of the notoriously corrupt British government of the eighteenth century as other than monarchical—or, conversely, of a monarchy as being other than corrupt. He was more accurate in saying that Hamilton was "so bewitched & perverted by the British example, as to be under thoro' conviction that corruption was essential to the government of a nation." Personally above corruption, Hamilton simply believed that

[66]Donald F. Swanson, "The Origins of Hamilton's Fiscal Policies," *University of Florida Monographs, Social Sciences* 17 (Winter 1963), 87; Broadus Mitchell, "Alexander Hamilton as Finance Minister," *Proceedings of the American Philosophical Society* 102 (Apr. 1958), 119.

[67]Earle, ed., *Makers of Modern Strategy*, 138; Joseph Charles, "Hamilton and Washington: The Origins of the American Party System," *W & M Quarterly* 3d ser., XII (Apr. 1955), 243–48. This essay, with two additional ones which appeared in succeeding issues of the *W & M Quarterly*, was published as *The Origins of the American Party System* (Williamsburg, 1956; New York, 1961). Citations hereafter are to the 1961 edition. Virgle G. Wilhite, *Founders of American Economic Thought and Policy* (New York, 1958), 233–80; William A. Williams, *The Contours of American History* (Cleveland, 1961), 163–71; Williams, "The Age of Mercantilism," 419–37; Dorfman, *Economic Mind* I, 404; Joseph Dorfman and Rexford Tugwell, *Early American Policy* (New York, 1960), 33.

[68]John A. Krout, "Alexander Hamilton's Place in the Founding of the Nation," *Proceedings of the American Philosophical Society* 102 (Apr. 1958), 124.

what one writer has called the "vicious practice and the virtuous theory" of the British Constitution were as a practical matter inseparable.[69]

In the Jeffersonian view, the United States was developing a society dedicated to the happiness and tranquillity of its citizens. Unsympathetic to so unheroic and passive an ideal, Hamilton sought to create a great nation along traditional lines, on the British model. Jefferson's foreign policy flowed from a sympathetic understanding of America's direction which Hamilton did not share.[70] During the wars of the French Revolution, President Washington's policy of neutrality never completely succeeded in suppressing the conflict between these opposing views of America's future.

[69]The "Anas," Ford, *Jefferson's Writings* I, 179–80. Robert R. Palmer, "The World Revolution of the West, 1763–1801," *Political Science Quarterly* 69 (Mar. 1954), 7.

[70]According to Dumas Malone, *Jefferson and the Ordeal of Liberty* (Boston, 1962), xv: Jefferson during this period "was seeking to preserve or restore the 'spirit of 1776', and . . . viewed the ordeal of the decade as that of Liberty herself."

## CHAPTER II

The Gironde
and American Neutrality

> The Americans are free men, they can hardly be
> ungrateful, they will support us. . . .
>
> GENET TO FOREIGN MINISTER, FEBRUARY 1793.

> Every consideration of the interest of the United
> States must lead them to avoid an interference
> which is not called for by the terms of the subsist-
> ing treaty, and must necessarily involve them in
> the most serious misunderstanding with this
> country.
>
> FOREIGN MINISTER GRENVILLE, FEBRUARY 8, 1793.

THE liberal, bourgeois philosophers of the Gironde, a French
Revolutionary party so named because many of its leaders came
from the department of Gironde (Bordeaux),[1] have usually been
regarded with sympathy by Americans. This has been true partly
because the Girondists represented an American-style republicanism purged of the Feuillant taint of aristocracy, and partly
because they never tired of pointing with admiration to the
American example. Attracted by the idealism and the drama provided by these new tribunes of the people, Americans did not and
could not investigate very closely the practical goals the Girondists were pursuing. Trans-Atlantic communications were difficult. News from France reached America late and intermittently,
and the most regular source of French news was the English
press, highly suspect because of its enmity toward the French

---

[1]Also called Brissotin after its leader, Jacques Pierre Brissot de Warville.

Revolution and because of its evident contempt for the United States.

The rise to power of the Gironde, however, filled a growing need of the emerging political parties in America. The fiscal and economic measures enacted under the leadership of Alexander Hamilton: the funding of the public debt, with its enrichment of speculators; the assumption of the states' debts by the federal government, which transferred the allegiance of creditors from the states to the federal government; the establishment of the Bank of the United States—all served to create a party of interest and privilege. Like the Hamiltonian measures themselves, this party reflected British practices and soon developed an elitist, antipopular tone. Against this pale reflection of British Whiggism, it was natural that opposition should gradually develop at the local and popular levels. The opposition, when it mobilized later on, was indigenous, and it stood on the solid ground of the principles of the Revolution and its understanding of those principles as codified in the Constitution.[2]

But the objections of James Madison and others to complicated financial measures could not easily arouse broad public support. Not only was it difficult to convert such technical and dull controversies into political principles, but the kind of party system which was being born was entirely new and depended first on the clarification of issues and the identification of leaders for its development. The stirring events in France seemed to present sharply defined issues of principle, and the public imagination was stirred by the French struggle to abolish despotism and to establish liberty.[3]

2Noble E. Cunningham, Jr., *The Jeffersonian Republicans* (Chapel Hill, 1957), 54; William N. Chambers, "Party Development and Party Action: The American Origins," *History and Theory* III (1961), 99–104; William N. Chambers, *Political Parties in a New Nation* (New York, 1963), 11; Ralph L. Ketcham, "France and American Politics, 1763–1793," *Political Science Quarterly* 78 (June 1963), 198–223.

3Cunningham, *Jeffersonian Republicans*, 54. "Hamilton, at the head of the speculators, with all the courtiers, are on one side. These I call the Party who are actuated by interest. The opposition are governed by principle. But I fear in this case interest will outweigh principle." William Maclay, *The Journal of William Maclay* (New York, 1927), 197.

Particularly after the continental despots, led by Austria, combined in the spring of 1792 in an effort to strangle the revolution in France, popular American sympathy for the French increased rapidly. The British minister to the United States, George Hammond, later reported to London that "the pernicious principles, which [the French Revolution] has tended to generate, have found here a soil adapted to their reception . . . . The dangerous notions of equality of rights have been imbibed with avidity by a people among whom there exists no great disproportion of property . . . ."[4] American reception of egalitarian principles was natural and indiscriminate, but it represented a theoretical alignment with the French cause rather than actual enlistment in France's struggle with its neighbors. For the most part, Americans were enthusiastic about promoting equality at home. Few thought that their country could or should become actively involved in expanding liberty and equality abroad.

The Girondist revolution had tremendous significance for Europe and for the United States. France was no longer dominated by experienced politicians seeking to deliver the country from the last shackles of feudalism and to lay the foundation of a modern constitutional monarchy. The new leaders were mostly idealistic young republicans with no experience in government. Gradually, as they hacked with fervid oratory at monarchy in France, they were drawn by the interrelationships of European royalty[5] into hostility toward monarchy in general. Their main political aim thus internationalized, these Utopian dreamers were impelled toward a crusade against monarchy everywhere, and it was from this point of view that they regarded all the world, including the United States.

Jean de Ternant, the last minister to the United States of monarchical France, and, Otto, even more, had coolly appraised the effect on America of war between France and Britain. But

[4] Hammond to Grenville, Mar. 7, 1793, F. O., ser. 5 (Instructions to and Dispatches from ministers to the U. S.), vol. 1, no. 5.
[5] The French queen Marie Antoinette, for example, was the sister of the Austrian emperor.

coolness was not a Girondist characteristic. Brissot de Warville and other Girondist leaders, anticipating war with England and Spain,[6] counted on the United States to make common cause with France. Their instrument was to be Edmond Charles Genet, a young man whose revolutionary enthusiasm had recently occasioned his expulsion from the court of Catherine the Great, where he had been secretary to the French minister to Russia since 1787. Girondist antimonarchical zeal furnished the theme of the instructions of the French Republic's first minister to America. In detail, Genet's instructions spelled out a grandiose plan of imperialist expansion in America, to be carried out with the cooperation of the United States.[7] Probably on the authority of Brissot, whose brief sojourn in America was the subject of three volumes published in 1791, the fraternity of France and the United States was taken for granted.[8]

The Gironde expected Genet to enlist the Americans in the rapid liberation of Spain's trans-Mississippi empire—"the deliverance of our former brothers of Louisiana from the tyrannical yoke of Spain"—the opening of the Mississippi to American trade, and even "the restoration to the American constellation of the beautiful star of Canada." Presumably the satisfaction of the old American goal of free navigation of the "father of waters" and French forbearance regarding Canada would be suf-

[6]Abolition of the French monarchy on Sept. 21, 1792, invalidated the Family Compact in Spanish eyes, and fear of French revolutionary ideas had overcome the Spanish court's traditional hostility toward Great Britain. In contrast to Girondist expectations of war, British Prime Minister Pitt included in his budget message of 1792 his famous prophecy of fifteen years of peace. See Alfred Cobban, *In Search of Humanity* (New York, 1960), 186.

[7]Genet's instructions are in Frederick J. Turner, ed., c. f. m. *Annual Report of the American Historical Association, 1903* II (1904), 200–11. Richard K. Murdock analyzes "The Genesis of the Genet Schemes" in *French American Review* II (Apr.–June 1949), 81–97. Genet and the Girondist ministers collaborated on the instructions during Dec. 1792, and the Provisory Executive Council, which Brissot dominated, approved them soon after. "Brissot then enjoyed an unlimited influence both in the Diplomatic Committee and in the Ministry." Louis-Guillaume Otto, "Considérations," ed. by Gilbert Chinard, in *Bulletin de l'Institut Française de Washington* XVI (Dec. 1943), 19.

[8]For a concise evaluation of Brissot which emphasizes his dedication to "the American dream," see Robert R. Palmer, *The Age of the Democratic Revolution: The Challenge* (Princeton, 1959), 260–63.

ficient to overcome American hesitations. This grand design, according to Brissot and his collaborators, would be a useful diversion to weaken England and Spain in the coming European struggle.

Genet was armed with blank French commissions for Americans, who could spread French revolutionary doctrine throughout Louisiana and other Spanish and English possessions in America, and for Indian chiefs, who could be persuaded to attack the Spanish garrisons at the mouth of the Mississippi. Before Genet eventually sailed for America, he received in addition two hundred and fifty letters of marque for American shipowners willing to privateer against France's enemies.

The National Assembly, by a decree of June 2, 1791, had directed the negotiation of a new commercial treaty with the United States as evidence of France's desire to increase mutually advantageous relations between the two countries.[9] In resurrecting this decree one and one-half years later, the Girondists determined that it should be "a national pact in which the two peoples would blend their commercial and political interests and establish an intimate accord to support the extension of the empire of liberty . . . ." Franco-American commercial partnership would "punish the powers which still maintain an exclusive colonial and commercial system by declaring that the vessels of these powers will no longer be received in the ports of the two contracting nations."

The Girondist crusaders for an emancipated international commerce deplored "the timidity of several chiefs of the American republic who, in spite of their acknowledged patriotism have always shown the strongest aversion for all measures which displease England." To counter their influence, France must insist upon the strictest fulfillment of the treaties of 1778, particularly the articles permitting the reception of French prizes in American ports and prohibiting American privateering against France,

[9]The Girondists assumed that the U. S. had not previously derived proper benefits from the French alliance, a consequence of "the liberticide treason of the cabinet of Versailles." Bernard Faÿ, *The Revolutionary Spirit in France and America* (New York, 1927), 164.

the outfitting of enemy corsairs in American ports. American Anglophiles would find these provisions onerous; to enforce them strictly, therefore, might overcome any hesitations concerning a new treaty.

Since the French interpretation of these articles included their converse—that is, the nonreception in American ports of the prizes of France's enemies and freedom for Americans to privateer on the side of France and to arm and provision corsairs in the service of France—American support of France was assured whether or not Britain forced the United States to enter the war formally. To eliminate any avenue by which the United States might evade its obligations, reaffirmation of the reciprocal guarantee of the possessions of the two nations, which the Girondists admitted had been "imperfectly stipulated in Article XI of the treaty of alliance of 1778," was requisite. France demanded this mutual guarantee as the *sine qua non* of that free commerce with the French West Indies on which American prosperity was believed to depend. Because of the great disproportion between French and American power, however, the United States' guarantee of France's possessions would be little more than nominal for a long time to come. The French guarantee of the United States, on the other hand, would be very real. The Girondists promised to provide French forces to protect American ports and commerce wherever necessary.

This gesture merely emphasized the unrealness of the Girondists' world. When they declared war on Britain soon after, necessity forced them to encourage the importation of American ships for sale in France, as well as to open all their West Indian ports to American commerce. Any evidence of awareness of the contradiction between these measures and their confident assumptions is lacking. They were consistent in offering the respective naturalization of French and American citizens for purposes of commerce. But this was a new inducement for the granting of exemption from the American tonnage duty, which French merchants demanded as compensation for losing their monopoly of the West India trade.

44

To finance Genet's mission, there was the American Revolutionary War debt to France. Étienne Clavière, Girondist finance minister, estimated that the debt, on January 1, 1793, amounted to almost thirty millions of livres. Since France was "occupied in defending her liberty and her independence, as the United States defended theirs when they borrowed the money," Genet was authorized to demand the liquidation of the entire debt. Genet figured his requirements for the first year at seventeen million livres, but he feared that the United States might not agree to a full reimbursement. Brissot's council waved away this caution, since Charles François Lebrun, the foreign minister, believed Genet could meet American requirements by engaging to spend the entire amount for American products. The council finally agreed that Genet could make whatever delegations of the debt he found necessary if the American government could not provide funds quickly enough.[10]

Genet's instructions contained the usual admonition to "follow scrupulously the established forms for official communications . . . and to permit no step, nor any proposal which might offend the free Americans . . . ." Since Genet's expulsion from Russia had been for flagrant violation of those forms, such a warning for once might have been appropriate, although the Council recorded its "complete confidence in the prudence, and in the acknowledged moderation of Citizen Genet"—as well it might, since Genet himself collaborated in framing his instructions. Otto later wrote that "these instructions, conceived and approved by men who burned to revolutionize the entire globe, would have suffered to turn the head of the new minister," were that possible.[11] Leaving aside Genet's fiery personality, the perfunctory caution to observe diplomatic protocol was so incompatible with the substance of his instructions as to be completely irrelevant.

If any of the French governments of the Revolution harbored designs inimical to American interests, and even to American in-

10AECPE-U, vol. 36, 502–504, 467–68, vol. 37, 7, 58.
11Otto, "Considérations," 19–20.

dependence, it was that of the Gironde. Yet it was only the agent whom Americans condemned. The resentments Genet aroused by his extravagances were to be revisited on perhaps the one French government of the Revolution which respected American interests.

Genet was at Rochefort awaiting a favorable tide when he received news of France's declaration of war against England, an event which he was sure would "serve the cause of liberty." His mission was now more vital and promising than ever: "The Americans are free men, they can hardly be ungrateful, they will support us . . . ." But, perhaps contemplating the long voyage across an ocean dominated by the British navy, Genet fleetingly viewed reality: the Americans "have hardly any navy."[12]

The aggressive fervor of the Gironde's American policy was matched by its expansionist policy in Europe. Genet's instructions, drafted in December 1792 and January 1793, were predicated on the inevitability of war with England. The British ambassador had been recalled the preceding August, when the French king was suspended, but the French ambassador was not dismissed from London until after Louis XVI was executed.[13]

On January 4, 1793, Foreign Secretary Grenville warned the British minister at Philadelphia of the imminence of war and ordered him to be particularly watchful of any French efforts to cultivate "a more intimate correspondence between the French government and the United States." Undersecretary James Bland Burges wrote to George Hammond the same day that the American minister at Madrid had received instructions to declare that the United States would feel obliged to support France in case of any aggression against her. Burges was misinformed, but Grenville hastened to send Hammond a sheaf of documents on the

[12]Aecpe-u, 37, 93–93vo, 97.

[13]Transmitting this intelligence to Hammond on Aug. 21, 1792, Grenville declared: "It is not His Majesty's intention in taking this step to depart from the line, which [he] has hitherto observed, of not interfering in the internal affairs of France or in the settlement of the government there . . . ." Bernard Mayo, ed., I. B. M., *Annual Report of the American Historical Association, 1936* III (1941), 32.

war's origins as soon as he learned that France, on February 1, 1793, had declared war. "These several papers," he wrote, "are sufficient to place in the strongest light the unjust and unprovoked aggression of France . . . ." According to Grenville, responsibility for starting the war was "indeed in itself so manifest, that I conceive the French government will hardly venture even to make any application to the United States for assistance, on the ground of their defensive treaty of alliance." America's course should be plain: "that every consideration of the interest of the United States must lead them to avoid an interference which is not called for by the terms of the subsisting treaty, and must necessarily involve them in the most serious misunderstanding with this country."[14]

Lebrun was as anxious as Grenville that the American government adopt a view favorable to his country. In a lengthy exposition written on February 3, he reminded Genet that England had many agents and partisans in the United States who would be tireless in her defense. Even more dangerous, the English gazettes in every part of the country would present the conduct of France in the most odious light. The reports of Morris and Short, who seemed to regret the passing of the old despotism in France, must already have prejudiced American leaders. Jefferson and Washington, Lebrun said, should be informed that the conduct of these two representatives continued to injure the interests of both countries.

Lebrun cited his futile attempts to gain the British government's promise of continued neutrality in France's conflict with the continental powers; the neglect of France's ambassador by the British court, while attentions were lavished on émigré intriguers; the British ambassador's recall; the stopping of French grain ships on the high seas; the lack of protection of French citizens in England; and the conduct of English representatives, particularly in Holland and Spain, who openly sought to raise

[14]Grenville, Burges to Hammond, Jan. 4, 1793, Grenville to Hammond, Feb. 8, 1793, *ibid.*, 33, 33–34, 34–35.

up all Europe against France. These and all the other hostile British acts, Lebrun declared, had forced France to accept London's challenge.

By a decree of January 31, the National Convention permitted French privateers to arm. "As there is reason to believe that at least for some time the Americans will observe an absolute neutrality," Lebrun informed Genet, the English would take advantage of the identity of language and their close commercial connections to use the neutral American flag to escape French corsairs. Since Spain's probable entry into the war would array against France all of Europe's maritime powers, the purchase of American ships was of the greatest importance, while the vastly increased needs of the Republic for all kinds of provisions would provide a very profitable speculation for American shipowners. For her own part, Lebrun assured America, France would persist in her resolve to cement with her blood the government she had formed.[15]

The question of responsibility for the outbreak of the new war was relevant to American affairs because of the treaty of alliance, "perpetual and defensive," between France and the United States.[16] Each of the two opposing political parties in America, whose mutual antagonisms were to be immeasurably intensified by the conflict, accepted the explanations which best fitted its preconceptions. The Republican leader, James Madison, was not sure, as late as February 23, that England intended war "tho' the affirmative is most countenanced by individual opinions." Jefferson did not believe England intended to intervene, but he had already rebuked Short on January 3 for repeated expressions of hostility toward the French government, asserting that enthusiasm for the French cause was felt by 99 percent of the American people.[17]

15AECPE-U, 37, 100–103.

16J. M. Thompson, *The French Revolution* (New York, 1943), ch. 18, concludes that neither France nor Britain was solely to blame for the outbreak of war. Alfred T. Mahan, *The Influence of Sea-Power upon the French Revolution and Empire, 1793–1801* 2 vols. (Boston, 1892), I, 115, notes Britain's unpreparedness for war, but this had already become a British tradition.

17Madison to Jefferson. Gaillard Hunt, ed., *Writings of Madison* 9 vols. (New

Hamilton admitted to Short one month later that "the popular tide in this country is strong in favor of the last revolution in France." But he argued that France was fighting an offensive war, conceding only that responsibility must probably be attributed to both sides.[18] The question seems to have occasioned less controversy than might have been expected, however, probably because it was academic as soon as it was raised. More important than any personal predilection was the fact that the principal figures of both parties were agreed on neutrality as the only practical course for the United States.[19] As both Lebrun and Grenville had foreseen, America would remain neutral if it were at all possible to do so. But a policy of neutrality remained to be formulated, and quickly, since many American shipowners would soon apply for French letters of marque to cruise against the former enemy and reap the quick profits of the privateersman.

The President was at Mount Vernon when news of the outbreak of war between France and England reached him, through both Jefferson and Hamilton. He replied that he would return to Philadelphia at once and enjoined both men to consider means "for the United States to maintain a strict neutrality between the powers at war." He had already heard that vessels in several ports were preparing to sail as privateers.[20] Six days later, Washington was at the capital city and addressed to his principal advisers the famous thirteen questions on the enforcement of neutrality.[21]

---

York, 1900–10), VI, 125. Jefferson to George Gilmer, Mar. 15, 1793; to Short, Jan. 3, 1793, Ford, *Jefferson's Writings* VI, 202, 153–57. Some Americans, especially in the west, rejoiced at the successes of the French "sons of freedom" against the "infernal league" and hoped these would nip in the bud "the growing aristocratical spirit in America." Jean Badollet to Gallatin, Jan. 30, June 6, 1793, Albert Gallatin Papers, New-York Historical Society, nos. 3, 13.

18Hamilton to Short, Feb. 5, 1793, *Hamilton Papers* XIV, 7.

19See Charles M. Thomas, *American Neutrality in 1793* (New York, 1931), 14–24.

20Washington to Hamilton, to Jefferson, Apr. 12, 1793, *Writings of Washington* XXXII, 415, 416. Hamilton's concern for continued good relations with Britain prompted a second note to the President on the outbreak of war: "... the whole current of *Commercial Intelligence* ... indicated thus far, an *unexceptionable* conduct on the part of the British government towards the vessels of the United States." Apr. 8, 1793, *Hamilton Papers* XIV, 296.

21The text of the questions is in *Writings of Washington* XXXII, 419–20, and in *Hamilton Papers* XIV, 326–27. They are discussed at length in Thomas, *American Neutrality* ch. 1.

Jefferson recognized the questions at once as ". . . not the President's, that they were raised upon a prepared chain of argument, in short, that the language was Hamilton's, and the doubts his alone. They led to a declaration of the executive, that our treaty with France is void." Hamilton was fully prepared when the cabinet met on April 19 to consider the questions, but the meeting was adjourned because the attorney general, Edmund Randolph, insisted that more time was necessary for reflection. The secretaries agreed to prepare written answers, except to two of the questions which were then decided unanimously: the first, in favor of receiving the new minister of the French Republic; the other, against convening Congress. Even Hamilton had no doubts concerning these decisions, though his reservations regarding the new French minister were soon to be revealed.[22]

Another question was decided after some debate. A proclamation was to be issued,

> forbidding our citizens to take part in any hostilities on the seas, with or against any of the belligerent powers; and warning them against carrying to any such powers, any of those articles deemed contraband, according to the modern usage of nations; and enjoining them from all acts and proceedings inconsistent with the duties of a friendly nation toward those at war.[23]

Jefferson, while completely in accord with the sentiments the President had already expressed in favor of neutrality, had not wished a proclamation to be issued at all. As in the Nootka Sound episode almost four years earlier, he thought he saw an opportunity to force concessions from the belligerents, perhaps a British evacuation of the western posts, and French concessions regarding West Indian trade. When Hamilton objected that such expectations were futile and would risk involvement in the war,

22"Anas," L & B, *Writings of Jefferson* I, 349–50. See Thomas, *American Neutrality*, 27–30. The American minister to France had already been instructed to recognize the French Republic (Jefferson to Morris, Mar. 12, 1793, Ford, *Jefferson's Writings* I, 208); hence Hamilton was attempting to reverse a decision already taken by the U. S. (DeConde, *Entangling Alliance*, 191). See also Malone, *Jefferson and Ordeal of Liberty*, 68–79; John C. Miller, *The Federalist Era* (New York, 1960), 129–30.
23*Hamilton Papers* XIV, 328; Ford, *Jefferson's Writings* VI, 217.

Jefferson fell back on the Constitution. The Executive, he insisted, had no authority to infringe the powers of the Legislature, to which the Constitution gave the power of declaring war—and therefore of determining peace. Outvoted on the question of a proclamation, Jefferson reluctantly acquiesced, on the understanding that the decision involved no usurpation of congressional prerogatives. This assurance was meaningless, however, as was the omission of the word "neutrality" in the document Randolph drafted. Washington's announcement was generally referred to as the Neutrality Proclamation from the day it appeared, on April 22, 1793.[24]

Two days earlier, Jefferson explained his view of American policy to the American minister at Paris:

> No country perhaps was ever so thoroughly against war as ours. These dispositions pervade every description of its citizens, whether in or out of office. They cannot perhaps suppress their affections, nor their wishes, but they will suppress the effects of them so as to preserve a fair neutrality. Indeed we shall be more useful as neutrals than as parties by the protection which our flag will give to supplies of provision. In this spirit let all your assurances be given to the government with which you reside.[25]

And Washington himself, in a letter to his English friend the Earl of Buchan, expressed similar sentiments, foreshadowing the Farewell Address issued three years later.

> . . . I believe it is the sincere wish of United America to have nothing to do with the political intrigues, or the squabbles of European nations; but on the contrary, to exchange commodities and to live in peace and amity with all the inhabitants of the earth. And this I am persuaded they will do, if rightfully it can be done. To administer justice to, and receive it from every power with whom they are connected will, I hope, be always found the most prominent feature in the administration of this country; and I flatter myself that nothing short of imperious necessity can occasion a breach with any of them.[26]

[24]L & B, *Writings of Jefferson* I, 403–405; Thomas, *American Neutrality*, 35–41, 43–47. The proclamation is in *ASP, FR* I, 140.
[25]Jefferson to Morris, Apr. 20, 1793, Ford, *Jefferson's Writings* VI, 217.
[26]Apr. 22, 1793, *Writings of Washington* XXXII, 428.

In December 1792, Washington told Jefferson that he believed the United States should draw closer to France.[27] The impact of the European war may already have induced second thoughts on the part of the President by the following April, but there is no indication that he shared Hamilton's almost instinctive loathing of the French Revolution. Hamilton's list of questions pointed to the abrogation of the treaties of 1778. He meant to use this occasion to break the legal and moral bonds between France and the United States, a purpose which was tacitly acknowledged in the opinions submitted to Washington by Jefferson, Randolph, and Hamilton himself.[28]

Hamilton's argument—that the treaties made with the royal government expired with the birth of the French Republic—could only be sustained by denying the right of revolution on which the independence of his own country depended. But Hamilton further contended that receiving the new minister of France, without suspending or renouncing the treaties, would of itself be a breach of neutrality.[29]

Jefferson took the "natural right" of revolution seriously. "Would you suppose it possible," he demanded of Madison, "that it should have been seriously proposed to declare our treaties with France void on the authority of an ill-understood scrap of Vattel . . . and that it should be necessary to discuss it?" The President shared Jefferson's surprise: he had never doubted the validity of the treaties, he said, but it had seemed proper to discuss the question once it had been raised.[30]

Jefferson concentrated his written argument against Hamilton's two principal theses: that the treaties involved only Amer-

27"Anas," L & B, *Writings of Jefferson* I, 327.

28Jefferson explained the omission of one from Secretary of War Henry Knox: "I believe Knox's was never thought worth offering or asking for." "Anas," L & B, *Writings of Jefferson* I, 351. He was mistaken, however, for Knox signed the letter transmitting Hamilton's opinion, described as "a joint answer." May 2, 1793, *Hamilton Papers* XIV, 364.

29*Hamilton Papers* XIV, 367–96.

30Apr. 28, 1793, Ford, *Jefferson's Writings* VI, 232; "Anas," L & B, *Writings of Jefferson* I, 351.

ica and Louis Capet, whose international obligations could not be inherited by a successor government; and that the republican government of France was not legitimate. In fact, Jefferson pointed out, both France and the United States had changed their forms of government. Hamilton had cited Vattel on the law of nations, but what Vattel really said was that one nation could absolve itself from commitments to another only when they constituted a great and immediate danger. Using Vattel as his yardstick, Jefferson demonstrated that the danger was not great and imminent; it was not even present. There remained, however, a right of noncompliance with particular treaty provisions as they proved immediately dangerous, as might conceivably arise from the American guarantee of the French West Indian possessions. But Jefferson doubted that this article would ever be invoked, or that it need involve the country in war if it were.

Jefferson's sharpest criticism was reserved for Hamilton's attack on the legitimacy of the new French government, which rested, as did the American, on the crucial right of revolution. Jefferson demonstrated that the greatest writers on the law of nations—Grotius, Pufendorf, Wolf, and Vattel—were unanimous in the opinion that "treaties remain obligatory notwithstanding any change in the form of government." In fact, Vattel maintained that every nation had the right to change its form of government and that it was wrong for another to oppose its doing so.[31]

The interpretation of the treaties faithfully adhered to in the months ahead was Jefferson's. Genet was to quarrel violently with parts of it, particularly regarding ARTICLE XXII of the treaty of commerce, which prohibited France's enemies from outfitting privateers or selling their prizes in American ports. Jefferson declared that "we are free to refuse the same thing to France, there being no stipulation to the contrary, and we ought to refuse it on principles of fair neutrality." Other treaty provisions relating to maritime warfare could not offend Britain, since

[31]Ford, *Jefferson's Writings* VI, 219–31.

they were prominent features of several international treaties, including the defunct Anglo-French treaty of 1786.[32]

Jefferson now turned to the enforcement of American neutrality. His hope of American gain from Europe's embroilment had been dashed because of the proclamation of neutrality adopted through Hamilton's intervention. "Hamilton," writes an administrative historian, "had triumphed in Jefferson's own domain."[33] Jefferson was left no diplomatic weapon anyway, because the intimacy between the secretary of the treasury and the British minister, George Hammond, had already provided His Majesty's government with the vital assurance that America's French connections need cause it no concern. Partly because Hamilton had been plotting with Hammond for more than one month to scuttle the Franco-American treaties, the British government was soon demanding that America pay for the privilege of remaining neutral.[34]

A Jeffersonian attempt at a diplomatic tour de force would have met with dismal failure. As Hamilton's most recent biographer remarks, Hamilton had already adopted the practice of aiding the agent of a foreign power in counteracting the secretary of state's policies. Hamilton's intervention in the sphere of his colleague was effected through indirect as well as direct means, with a complete absence of scruple either way.[35]

Instead of the diplomatic freedom of maneuver he had contended for, Jefferson was circumscribed on every side. Hammond was able to place absolute confidence in Hamilton's disclosures because "... any event which might endanger the *external* tranquility of the United States would be as fatal to the systems he has

32Since France had hardly then presented a threat to Britain's domination of international trade, London had consented to the inclusion in that treaty alone of the modern, liberal provision that free ships made free goods. Jefferson, of course, did not add that this single British departure from traditional policy was nullified by the war.

33Leonard D. White, *The Federalists* (New York, 1948), 214. But see Lycan's account, *Hamilton & American Foreign Policy*, 152–61.

34Hammond to Grenville, Mar. 7, 1793, F. O. 5, 1. Nathan Schachner, *Alexander Hamilton* (New York, 1946), 316–17; Bemis, ed., *American Secretaries of State* II, 34–36; Malone, *Jefferson and Rights of Man*, 412–19; I. B. M., 36–43.

35Miller, *Hamilton*, 368.

formed for the benefit of his country, as to his present personal reputation and to his future projects of ambition."[36] Probably Jefferson was only beginning to realize fully how inextricably Hamilton was tying the United States to Britain's commercial system, or, to put it another way, how rapidly Hamilton's economic system was restoring the United States to its former status under British mercantilism. As Hammond saw clearly, Hamilton and his Federalist supporters would permit no step on the part of the United States which might displease Britain. London thus held a virtual veto power over the actions of the American government.

To complicate Jefferson's problems even further, he would have as little aid in maintaining an honorable neutrality from France, whose policy now was to extract from its engagements with America every possible advantage, regardless of the consequences. The Girondists meant to enlist the United States in their crusade against the archenemy of liberty, whether war against Britain should be formally declared by the American government or not. France had already decided America's course: as an ally and a sister republic, the United States was to share in the deliverance of Europe and Europe's dominions from the twin fetters of monarchy and aristocracy. The Gironde's agent was on his way, but it would be some time before Jefferson, who entertained no illusions concerning British intentions, would reluctantly face squarely the danger from France.

[36]Hammond to Grenville, Mar. 7, 1793, F. O. 5, 1. The New York merchant and speculator William Constable quoted Lord Hawkesbury as having said on Aug. 19, 1792: "Mr. Jefferson is a Party man & we know it." Hawkesbury had gone on to reassure his interlocutor, who had reported concern in "the city" over the possibility of war with America: "Not the smallest be assured of it, as long as Washington is at the head of the Executive & the Federal Party prevail . . . ." Unsigned, undated memorandum of conversation with Lord Hawkesbury, apparently enclosed in a letter from Constable to a friend who passed it to Hamilton. Hamilton Papers, Library of Congress, XVII, 2310.

CHAPTER III     Citizen Genet

> A fair neutrality will prove a disagreeable pill to
> our friends, though necessary to keep out of the
> calamities of a war.
>
> JEFFERSON TO MADISON, APRIL 28, 1793.

> All the old spirit of 1776 is rekindling.
>
> JEFFERSON TO MONROE, MAY 5, 1793.

JEFFERSON realized, as he told Madison, "that a fair neutrality
will prove a disagreeable pill to our friends, though necessary
to keep out of the calamities of a war." The arrival of the new
French minister, however, would afford the people an opportunity to display their sympathies and somewhat sweeten the pill.
Madison agreed that peace should be preserved "at any price that
honor and good faith" would permit and seconded his friend's
hope that the reception of Genet "may testify what I believe to
be the real affections of the people. It is the more desireable as a
seasonable plum after the bitter pills which it seems must be
administered."[1]

Genet landed on April 8, 1793, at Charleston, South Carolina,
where an immense crowd, with the French consul, Michel Ange
Mangourit, met him at the dock and escorted him to the mansion
of Governor William Moultrie. His charm appeared irresistible.
Reporting to Hamilton, a hostile observer described "the man
that we are all affraid [sic] of" as of "a good person, fine ruddy
complection, quite active and seems always in a bustle, more like
a busy man than a man of business, [who intends] to laugh us

[1]Apr. 28, 1793, Ford, *Jefferson's Writings* VI, 232; May 8, 1793, *Writings of
Madison* VI, 127–28.

into the war if he can." Governor Moultrie entered into the spirit of Genet's reception and, at the latter's suggestion, obligingly ordered the harbor defenses strengthened and promised to permit the arming of privateers. Four ships—the *Républicain*, the *Sansculotte*, the *Anti-George*, and the *Patriote Genet* (later renamed the *Citizen Genet*)—were being fitted for action against France's enemies, one having already put to sea.[2]

Flushed with his initial success, Genet proceeded northward by land. His arrival at Philadelphia, he reported, was a "triumph for liberty," after one month's journey which was "an uninterrupted succession of civic fêtes." He learned of the neutrality proclamation at Richmond, however, and hurried on so fast that he missed the public dinner prepared for him at Fredericksburg. The only sour note, according to Madison's information, was Alexandria, where "the fiscal party . . . was rather an overmatch for those who wished to testify the American sentiment." But this deficiency was repaired by Georgetown. Already, Genet was prepared to defy the American government: he promised to send to Paris proofs of his complete conquest of American sympathies, so that France could "judge the value of the declarations of neutrality" which had been thrust upon the American people.[3]

Jefferson rejoiced that "all the old spirit of 1776 is rekindling." But he hoped "that we may be able to repress the spirit of the people within the limits of a fair neutrality." Hamilton, however, was struggling mightily against the popular enthusiasm for France, and Jefferson described him as "panic struck if we refuse our breach to every kick which Great Britain may chuse to give it." Even a "sneaking neutrality" would be difficult to

[2]Apr. 16, 1793, C. F. M., 211–13; John Steele to Hamilton, Apr. 30, 1793, *Hamilton Papers* XIV, 359. See Frederick J. Turner, ed., "The Mangourit Correspondence in Respect to Genet's Projected Attack upon the Floridas, 1793–94," *Annual Report of the American Historical Association, 1897* (1898), 570.

[3]Genet to Minister of Foreign Affairs, May 18, 1793, C. F. M., 214–15; Madison to Jefferson, May 27, 1793, *Writings of Madison* VI, 130; Thomas, *American Neutrality*, 82–84. See also John B. McMaster, *A History of the People of the United States from the Revolution to the Civil War* 8 vols. (New York, 1883–1913), II, 100–101, and Claude Bowers, *Jefferson and Hamilton: The Struggle for Democracy in America* (Boston, 1925), 217–20.

maintain, and that only because of the President, for Jefferson was always outvoted by "2½ against 1½." This, he explained to Madison, was owing to Randolph's indecision, which was also the cause of "the pusillanimity of the proclamation."[4]

Jefferson had high praise for Genet's conduct: "it is impossible for anything to be more affectionate, more magnanimous." He took Genet at his word and approvingly quoted him:

> We know that under present circumstances we have a right to call upon you for the guarantee of our islands, but we do not desire it. We wish you to do nothing but what is for your own good and we will do all in our power to promote it. Cherish your own peace and prosperity. You have expressed a willingness to enter into a more liberal treaty of commerce with us; I bring full powers (and he produced them) to form such a treaty, and a preliminary decree of the National Convention to lay open our country and its colonies to you for every purpose of utility, without your participating in the burthens of maintaining and defending them. We see in you the only person on earth who can love us sincerely and merit to be so loved.[5]

Some of Genet's extravagant talk appeared in the Paris press, as on July 17, when compliments exchanged on May 20 between Genet and a delegation of Philadelphians were reported in the *Gazette de France Nationale*. "Although America can take no part in the present war," the delegation offered its most earnest prayers for French success. Genet replied: "I should declare to you frankly . . . that France has never thought that America, separated from her by so great a distance, could take part in the present war."[6] As Jefferson concluded, Genet offered everything and asked nothing.

Perhaps to capitalize as quickly as possible on the resounding din of his popular reception, Genet sent his letter of credence to Jefferson and asked for an appointment with the President the

[4]To Monroe, May 5, to Madison, May 19, 1793, Ford, *Jefferson's Writings* VI, 239, 259–61. Lawrence S. Kaplan, *Jefferson and France* (New Haven, 1967), 38–39, suggests that Jefferson's "championing of the French Revolution . . . was inspired in part by an understandable jealousy of his adversary's brilliance."
[5]To Madison, May 19, 1793, Ford, *Jefferson's Writings* VI, 259–61.
[6]AECPE-U, 37, 297–97vo.

day after three hundred of Philadelphia's merchants formally presented their thanks to the President for the neutrality proclamation.[7] The attitude of the "Anglophiles" at Alexandria had already forewarned Genet of substantial opposition to his plans.

On May 18, President Washington received Genet, who presented a reassuring letter from the President of the National Convention. "The immense distance which separates us," the Girondist leader had written, "prevents you from taking the part in that glorious regeneration of Europe which your principles and your past battles reserved for you." But the letter hinted that American participation might be demanded at some future time:

> The day is doubtless not far off when political sanity will establish the bases of commerce. . . . It depends on the courage of the United States to accelerate this happy moment, and the French Republic will hasten to cooperate in every effort to strengthen the political and commercial bonds of two nations which can have only a common sentiment, since their principles and interests are the same.[8]

A "Report on the Mission of Citizen Genet" drawn up by the Executive Council of the Republic prior to the minister's departure omitted the innocent protestations:

> The Council has indicated to [Genet] the path he must take to induce the Americans to forge again the links that bind them to the French nation, in order to arouse them to join their cause to ours and to second, as much as will be in their power, the efforts that we will be obliged to make in all parts of the world in the struggle against the hostile activities of England and Spain . . . .[9]

Jefferson's desire to believe the self-denying reassurances of Genet blinded him for a while to the contrast between the Frenchman's words and deeds. Hamilton would have doubted Genet's promises even if they had been genuine, however, and he at once professed to see "a snare into which he hopes we shall

[7]Ford, *Jefferson's Writings* VI, 260; Washington to the Merchants and Traders of the City of Philadelphia, May 17, 1793, *Writings of Washington* XXXII, 460–61.
[8]AECPE-U, 36, 473–74vo.
[9]Jan. 4, 1793, *ibid.*, 37, 20.

not fall." Knox, as usual, seconded Hamilton, and Randolph was clearly suspicious, as was Washington. Jefferson seems at first to have attributed Genet's indiscretions to the rashness of youth and republican zeal, which could be tempered through sympathetic advice. He was more concerned over what Madison called the "secret Anglomany" behind the "mask of neutrality."[10]

The Washington administration's policy regarding the European war had been determined before Genet reached Philadelphia. Because of rumors that an assault on Louisiana from Kentucky was being organized, the cabinet decided on March 10 to issue a proclamation warning against such an expedition, to alert the governor of Kentucky as well as Congress, and to instruct General Wayne to use force if necessary to intercept it. Jefferson objected to the last point, perhaps thinking it unnecessarily provocative, but he clearly recognized the dangers of such adventures to the honor and tranquillity of the United States. The secretary of state was even then sending to American representatives all over the world, from Samuel Shaw, consul at Canton, China, to Thomas Pinckney, minister at London, instructions on the protection of America's rights as a neutral.[11]

The question of prizes, too, had already caused some difficulty. After depositing Genet at Charleston, the frigate *Embuscade* resumed its journey to Philadelphia. On April 27, Jefferson wrote to his friend George Wythe: "We understand that a French frigate has taken several English vessels off the capes of Delaware, within two or three days after they had left Philadelphia." In what turned out to be something of an understatement, Jefferson added: "We shall be a little embarrassed occasionally till we feel ourselves firmly seated in the saddle of neutrality."[12]

---

10To Madison, May 19 and 27, 1793, Ford, *Jefferson's Writings* VI, 261, 168–69; "Anas," L & B, *Writings of Jefferson* I, 347–48; to Jefferson, May 27, 1793, *Writings of Madison* VI, 130.

11"Cabinet Opinion on Filibusters," Ford, *Jefferson's Writings* VI, 198; Jefferson to Samuel Shaw, Mar. 21, to David Humphreys, Mar. 22, to Carmichael and Short, Mar. 23, to C. W. F. Dumas, Mar. 24, 1793, L & B, *Writings of Jefferson* IX, 49–57.

12Ford, *Jefferson's Writings* VI, 218.

One of the *Embuscade*'s prizes was the *Grange*, captured inside
Delaware Bay. Jefferson accepted the British minister's prompt
protest on May 2. "The United States being at peace with both
parties," he assured Hammond, "will certainly not see with indifference its territory or jurisdiction violated by either . . . ."
Jefferson immediately advised Ternant, demanding that he im-
pound the *Grange*, but the outgoing minister had already determined to defer any action until Genet's arrival, in order not to
create an inconvenient precedent for his successor.[13]

This was the most clear-cut of the many prize cases which followed. One result was a report drafted by Randolph claiming the
entire Delaware Bay—and inferentially the Chesapeake as well—
as American territorial waters. The capture was therefore illegal,
and so Jefferson informed Ternant. He then asked Hammond to
note this proof of American "justice and impartiality to all parties" and pointedly expressed the hope

> that it will insure to their citizens pursuing their lawful business
> by sea or by land, in all parts of the world, a like efficacious inter-
> position of the governing powers to protect them from injury,
> and redress it, when it has taken place.[14]

Jefferson had by now virtually given up hope of extracting
from England even just treatment as a price of America's neutrality. He complained to Monroe that

> Gr Br has as yet not condescended to notice us in any way. No
> wish expressed of our neutrality, no answer of any kind to a
> single complaint for the daily violations committed on our sailors
> and ships. Indeed we promise beforehand so fast that she has not
> time to ask anything.[15]

At present he could only appeal to British fairness, in which he
had little confidence. But he had already suggested to Madison
another mode of appeal to Britain, one which testified to Jeffer-

---

[13]Jefferson to Ternant, to Hammond, May 3, 1793, *ibid.*, VI, 236–37; Ternant
to Minister of Foreign Affairs, May 1 and 10, 1793, C. F. M., 196–97, 197–99.

[14]Jefferson to Ternant, to Hammond, May 15, 1793, Opinion of the Attorney
General, May 14, 1793, *ASP, FR* I, 147–49.

[15]May 5, 1793, Ford, *Jefferson's Writings* VI, 240.

son's abhorrence of war as well as to his concern for the larger and more permanent interests of the United States.

> The idea seems to gain credit that the naval powers combined against France will prohibit supplies even of provisions to that country. Should this be formally notified I should suppose Congress would be called, because it is a justifiable cause of war, & as the Executive cannot decide the question of war on the affirmative side, neither ought it to do so on the negative side, by preventing the competent body from deliberating on the question. But I should hope that war would not be their choice. I think it will furnish us a happy opportunity of setting another example to the world, by showing that nations may be brought to do justice by appeals to their interests as well as by appeals to arms. I should hope that Congress instead of a denunciation of war, would instantly exclude from our ports all the manufactures, produce, vessels & subjects of the nations committing this aggression, during the continuance of the aggression & till full satisfaction made for it. This would work well in many ways, safely in all, & introduce between nations another umpire than arms.[16]

In effect, Jefferson wanted to use measures of economic coercion to force Britain to accept the doctrine of "free ships, free goods," which would permit freedom of commerce for American ships with all the warring powers. He recognized, of course, as he once had to explain to Genet, "that by the general law of nations, the goods of a friend found in the vessel of an enemy are free, and the goods of an enemy found in the vessel of a friend are lawful prize." Britain had thus far been determined to adhere to "this rigorous principle," but Jefferson hoped its own interest could be enlisted to bring about the denied "modification," as he called it.[17] Jefferson knew that Britain was the United States' best customer. But the reverse was also true, and this was the basis for Hamilton's irreconcilable opposition to Jefferson's views.

The secretary of the treasury, whose views usually commanded a majority in Washington's cabinet, appeared to be motivated

[16]Mar. 1793, *ibid.*, VI, 192–93.
[17]July 24, 1793, *ibid.*, VII, 456–59. Jefferson's recognition of fact, however, did not amount to the abandonment of "free ships, free goods" adduced by Ritcheson, *Aftermath*, 285.

by two factors: a growing detestation of the French Revolution and, more important, the conviction that American trade with Britain, on which his fiscal system and especially the revenue which supported the federal government was based, was vital to the nation's survival. Jefferson rejected both of Hamilton's assumptions, but his own remedies were not to be tried until he became President. Meanwhile, Grenville's diplomacy, with the inestimable advantage of Hamilton's confidential relationship with Hammond, and the recklessness of the Girondist government of France and its agent, combined to nullify Jefferson's best efforts.

Britain was not interested in American complaints or in purchasing American neutrality. Grenville possessed as sure an understanding of France's intentions as he did those of the United States, as his instructions to Hammond demonstrated. On March 12, 1793, he ordered his minister to watch particularly for shipments to France of corn, flour, and naval stores. These items were contraband, according to British maritime practice, and Grenville specifically rejected the modern principle of "free ships, free goods." Britain would not tolerate the fitting out of French privateers in American ports and, since she intended to blockade French ports, American ships would risk confiscation by attempting to enter those declared blockaded. A prohibition against financial aid to France through advance payments on the American debt completed Grenville's rules for American good conduct, which was to be guaranteed by Hammond's support of those influential Americans who shared Britain's abhorrence of "principles similar to those which have been so generally and so fatally propagated in France.[18]

18I. B. M., 37–40. Hammond's *Most Secret and Confidential* dispatch No. 11, Apr. 2, 1793, justified Grenville's confidence. Hammond assured his chief that the U. S. would adopt "as strict a neutrality *as may not be directly contrary*" to its treaties with France. It would receive Genet but would not give him *de facto* recognition and would make no new engagements with France. This, of course, from Hamilton, whom Hammond now identified in cipher. Proof of Hamilton's reliability, said Hammond, was evident in his fulfillment of his promise to refuse any advance to France on the American debt. A further interesting revelation was Hammond's suggestion that Jefferson, whom he regarded as "the devoted instru-

Still basking in the warmth of his popular reception, Genet thought he could afford to be generous regarding the *Grange*. "The learned conclusions of the Attorney General of the United States, and the deliberations of the American Government," he declared, "have been on this subject the rule of my conduct." The prize had been surrendered

> as a proper means to convince the American Government of our deference and of our friendship. The French republicans ... will seize every occasion of showing the sovereign people of the United States their respect for their laws, and their sincere desire to maintain with them the most perfect harmony.[19]

Genet had more important matters to attend to. He had first to derive benefit from the French decree of February 19 opening French West Indian ports to American ships and equalizing French import duties paid by American and French shipowners. Jefferson informed Monroe on May 5 of "a most advantageous decree of the French National Assembly in our favor" which, as Lebrun had noted, "offers the Americans all the advantages that they could desire." However, Lebrun told Genet, "this new proof of fraternal sentiment" was deserving of reciprocity—the least the American government could do, in fairness if not in gratitude, was to grant the long-denied exemption from the tonnage duty.[20]

Less visionary than the Brissotin inner circle, Lebrun did not rely on the good disposition of the government of the United States. He ordered Genet ". . . to direct public opinion by anonymous publications and . . . draw forth all the advantage you can from the first reaction to the decree of the National Convention."

---

ment of a French faction," had already violated his trust in subverting policies of his government, though "the proofs of his criminality are not easily obtained." F. O. 5, 1. It is not unreasonable to attribute these inferences to Hamilton and, though they failed to damage Jefferson personally, they clearly foreshadow the campaign of innuendo which later was so markedly successful against his successor, Randolph.

19To Jefferson, May 27, 1793, *ASP, FR* I, 149–50.

20Ford, *Jefferson's Writings* VI, 239; Lebrun to Genet, Apr. 10, 1793. AECPE-U, 37, 132–33. The decree of the National Convention is in *ASP, FR* I, 147.

He advised using the gazettes of Boston and Baltimore, in order to "diminish the suspicion that you wrote them yourself." Genet could place complete confidence, according to Lebrun, in President Washington, in Jefferson,[21] in Senator Pierce Butler of South Carolina and in Madison, all of them Southerners, but special efforts would be needed "to direct the sentiments of the New Englanders."[22]

Lebrun's first concern was the procurement of American supplies and provisions, which the February decree was intended to facilitate. Since the French merchant marine could not hope to supply France while the British navy ruled the waves, that decree bespoke national necessity rather than generosity. By April 10, Lebrun had still heard nothing of Ternant's application for three millions of livres to purchase salt and beef—a substantial test of American gratitude to France—and also to liquidate the remaining American debt promptly.[23]

On May 22, Genet formally presented to Jefferson a request for repayment by the United States of the balance of its debt to France. This precipitated another cabinet controversy, with Jefferson and Hamilton as usual pitted against each other. Hamilton favored a flat rejection of the request, without assigning any reason for it. Jefferson agreed on the necessity of refusing but saw no reason to add a gratuitous insult. Observing that the best reasons for a refusal were best unmentioned, Jefferson suggested that Hamilton could easily adduce practical objections and proposed that debt installments due during the current year be met ahead of schedule in order to ensure the continued good will of France. Washington as usual tried to steer midway between his two secretaries: Hamilton drafted a refusal of the application,

21Commenting on Ternant's report of Jefferson's intention to retire, Lebrun wrote: "We know what is responsible for the disagreements that he has experienced for some time past." A successor to Jefferson might be "a man less attached to our alliance and less prejudiced against England." Genet therefore should prevent his post falling to "a man won by England or linked to Mr. Hammond." To Genet, Apr. 10, 1793, AECPE-U, 37, 208–209vo.
22Feb. 24, 1793, ibid., 37, 132–33.
23Lebrun to Genet, Apr. 10, 1793, ibid., 37, 208–209vo.

ascribing it to the inadequacy of the treasury's resources, but no offer of advance payments was included.[24]

This refusal went beyond Genet's most pessimistic expectations. By the middle of June, moreover, the financial requirements of projects already set in motion had become pressing, and he appealed to Jefferson again. He would not expose himself twice to a refusal, he said, and was therefore serving notice that he would begin giving assignments of the American debt in payment to his creditors. Now Jefferson hastened to inform Genet that the President had authorized the settlement of installments due that year. This arrangement was just and desirable for both parties, he added, although the government had not expected to be able to oblige so soon. But Genet must reconsider his plan for assigning portions of the debt. Jefferson thought this would be harmful to the interests of both nations and insisted "that what is of mutual concern will not be done but with mutual concert." His gesture of good will was gained after all, and Genet's financial straits were momentarily relieved.[25]

Genet next invited Jefferson to negotiate a new treaty. Following the inevitable grandiloquent preface, Genet announced the recent decrees of the National Convention, implying that it was now the turn of the United States to offer a *quid pro quo*. Although it does not seem to have occurred to Genet, the French decrees (that of February 19 was "explained" by another of March 26) really made the question of a new treaty superfluous. The exigencies of her position had already forced France to yield to American commerce all the privileges for which Jefferson and others had been contending for almost a decade. Lebrun saw this, and on April 11 he had ordered Genet to counteract it with the observation that the new privileges rested upon a law which could be revoked if Frenchmen were not put on the same foot-

24 *ASP, FR* I, 142–46; Washington to Hamilton, June 3, 1793, Draft of Report on the French Debt, June 5, 1793, *Hamilton Papers* XIV, 514–16, 518–21; Jefferson to Washington, June 6, to Genet, June 11, 1793, Ford, *Jefferson's Writings* VI, 287–89, 294–95.

25 Genet to Jefferson, June 14, Jefferson to Genet, June 19, 1793, *ASP, FR* I, 156–57.

ing as Americans in American ports, as the decree specifically required.[26]

Lebrun probably realized that this could be no more than a gesture. Any concessions to France would necessarily jeopardize American neutrality. And most dangerous, from the American point of view, would be the strengthening of the colonial guarantee which Genet was to insist upon. Even an exemption from the tonnage duty in favor of French ships, though it could have but little value, would certainly be interpreted as an act of hostility by Britain. This difficulty had been foreseen in Genet's instructions, and Lebrun would have been happy if the United States had been willing to enter the European war at once, rather than become involved by degrees. Jefferson, though he seemed to Genet "impressed . . . with the necessity of contracting new political and commercial links with us," preferred to leave well enough alone and avoided a formal reply. At the end of the year, when he submitted to Congress his long-deferred report on commerce, he referred to Genet's overtures and attributed their non-acceptance to internal disturbances in France.[27]

By the end of May, Jefferson already had his hands full working out the practices of neutrality and trying to restrain the flamboyant minister. Genet was feverishly engaged in executing the many projects which, as Lebrun reminded him, "demand the greatest activity of you." These, and multiplying difficulties which were largely unforeseen, gave Genet little time for wasted endeavors, especially since he would soon choose to spend many precious hours vainly seeking to controvert the policies of the American government.[28]

Genet's subsequent career was to illustrate abundantly the Brissotin intention of revolutionizing the globe. It was ironic that Americans continued to trust the leaders of the Gironde,[29]

26Genet to Jefferson, May 23, 1793, *ibid.*, I, 147; AECPE-U, 37, 210-11.
27Genet to Minister of Foreign Affairs, Oct. 5, 1793, C. F. M., 258; "Commercial Privileges and Restrictions," Dec. 16, 1793, *ASP, FR* I, 304.
28Lebrun to Genet, Apr. 10, 1793, AECPE-U, 37, 132VO.
29See Jefferson to Brissot, May 8, 1793, Ford, *Jefferson's Writings* VI, 248-49.

despite their callous determination to use the United States as a pawn in the execution of their grand designs.

Genet wrote to Lebrun on June 19, 1793, that if he had not landed at Charleston and there been able to mobilize public opinion in his support, he probably would not have been received at Philadelphia at all.[30] He was completely wrong about this and instead might have blamed that circumstance as the beginning of his troubles, because what he did there was to plague his relations with the government from the moment he arrived at Philadelphia.

Jefferson begin his official correspondence with Genet by laying down the principles which would guide the United States in cases affecting American neutrality. He evidently expected that the new French minister would be grateful for "explanations" which would serve as a "rule of action" for him as well as for the American government. The first rule concerned the court of admiralty which Genet had ordered Mangourit to set up at Charleston, a consular court which had since condemned a British vessel captured by a French frigate. Jefferson agreed with Hammond, who claimed that this was not warranted by the usage of nations nor by treaty stipulations between France and the United States. He warned Genet that the United States could not tolerate such an assumption of jurisdiction by any officer of a foreign power; and while it would be regarded in this instance as "an error in judgment in the particular officer," Genet would be relied upon to prevent any repetition.[31]

Hammond had also charged that a vessel had been fitted out and manned at Charleston and commissioned to cruise against Britain. Regarding Hammond's assertion that some of the crew were Americans, Jefferson stated that the government had already expressed its "highest disapprobation" of such conduct and would discover and punish any offenders. The friendship of the United States with all the belligerents, its desire for peace as the surest path to prosperity, and its intention to prevent the corrup-

30C. F. M., 217.
31Jefferson to Ternant, May 15, 1793, *ASP, FR* I, 147.

tion of the morals of its citizens through participation in lawless plunder and murder[32] were security for the good faith and vigilance of the government. Jefferson was unwilling to believe that the French nation was lacking in respect and friendship for the United States, but such charges demanded attention.[33]

Genet replied to Jefferson's friendly letter on May 27, and it was obvious at once that he had no intention of accepting advice on faith. The condemnation of prizes at Charleston, he claimed, was merely the exercise of a right belonging to France under the Treaty of Commerce of 1778. As for the arming of privateers at Charleston, they were all ships belonging to French commercial houses, and he had authorized their armaments and commissioned them after the governor of South Carolina had agreed with him that there was no law prohibiting such action. Furthermore, the vessels were manned and commanded by French citizens or by Americans who, at the moment when they entered the French service, knew no article of the treaties or laws of the United States which forbade it. These explanations, Genet asserted, were "a sincere exposition of my conduct, to put you in a capacity to judge whether I have encroached on the sovereignty of the American nation . . . ."[34] Much of this account could not be contradicted because the neutrality proclamation was not known in Charleston at the time. But Genet had exposed himself to severe criticism by exercising the functions of his office, and the most questionable ones at that, before he had even been received. Two days later, he thought it best to revise the instructions he had given the consuls of France, "as it is essential at this time to avoid all that could contravene the principles

[32]Ternant had proposed an article suppressing privateering as one of the bases for the new treaty he hoped to negotiate in the fall of 1792. Since it was based on antiprivateering articles in U. S. treaties with Portugal and Prussia, Ternant was hopeful, reporting to his government that Jefferson much favored this "humanitarian principle." Jefferson to Ternant, Oct. 16, 1792, Ford, *Jefferson's Writings* VI, 122; Ternant to Dumouriez, Sept. 10, Oct. 11 and 17, 1792, C. F. M., 158, 160–62.

[33]Jefferson to Ternant, May 15, 1793, *ASP, FR* I, 147–48. Grenville expressed satisfaction at "the tone and purport" of Jefferson's reply. To Hammond, July 5, 1793, I. B. M., 42.

[34]*ASP, FR* I, 149–50.

of neutrality that the American government appears to have adopted provisionally." But he still claimed exactly what he had already defended as his country's right.[35]

The points at issue here brought up at the outset, in one form or another, all the principal problems of neutrality which were to vex relations with Genet for the rest of his mission. The question of admiralty jurisdiction arose from conflicting interpretations of the treaties between France and the United States; this was part of a larger question, that of the limits of American territory. There was no question of the right of French armed vessels to bring their prizes into the ports of the United States,[36] but Genet claimed for the French consuls the right of passing on the validity of the prizes after a question had arisen involving the territorial jurisdiction of the United States. Jefferson rejected this claim, asserting that questions involving American jurisdiction were a matter of sovereignty which could be surrendered only by special arrangement. Genet reiterated his claim on June 14, and again on June 22, but the futility of it was acknowledged in his complaint that "our treaties have been unfavorably represented: arbitrary orders have directed against us the action of the tribunals."[37]

Answering Genet on June 5, Jefferson stated the conviction of the government that it was "the *right* of every nation to prohibit acts of sovereignty from being exercised by any other within its limits, and the *duty* of a neutral nation to prohibit such as would injure one of the warring powers." The case of admiralty jurisdiction involved its duties as a neutral nation, and it was with the duties of the United States that Washington's administration was primarily concerned. In his opinion in the case of the *Little Sarah*,[38] Jefferson conceived it the duty of the United States,

---

[35]Circular letter to French consuls, May 29, 1793, AECPE-U, 37, 325–26.

[36]In a circular letter to the collectors of the ports of May 30, 1793, Hamilton stated that French prizes could be brought into American ports and sold, provided that they paid the regular duty required by the tonnage law. Other belligerents could not do so, however, because it was prohibited by ARTS. 17 and 22 of the treaty with France. *Hamilton Papers* XIV, 499.

[37]Genet to Jefferson, May 27, June 14 and 22, 1793, *ASP, FR* I, 149–50, 152, 155.

[38]The *Little Sarah* was an English brig which had been captured by one of the

since its treaty with France forbade the fitting out of privateers for her enemy, to prohibit the same to France. The treaty not granting France the privilege, it was a case of "the refusal being necessary to preserve a fair and secure neutrality." But the arming had taken place before the government had been able to take measures to prevent it or even to make known its policy, and therefore it would be unjust to require restoration of the prize. Britain, he said, should be satisfied with a "very moderate apology" and the knowledge of the disapproval of such acts in the future by the government of the United States.[39]

Hamilton was more concerned with Britain's rights. He was for forcing the French to make restitution of the prize, and thought that "a decided conduct appears most consistent with our honor and with our future safety." Rather than being consistent with American future safety, however, such a course would very quickly have embroiled the United States with France, because the *Little Sarah* was only the first such case and several privateers had been fitted out at Charleston at about the same time and had since been busily taking English prizes. Jefferson suspected Hamilton of aiming at such an embroilment with France and he struggled against it constantly. Presumably it was on account of such a possibility that Washington decided to say nothing of the prizes, but to order out of American ports all privateers which had been armed there. Jefferson did not think even this right, though he was relieved that Hammond, supported by Hamilton, was not to win restitution.[40]

Jefferson informed Hammond on June 5 of the President's decision. He reported it to Genet at the same time, adding that the friendly sentiments already expressed by the minister left no room to doubt his speedy compliance. Little more than one week later, however, Genet complained indignantly that the seizure

privateers outfitted at Charleston, probably the *Citizen Genet*. McMaster, *History of the People of the United States* II, 100. See Thomas, *American Neutrality*, 188–96.

[39]"Opinion on Little Sarah," May 16, 1793, *ASP, FR* I, 150.

[40]May 15, 1793, *Hamilton Papers* XIV, 451–60; Jefferson to Madison, June 2, 1793, Ford, *Jefferson's Writings* VI, 277.

of a French armed vessel by order of the governor of New York was a "signal violation of the laws of neutrality." Jefferson at once reminded Genet of the decision communicated one month earlier and warned him that all persons involved in this second breach of neutrality would be prosecuted in the courts. Hammond had also asked whether the French privateers ordered out of American ports were to be allowed to return or to send in their prizes. The cabinet merely agreed, however, that the privateers must depart to French ports; nothing was to be said concerning their subsequent proceedings.[41]

Hammond wrote on July 7 that ever since Genet's arrival "he has, in his communications with the government, assumed a tone of authority unexampled in any independent nation."[42] Genet had indeed, but initially his arrogance was tempered with conciliation. By the beginning of June, Genet was openly fighting the United States government in American courts. This contest involved an American citizen, Gideon Henfield, who, having enlisted on the crew of the *Citizen Genet*, was arrested at Charleston for engaging in hostile action against a nation at peace with the United States and was tried and eventually acquitted. Genet insisted that Henfield and another American, John Singletary, by their act of enlistment, had renounced their American citizenship and placed themselves under French protection. Jefferson, supported by a tart opinion of Attorney General Randolph, contended that an act which was itself the commission of a crime could not transfer citizenship. When the defendant was acquitted, notwithstanding the charge of the court recognizing the offense as punishable, Jefferson rationalized the result as the jury's exercise of the executive authority's right of pardon, because the crime was not knowingly and willfully committed.

41To Genet, to Hammond, June 5, to Genet, June 17, 1793, Ford, *Jefferson's Writings* VI, 282–83, 285–87, 307–11; Genet to Jefferson, June 14, 1793, *ASP, FR* I, 152–53; "Anas," June 17, 1793, L & B, *Writings of Jefferson* I, 359.

42To Grenville, F. O. 5, 1. See John A. Carroll and Mary W. Ashworth, *George Washington: First in Peace* (New York, 1957), 84ff. for the President's view of Genet.

More accurately, Hammond reported to Grenville that the jury was packed.[43]

The result of the Henfield affair was not entirely satisfactory either to the government or to Genet. Genet could still report to Lebrun that "the voice of the people continues to neutralize the declaration of neutrality of the President," although the Fayettist Washington," a much changed man from the hero of former years, impeded his mission in a thousand ways. Jefferson, despite his good qualities, was weak-kneed enough to subscribe to measures in which he did not believe. But Congress would soon voice the sentiments of the people. Full speed ahead, therefore:

> In the meantime I provision the Antilles, I excite the Canadians to throw off the yoke of England; I arm the Kentuckians, and I prepare an expedition by sea which will second their descent into New Orleans . . . . The *Embuscade* and our corsairs, whose number is augmented by the *Vainqueur de la Bastille*, the *Petite Démocrate*, and the *Vieux-Whig*, desolate the commerce of our enemies.[44]

The *Petite Démocrate*, formerly the *Little Sarah*, had an important place in the plan against New Orleans, but meanwhile it had attracted the notice of the government.

The President's cabinet heard on July 6 that the *Little Sarah* was being armed at Philadelphia, under its very nose, and immediately asked Governor Thomas Mifflin of Pennsylvania to investigate. Two days later, Mifflin presented his report and asked what he should do. The brig had indeed been fitted out and was armed with fourteen cannon, which Genet said were French property. The Governor knew that some of them, at least, had been purchased at Philadelphia. The vessel had recently dropped down the river toward Mud Island, but Genet told Jefferson that it was not yet ready to sail. Jefferson tried to extract a promise

---

[43]Genet to Jefferson, May 27, 1793, AECPE-U, 37, 315vo–16; Genet to Jefferson, Jefferson to Genet, June 1, Randolph to Jefferson, May 30, Jefferson to Morris, Aug. 16, 1793, *ASP, FR* I, 151–52, 168–69; July 7, 1793, F. O. 5, 1. See Thomas, *American Neutrality*, 165–76, and Malone, *Jefferson and Ordeal of Liberty*, 119–21.

[44]May 31, June 19, Aug. 15, 1793, C. F. M., 216, 217–18, 241.

from Genet that it would not depart until the President returned to Philadelphia, but the minister refused. Jefferson was confident, however, from Genet's declaration, that the ship could not leave before that time.

Hamilton and Knox wanted to set up a battery on Mud Island to interdict the sailing of the vessel, firing on it if necessary. Jefferson objected to this action as liable to produce the event it sought to prevent, which, because of the ship's unready state, would not otherwise occur. Firing on the *Petite Démocrate* might result in a commencement of hostilities and, since there were reported to be Americans in the crew, no one could foretell the consequences. Also, such a measure would be most inconsistent, in view of the patience of the government in suffering the insults and injuries inflicted by England. Hamilton and Knox were not convinced by this argument, replying that the government was in duty bound to prevent the sailing of the vessel, or England would have grounds for declaring war. Besides, there would be no trouble if the vessel remained where it was. Since the President was expected back from Mount Vernon within forty-eight hours, however, they agreed to postpone the matter pending his decision.[45]

The President returned to Philadelphia on July 11. He was immediately apprised of these facts and the next morning summoned his cabinet. Jefferson had received a letter from Genet regarding the intentions of the *Petite Démocrate*, which Genet said would be dispatched "when ready." The case, he continued, could not create any difficulty: "When treaties speak, the agents of nations have but to obey." Genet was sticking to his own interpretation of the treaties and, if further proof were needed, there were two other letters Jefferson had received in the interval. One, written at the same time the cabinet was debating the fate of the *Petite Démocrate* (July 3), demanded the restitution of the *Vainqueur de la Bastille*, which had eluded the unenthusiastic vigilance of Governor Moultrie at Charleston and had

45"Cabinet Opinion on 'Little Sarah,' " July 8, "Reasons for his Dissent," July 9, 1793, Ford, *Jefferson's Writings* VI, 339–44.

been seized, with a British prize, when she entered the port of Wilmington, North Carolina. The other was a peremptory summons to cause Governor Mifflin to order out of the port of Philadelphia the English ship *Jane*, which Genet asserted to be a privateer. With these and several other matters before them, the President and his advisers decided to consult judicial authority. A list of questions would be submitted to the Supreme Court covering all the problems which were still being contested. In the meantime, all the ships involved would be expected not to depart until the further orders of the President.[46]

Six days after this decision, twenty-nine questions on the practice of neutrality were submitted to the justices of the Supreme Court, but in the meantime the *Petite Démocrate* had been sent to sea by Genet to cruise off the American coast. Unfortunately for the harassed cabinet officers and their chief, the justices refused on constitutional grounds to answer the questions, and they had to be taken up again.[47]

[46]"Cabinet Opinion on Privateers and Prizes," July 12, 1793, *ibid.*, VI, 344–45; Jefferson to Genet, July 12, 1793, *ASP, FR* I, 163.

[47]To the Chief Justice and Judges of the Supreme Court of the U. S., Questions for Judges, July 18, 1793, Ford, *Jefferson's Writings* VI, 351–52, 358–60; Thomas, *American Neutrality*, 150; Jefferson to Morris, Aug. 16, 1793, *ASP, FR* I, 169–70. In contrast to Genet's conduct in regard to the *Petite Démocrate*, Hammond agreed to detain the *Jane* at once. After an exchange concerning some additional guns which had been mounted, Consul General Phineas Bond ordered the new armament dismounted and the vessel was released. Reporting the incident to Grenville, Bond referred to the French privateer which "was permitted to sail," but he added: "... the fact is ... that the inability of the United States to enforce any measures in opposition to the views of the French faction existing here has induced the exercise of a caution, not very favorable to the dignity of the government, but deemed inevitably necessary." Aug. 5, 1793, J. Franklin Jameson, ed., "Letters of Phineas Bond, British Consul at Philadelphia, to the Foreign Office of Great Britain, 1790–1794," in *Annual Report of the American Historical Association, 1897* (1898), 535–36.

CHAPTER IV     Genet's Undoing

> If the Americans are neutral it is certainly difficult
> for them to preserve the peace and tranquillity of
> neutrality. The English menace and insult them;
> the French excite and disturb them.
>
> COMTE D'HAUTERIVE, 1793.

JEFFERSON had been rapidly undeceived respecting Genet by the *Petite Démocrate* incident. He unburdened himself to Madison in unusually bitter terms:

> Never in my opinion was so calamitous an appointment made, as that of the present Minister of F. here. Hot-headed, all imagination, no judgment, passionate, disrespectful & even indecent towards the P. in his written as well as verbal communications, talking of appeals from him to Congress, from them to the people, urging the most unreasonable & groundless propositions, & in the most dictatorial style etc, etc, etc. If ever it should be necessary to lay his communications before Congress or the public, they will excite universal indignation. He renders my position immensely difficult.[1]

What was most unfortunate was that the Republican party had received Genet so wholeheartedly and espoused his cause so warmly that its existence was now threatened by the excesses of its colorful hero.[2] The reception being accorded the papers written by Hamilton, under the pen name "Pacificus," plainly illustrated the danger. Those papers, as Adet explained to his

[1] July 7, 1793, Ford, *Jefferson's Writings* VI, 338–39.
[2] Jefferson explained to Monroe on June 4, 1793: "Parties seem to have taken a very well defined form in this quarter.... The war has kindled & brought forward the two parties with an ardour which our own interests merely, could never excite...." *Ibid.*, VI, 281–82.

superiors two and one-half years later, were really an extenuation and explanation based on the thirteen questions Hamilton had drawn up for Washington in April. With the advantage of Genet's scandalous conduct as a running commentary, Hamilton's argument had become more persuasive. Never one to underestimate an opponent, Jefferson selected Madison as the only journalistic debater equal in talents to Hamilton. "Nobody answers him, & his doctrines will therefore be taken for confessed. For God's sake, my dear Sir, take up your pen, select the most striking heresies and cut him to pieces in the face of the public."[3]

Madison answered on July 18 that the letters of "Pacificus" caused him "equally surprise & indignation." He doubted that he could do the subject justice, however, since he was not in possession of some important materials and hoped someone else had already assumed the task. But within a few days he started to work, though he soon found the task "the most grating one I ever experienced." In contrast to Hamilton, he was handicapped by ignorance of pertinent transactions of the government, since Jefferson believed himself bound to protect the secrecy of cabinet proceedings. Madison nevertheless published five installments of his reply to "Pacificus" in August and early September, under the nom de plume "Helvidius." But fever and the oppressive heat of the Virginia summer cut short his labors before he had finished. It did not matter much anyway, for Genet had already done to himself what his most rabid antagonists could never have accomplished without his help, and the tireless Hamilton had seized the opportunity to open a new attack against France and her sympathizers under the pseudonym "No Jacobin."[4]

[3]Adet to Committee of Public Safety, Jan. 17, 1796, C. F. M., 816; July 7, 1793, Ford, *Jefferson's Writings* VI, 338. The "Pacificus" papers are in *Hamilton Papers* XV, 33–135. Seven numbers appeared in the *Gazette of the United States*, beginning on June 29 and concluding July 27, 1793.

[4]To Jefferson, July 18, 22, 30, 1793, *Writings of Madison* VI, 135–38. The "Helvidius" papers are in *ibid.*, VI, 138–88. Jefferson reported that he was "charmed" with No. V on Sept. 8, but he did not press Madison to continue. Ford, *Jefferson's Writings* VI, 417. Madison's letters to Jefferson of June 10 and 13 contain the gist of the arguments he elaborated as "Helvidius." See *Writings of Madison* VI, 127–28, 130–33, and Neal Riemer, "The Republicanism of James Madison," *Political*

More serious than Hamilton's heresies was the fanatical conduct of Genet. Madison appealed to Jefferson: "he must be brought right if possible. His folly will otherwise do mischief which no wisdom can repair." Jefferson had already told Monroe that Genet's conduct was "indefensible by the most furious Jacobin" before Genet doomed himself by sending out the *Petite Démocrate.* The only thing to be hoped, Jefferson continued, was that Americans generally would distinguish between Genet and the nation he represented. On August 3, Jefferson told Madison that Genet must be disowned, because "he will sink the republican interest if they do not abandon him." He himself had already done so, for "we have decided unanimously to require the recall of Genet."[5]

If Jefferson had reached such conclusions, to what degree was Washington's patience taxed? On July 31, the President wrote to Jefferson that the cabinet would the next day consider what to do with Genet. Jefferson was requested to bring along all his correspondence with the exasperating minister. It was unanimously agreed to send to Gouverneur Morris a full statement of Genet's conduct to be communicated to the Executive Council of France, including a stipulation requiring Genet's recall. Knox

---

*Science Quarterly* LXIX (Mar. 1954), 45–64. Hamilton's "No Jacobin" letters appeared from July 31 through Aug. 28, 1793, and are in *Hamilton Papers* XV, 145–306 *passim.* Edward S. Corwin, *The President: Office and Powers, 1787–1957* 4th rev. ed. (New York, 1957), 427, quotes John Quincy Adams on Madison: "He therefore entered the lists against Mr. Hamilton in the public journals and in five papers under the name of Helvidius, scrutinized the doctrines of Pacificus with an acuteness of intellect never perhaps surpassed and with a severity scarcely congenial to his natural disposition and never on any other occasion indulged." Adams also noted that Madison's "most forceful arguments are pointed with quotations from the papers of *The Federalist* written by Mr. Hamilton." See John Q. Adams, *Eulogy on James Madison* (Boston, 1836), 45–48. Charles G. Fenwick, *The Neutrality Laws of the United States* (Washington, D. C., 1913), 5–25, shows that the bases of Jefferson's neutrality policy were correct according to eighteenth-century practice. Concerning Madison's principal argument, that Congress rather than the President had the constitutional power to determine peace as well as war, Corwin states: "In 1794 Congress passed our first neutrality act, and ever since then the subject of neutrality has been conceded to lie within its jurisdiction." *President,* 181.

[5] July 18, 1793, *Writings of Madison* VI, 135; July 7, 1793, Ford, *Jefferson's Writings* VI, 339, 361–62.

proposed to dismiss Genet, but no one else supported so abrupt a measure. It was agreed, however, to inform Genet that his recall had been "required." Jefferson opposed this procedure, foreseeing that "it would render him extremely active in his plans," but he was overruled. Hamilton then made a "jury speech" proposing to publish the whole correspondence with Genet "by way of appeal to the people." Randolph's opposition to this transparent attempt to use Genet for Federalist party advantage forced a continuance of the discussion until the following day, when Jefferson answered Hamilton's second speech. Knox then introduced recently published attacks on Washington by the Jeffersonian press, obviously hoping thus to enlist the President's support of this stratagem to involve the Republican friends of France in the minister's ruin. But Washington ultimately preferred to leave the issue to the course of events.[6]

Though this scheme to arouse the people against France and her sympathizers through the publication of Genet's correspondence failed for the time being, Genet himself had given his enemies a handle which would suit the same purpose. When Alexander J. Dallas, Governor Mifflin's secretary, had hurried to Genet with the governor's request to detain the *Petite Démocrate* in port, Genet had flown into a rage. In the course of a violent diatribe against the treatment he had received from the government, he threatened to appeal directly to the American people. This threat was reported to Mifflin, who let it slip to Hamilton, who told his friends, Chief Justice John Jay and Senator Rufus King of New York. Apparently Hamilton and King, with Jay's complicity, decided to make something of it after Hamilton had lost his fight to make an appeal to the people. Hamilton wrote King that "the present question may be pursued independently," since the correspondence, when turned over to Congress, would probably include nothing not strictly official.[7]

6Aug. 1 and 2, 1793, L & B, *Writings of Jefferson* I, 379–83; Carroll & Ashworth, *Washington: First in Peace*, 109–13.
7Hamilton to King, Aug. 13, 23–24, 1793, *Hamilton Papers* XV, 233–42, 267.

King and Jay then came forth with a public charge that Genet had threatened to appeal over the head of the President to the people, and the Federalist newspaper took it up with a vengeance. Genet continued to play into Federalist hands, first by emphatically denying the charge, and immediately thereafter by threatening to appeal to the arbitration of Congress. Then Dallas refused to substantiate the story of Jay and King, and Mifflin and Jefferson refused to say anything at all. Genet demanded that his accusers be prosecuted for libel, and Jefferson replied that the President had referred his complaint to the attorney general. At this point, Jay and King were insulted and demanded an explanation from the President for this unfavorable inference, and the comedy of affidavits rolled merrily on into the next year.[8]

The threat to appeal over the head of the President was included in the stinging indictment of Genet's conduct which Jefferson addressed to Morris on August 16. The threat must have appeared even more incredible in the light of the French National Convention's decree of April 13, which Genet belatedly forwarded to Jefferson on September 24. This decree announced the general French policy of not meddling in the affairs of foreign governments, and to permit no interference in the internal administration of the Republic.[9] Genet, however, was probably too obsessed with his plans to see the humor of it. Jefferson had correctly foreseen the reaction of the French minister to this crowning disaster on top of his pyramiding misfortunes.

The party of Jefferson and Madison was jettisoning Genet in

[8]Dallas had told Jefferson of the threat and the latter had repeated it in a cabinet meeting. Jefferson assured Madison (Sept. 1, 1793) that the charge was true. Ford, *Jefferson's Writings* VI, 403. Much of the correspondence concerning this affair is printed in Charles R. King, *Life and Correspondence of Rufus King* 6 vols. (New York, 1894–1900), I, 455–80. See also Meade Minnigerode, *Jefferson, Friend of France* (New York, 1928), 325, who claims the last laugh for his hero, Genet, when he admits that the Frenchman's "whole procedure was a continuous appeal to the people."

[9]*ASP, FR* I, 171, 165. Jefferson's performance on this occasion, according to one of Hamilton's closest friends in New York, entitled him to absolution from all his past sins and rendered his continuance in office necessary "until the clouds which threaten a storm be dispersed." Robert Troup to Hamilton, Dec. 25, 1793, *Hamilton Papers* XV, 587–89.

the nick of time. Hamilton's motives in seeking to bring Washington's enormous prestige to bear against their party (a tactic which would be employed with increasing frequency and success) in the business of Genet's recall were evident. But he was much more candid with the British minister than he had been with his chief and his colleagues. One week after Genet's fate had been sealed, as far as the American government was concerned, Hammond reported the unanimous decision: should the French National Convention refuse to recall Genet or disavow his schemes, Hammond quoted Hamilton, "This order of things must issue in a war between France and this country, an event to which I know this government looks forward, as neither improbable nor distant." Hamilton, according to Hammond, claimed that he had done everything possible "towards the production of this condition of affairs in the existing relations between France and the United States."[10]

Jefferson recorded in his "Anas" on July 5 that Genet had called on him and rapidly read instructions he had prepared for the French botanist André Michaux, whom he was sending to Kentucky, and addresses to the inhabitants of Louisiana and of Canada. Besides inciting the people of the latter two provinces to insurrection, Genet had mentioned two American generals in Kentucky who had offered to capture New Orleans if he would finance the expedition. He would not advance the money required, but promised to reimburse them after the campaign was over. The officers would be commissioned in Kentucky and Louisiana and, with what Indians they could enlist, would undertake the expedition against New Orleans, after which Louisiana would be established as an independent state. Jefferson answered that he did not care what disturbances were excited in Louisiana, but that enticing Americans from Kentucky to attack Spain was the same as hanging them, for that would be their fate if they started hostilities in violation of their country's neutrality.[11]

10Hammond to Grenville, Secret, Aug. 10, 1793, F. O. 5, 1.
11July 5, 1793, L & B, *Writings of Jefferson* I, 361–62.

81

The indefatigable Frenchman had already been busy arranging campaigns against the enemies of France all over the American continent. At Charleston, he and Mangourit had made plans for the recruiting of Americans and Frenchmen in Georgia and the Carolinas for attacks on the Spanish Floridas. Mangourit was entrusted with the organizing of this expedition.[12]

One of Genet's first acts after reaching Philadelphia had been to send one of his secretaries, Mézières, to Canada to find out whether conditions there were favorable to a revolution against English rule. Mézières sent Genet a highly optimistic report, but a Frenchman whom Mézières sent to Montreal to start a French newspaper was so badly received that he did not dare publish Genet's proclamation. By September, Mézières was forced to confess his miscalculations, writing to Genet that "it is useless to shine all at once the light of liberty at its fullest before a people completely submerged in the black night of ignorance and slavery."[13]

According to the vague plans of the Girondist visionaries, Canada, when separated from England, was to be awarded to the United States. Genet, though interested in this result, was far more concerned with the long-dreamed-of recovery of the French empire in Louisiana from Spain. Too, this project held greater promise of success in view of the difficulties the United States had been experiencing with the Spaniards over the navigation of the

[12]See Frederick J. Turner, *The Significance of Sections in American History* (New York, 1950), chs. 3 and 5, "The Origins of Genet's Projected Attack on Louisiana and the Floridas" and "The Policy of France toward the Mississippi Valley in the Period of Washington and Adams," reprinted from *American Historical Review* III (July 1898) and X (Jan. 1905). The most recent treatment is Richard K. Murdock, "Citizen Mangourit and the Projected Attack on East Florida in 1794," *Journal of Southern History* XIV (Nov. 1948), 522–40.

[13]AECPE-U, 37, 419–23vo; L. Didier, "Le Citoyen Genet," *Revue des Questions Historiques* 92 (1912), 72–73. Didier blames the complete failure of Genet and Mézières in Canada on Genet's dislike of Indians and neglect of the potentialities for using the large tribes north of the Ohio who were ancient friends of France. In addition, Mézières had totally misunderstood the Roman Catholic Canadians, whom he reported enthusiastic for the French Revolution and contemptuous of their priests.

Mississippi and the belligerent attitude of the western settlers toward the obstinate officials at New Orleans. Ternant had already received an offer from George Rogers Clark, a hero of the American Revolution who had been embittered by Virginia's ingratitude for his services, to conquer the province for France. General Clark promised to take Upper Louisiana with 400 men, and New Orleans with 800, plus the Indian tribes which he would enlist. He estimated the expense of the whole expedition at not more than 3,000 livres sterling. Ternant put this letter into the hands of Genet on the latter's arrival at Philadelphia, and by July, Genet was ready to send Michaux to Kentucky to coordinate plans with Clark and gain the cooperation of Kentucky's Governor Isaac Shelby.[14]

The affairs of the strife-torn French colony of Saint-Domingue now claimed Genet's attention, but circumstances were shortly to join them to the Louisiana project. Early in June, Jefferson was relieved to hear from Genet that France did not wish to involve the United States in the European war by its guarantee of the islands. Just as heartening was the news that Saint-Domingue and Martinique were both willing and able to defend themselves against British attack, though a prolonged blockade would have serious consequences. On June 19, Genet reported that the news from the Antilles continued good: Saint-Domingue was calm at last, Martinique and Guadeloupe had already repulsed English attacks, and reinforcements had arrived in all those islands. Tobago had fallen to the English, however, as had St. Pierre and Miquelon opposite the Gulf of St. Lawrence, but 200 French marines had escaped from the last two islands and reached Philadelphia.[15]

A new outbreak of violence erupted at Saint-Domingue at the end of June. Aroused by a civil conflict between separate French

14 Ternant to Minister of Foreign Affairs, May 10, Genet to Minister of Foreign Affairs, July 25, 1793, C. F. M., 199, 222; L. Didier, "Le Citoyen Genet," 76–77.

15 Jefferson to Madison, June 9, 1793, Ford, *Jefferson's Writings* VI, 293; Genet to Minister of Foreign Affairs, June 19, 1793, C. F. M., 218.

authorities at the island's capital, the blacks had risen again. Cap
Français (now Cap Haïtien) was virtually destroyed in a three-day
orgy of killing, looting, and burning. The whites who escaped
fled to the shelter of the ships in the bay, American merchantmen as well as French warships now under the command of the
expelled governor of the colony, General T. F. Galbaud. Bulg-
ing with refugees, the pathetic fleet sailed for America and, by
the middle of July, dropped anchor in Chesapeake Bay. Galbaud
sent two admirals from the French squadron to report their
plight to Genet in Philadelphia.[16]

The refugees received a fraternal and hospitable welcome in
the United States,[17] but the French squadron was in such a state
of disrepair that Genet sent it to New York for refitting. Genet's
own sympathies were all on the side of the National Convention's commissioners in Saint-Domingue who had driven out the
governor, and he decided to get rid of Galbaud's adherents
among the French sailors. His fertile brain had quickly devised
plans for the squadron which, he promised his government, "will
rapidly change the face of our affairs in America." Previously,
he had intended the *Embuscade* and the *Petite Démocrate* as
naval support for General Clark's attack on New Orleans; now
the squadron from Saint-Domingue could also assist in that en-
terprise. That campaign could not begin until October, however,
and first he would send the fleet north to retake St. Pierre and
Miquelon, destroy the English base at Halifax, and disrupt British fishing operations in the Newfoundland fisheries. This mission could be accomplished in time for the fleet to return for
repairs to New York before sailing for New Orleans.[18]

[16]Genet to Minister of Foreign Affairs, July 6, 1793, c. f. m., 219. A detailed account of the disaster at Saint-Domingue is Ludovic Sciout, "La Révolution à Saint-
Domingue — les Commissaires Sonthonax et Polverel," *Revue des Questions Historiques* 64 (1898), 424–44. See also Mary Treudley, "The United States and Santo
Domingo," *Journal of Race Development* VII (July 1916), 112–13.
[17]The problem of French refugees from Saint-Domingue as well as from France
occupied much of the time of French agents in America throughout the Revolution. See Frances S. Childs, *French Refugee Life in America, 1790–1800* (Baltimore,
1940), 160–85.
[18]Genet to Minister of Foreign Affairs, July 28, Aug. 2, 15, 1793, c. f. m., 227,
234, 238–40. See McMaster, *History of the People of the United States* II, 124–25.

"The plan will appear very grandiose to you," Genet admitted, "but I am convinced that it will succeed." An important reason for his confidence was Genet's belief that "the American people, enlightened as to their true interests by our attentions, want war despite their worthless government." And an even greater design had appeared in the soaring imagination of the "veritable proconsul," who thought nothing of equipping fleets and armies on foreign soil in defiance of that nation's government. "My zeal will never be satisfied until I shall have drawn [the American people] into the war at our side. The whole new world must be free and the Americans must support us in this sublime design."[19]

The Saint-Domingue squadron, however, failed to exhibit the cooperation and enthusiasm without which it could be nothing but a burden on Genet's resources and a threat to his ulterior plans. The crews remained disaffected, and General Galbaud was soon implicated in a plot of royalist refugees to use the fleet to take them back to the colony for the purpose of effecting a counterrevolution. Genet discovered the intrigue in time to prevent its fruition, but Galbaud escaped to Canada with a few lieutenants, despite the efforts of Governor Clinton to capture him and turn him over to Genet. This occasioned another combing of the fleet, and soon the ebullient minister was sure that he had "shown the light to the misguided crews," and "re-electrified their patriotism." Precious time had been lost, he added, but it was still possible to repair the damage.[20]

After weeks of frenzied activity, Genet was ready to set in mo-

[19]Genet to Minister of Foreign Affairs, Aug. 2, 1793, C. F. M., 234–35; Didier, "Le Citoyen Genet," 82. One of many plans for the reconquest of Louisiana presented to the French government had concluded in words similar to Genet's: "an important observation is that such an expedition, although made without the consent of the United States, would be regarded by England and Spain as very hostile and would *inevitably force America to enter the war on our side*." Frederick J. Turner, ed., "Selections from the Draper Collection in the possession of the State Historical Society of Wisconsin, to elucidate the proposed French expedition under George Rogers Clark against Louisiana, in the years 1793–94," *Annual Report of the American Historical Association, 1896* I (1897), 956.

[20]Genet to Minister of Foreign Affairs, Sept. 19, 1793, C. F. M., 242; Treudley, "United States and Santo Domingo," 118–20.

tion the grand designs which were to cover him with glory and force a reorientation of the policy of the American government. He dispatched part of his fleet northward to retake St. Pierre and Miquelon, destroy the Newfoundland fishing bases, and burn Halifax. The remainder sailed for the Georgia coast to embark American volunteers recruited by Mangourit for the conquest of Florida. The two divisions would rendezvous later for the attack on Louisiana.[21]

Genet was sure these projects would succeed gloriously, and their obvious utility to the United States, especially in regard to Louisiana and Florida, would reverse the attitude of the American government toward him. But as his principal assistant at New York, the consul Alexandre Maurice Blanc de La Nautte, comte d'Hauterive, told his diary, Genet was infatuated with glittering generalities. No proper precautions regarding friendly ports, supplies, or other necessities had been taken, and Genet planned to use a fleet to accomplish what the English had done with a frigate and a ship's boat. "The conquest of Florida is a chimera which makes up for everything: there are two thousand men here and six hundred there. Michaux is in Kentucky and the frigates will be able to stand broadside to St. Augustine. . . . Canada is ours: two hundred Frenchmen are enough to expel the English from the posts. . . . Genet always decides on a course before having calculated the consequences. Nothing is thought through." And in New York: "We have here supplies of stores, a military hospital, an arsenal, sentinels going and coming, rifles on their shoulders: it is as Mr. Jefferson says, a sovereignty within a sovereignty."[22]

What was more serious for the French cause, Genet insisted on carrying on "a veritable war of words" with the American government, and he admitted that he aimed to overturn it. He thus opened wide the door to the complete justification of the Presi-

21Genet to Minister of Foreign Affairs, Oct. 7, 1793, C. F. M., 265. Genet reported that he had on July 31 ten naval vessels, including two ships-of-the-line, and thirteen privateers. AECPE-U, 38, 144–45.

22Genet to Minister of Foreign Affairs, July 25, 1793, C. F. M., 220; "Hauterive Journal" (New-York Historical Society), 27, 30, 31–32, 36, 41–42. See Frances S. Childs, "The Hauterive Journal," *The New-York Historical Society Quarterly* XXXIII (Apr. 1949), 69–86.

dent. But, "how to give advice to a man who airs his thoughts without thinking of the consequences?" Hauterive found it impossible, as Jefferson had months earlier: "If some one gives him advice, he will not listen unless they are views that he himself has already expressed." Especially was this true of the "war of the gazettes" which Genet insisted on waging, against the advice of his friends. Genet was at a disadvantage in every respect, and he could not put his money and his time to worse use than in these contests, where it was "ridiculous to triumph and shameful to be defeated." By November, Hauterive was sure that hostilities between France and America were as good as begun. Agreeing with Genet in his interpretation of the treaties and in his opinion of the course the American government insisted upon following, he nevertheless had to add that "it is certain that the public abuse, the accusations, the denunciations against the members of the government are acts of hostility on the part of an ambassador . . . ."[23]

Though solidly grounded, Hauterive's fears were premature, for on November 3 Genet heard that most of the squadron had sailed for France. "The whole build-up of a great project has collapsed like a house of cards: Canada, St. Pierre, Newfoundland, Acadia have vanished in smoke. All this had been predicted,

[23]"Hauterive Journal," 31, 45–48. Unlike Genet, whose writings and actions so often betrayed the thorough contempt he felt for the country, as well as for its government and leaders, while at the same time he "plots, contracts and spends with the ease, the prodigality and thoughtlessness of kings," Hauterive had a genuine affection for and understanding of America. "If the Americans are neutral it is certainly difficult for them to preserve the peace and tranquillity of neutrality. The English menace and insult them; the French excite and disturb them; and the colonials have chosen their country as the field for their harangues, their conspiracies and their debates. If it were permissible to stop being a Frenchman for one moment, this is how I would counsel them: Answer the English with pride, seize the forts they are holding from you, announce to their Minister that you are masters in your own country. Chase out the colonials, let not one of these agitators come to dishonor your territory by his offers, his complaints, his supplications. Announce to the French that you are neutral, they may trade freely, live in peace, prosper in the shade of your laws, but they may not negotiate; . . . Say to all the earth: we are neutral, and be it in truth, and I swear to you that you will be, and that in this firm and generous attitude you will ride out the tempests of war, everywhere welcome, everywhere respected, and that you will hold yourselves as far above the circumstances of your position as you are now actually beneath them." *Ibid.*, 56, 60–61.

however, by every one; but the foresight of misfortune will never enter a head so fascinated with flattering illusions." Genet's bubble had burst and, despite the activity he had inspired along the frontiers, his projects were doomed, the remnants of his forces disbanding in disgust a few months later.[24]

In a lengthy dispatch of October 7, Genet attempted to justify himself. He had been forced into open defiance of the American government, he said, because it was dominated by an English faction which continually refused to France her rights under the treaties, while it accepted supinely all the insults which England chose to give it. The aristocratic and monarchical bias of the government was so pronounced that "America is lost to France if the purgative fire of our revolution" were not to sweep the country. He had chosen the only course possible under the circumstances and was encouraged by the fact that he was supported by all honest Americans, who were more attached to the basic interests of America than to those of the selfish mercantile group. Jefferson, who at first had seemed to second his views, had turned out to be a man of straw. In the bitterness of his self-pity, Genet concluded that Jefferson's only real concern was to keep his place, whatever the issue of events.[25]

This querulous letter was entrusted to the first secretary of legation, Pascal, whom Genet was sending to Paris to plead his case. The minister knew that his recall had been demanded, and that his friends Brissot and Lebrun were no longer in a position to support him. He concluded: "If you believe it expedient to sacrifice me to Washington, at least send in my place a minister who will not abandon the Republicans . . . ." Genet persisted in the fiction that he was being persecuted for his devotion to the principles of liberty and equality, and grandiloquently offered himself as a martyr to the cause.[26]

Genet's concern for the Republicans was wasted. Aware of the political danger their former sponsorship of Genet now pre-

[24]*Ibid.*, 37.
[25]Genet to Minister of Foreign Affairs, Oct. 7, 1793, C. F. M., 244–52.
[26]*Ibid.*, 252.

sented—William Smith of South Carolina wrote to Hamilton from Boston: "You will be delighted with the Anti-Gallican Spirit which has lately burst forth"—the Republicans for some time past had been vigorously disassociating themselves from him. Jefferson, reporting Genet's public campaign against the President to Madison, was not sure that "some of the more furious republicans may not schismatize with him." That was in August, but by the middle of September, Madison reported to Monroe that the "mad-man" had been abandoned "even by his votaries in Philada." Madison was now at work on a campaign "to distinguish between the nation & its agent, between principles and events." The American people, Madison was convinced, were attached to the Constitution, to the President, to France and her revolution, and "to peace as long as it can be honorably preserved...." He was getting unexpected help in his campaign, for "the Anglicans & Monocrats... are betrayed by the occasion into the most palpable discovery of their real views. They already lose sight of the agent; and direct their hostilities immediately against France." Perhaps Genet realized what all this meant for him. Jefferson, passing on to Madison a report that Genet was to marry a daughter of Governor Clinton, concluded that the minister was afraid to return to France.[27]

In the first days of June 1793 the French government underwent another revolutionary change. The Jacobins seized power and displaced the Gironde. Lebrun carried on his functions under guard for a few days after the downfall of his party, but by June 14 the Mountain had installed one of its own men, François Louis Michel Deforgues, in the Ministry of Foreign Affairs. When Genet's first dispatches were received at the end of July, the

27Smith to Hamilton, Aug. 22, 1793, *Hamilton Papers* XV, 262–63; Aug. 25, 1793, Ford, *Jefferson's Writings* VI, 397–98; Madison to Archibald Stuart, Sept 1, to Jefferson, Sept. 2, to Monroe, Sept. 15, 1793, *Writings of Madison* VI, 188–89, 191–95, 197–98; Nov. 2, 1793, Ford, *Jefferson's Writings* VI, 440. The second rank of Republican leaders was similarly disillusioned: "Genet's conduct is really extravagant. I do not so much object to his matter, as to his manner, of complaint. I think, amidst all his rant about the rights of man, I can discern a care about self; . . ." Alexander J. Dallas to Albert Gallatin, Nov. 8, 1793, Albert Gallatin Papers, New-York Historical Society, 1793, No. 22.

new minister at once wrote a blistering lecture to Genet. Comparing Genet's letters with American newspapers, Deforgues noted with satisfaction the generous hospitality of his reception, which had been the more enthusiastic because he was the first representative of the Republic. But there was nothing to justify the minister's assumption that he could direct political activities in the United States and force it to make common cause with France in defiance of its government. The Executive Council (Girondist) could never have authorized its representative to exercise proconsular powers in a friendly and allied nation; it had, on the contrary, ordered him to treat with the government and not with a portion of the people. Neither had Genet been instructed to set himself up as the chief of an American party, nor to antagonize Washington, without whose good will and cooperation any supposed success would be illusory. It appeared to Deforgues that Genet, ever since his arrival at Charleston, "had been surrounded by men who were either misinformed or very designing." Genet's activities in contravention of the expressed policy of the American government were explicitly censured, and Deforgues ordered him to apply himself to the task of gaining the confidence of the President and Congress, without which he could never attain "the patriotic and laudable goal that you have in view."[28]

Deforgues had more than Genet's dispatches and American newspapers by which to judge his envoy's conduct. He read accounts of Genet's activities in the English press. And in October, ships of the fleet which Genet had expected to use for the conquest of enemy territories in America began to arrive in French ports, carrying most unfavorable reports of the minister's conduct. The first ship to arrive had come straight from the Chesapeake, where it had heard of Genet's plan to retake St. Pierre and Miquelon. Assigned to convoy a fleet of provision ships to France, it had been commandeered by Genet for his schemes but had escaped. The port officials of Lorient and Brest addressed a diatribe

<hr />

[28]July 30, 1793, C. F. M., 228–31. Genet's successor, Joseph Fauchet, and Otto both became convinced that Genet's American intimates were motivated more by hatred of Washington than by love of France. Commissioners to Minister of Foreign Affairs, Mar. 21, 1794, *ibid.*, 314; Otto, "Considérations," 73.

against "the unauthorized and treasonable actions of Genet" to the foreign minister, venturing the opinion, as good Jacobins, that no better could be expected from a friend of the dictatorial Brissot. More important, what about the provision fleet which was probably still in the Chesapeake awaiting a convoy?[29]

This question much interested Deforgues. Provisions from America, he wrote to Genet on September 28, were needed immediately. Genet's neglect of this subject, despite his instructions and Lebrun's correspondence, was inexcusable. Genet was ordered to explain at once, and meanwhile to place himself under the instructions of Deforgues' emissary, who had a commission from the minister of the interior for another three million livres in provisions.[30] Unimpressed by Genet's flamboyant schemes, the Jacobin minister emphasized from the first France's true interest in America—as a primary source of provisions. Genet, seeking to carry out the plans of his erstwhile masters, had lost sight of this elementary fact in his zeal for military conquests, which tended to contravert the American neutrality on which the carriage of provisions depended.

The Jacobin government had already decided to get rid of the disturbing minister when Pascal reached Paris late in November with a trunkful of correspondence from Genet. Deforgues asked the Committee of Public Safety what to do about the papers; before the committee asked for them, Pascal was in jail. One month earlier, Captain Bompard, Genet's erstwhile friend of the *Embuscade*, had reached Rochefort in command of the division which Genet had ordered to St. Pierre. Now thoroughly disgusted with Genet, Bompard was so loud in his denunciations

29London *Gazeteer*, Sept. 4, 1793, Officials of Brest and Lorient to Committee of Public Safety, Oct. 2, 1793, AECPE-U, 38, 58–58vo, 286–86vo.

30*Ibid.*, 38, 277–77vo. The commission for three millions sent Ternant the previous year had been filled, but Genet had received a total of 13,835,000 livres in orders for provisions, from which nothing had been received. The U. S. had made all payments on the debt due in 1793 by Nov. 1, when Genet asked that he be allowed to draw on installments due the next year. The day following this request he complained to Jefferson that drafts he had issued in anticipation of a favorable response had been refused by the Treasury, but it was another week before he received Hamilton's formal refusal. *ASP, FR* I, 158–59, 185–86, AECPE-U, 39, 253–54.

that the agent at the port joined in denouncing Genet to Deforgues, to which Deforgues answered that measures had already
been taken to replace Genet.[31]

Betrand Barère, a ubiquitous politician who exercised a decisive influence over diplomatic affairs in the Committee of Public
Safety, had plucked Deforgues from a minor post in the War
Ministry to head Foreign Affairs. Barère and Hérault de Sechelles made policy, though even they were careful to follow
the lines laid down by the Jacobin chief, Robespierre.[32] Barère
had discussed American affairs with Thomas Paine, the famous
American propagandist for liberty who had just relinquished a
seat in the Convention, and Paine had helped prepare a paper on
relations with the United States which Barère presented to the
committee on September 13.

Barère reported a rumor that the United States had embargoed
English ships and that Thomas Pinckney was preparing to leave
London in anticipation of war between the two countries. If this
were true, immediate measures should be taken to exploit the
situation. With Genet's recklessness in mind, he suggested that
two commissioners be sent to the United States to treat with its
government: "much dignity, great tact, and, if possible, a knowledge of the English language is necessary." Paine, he suggested,
could be useful as a guide and interpreter, but he had too many
enemies in America to succeed as a principal agent. The advantages Barère expected to accrue to France from America's imminent participation in the war were almost identical to those
sought by the Girondists, but the fervor for world revolution had
given way to calculations for the improvement of the external
position of France.[33]

Barère's expectations of an Anglo-American rupture did not
materialize, but his *mémoire* first suggested the use of commis-

[31]Deforgues to Committee of Public Safety, Dec. 22, Representatives of the
People (Rochefort) to Minister of Foreign Affairs, Nov. 11, Deforgues to Representatives Lequiner and Laignelot, Nov. 19, 1793. AECPE-U, 39, 457, 230, 301.
[32]Frédéric Masson, *Le Département des Affaires Étrangères pendant la Révolution, 1787–1804* (Paris, 1877), 285–88.
[33]AECPE-U, 38, 215–17vo.

sioners to repair the damage done by Genet. In spite of the latter's conduct, however, Barère opposed his recall: Genet knew what was happening in the United States, had many friends there, and the explanations of the commissioners would suffice to mollify the American government. Barère proposed that Hérault head the commission, since Hérault had been "particularly intimate with Jefferson during the latter's stay in France." The commission would be a sort of supermission, in effect reducing Genet to the position of a secretary. It would have powers to conclude a new treaty of commerce and to arrange the closest cooperation between the two nations during the war, but the proposal for a new treaty of perpetual alliance also suggested by Barère was rejected by the rest of the committee when the subject was reviewed one month later.[34]

Thanks to the fact that Genet's later dispatches only straggled into the Foreign Office in unrelated and nonsequential groups after September 28, his superiors did not know that retaining Genet in Philadelphia in any capacity was now out of the question. Gouverneur Morris, the American minister to France, received Jefferson's long exposition of Genet's misconduct on October 5, and three days later he related it to Deforgues, who promised to recall the offending minister immediately. On October 10, Deforgues answered Morris officially, assuring him that the council would regard "the strange abuse of their confidence by this agent, as I do, with the liveliest indignation." Deforgues promised that Genet would be punished, but Morris assured him that he was instructed only to request his recall. Reporting this to Jefferson on October 19, Morris added that the French government planned to send a commission of three or four persons to replace Genet, who would be sent back to France under arrest.[35]

Despite Deforgues' assurances, there were difficulties involved in recalling Genet. As Otto, now back in Paris, pointed out: "Since his operations in finance and other matters are very ad-

---

[34]*Ibid.*, 39, 466–69vo. This is a copy of the Barère-Paine *mémoire* already cited, but with annotations of the committee.

[35]*ASP, FR* I, 372, 373, 374–75.

vanced it would be dangerous to recall him," although "he is clothed with powers all the more dangerous since there is some doubt of the sincerity of his patriotism." Genet was no longer acceptable to the American government, but he still enjoyed great popularity. The Jacobin charge of Girondist treason had begun to incriminate Genet, but Otto, at least, seemed to prefer waiting for the success or failure of Genet's schemes before throwing his fate into the political vortex. His solution was a simple one, similar to Barère's: "Give him without delay two adjuncts under the title of commissioners and order him to work only in concert with them.'" Robespierre, however, had made up his mind, and "Recall" was entered in the margin of Otto's report. Beside the names of Pascal, "a very good patriot, intelligent, but without experience," and Bournonville, "a very young man," the same word was entered.[36]

Robespierre could not resist the temptation to continue the attack on the already guillotined Girondist leaders by repudiating their foreign policy and branding as traitors their agents abroad.[37] In a speech to the Convention on November 17, framed in the form of a report to the Committee of Public Safety, Robespierre laid down the new line. He began by cleverly establishing a common identity between Girondist and English policy. Both, he said, were trying to separate North from South in France and in the United States. England's Pitt, like the federalist Girondists, wanted to fragmentize the American union, and the agents of the traitors France had just punished still pursued the same policy in the United States. The brother-in-law of Brissot himself was French consul general in the United States, and the friend of Brissot and Lebrun, Genet,

> has fulfilled faithfully the views and the instructions of the faction which chose him. He has used the most extraordinary

[36]AECPE-U, 39, 193.

[37]Otto wrote in June 1797: "However atrocious and imperious the policy of Robespierre, of S. Just, of Colot and of Barère, then all-powerful in France, was, they could not refuse a demand so just. But always extreme and tyrannical in their measures they ordered the minister and his advisers put in irons and sent back to France on board a frigate." "Considérations," 22.

means to antagonize the American government against us; he has dared to speak to it, with no pretext, in a threatening tone, and to make propositions equally contrary to the interests of both nations; he has endeavored to render our principles suspect or dangerous . . . .[38]

It is easy, almost unavoidable, to disparage this *"opéra bouffe bungler,"* as one historian has dubbed Genet,[39] but at the same time his fanatical zeal and almost superhuman energy command a measure of wonder, if not admiration. Hamilton, who was himself endowed with a capacity for tremendous bursts of sustained activity, called Genet a "burned out comet" at the end of his mission. And so he was. He retired to a small farm on Long Island to escape paying at Paris the price of his colossal failure, married the daughter of Governor Clinton, and spent the rest of his life in a self-imposed martyrdom which he nourished self-consciously.

The plans of the Gironde, under existing circumstances, were impossible of fulfillment. They and their unhappy minister were victims of changing standards in the conduct of neutral nations toward belligerent powers. According to previous international practice, Genet had a right to expect from Washington's government a pro-French neutrality rather than a truly impartial one. Jefferson's sense of international justice and Hamilton's extreme fear of antagonizing Britain, with the concurrence of both in the national interest in preserving peace, led to Genet's utter frustration. Unable to fulfill his mission by regular diplomatic means, Genet chose to carry it out in the only other manner which presented itself. Robespierre was less than frank, however, in imply-

38AECPE-U, 39, 280–84vo. For the reasoning which linked the Girondins to English policy, Robespierre was indebted to Ducher, whose pamphlet "les Deux Hémisphères" had already been published in Paris with Robespierre's approval. Ducher's main object, however, was to arrest the neglect of the West Indian colonies which, he warned, was leading to their "Anglo-Americanization." He approved of America's neutrality as the most realistic course, but he insisted that its benefits to France would not be increased by abandoning the colonies to the U. S. AECPE-U, 39, 201–204vo.

39Thomas A. Bailey, *A Diplomatic History of the American People* 3d ed. (New York, 1946), 78; Samuel F. Bemis, *A Diplomatic History of the United States* 5th ed. (New York, 1965), 103.

ing disapproval of the ends Genet sought to attain, at least as far as they included measures calculated to obtain for France a more beneficent neutrality.[40]

It would be misleading to assume that the Jacobin government had marked Genet for destruction as a consequence of its accession to power, as it undoubtedly had Brissot and his intimates. It was the magnitude of Genet's failure and the necessity for reversing the reaction against France in the United States which caused Robespierre to move so dramatically against him. "To upset the perfidious maneuvers used by its enemies to alarm the faithful allies of the French nation, the Swiss cantons and the United States, as to [France's] intentions," Robespierre presented a decree which was at once seconded by his committee and adopted by the Convention. It was the constant resolution of the French Republic, decreed Robespierre, to be "terrible towards its enemies, generous towards its allies, just towards all peoples." The treaties which bound the French people to the Americans and Swiss would be faithfully executed, and changes in those treaties required by the Revolution and by the war would be made "on the basis of reciprocal loyalty and common interest." All French officials would respect the territory of all neutral or allied nations, and the Committee of Public Safety would find means of strengthening the bonds between France and the United States. Finally, in all her discussions with these powers, France would be guided by "principles of equity, generosity and esteem." An evident attempt to undo the mischief caused by Genet, the decree was to be translated into many languages and distributed everywhere. That this was not too much to do was obvious when news arrived that Genet, in order to justify himself, had published parts of his instructions. They showed, in the words of Otto, "that the French Government had constantly betrayed the Americans, whom it wanted to raise to the loftiness of our principles in order to drag them into the war."[41]

[40]Charles S. Hyneman, "The First American Neutrality," *Illinois Studies in the Social Sciences* XX, Nos. 1 & 2 (1934), 153; DeConde, *Entangling Alliance*, 305.

[41]Report to the Committee of Public Safety on the Political situation of the Republic, Nov. 17, 1793, AECPE-U, 39, 292–93vo; Otto, "Considérations," 23.

Despite Robespierre's soothing assurances, however, French aims had not changed a whit. The missionary zeal for world revolution of the Gironde had been replaced by a nationalistic self-interest, and a new practicality was evident. The new situation, as it affected the United States, was outlined by the Committee of Public Safety, on November 25, in a memorandum entitled "Means of attacking and destroying the influence of the English on the American continent." French agents, according to the committee, must demonstrate to Congress, and convince the American government, that the fate of America was dependent on that of France. English capture of the French islands would close them to American commerce forever,[42] and it was therefore in America's interest to do all in her power in their defense. Congress should be persuaded to join with France in expelling England from Canada and Nova Scotia in retaliation for the shameful conduct of Britain in retaining the Northwest posts in violation of the peace treaty of 1783, and Canada and Nova Scotia would then be free to join the American Union. In addition, the United States should be sufficiently encouraged by recent French successes to remonstrate against English insults less timidly.

In the economic sphere, the United States, after ministerial agreements with France, should publicize its trade figures with England. That country's favorable balance of two to three millions sterling a year would arouse public opinion in support of a 15 or 20 percent tax on British imports. The proceeds from these duties could be used to encourage native manufactures, and both results would combine to turn English merchants against Pitt. And, an additional motive for American cooperation: "England concerts with Spain to keep the United States from the navigation of the Mississippi River."[43]

42Two of the ports of Saint-Domingue had been surrendered to the English in September by their royalist inhabitants. Genet to Minister of Foreign Affairs, Oct. 10, 1793, C. F. M., 283; *ASP, FR* I, 187–88. For an analysis of English strategy in the West Indies at this time, see Mahan, *Influence of Sea-Power upon the French Revolution* I, 110–11.
43AECPE-U, 39, 324–25vo.

An ambitious program, but not one likely to commend itself to a government dedicated to avoiding Europe's embroilments. The United States was with difficulty adhering to its treaty obligations with France, despite the provocations of Genet.[44] But the Jacobin emphasis on economic nationalism for the United States was new. Perhaps Hérault's earlier intimacy with Jefferson had supplied this argument, for it was very similar to the program which Jefferson was soon to propose to Congress. But meanwhile, France had an American Genet to deal with.[45]

[44]It was true, as Mahan says, that the U. S. "then observed a benevolent partiality for French cruisers and their prizes," but this was in fulfillment of explicit treaty stipulations. *Influence of Sea-Power upon the French Revolution* I, 111. Britain was so far from resenting this that Grenville wrote to Hammond in January 1794: "... with respect to the conduct of the present Government of America His Majesty's Ministers think that there appears to have prevailed in it's general tenor a desire for the maintenance of a fair Neutrality and even a disposition friendly towards this Country." I. B. M., 44.

[45]Ulane Bonnel characterizes Gouverneur Morris as "counterpart to Genet, and as clumsy as he was." *La France, Les Etats-Unis, et la guerre de course (1797–1815)* (Paris, 1961), 39n.

## CHAPTER V

An American Aristocrat
in Revolutionary France,
1792–1794

> I felt myself degraded by the communications I
> was forced into with the worst of mankind.
>                    GOUVERNEUR MORRIS TO WASHINGTON,
>                                    DECEMBER 30, 1794.

IN his foreword to an edition of Talleyrand's letters in America,
Frederick L. Nussbaum noted that statesmen of the last century
were familiar with the idea that the international financiers were
"the Sixth Great Power," a catholic community outside the con-
fines of the nation-state.[1] This power "was somewhat like a feudal
society with its suzerains and vassals bound together by a complex
of mutual loyalties and common interests." Although it eventually succumbed to the totalitarian impulses of the national states,
in the eighteenth century it was an international community
whose members maintained a double citizenship and operated in
areas beyond the range of the still incomplete authority of the
individual states. Members of the international financial community frequently assumed national offices, in which their importance as members of the "Sixth Power" might transcend their
authority as representatives of a perhaps relatively insignificant
nation.

An American junior member of "the Sixth Great Power" was
Gouverneur Morris, whom President Washington nominated at

[1] Hans Huth and Wilma J. Pugh, trans. and eds., "Talleyrand in America as a
Financial Promoter, 1794–96," *Annual Report of the American Historical Association, 1941* 2 vols. (1942), II, v–vii.

the end of 1791 as minister plenipotentiary to a France in revolution. Morris' actions in France appeared to his critics as the result of a rigid ideological bias combined with a sentimental attachment to the privileges of royalty. In his own view, however, he was a representative of an order fighting to maintain a semblance of international financial stability and the concomitant social amenities against a revolutionary trend which increasingly threatened chaos.

Morris' aristocratic propensities caused an acrimonious debate in the Senate over his nomination. Washington was wasting his time when he told his friend of the senatorial objections to him and warned him against "imprudence of conversation and conduct." Morris' promise in reply that he would henceforth observe "that circumspection of conduct," which had hitherto been lacking, and refrain from the busy meddling in French affairs which had already made him suspect at Paris, was at least disingenuous. At the very time the Senate voted, on January 12, 1792, to approve his appointment, by a vote of sixteen to eleven, Morris was up to his neck at Paris in a plot to effect King Louis XVI's escape from France.[2]

William Short, chargé d'affaires at Paris since Jefferson had returned home, was bitterly disappointed at not receiving the appointment himself. Privately, he believed Morris' attitude had disqualified him, and he regarded Morris' open contempt for the

---

[2]Malone, *Jefferson and Rights of Man*, 400–403; Washington to Morris, Jan. 28, 1792, *Writings of Washington* XXXI, 468–69; Morris to Washington, April 6, 1792; Morris, *Diary and Letters* II, 402–404. Senator James Monroe wrote to Jefferson: "The appointment of Gouverneur Morris . . . is so generally reprobated that no one appears to vindicate it . . . . It is said that it would have been difficult to have found a more unfit person for that station, even if some industry had been used to select him out." June 17, 1792, Stanislaus M. Hamilton, ed., *Writings of James Monroe* 7 vols. (New York, 1898–1903), I, 232. More than one year earlier, Senator William Maclay had confided to his diary a pungent premonition of such an event: "Mr. [Robert] Morris wishes his namesake, Gouverneur, (now in Europe selling lands for him) placed in some conspicuous station abroad. He has acted in a strange kind of capacity, half pimp, half envoy, or perhaps more properly a kind of political eavesdropper about the British court, for some time past. Mark the end of it." Feb. 25, 1791, *Journal of William Maclay*, 389. See Morris, *Diary and Letters* II, 387n.

French Revolution as dangerous to his country's interests.[3] But Short had been named minister resident to The Hague. With Morris in Paris, he asked Charles François Dumouriez, the able soldier of fortune then presiding over the Ministry of Foreign Affairs, for an interview to present the new minister and to deliver his own letter of recall. Dumouriez replied politely a few days later that the representative of the American people "will be precious to me above all the ministers of foreign powers," but it was obvious to Morris that the minister entertained reservations. During the interview which followed, Morris tried to remove the prejudice against himself with the frank statement that he had previously tried to effect changes in the new French constitution out of his regard for France, and that he had resolved henceforth not to meddle in her affairs. Dumouriez remained unconvinced, however, and despite the promptings of the court delayed another two weeks before presenting Morris to the King.[4]

Jefferson, in his instructions to Morris, had written that "to you it would be more than unnecessary for me to undertake a general delineation of the functions of the Office to which you are appointed." Nevertheless, he went on to remind Morris that those functions were to be

> constantly exercised in that spirit of sincere friendship and attachment which we bear to the French Nation .... With respect to their Government, we are under no call to express opinions which might please or offend any party, and therefore it will be best to avoid them on all occasions, public or private. Could any circumstances require unavoidably such expressions, they would naturally be in conformity with the sentiments of the great mass of our countrymen, who having first, in modern times, taken the

3 Jefferson told Madison that he had already received "letters from France concerning the appointment there in the severest terms." June 1, 1792, Ford, *Jefferson's Writings* VI, 69. Soon after, however, he reported seeing a letter from Morris to the President containing promises "which mark him properly and gratefully impressed with the counsel which had been given him pretty strongly, as you know." To Madison, June 21, 1792, *ibid.*, VI, 90.

4 Short to Dumouriez, May 8 and 11, Dumouriez to Short, May 13, Deségueville to Dumouriez, May 17, 1792, AECPE-U, 36, 206–206vo, 224–24vo, 226, 231; Morris, *Diary and Letters* II, 429–30.

ground of Government founded on the will of the people, cannot but be delighted on seeing so distinguished and so esteemed a Nation arrive on the same ground, and plant their standard by our side.

Jefferson, too, had reservations concerning Morris, although there is no indication that he credited Morris' appointment to the influence of Hamilton. Had he known that Morris had immediately acknowledged this debt with an appeal to "water the Tree which you have planted" through a confidential correspondence by-passing the secretary of state, he might have derived less comfort from Morris' promises of good behavior to President Washington. As it turned out, Jefferson wished in vain to prevent Morris from indulging his personal sentiments in favor of a properly republican line. He was beginning to be disturbed at President Washington's gradual cooling toward the French Revolution, and with reason he blamed Morris' private letters for this attitude.[5]

Morris was particularly instructed to consider, "as the most important of your charges, the patronage of our Commerce and the extension of its privileges, both in France and her colonies, but most especially the latter." Dumouriez, disgruntled at the course of politics in Paris, had resigned and gone off to command an army at the frontier, so Morris, on July 9, 1792, addressed his successor, Chambonas: Congress had just shown its regard for French commerce in exempting French wines from a general increase in port duties, but there was widespread discontent in America at the late decrees restricting commerce in regard to tobacco and ships. The new commercial treaty recommended by the Constituent Assembly could remove such irritations by establishing commerce on a just and reciprocally useful basis. The United States would welcome any such overtures, which Morris clearly implied should properly be made at Philadelphia. Two

[5] Jan. 23, 1792, Ford, *Jefferson's Writings* V, 428; Morris to Hamilton, Mar. 24, 1792, Hamilton Papers, Library of Congress, XIV, 2074; Malone, *Jefferson and Rights of Man*, 403–404. It was likewise Hamilton, along with Chief Justice John Jay, who had prevailed upon the President to use Morris as unofficial agent in London in Oct. 1789. Ritcheson, *Aftermath*, 94.

weeks later, Chambonas replied evasively in language which clearly betrayed the ministry's coolness to the idea of a new treaty.[6]

Morris had no more luck with the debt question. He asked for an accounting from the records of the French treasury, so that he and Chambonas could settle past payments and regulate the terms of the aid Hamilton had advanced to Ternant for Saint-Domingue. Chambonas promised to assemble the documents and attend to the business as soon as possible. Morris believed that Chambonas wanted to settle every issue between the two countries, but he knew that the minister's position was too precarious to undertake anything. The Assembly was openly at war with the ministry and would almost certainly reject any arrangements made by any but its own leaders. When not engaged in factional maneuvering, the assemblymen were too busy thinking about the hostile troops massing on the frontier to give any attention to less critical affairs. Morris did receive, however, an account of the debt from the commissioners of the treasury, and he could work out adjustments for future discussion from it. Nothing further could be done for the moment.[7]

Affairs in Paris were approaching a climax, and the state of suspense could not last much longer. The expected outbreak came on August 10, when the Paris populace stormed the Tuileries, where the royal family was living. The King fled to the Assembly for protection, but it was forced to surrender him, and he was imprisoned with his family by the Paris Commune. The Assembly then suspended the unfortunate monarch and Morris recognized that France would soon be a republic, if the invading foreign armies could be repulsed. The ministry had evaporated again, the latest foreign minister, Sainte-Croix, fleeing to Morris' house for asylum, his predecessor having escaped to England just one week earlier. This latest revolution installed an all-Girondist ministry, which repudiated the constitution of 1791 and pushed

[6]*ASP, FR* I, 332–33, 333.
[7]Morris to Chambonas, July 18, Chambonas to Morris, July 20, 1792, AECPE-U, 36, 303, 308; to Jefferson, July 10, 1792, Morris, *Diary and Letters* II, 464–65.

a call for a national convention through the Assembly. France was declared a republic on September 21, 1792.

While elections for the National Convention went forward and the Girondists hunted down the Assembly's former leaders to be punished summarily for the crime of Feuillantism, the new ministers proceeded to duel with Morris over the problem of the debt. In April, Short had arranged with Dumouriez and his colleagues to turn over a substantial payment on the American debt at Philadelphia, where it would be used to purchase supplies for the relief of Saint-Domingue. But none of the ministers was willing to conclude the agreement without specific authority. By the time they had decided to ask the Assembly for legislative permission, Short thought the plan had been abandoned and had made the payment in the usual way at Amsterdam. The Assembly did issue a decree, on June 26, appropriating four millions of livres to the relief of Saint-Domingue, and Lebrun, the new Girondist minister of foreign affairs, used this in an attempt to get an advance of $400,000 for Saint-Domingue relief from Morris. Accepting Lebrun's invitation of August 28 to a conference with himself, Étienne Clavière and Gaspard Monge, ministers of public contributions (finance) and marine and colonies, respectively, Morris was asked to enter into the same contract which Short had agreed to five months before. This he refused to do, insisting that he had powers only to regulate the exchange of funds already advanced to Ternant. Pressed by Clavière, Morris asserted that he had no powers to treat with France's republican government at all.[8]

Morris' reflection on the legality of his government exasperated Lebrun, who pointed out to Morris the inconvenience of a position which made his functions useless. Such a stand, he insisted, could not be taken by a minister without orders from his government, and orders could not have arrived since the estab-

[8]Minister of Marine to Dumouriez, Apr. 19, 1792, Commissioners of Colonial Assembly of Saint-Domingue at Paris to the Colonial Assembly, Apr. 24, 1792, AECPE-U, 36, 169–69vo, 181–81vo; *ASP, FR* I, 336–37; Morris to Jefferson, Aug. 30, 1792, Morris, *Diary and Letters* II, 520–22.

lishment of the Republic. Morris was told by Talleyrand, former bishop, sometime diplomatic agent, and financier who was soon to flee his country, that Lebrun's letter had been written by Brissot himself, chief of the Girondists, and that the object was really to force Morris to commit the United States to recognition of the new regime. Morris was furious at the tone of the letter and had no intention of offering recognition to a government he abhorred. He alone of the foreign diplomatic corps had intended to remain in Paris, he told Lebrun, but the "style" of his letter obliged him to ask for his passport. He would leave France and go to England to await his government's orders.[9]

Morris' defiant reply alarmed the ministers, and Lebrun decided to placate him. The petty annoyances he had experienced were caused by "the agitation inseparable from a great revolution," Lebrun wrote on September 16, and increasing stability would prevent their reoccurrence. His letter had been misinterpreted, and he was chagrined that the representative of a nation founded on the same principles as those of France's new government should act like other foreign ministers. He hoped Morris would remain, but he would send his passport if he still wanted it. Monge told Lebrun that, since it appeared impossible to obtain more funds for Saint-Domingue from the United States, he had asked the Assembly to provide what was needed from other sources.[10]

Morris noted in his diary on September 8 that he had received "from the Minister an indirect apology for his impertinent letter and therefore I shall stay." He wrote Lebrun on September 17:

> I had the honor to receive your letters of the 8th and 16th. In consideration of the explanations contained in the latter I will

9 *ASP, FR* I, 338, 338–39; Lebrun to Morris, Aug. 30, Morris to Lebrun, Sept. 1, 1792, Morris, *Diary and Letters* II, 536, 523–27. Morris had anticipated Jefferson, who wrote on Oct. 15 ordering him to suspend all payments to France until further orders. Morris expressed his relief in his answer of Dec. 21, adding, "on this point I have been hard run." Ford, *Jefferson's Writings* VI, 120; Morris, *Diary and Letters* II, 590. Jefferson wrote on Dec. 30 that the suspension was revoked, since the Convention was invested with full powers to do the business of France. Ford, *Jefferson's Writings* VI, 149.

10 *ASP, FR* I, 339–40; Sept. 8, 1792, AECPE-U, 36, 380.

not again refer to yours of August thirtieth, and as it was that which decided me to leave France I resume my intention of staying on and awaiting the orders of my Court.

Morris' reference to his "Court" may have been an unintentional slip, but it must have irritated the militant republicans of the ministry. Clavière whom Morris had suspected of trying to feather his own nest, recognized that Morris had to be handled with care, but he demanded that his recall be applied for, "to save us from the artifices of a dangerous man, on account of his talents and the sinister use he seems set on making of them."[11]

Aside from personal animosities, the ministers' conviction that Morris was involved in royalist intrigues was only too well founded, for Morris was again hatching a scheme to rescue the King and his family. His diary for July and August records the development of the plot, and his own house was a royalist headquarters. The plain failed, but Morris had accepted custody of the King's funds, which he turned over to the King's heiress in Austria more than four years later. All of this was only suspected in the summer and fall of 1792, but it was enough to account for the fear and hostility with which Morris was regarded.[12]

Lebrun agreed with Clavière, and his first charge to Ternant was to demand Morris' recall. Lebrun feared the effect of Morris' dispatches in the United States and asked Ternant to report carefully the impression they made on American officials. Ternant at length turned over Lebrun's complaints to Jefferson because rumors concerning the rift between Morris and the ministry were already current. Jefferson at once laid the matter before the President, who agreed that Morris' usefulness at Paris was ended. The question of replacing him, however, was not soon to be answered.[13]

---

11 Morris, *Diary and Letters* II, 541; *ASP, FR* I, 340; Clavière to Lebrun, Sept. 10, 1792, AECPE-U, 36, 381–84vo.

12 Morris to Princess of France, Dec. 1796, Morris, *Diary and Letters* I, 561–64.

13 Lebrun to Ternant, Sept. 13 and 19, 1792, AECPE-U, 36, 387–88vo, 399–403vo; Ternant to Minister of Foreign Affairs, Feb. 13, 1793, C. F. M., 170–73; Feb. 20, 1793, L & B, *Writings of Jefferson* I, 334–35.

Lebrun henceforth avoided all active altercation with Morris, and an uncomfortable *modus vivendi* was imposed upon both parties by the exigencies of their respective situations. Morris told Jefferson that he was trying to maintain a strict neutrality between factions and governments in the unpredictable progress of the Revolution: a difficult thing when to do nothing often was to take sides. He was handicapped, he told Rufus King, in not being able "as heretofore to peep behind the scenes," but all desire to take part in French affairs went with the abolition of the monarchy. He appended a laconic footnote to his former activities in a remark to Washington: "History informs us that the Passage of dethron'd Monarchs is short from the Prison to the Grave."[14]

Despite President Washington's decision to replace his offensive minister at Paris, Morris retained his post for another year and a half. Washington tried to persuade Jefferson, who had recently postponed his retirement at his chief's earnest request, to accept another mission to France. Jefferson refused, saying that he was determined upon retirement and would never again cross the Atlantic in any case. Besides, the post at Paris had lost much of its importance: Philadelphia "was likely to be the scene of action, as Genet was bringing powers to do the business here." Jefferson had good reason to prefer handling relations with France himself at Philadelphia and there were additional reasons for putting off selection of a successor to Morris.[15]

The uneasy diplomatic truce between the Girondist ministry and Morris was maintained because all important matters were confided to Genet. The ministers ignored Morris as much as possible, particularly after adoption of the decrees of February 1793 in favor of American commerce. These, Morris reported on March 7, "contain, I believe, all that we want."[16]

---

14 Morris to Jefferson, to King, to Washington, Oct. 23, 1792, Morris, *Diary and Letters* II, 564, 566, 569.

15 "Anas," Feb. 20, 1793, L & B, *Writings of Jefferson* I, 335–36.

16 *ASP, FR* I, 355. Colonel W. S. Smith told Jefferson that "the French ministers are entirely broken with Gouverneur Morris; shut their doors to him, and will never receive another communication from him." "Anas," Feb. 20, 1793, L & B, *Writings of Jefferson* I, 334.

Morris was diligent in protesting seizures of American vessels by French privateers and warships, and Lebrun regularly assured him that the minister of marine would take "the most speedy measures for procuring . . . satisfaction." On one occasion, however, Lebrun could not resist commenting that the difficulty of distinguishing American from English vessels proceeded, in part, from "the probable connivance between several individuals of those two nations in making disguised shipments."[17]

Informing Genet of such difficulties on March 31, Lebrun said that "without doubt M. Morris will have taken advantage of them to present the conduct of France in an odious light." The ships complained of had been released without delay, he explained, and the indemnities demanded under the treaty would be granted. To reduce the danger of further seizures, the American government should provide national ships with the passports prescribed by the commercial treaty of 1778. As for Morris, his "manner of thinking, generally known here," rendered him obnoxious: Genet should repeat the demand that the American government have a representative at Paris who would "work in concert with the executive Council of the Republic in maintaining the good understanding between the two nations."[18]

Suddenly, on May 9, 1793, the Convention aimed a powerful blow at Franco-American understanding. It declared that all foodstuffs bound for any enemy port on a neutral ship, or enemy merchandise found on a neutral ship, were lawful prize. Morris warned Lebrun that Britain would immediately adopt this system,[19] which in France's case was specifically prohibited by the "free ships free goods" stipulation of the treaty of 1778. Lebrun informed the president of the Committee of Public Safety that Morris was right and that "justice and the interest of the Republic equally demand that the flag of the United States be treated

17Lebrun to Morris, Mar. 29, Apr. 8, 1793 (enclosing copy of letter from Minister of Marine to Minister of Foreign Affairs, Apr. 7, 1793), *ASP, FR* I, 359–60, 361–62.

18AECPE-U, 37, 194–95vo.

19As early as Feb. 13, Morris had told Jefferson that he expected England to adopt such a policy. *ASP, FR* I, 350.

with care and, moreover, that we furnish no taint to a treaty which we will often have occasion to invoke in the course of the present war." The committee agreed, for on May 17 Lebrun informed Morris that it would propose an exemption to the provision decree in favor of American commerce, which it did in a decree of May 23.[20]

Within one week, however, the Convention again reversed itself and repealed the May 23 exemption. Morris was sure that the whole business resulted from the corruption of certain members of the Convention who represented interests having a stake in the fate of valuable American cargoes already seized. He could make no accusations yet, since his evidence was wholly circumstantial and hearsay.[21]

Whatever Morris really thought of the motive behind the provision decree, its utility was defended in a report written by Otto sometime in June. Otto admitted that, according to ARTICLE XXIII of the treaty of 1778, Morris was right in claiming that American vessels carrying enemy goods were not liable to seizure. But the preamble to the treaty granted each party "perfect reciprocity" and "liberty to make rules of convenience," in order that the treaty should guarantee "reciprocal usefulness." These friendly passages, he continued, had been ignored by the American minister.

The provision decree was provoked by circumstances not foreseen at the writing of the treaty. It could not have been intended to permit the seizure of all neutral ships bound for France by Britain, while France was prevented from retaliating in kind. France had adopted reprisals against Britain in the hope that the latter would modify her policy, and the decree provided for its own repeal in that eventuality. On the contrary, England had recently ordered the seizure of all neutral ships loaded with pro-

20Lebrun to Committee of Public Safety, May 15, 1793, AECPE-U, 37, 269–69vo; *ASP, FR* I, 364–65.

21Morris to Lebrun, May 14, to Lebrun, June 19, to Jefferson, June 25, 1793, *ASP, FR* I, 364, 367–68, 366. Samuel F. Bemis has summarized the alternating French commercial decrees in "Washington's Farewell Address: A Foreign Policy of Independence," *American Historical Review* XXXIX (Jan. 1934), 252–53n.

visions for France.[22] It was bad faith on the part of the United States, therefore, to insist on a treaty stipulation which would provision France's enemies at French expense, especially in view of the sacrifices France had made when the United States had been in a similar position.

Otto recurred once more to the old squabble over the American tonnage act to prove that "often great political proprieties can modify the rigorous stipulations of a national pact." According to ARTICLE V of the treaty of 1778, he asserted, French ships should not pay the duty; according to ARTICLE IV, France should be the most-favored-nation with respect to American commercial regulations. But the United States favored no nation. Instead of insisting on her rights, France had attributed these to "political expedients," which friendship caused her not to resist. This good faith was absent from the demands of the American minister, "who consults more the temporary interest of his constituents than the well-being and respect that friendly powers owe to each other."[23]

The two self-contradicting decrees of late May, for practical purposes, might as well not have passed, for American ships were being brought into French ports for adjudication in increasing numbers. An American ship, the *Ruby*, loaded with rice for London, was brought into Morlaix on June 14 and adjudged the same day. The cargo was confiscated according to the provision decree, but the captain was paid the full price for it and his ship was restored to him as soon as it was unloaded. The case of the *Little Cherub*, however, was as complicated as that of the *Ruby* was simple. Morris protested to Lebrun on June 19 that the *Little Cherub* had been seized near Dunkirk after discharging a number of French refugees from Spain, and that the ship's mate had been wantonly murdered and the captain and crew very badly treated, although they had made no resistance. Morris was also

---

[22]This referred to the British Order-in-Council of June 8, 1793. The British government's rejection of the "free ships, free goods" doctrine had been explained to Hammond in March. I. B. M., 38.

[23]AECPE-U, 37, 270–73.

"astonished" at the reinstatement of the provision decree. Lebrun, in one of his last official communications, told Morris on June 21 that he was "infinitely wounded" at what had happened on the *Little Cherub*, and enclosed a copy of the report he had sent to the executive council. This report merely reiterated Morris' recital of facts and advocated full satisfaction for the captain of the vessel, as well as restoration of the exemption of American ships from the provision decree. The report ended, however, with the significant proposition that the United States should only receive the benefits of its neutrality, "as long as that neutrality assures the supplies of the Republic and of her colonies."[24]

Deforgues entered the Foreign Office determined "to leave no motive standing which could alter the good dispositions of the United States toward France." He asked the Committee of Public Safety at once to obtain from the Convention a decree ordering reparation to the captain of the *Little Cherub* and punishment for the murder committed. He also told Morris on June 27 that the change in ministers would have no effect on the friendly dispositions of all Frenchmen toward their American allies. Exemption from the provision decree was referred to the Committee of Public Safety, and on July 1 the Convention once again exempted American ships from its provisions. On the same day the immediate release of the *Little Cherub* with indemnification for her delay was also decreed. In addition, the minister of justice was ordered to investigate the murder and determine the amount of indemnity due the family of the murdered man.[25]

Though Morris told Deforgues that "I learn with satisfaction

24President of Tribunal of Commerce of Morlaix to Lebrun, June 14, 1793, AECPE-U, 37, 424–25vo; *ASP, FR* I, 367–68.

25Deforgues to Committee of Public Safety, to Morris, June 27, 1793, AECPE-U, 37, 463, 464–64vo; *ASP, FR* I, 371. The minister of justice reported two weeks later that the mate of the *Little Cherub* had resisted a sentinel on the ship, who had killed him in performance of his duty. Also, the ship had been cleared for Hamburg on the basis of false papers, really intending to go to Cadiz. It had been intercepted because it did not leave the list of the crew as required when it touched at Le Havre. The council eventually rescinded the indemnity, released the ship, and purchased the cargo under the provision decree, paying the freight charges as well. Reports of Minister of Justice, July 1793, others undated, AECPE-U, 37–38, 40, 94–97, 133–33vo.

of the daily arrival of wheat and flour sent to you from America," the quantities were far from sufficient to the need. At the end of May a ship, the *Patty*, with a cargo of flour destined for the town of St. Valéry, was stopped outside Cherbourg and forced to enter that port. In answer to Morris' protests, Deforgues asserted that the minister of the interior would render justice to the owners. Meanwhile, on Morris' demand, Deforgues ordered the release of an American at Boulogne who had been arrested on suspicion of being English. On July 2, he wrote to the minister of marine that he had noticed in the gazettes that two American vessels were listed among enemy prizes taken by French ships. There must be particular circumstances to account for these seizures, Deforgues insisted; otherwise they would be violations of neutral rights and contrary to the interests of the Republic. He asked the minister to supply the particulars and to cause the gazettes in future to distinguish between enemy prizes and neutral ones, "so the United States will not be misled by detractors of the Republic."[26]

On July 27, the Convention again applied the provision decree to vessels of the United States. Morris told Jefferson on August 13 that the whole question had been "bandied about in a shameful manner," and he presented evidence to support his opinion that corruption in the Convention was the cause of the frequent reversals of policy. To Deforgues, Morris wrote on August 6 that prior knowledge of the provision decree at Le Havre indicated a "pernicious influence" which should be removed, but by October 1 he had returned to his original argument that the decree violated the treaty of 1778.[27]

The Committee of Public Safety was not impressed with Morris' insinuations. On October 17, Deforgues defended the law of May 9 to Morris on the ground of "painful necessity." The "extreme rigor" with which England treated all neutral vessels bound for France, he wrote, had forced the latter to take in re-

[26]Morris to Deforgues, June 27, Deforgues to Morris, July 3 and 29, 1793, *ASP, FR* I, 369, 370, 372; Deforgues to Morris, July 10, to Minister of Marine, July 2, 1793, AECPE-U, 38, 27, 6–6vo.

[27]*ASP, FR* I, 369, 374; AECPE-U, 38, 170–71vo.

prisal the provisions belonging to her enemies. The French law was conditional, while that of England was positive and frankly intended to starve millions of victims. It was not reasonable, in these circumstances,

> that France, attacked on all sides, abandoned to its own strength, without allies, without foreign succor, should confine herself scrupulously to the maxims of the law of nations, so cruelly violated by her enemies. Hence it would result, that the neutrality of several powers would be partial; that it would operate only in favor of our enemies, whose commerce would be peaceably carried on under the shelter of a borrowed flag, while ours could not be, under any flag whatever.

These observations, continued Deforgues, applied to the larger part of the claims addressed to him. He had done all that he could to obtain an exception to the general rules in favor of Americans, and he had been successful in several cases. Furthermore, "when the particular circumstances of the republic permitted the administration to favor your countrymen, it was eager to give them testimonies of the desire which it always has had, of bringing closer and closer the citizens and the interests of the two countries."[28]

Deforgues had not tried to justify this violation of the treaty, as Otto had, but placed his explanation squarely on the grounds of dire necessity. Morris haughtily answered a few days later that, while he could not agree, he would refrain from further discussion of the matter, referring it instead to his government. He reminded Deforgues, however, that the question involved the explicit stipulations of a treaty and not the law of nations, and he pointed out the hardship of American merchants, required to honor the treaty at home, and having the advantage neither of the treaty nor of the law of nations elsewhere. To Jefferson, Morris reported that Deforgues, unable to procure the repeal of the

---

28*ASP, FR* I, 376–77. Morris' suspicions concerning the corrupt influence at Le Havre were substantiated in a report the Committee of Public Safety adopted and ordered printed the following February. But in scolding those responsible and ordering justice rendered the Americans, the committee did not question the provision decree. AECPE-U, 40, 101vo.

decree, had been driven "to the necessity of excusing a step which it is not possible to justify." He could only, therefore, "leave it to you in America to insist on a rigid performance of the treaty, or slide back to the equal state of unfettered neutrality."[29]

Deforgues himself, early in August, had deprecated the restoration of the provision decree. "It is a fact," he insisted, "that at the present time the violation of the treay of commerce of 1778 would be infinitely prejudicial to the interests of the Republic. We have the greatest need of provisions from the United States . . . ."[30]

Meanwhile, in accordance with a decree of November 8, settlement of American claims had been turned over to the Provisory Executive Council in order to relieve the Committee of Public Safety, which had preempted most of the power the council had enjoyed under the Gironde, from the mass of detail each case involved. The council now ordered at least one ship with its cargo restored, considering that it was due "the justice of the French Republic to respect the neutrality of the United States and to maintain faithfully the treaty of 1778." The cargo, however, being "articles of first necessity" (i.e., foodstuffs), would be paid for at the price prevailing at their intended destination, and an indemnity for freight charges and for the nine months' delay was allowed. Thus, in spite of the reassuring words of Robespierre, who dominated the all-powerful Committee of Public Safety, the provision decree remained a part of French commercial war policy.[31]

Morris, by the end of October, received complaints from American captains of new and old seizures almost daily. He continued to refer to them to Deforgues, but the latter was helpless in the face of the chaotic and unruly condition of the French prize courts. Morris was soon telling Jefferson that consuls and

29 Morris to Deforgues, to Jefferson, Oct. 19, 1793, *ASP, FR* I, 378, 374–75.
30 AECPE-U, 38, 173–73vo, 273–74.
31 *Ibid.*, 39, 476, 299–300, 455–55vo, 447–47vo. The council ordered the *Hope* and her cargo restored but ordered the privateer which captured her indemnified, because it had "acted correctly under the decree of May 9." "Deliberation of Executive Council," Oct. 1793, *ibid.*, 39, 174–75.

vice-consuls should be appointed in all the ports and in Paris, so that the courts and the committees could be followed up continuously, "so as to plague them into decisions."[32]

Although Morris could with perfect justice complain about the provision decree and its alternating reinstatement, domestic French policy which affected foreign commerce presented a more complicated problem. In order to conserve the national produce for domestic consumption, the Jacobin government in the summer of 1793 placed an embargo on all exports from France. France sorely needed provisions from America but, as Morris pointed out to Deforgues on August 20, forcing American vessels to depart in ballast for the return trip home or to the West Indies would soon discourage all trade between the two countries. Dissatisfied with the results of Morris' efforts, a number of American captains held up at Bordeaux wrote directly to the French Convention, even hinting that the provision decree was unobjectionable as long as they were permitted to take on return cargoes of French goods.[33]

Continuing its ban on exports, by October the Convention extended its domestic economic policy by fixing maximum prices for essential commodities, a striking indication of French economic distress and the widening impact of the national war effort. Deforgues now was seriously concerned. He had observed that "the Americans have not complained as long as we paid for the cargoes and the transportation charges" of ships seized under the provision decree, but enforcing price controls on American imports clearly threatened their total stoppage.[34]

[32]Morris to Deforgues, Oct. 21, Deforgues to Morris, Oct. 23, 1793, *ibid.*, 39, 180–81vo, 186–86vo; Jan. 21, 1794, *ASP, FR* I, 402–403. Morris frankly told Jefferson that he privately rejoiced at French violations of the treaty. "My efforts to support the treaty have been constant and persevering," he wrote on Oct. 10, "although, in my private judgment, the breach of it on the part of our allies, by releasing us from the obligations it has imposed, could not but be useful under the present circumstances." *ASP, FR* I, 373.

[33]Captains of vessels of the U. S. to the National Convention of France, Aug. 22, 1793, *ASP, FR* I, 373–74.

[34]Morris to Deforgues, Oct. 13, 1793, *ibid.*, I, 376; Deforgues to Quezno, Dec. 10, to President of National Convention, Oct. 13, 1793, AECPE-U, 39, 443vo, 153–53vo. See Robert R. Palmer, *Twelve Who Ruled* (Princeton, 1941), ch. 10.

The Committee of Public Safety soon had to modify its policy. On November 7 it decreed that articles of the "first necessity" were to be sold directly to agents of the government by private contract. Neutral carriers would then be allowed to purchase French goods for export. This concession was absolutely necessary, as Morris reported to Washington, "because America is the only source, from whence supplies of provisions can be drawn to feed this city, on which so much depends."[35]

At the end of November, however, ninety-two American ships were still detained at Bordeaux. The members of the Convention "on mission" refused to open the port, and not even the Committee of Public Safety could interfere. Unless something were done, Morris was sure that "all commerce between this country and America must soon terminate." He explained to Jefferson that these commissioners in the departments had almost unlimited powers; otherwise it was "almost impossible that this grievance should be continued." He expected it would be, however, despite the promises made to Joseph Fenwick, United States consul for the French Atlantic ports, by the commissioners. The minister of foreign affairs reported to the Committee of Public Safety on January 1, 1794, that the treatment of American commerce at Bordeaux "will ruin prospects for spring deliveries of grains when they will be needed most." Deforgues feared also that American merchants would be tempted to retaliate in the United States by obstructing the efforts of French purchasing agents there. The next day, Deforgues told Morris that he expected the embargo to be lifted very soon, but it was not until April that Fenwick finally obtained an explicit decision, "after a sedulous attendance on the *Comité de Salut Public.*" There still remained the matter of claims against France for the losses occasioned by the detentions, although the committee had already decided that indemnities should be granted.[36]

[35]*ASP, FR* I, 398; Nov. 12, 1793, AECPE-U, 39, 226–26vo.

[36]Morris to Jefferson, Nov. 26, 1793, Mar. 6, Apr. 15, 1794, *ASP, FR* I, 400, 404–405, 407; Report on embargo of American ships at Bordeaux, Jan. 1, Deforgues to Morris, Jan. 2, 1794, AECPE-U, 40, 3–7vo, 9–10. Deforgues told the Committee of Public Safety on Mar. 24 that indemnities claimed already exceeded five million

It is apparent that Deforgues' intentions were all that Morris could reasonably have wished, and his indifferent success in carrying out France's treaty obligations toward the United States was due more to confusion and threatening food shortages than to any malevolence on the part of French officials. Morris repeatedly alluded to both of these factors in his dispatches home, and even outlined the British policy which was framed to exploit them.[37]

The Jacobin government at length lost patience with Morris, when he tried in November to shield an old royalist friend from the inquisition of the Committee of General Security. The Countess de Damas, fleeing the committee's warrant, sought refuge at Morris' country home, and the sympathetic minister wrote the committee to ask dismissal of the charges against her. The committee replied that the inviolability of his house could not protect her and demanded that she be surrendered. Politely, the committee added that the matter did not concern him and that the question of her guilt was not his to decide. Morris at once denied any intention of interfering and added that he would have given her up had he been asked, but the inviolability of his house prevented her being arrested there. He asked consideration of his arguments in her behalf as a favor, not as a right. Meanwhile, the countess had given herself up, but Morris was furious when the officers of the committee forced their way into his house and put seals on trunks the countess had left behind.[38]

---

livres. The committee raised the embargo a few days later, gave advances to the American captains on indemnities due, and ordered a commission to fix final amounts. AECPE-U, 40, 319, 347–48, 371–71vo. Despite the committee's good intentions, however, the claims were not liquidated.

37Morris wrote to the President after leaving Paris that "I felt myself degraded by the communications I was forced into with the worst of mankind, in order to obtain redress for the injuries sustained by my fellow-citizens, [but] the conduct of Britain rendered a temporizing conduct with France indispensable." Dec. 30, 1794, *ASP, FR* I, 412.

38Committee of General Security to Morris, Nov. 18, Morris to Committee of General Security, Nov. 22, 1794. AECPE-U, 39, 298–98vo, 308–309. This incident provides an interesting contrast to Morris' action following the arrest of Thomas Paine in Dec. 1793. Paine insisted that Morris effect his release, though Morris told Jefferson that Paine's best hope lay in remaining quiet and forgotten lest he share

At this point, Deforgues took a hand, requesting the committee to remove the seals from Morris' house at once, so that his government would have no grounds for complaint. To Morris, Deforgues wrote that he had arranged to have the seals removed at whatever time the minister should specify, but he agreed with the committee in insisting that diplomatic immunity applied only to the minister and his own employees. The matter might have ended there, but Morris was determined to have the last word. He renewed the argument regarding the inviolability of his house with Deforgues, but the latter refused to become involved any further and merely forwarded the letter to the committee.[39]

This affair was the last straw as far as the French government was concerned, and Deforgues hastened to use it as a conclusive argument for Morris' recall. Early in November 1793 he wrote to Fauchet that Morris had consistently shown his hostility to the French Revolution; the latest example of this malevolence demonstrated that he could no longer be tolerated. On second thought, as a friend of Washington's and other influential Americans, Morris would be more dangerous in the United States than at Paris. But by the end of the month, Deforgues could wait no longer. He now told Fauchet that it was beneath the dignity of the Republic to demand Morris' recall, but he should use the earliest opportunity to suggest that Morris be replaced by someone "more worthy to follow Franklin and Jefferson."[40]

Jefferson himself had fixed the end of the year as the date of his retirement and wanted to clear up unfinished business before his successor took office. On December 11, prompted by a

---

the fate of his Girondin friends. Such a course was impossible for the author of *The Age of Reason*, who, according to Morris, "amuses himself with publishing a pamphlet against Jesus Christ." The Committee of Public Safety ignored Morris' request, but Deforgues replied that Paine was considered a French citizen. Morris to Jefferson, Jan. 21, Mar. 6, 1794, *ASP, FR* I, 402, 404; Morris to Deforgues, Feb. 14, Deforgues to Morris, no date, AECPE-U, 40, 91, 102.

[39]Deforgues to Committee of General Security, Nov. 24, to Morris, Nov. 25, Morris to Deforgues, Nov. 25, Deforgues to Committee of General Security, Nov. 26, 1794. AECPE-U, 39, 313–13vo, 316–17, 326–26vo, 327.

[40]Deforgues to Fauchet, Nov. —, 21, 1794, *ibid.*, 39, 297–97vo, 302–302vo.

heated reference to Morris in a letter from Genet, he wrote to the President to remind him of the persistent hints of French dissatisfaction with Morris. The President would recall the informal representations of Ternant, and Jefferson now desired to inform him that Genet had hinted to the same effect in informal conversation shortly after his arrival. The subject had not been pursued at the time, Jefferson continued, but now his approaching retirement made it necessary that the President should know all the circumstances.[41]

As before, Washington admitted the inconvenience of keeping Morris at Paris, but there was still the problem of finding a successor. He determined that Morris should be recalled, but the sealed letter demanding Morris' recall, which Fauchet brought him from the Committee of Public Safety in the middle of March 1794, found him still engaged in the search for a suitable replacement. The best arrangement he could conceive was a variation of Jefferson's earlier suggestion, that he ask Jay to go to London so that Pinckney would be free to take Morris' place at Paris. At the same time, he offered the Paris appointment to Robert R. Livingston, who declined. Edmund Randolph, who had succeeded Jefferson the first of the year, worked for the nomination of James Monroe, then senator from Virginia. After some discussion with Randolph over the supposed previous claim of Aaron Burr, Monroe accepted. He was nominated on May 27, and the Senate approved his appointment three days later.[42]

Morris had been fully aware of Jefferson's disapproval of his principles, and he reciprocated in kind quite heartily. Jefferson's retirement was something of a personal boon to him, and on April 15 he congratulated Randolph on his appointment, which would be "useful to the United States." It would be the more

---

41Ford, *Jefferson's Writings* VI, 465–66.

42Washington to Jay, Apr. 29, to Livingston, Apr. 29, May 14, 1794, *Writings of Washington* XXXIII, 345, 346, 364; Moncure D. Conway, *Omitted Chapters of History Disclosed in the Life and Letters of Edmund Randolph* (New York, 1888), 240. Fauchet reported on June 9 that he knew that one of the sealed letters he had delivered to the government had contained the demand for Morris' recall, but that this had been decided before his arrival. C. F. M., 391.

so, he continued, "as your convictions respecting our form of government will restore . . . harmony to our Executive departments . . . ." That Randolph might have no misconceptions about the abilities of his predecessor, Morris carefully implied that Jefferson's attention to duty had not been exemplary as far as he was concerned.[43]

Morris felt even less need for caution after Jefferson had removed himself from the scene. He was always a tenacious asserter of American rights in France, but he apparently had learned nothing from the case of his friend the countess about French concern for their own prerogatives. When another of his friends, a lady named Langeron, was arrested by the Committee of General Security, he asked Deforgues to intercede in her behalf. Deforgues was having no more such interference, however, and merely scribbled a "note for reply" on Morris' letter—since the lady was a French citizen the matter was none of his concern and his request could not be considered.[44]

Despite these personal frustrations, Morris could find no legitimate grounds for criticism of the honest attempts of Deforgues to maintain friendly relations. Having learned that Genet had been instructed to effect his replacement, he told Deforgues that if the French government desired another minister, it had only to tell him and he would apply for his own recall. Deforgues had answered with assurances of esteem, Morris reported to Randolph on July 23, 1794—barely one week before Monroe arrived to succeed him.[45]

Morris saw without concern the arrest of Deforgues and his replacement by a commissioner of external relations. On April 15, 1794, a few days after the event, he wrote to Randolph that the change in the administrative system would in future make the department (now commission) heads "in name what they were before in fact"—an accurate comment on the complete subordination of all executive branches to the all-powerful Committee

[43] *ASP, FR* I, 406.
[44] Morris to Deforgues, Jan. 31, 1795, AECPE-U, 40, 55.
[45] *ASP, FR* I, 411.

of Public Safety. The new commissioner, Buchot, could accomplish nothing in any case, for Robespierre and his lieutenants were busy eliminating threats to their continuance in power. The purges of the Dantonists and of the Hébertists occupied the attention of the Committee of Public Safety and were soon followed by the Thermidorean reaction, which encompassed the fall of Robespierre himself. Before that time, however, news arrived that President Washington had bowed to the will of the Convention and was replacing Morris.[46]

Monroe reached Paris on August 2, 1794, and was presented to Buchot as soon as Morris could hurry in from his country home. On August 10, Buchot informed the Committee of Public Safety of Monroe's arrival, quoting the President's letter to the committee, to the effect that Morris' replacement was in reciprocation for the speed of the Republic in replacing Genet. The government was in an uproar because of the recent demise of the Robespierrists, but Buchot asked that Monroe be received by the purged committee as soon as possible, "because of the regard the Convention has always had for the United States."[47]

So ended the unfortunate mission of Gouverneur Morris to France.[48] As if to justify his critics, he spent the next few years in Germany and Austria, hobnobbing with French émigrés and acting as a sort of wandering unofficial informant for the British foreign office. It was this kind of diplomatic task for which his talents and his financial connections best qualified him, and from which he derived the greatest pleasure. He was not a diplomat in Paris, but a censor constantly seeking to satisfy his own animosity. *Persona non grata* even before his appointment as minister,

46*Ibid.*, I, 407; Morris to Commissioner of External Relations, Apr. 15, Washington to Committee of Public Safety, May 28, 1795, AECPE-U, 40, 420–20vo, 41, 101–101vo.

47Monroe to Randolph, Aug. 11, 1794, *ASP, FR* I, 670; AECPE-U, 41, 276–76vo. The President assured Morris of his own undiminished respect and esteem and Morris, replying gratefully, promised to keep him informed of European affairs as long as he remained there. Washington to Morris, June 19 and 25, Morris to Washington, Dec. 30, 1794, *ASP, FR* I, 409–10.

48Morris' earlier unofficial mission to the British government had been equally unsuccessful. Ritcheson, *Aftermath*, 108.

his well-known antirepublican attitudes denied him the exercise of the highest functions of his office. The small successes he did achieve for American commerce were won in spite of, rather than because of, his efforts. Successive French republican governments regarded him as an enemy scheming against their security, and he despised them all heartily in turn.[49]

Morris' mission was therefore foredoomed to failure. At a time when an understanding between France and the United States was indispensable, he had already aligned himself with France's enemies. Had he possessed the confidence of the government to which he was accredited, as Franklin and Jefferson had in their times, he might have tempered the misconceived policy of the Gironde. In 1793 in Paris, he was out of time and out of place. He unwittingly encouraged both France and England to continue the game of makeweight with America, and he vastly increased the difficulties of establishing American neutrality.

[49]Nearly two years earlier, the daughter of Vice President John Adams had reported from London that Morris "renders himself very obnoxious by an active and officious zeal in favour of the aristocracy." If Morris had not been an American and the minister of George Washington, she continued, the Jacobins would "have had his head on a pike long ago." Abigail to John Adams, Feb. 9, 1793, Adams Papers, Massachusetts Historical Society (microfilm copy, University of Tennessee Library, reel 1376), Letters received, 1793.

CHAPTER VI  French Conciliation
and English Aggressions,
1793–1794

But now a chain of despots bring
Their troops to avenge poor Gallia's King—
That is—since Louis' head is gone,
They tremble stoutly for their own.

NEW YEAR'S GREETING TO SUBSCRIBERS TO
THE *Connecticut Courant*, JANUARY 1,
1794.

My opinion of the British govt is, that nothing
will force them to do justice but the loud voice of
their people, & that this can never be excited but
by distressing their commerce.

JEFFERSON TO WASHINGTON, MAY 14, 1794.

ROBESPIERRE's first foray into American policy settled Genet's fate. It seemed probable that a commission would soon be sent to supersede Genet: Barère and Paine had already nominated Hérault de Sechelles (probably to remove a rival to Barère as foreign policy oracle on the ruling committee) to head the commission; and it was said that Deforgues coveted that place for himself. The famous archaeologist Constantin F. C. B. Volney volunteered to go to America as an "observer of all aspects of life" and to refute "the attempts of the enemy to slander France." But Volney, a Girondist, went to prison instead, though he was to escape the guillotine and reach America two years later.[1]

---

[1] Volney to Deforgues, Oct. 17, Deforgues to Minister of Interior, Nov. 2, 1793, AECPE-U, 163–63vo, 221.

Robespierre probably had decided on the personnel of the commission by October 22, 1793, when the commissioner of marine at Le Havre was ordered to find passage at once on an American vessel for a party of important "voyagers." On Robespierre's initiative, the Committee of Public Safety had already (October 16) issued a decree ordering a four-man commission to sail for Philadelphia "in the greatest secrecy" to arrest Genet and his collaborators. The commission was to be composed of a minister plenipotentiary, a consul general, a consul for Pennsylvania, and a secretary of legation. Its actions were to be determined by decision of the majority, and at least three of the commissioners would be required to sign its reports. The experience of Genet, the committee declared, demonstrated the danger of confiding to one man the interests of a nation so far away.[2]

Joseph Fauchet, formally appointed minister on November 18, was to have the right of initiative in purely political questions. His letter of credence expressly disavowed Genet and added the hope that Fauchet would merit confidence. Fauchet also carried a letter informing Genet of his recall, because of "the very serious complaints" of the United States. The commission was to disarm the privateers outfitted by Genet and forbid all Frenchmen to violate the neutrality of the United States. Any consul who had taken part in the arming of corsairs or in the condemnation of prizes was to be replaced, and the commission was given the power to appoint commercial agents provisorily, until they could be replaced in the regular manner. Antoine-Réné-Charles Mathurin, comte de La Forest, who had urged the committee to reestablish normal relations with the United States, "an ally in truth not powerful, but at least the most useful of neutral nations," was once more to be consul general; Pétry, consul for Pennsylvania, and Régis Le Blanc, secretary of legation, completed the commission.[3]

[2]Decrees of Committee of Public Safety, Oct. 16 and Nov. 15, 1793, *ibid.*, 39, 194; C. F. M., 287–89; James A. James, "French Diplomacy and American Politics, 1794–1795," *Annual Report of the American Historical Association, 1911* I (1914), 154.
[3]Fauchet's letter of credence, dated Nov. 15, Deforgues to Genet, "Brumaire"

This outline of policy was probably adopted before the "Incorruptible" perceived the opportunity the situation offered of completing the ruin of the Gironde, whose followers were even then engaged in large-scale insurrections in the Vendée and scattered parts of the provinces. On November 17, Robespierre used Jefferson's recital of the misdoings of Genet for another assault in the Convention upon his enemies. Fauchet's letter of credence and the instructions to the commissioners, though not signed by Robespierre, follow closely the line he marked out to rectify Girondist crimes.

The most important task committed to Fauchet and his partners was the expedition of provisions purchased by agents of the Commission of Subsistences and Provisions. They were charged with obtaining a statement of the American debt, after an accounting of the advances already made by the American government. And Fauchet was to see that the treaties of 1778, especially the articles dealing with maritime prizes, were faithfully observed. This requirement involved a reversal of the American decision to forbid the sale of French prizes, but the minister was required to insist upon it so that prizes could be used for shipment of provisions to France.

By way of dispelling American resentment of the provision decree, "which has been the subject of so many remonstrances," the commissioners were to plead the necessity for French retaliation in kind against Britain's policy of depriving her of all importations of foodstuffs from abroad. As a matter of fact, that article of the treaty, under present circumstances, was incompatible with the general object of that treaty, "which excluded all *onerous preference* and which is based on the most perfect reciprocity." The provision decree actually tended indirectly to support the rights of neutrals because it provided for its own nul-

---

(Oct. 22–Nov. 20), decree of Provisory Executive Council, Nov. 17, Deforgues to Fauchet, to Le Blanc, Nov. 18, "Mémoire on re-establishing regular correspondence with the United States," by La Forest, Oct. 29, 1793, AECPE-U, 39, 261–61vo, 262, 277–77vo, 295–95vo, 296, 216–17; "Orders of the Committee of Public Safety," Oct. 11, 1793, C. F. M., 287–89.

lification as soon as France's enemies agreed to recognize as non-seizable provisions found on neutral ships. Also, American ships were subsequently specifically exempted from seizure under the decree as a proof of good will.

Further to show France's determination to respect America's position, Genet's expedition against New Orleans, "manifestly compromising to the strict neutrality of the United States and contrary to the views of the council on the employment of our naval forces," was to be prevented. The commissioners would endeavor to win the confidence of the President and his administration, observe scrupulously the forms established for official communications between the President and foreign agents, and take no step which might offend Americans by seeming to lack respect for their government. Above all, the commissioners were to be mindful of the Republic's determination not to interfere in the government of other nations.

But France could not approve of American negotiations with Spain concerning the navigation of the Mississippi under present circumstances, nor would France see without concern the conclusion of a commercial treaty with England. The better to repel the advances of the enemy coalition, the commissioners were authorized to propose to the United States a new treaty of commerce founded on more solid bases than that of 1778. A primary requisite was to be the long-sought exemption from the American tonnage duty, but the respective naturalization of French and American citizens, "proposed by Jefferson and desired by the French nation," would gain this object without giving cause of offense to other powers.

The Jacobins expected that great advantages would accrue to the United States from the Navigation Act passed by the Convention on September 21, 1793. This would free American navigators from the sufferance of the English and Dutch. The American government should appreciate this evidence of France's successful resistance to the "vast system of brigandage" of the monarchs coalesced against her. French successes against the attacks of so many enemies from without, and the reduction of the insurgents within, should inspire appreciation of the "incalculable resources" and the "heroic energy" which gave stability to a government "founded on the vigor of the French people and on their inexhaustible resources."[4]

These instructions differed little from those of the despised Genet, except in their defense of the new Jacobin commercial policy. France still demanded all her prerogatives under the old treaties and desired a new treaty which would establish more securely those heretofore evaded or refused. With the lesson of Genet's failure before it, however, the Committee of Public Safety was careful to stress the warning against involvement in American politics. And most noteworthy, the Girondist crusading enthusiasm for the propagation of French ideas of freedom was gone. It had been replaced by a nationalistic self-interest which sought to ensure American support of France by appeals to her ally's interests, and by demonstrating the value of French support to American interests in Europe.

The basis of French policy toward the United States was succinctly summarized in a report from the Ministry of Foreign Affairs to the "great committee" at the beginning of 1794. "America is the only place where the French revolution has found ardent supporters, in the government as well as among the mass of the people," it began, and noted that Congress itself adjourned to celebrate the news of the recapture of Toulon. After the Swiss, America was France's most natural ally: the Committee of Public Safety had realized this in rendering justice to American sufferers from the Bordeaux embargo and from the insults of French corsairs. All the Americans had departed satisfied, many with new contracts. This was most important because "American navigators render to the Republic the most essential services." Their hardihood and energy were well known, and their activities so manifold that some even brought English raw materials into France—potash, for example.

The main object of the commissioners' instructions, the re-

[4]The instructions to the commissioners, dated Nov. 15, 1793, are in C. F. M., 288-94.

port concluded, was to nourish and to protect American commerce as much as possible. But the commissioners needed help because "American commerce is paralyzed in southern Europe" as a result of "Pitt's arrangement of a Portuguese-Algerian truce." The committee had decided to intervene with the Regency of Algiers and had named envoys for the mission more than two months before, but they had not yet been sent. Such an interposition of French good offices would have the double advantage of increasing French provisions from America and of tightening Franco-American bonds. It was "important to the Republic to negotiate a truce with the Algerians in favor of American ships without delay."[5]

Foreseeing the effect of this English maneuver on American opinion, the writer suggested that it was "possible that English insolence will force the United States to fight." France would welcome "this useful event" because of the harm it would do to English commerce, but it would cause her hardship since it would be more difficult to get provisions from America, "and we would have to protect an ally strong only at home, with little means of playing a role of maritime power."[6]

[5]Portuguese-Algerian hostilities had been limited to a Portuguese blockade of the Straits of Gibraltar, preventing the Algerians from plying their piratical trade beyond the Mediterranean. Immediately after the truce had been arranged by the British consul at Algiers, an Algerian fleet sailed into the Atlantic and quickly demoralized American commerce. Edward Church, American consul at Lisbon, wrote to the French Foreign Office in Oct. 30, 1793, of the British intrigues which had made the truce possible. Church thought that Portugal would welcome an alliance with France "to save her from the millstones of England and Spain" and offered himself as a correspondent for France. On Jan. 11 following, Deforgues answered Church, thanking him and inviting further information. AECPE-U, 39, 218–20, 40, 31; Humphreys to Secretary of State, Oct. 12, 1793, *ASP, FR* I, 295, 296. Pinckney had already suggested to Grenville in London that the U. S. would consider the truce "as a measure calculated to distress the American commerce," an assumption which proved accurate. Grenville instructed Hammond in Jan. 1794 to combat this "disagreeable sensation" with the argument that England had intervened at Portugal's request, merely in order to free Portuguese naval forces "to act more effectively against the common enemy." Hammond was to disclaim any intent to injure America: even if that were British policy, said Grenville, it could have little effect on the supply of France and exposed English property on American ships to the same risks to which American vessels were liable. I. B. M., 49–50.

[6]AECPE-U, 40, 11–13.

The commissioners, meanwhile, had started on their trans-Atlantic journey. They left Paris at the end of November 1793, but did not sail from Brest until one month later. They reached Philadelphia toward the end of February 1794, to find themselves in the midst of a great debate over American commercial policy, which was being conducted in an atmosphere approaching war hysteria. The United States was seething with indignation at the conduct of England, and the small band of followers who remained loyal to Hamilton's pro-British policy were fighting a delaying action in Congress to save England's commercial dominance in America. Fauchet and his colleagues, therefore, were favored by a reaction in popular opinion in France's favor, a reaction which their formal liquidation of the mission of Genet tended to promote.[7]

The Navigation Act voted by the Convention on September 21, 1793, was the cornerstone of Jacobin commercial policy. Barère, reporting on the act to the Convention the same day, noted that it had twice before been proposed, on July 3 by Marec, on behalf of the committee on commerce, and on May 29 by the Committee of Public Safety itself. The committee, said Barère, had submitted its report of May 29 "as a means of regenerating our navigation, reviving our commerce, encouraging shipbuilding, increasing the fishery, and doubling our carrying trade, by destroying the intermediate freights and the interference of all direct navigation in the maritime transportation of the commodities we exchange with foreign nations." Nothing was done, and a supplementary report one month later was scarcely discussed, many then fearing that such a measure would injure the commercial relations of France with the neutral powers.

Such an attitude was unrealistic, asserted Barère. The demands of war and the position of neutral powers made such a policy "inevitable" and "rightful." Furthermore, in contrast to the atrocious navigation act of England, which "bears the impression of the despot who created it," that of France "will bear the impres-

[7]Fauchet to Minister of Foreign Affairs, Dec. 9, 22, 1793, Commissioners to Minister of Foreign Affairs, Mar. 21, 1794, C. F. M., 295–97, 289–302, 306–17.

sion of liberty and equality, which produced it." On September 21, 1792, he concluded, the Convention had proclaimed the liberty of France and of Europe; on September 21, 1793, it should proclaim the liberty of commerce—the freedom of the seas. The Convention was not in the hands of the Jacobins on May 29, and their control was not perfect by July 3. By September 21, however, the Convention was little more than a ratificatory organ of the Committee of Public Safety. The Navigation Act was introduced with a flourish and passed at once.[8]

Thus ended in victory the long, determined struggle of Jacobin protectionists, led by G. J. A. Ducher, to extend the new French nationalism to the economic sphere. It represented a complete retreat from the liberal commercial views of the French government of 1786, which, according to Barère, had "enslaved" France by "a ridiculous predilection for England, a ruinous and disgraceful commercial treaty purchased from the ministers of Capet." France therefore ought to extend the war with England to international commerce, long recognized as the source of that nation's great wealth. Another and no less important advantage to be realized from this measure was its tendency to place France in the position of protector of neutral nations from English commercial exploitation.[9]

A part of this favorable position is to be seen in Fauchet's instructions on a new commercial treaty with the United States, and in the injunction to frustrate expected British attempts to negotiate a commercial treaty with the United States. The Committee of Public Safety probably feared that their ally might in turn be "enslaved" by Britain by means of "a ruinous and dis-

---

[8]Secretary of State to Vice President of the U. S. and President of the Senate, Jan. 28, 1794, transmitting translation of the French Navigation Act of Sept. 21, 1793, *ASP, FR* I, 316–21. Ducher had insistently promoted such a policy for more than two years, and Marec paid tribute to him in his report of July 3. Formerly vice-consul at Charleston, Ducher was a staunch advocate of closer relations with the U. S. One of his early pamphlets commending a protectionist commercial policy was entitled "Alliance between the French and American Republics." AECPE-U, 37, 154–55vo, quoted in part in Nussbaum, *Commercial Policy in the French Revolution*, 88.

[9]*ASP, FR* I, 316.

graceful commercial treaty," fears which were to be recalled bitterly after the negotiation of the Anglo-American treaty one year later. Fauchet was soon to suggest to the American government the passage of an American navigation act which would complement that of France and make reciprocal the commercial policies of the two nations.

Late in September 1793, the minister of foreign affairs, in a circular letter to the political and commercial agents of the republic in foreign countries, explained the reasons behind the new commercial policy. Instead of the commercial position France should have enjoyed by virtue of her central position and "the genius and activity of her inhabitants," she had, for more than one century, carried only three-tenths of her own trade. Because of French torpor, the Dutch and English had been enabled to raise at the expense of France, in time of peace, the financial resources necessary to wage war against her. The commercial treaty of 1786 with England had been the final step toward the strangulation of French industry and navigation, and France, devoured by foreign merchants, found herself in the final stage of exhaustion. The Convention had rescued her by the Navigation Act, which was expected to fulfill "the double object of re-establishing our maritime commerce gradually and of punishing the conspiracies of our enemies."[10]

An undated paper, apparently written about the same time, explained the strategy to be employed by France in her maritime war against England and Holland. The Americans were gaining from the war the advantage they should already have received from a direct trade with France. France, therefore, should permit the importation of goods from the United States in French and American ships only, abolishing the indirect trade "which is the source of England's wealth." Privateers should be given every encouragement and all French commerce should be protected

[10]AECPE-U, 38, 202–202vo. Of the 16,225 ships in the French carrying trade, only 3,763 were French owned. Only one-fifth of French commerce was carried in national bottoms, therefore, while twice that amount was carried by Britain. Shepard B. Clough, *France: A History of National Economics, 1789–1939* (New York, 1939), 46.

by convoys, although French warships should avoid naval battles with the enemy wherever possible. Thus, "the English would see that their navy has more *éclat* than utility," English and Dutch merchants would lose their immense profits, the British government would fall, and an English republic emerge.[11]

Thus, whereas the imaginations of Brissot and his colleagues had anticipated the overthrow of the British monarchy through the stimulus of abstract political principles, the Jacobins would achieve the same result by applying economic pressure to the source of British wealth. Other nations had heretofore operated under a vague kind of outmoded economic internationalism, and, for France, this practice had culminated in the disastrous Eden Treaty of 1786. The treaty had already been abrogated at war's outbreak, but now the Jacobins were determined to "nationalize" France's foreign commerce as a weapon for the economic strangulation of "the isle of shopkeepers." The Jacobins were sure that the United States had suffered similarly from British exploitation and would welcome this French initiative. As a matter of fact, that subject was on the point of erupting in America, in a Congress exasperated almost beyond endurance by British maritime restrictions.

When Edmund Randolph sent to the Senate, on January 28, 1794, translations of the French Navigation Act and the reports to the Convention of Barère and Marec, the long expected fight over American commercial policy had erupted in the House of Representatives. The subject had been smoldering ever since February 1791, when a message from the President informed Congress that Great Britain refused to respond to overtures for a commercial agreement. That announcement gave such impetus to Madison's anti-British discrimination campaign that the pro-British group, directed by Hamilton, barely defeated it by referring the whole subject to Jefferson for study and report.[12]

Britain's purpose at that time appears to have been to bind the

---

[11]AECPE-U, 38, 278–79.

[12]*ASP, FR* I, 316; Brant, *Madison: Father of Constitution*, 389; Setser, *Commercial Reciprocity*, 104–109.

United States to her by a treaty of alliance, and to include commercial arrangements which would make the negotiation more palatable to American patriots reluctant to abandon their connection with France. Phineas Bond, British consul general in the United States and confidential informant of Lord Grenville, wrote on October 8, 1791, that American leaders whom he had sounded out on the subject did not think the United States could "enter at this time into a treaty offensive and defensive with Gt. Britain." But, Bond continued, "they add that in a series of time the advantages of a commercial connection with Gt. Britain would be so extensively felt that every part of the Union would see the expediency of the closest alliance between the two countries." There is no reason to doubt that this report accurately reflected the view of the secretary of the treasury, with whom Bond was on cordial terms. Bond proposed that England allow the Americans to sell some ships there "as some equivalent for the carrying trade to the West India Islands," forbidden to Americans. This "indulgence" would "infallibly promote great and extensive nay increasing advantages to the manufactures of Gt. Britain by securing the continuance of that predilection which avowedly prevails in their favor."[13]

Hamilton had earlier been equally frank with Colonel George Beckwith, the special agent who served as London's liaison with pro-British official circles in America in the absence of an accredited minister. As a result of several long conversations with Hamilton, Beckwith had concluded that Britain could undermine the French position in America by negotiating the Anglo-American treaty of commerce the United States had so long desired. This agreement would pave the way for "whatever other treaty" the ministry wanted; however, a treaty of alliance would be acceptable only after conclusion of a commercial treaty. Beckwith, obviously underestimating Hamilton and his friends, feared that Britain's failure soon to grant a treaty of commerce would result in the adoption by Congress of restrictive commercial regula-

13"Letters of Phineas Bond," 492–93.

tions damaging to British trade. Not presuming to estimate the importance to Britain of the American market, Beckwith nevertheless stated that he considered "the birth of every child from New Hampshire to the river Mississippi, as the production of a being destined to extend the manufactures of the Empire; the value of their consumption the States may overrate, but the difficulties will be augmented by delay."[14]

The political scales in America were delicately balanced, Beckwith said: Hamilton headed a pro-English party; Jefferson, a pro-French. Washington, whose "talents . . . are greatly overrated in the world," vacillated helplessly between the two, with no knowing which way he would lean. Beckwith wanted a commercial treaty negotiated at Philadelphia in order to take advantage of Hamilton's influence.[15]

Beckwith's reports appear at least to have convinced London that an official representative at Philadelphia would be useful. George Hammond presented his credentials on November 11 and, benefiting from the confidential relationship with Hamilton bequeathed by Beckwith, he set to work to defeat the anti-British discrimination movement. In a transparent and unsuccessful maneuver designed to intimidate Congress, he urged an extreme and unwarranted interpretation of the English navigation act to impress upon Americans the "precarious indulgence" their commerce enjoyed in his country. Ternant was happy to report to his government that the Americans had failed to take the bait, and that Jefferson had refuted Hammond's claims with ease.[16]

Jefferson was much disappointed at the failure of Madison's attempts to inaugurate a positive program to counter British commercial policies. He set to work at once to gather from over-

14Beckwith to Grenville, Mar. 3, 1791, F. O. 4, 12. Ritcheson, *Aftermath*, 103, suggests that an Anglo-American alliance was Hamilton's idea, not Beckwith's.

15Beckwith to Grenville, Mar. 11, 1791, F. O. 4, 12. See Boyd, *Number 7*, especially ch. 7, for a thorough discussion of the Hamilton-Beckwith relationship.

16I. B. M., 20n; Ternant to Lessart, Apr. 15, 1792, C. F. M., 117–19. For Hammond's instructions concerning a commercial treaty with the U. S., see I. B. M., 9–23 *passim*. The question of sending a minister to the U. S. is discussed in Ritcheson, *Aftermath*, 138–44.

seas the information required by Congress, but the threatening aspect of affairs in Europe caused it to be held up. Jefferson also wished to present his report at the most propitious moment for Madison's program, but general expectations of a new Anglo-French war at the beginning of 1793 rendered it inadvisable to delay longer.[17]

On February 13, 1793, Jefferson addressed a circular letter to the foreign ministers residing in Philadelphia. His report on commerce had to be submitted to Congress within a few days, he said, and the ministers were requested to make such corrections or additions to the parts relating to the commerce of the United States with their particular nations as would contribute to the truth and accuracy of the report. E. P. Van Berckel for Holland and José Ignacio de Viar and José de Jaudenes for Spain found little upon which to comment, but Ternant objected to Jefferson's view of the effect of the duty on tobacco lately decreed by France. Hammond strongly objected to the facts in the report relating to Britain. Jefferson sent Hammond's letter to the President, observing that "it is sometimes difficult to decide whether indiscretions of this kind had better be treated with silence, or due notice. The former perhaps would be best, if it were not that his letter would go unanswered to his court, who might not give themselves the trouble of seeing that he was in the wrong." Apparently, Washington decided that the facts had been so mishandled by Hammond as not to deserve a reply, but Jefferson sent Ternant a polite answer disagreeing with his objections.[18]

Jefferson's report on commerce was put off again, this time by a decision of a committee of the House of Representatives. Hammond suspected that Jefferson had planned this delay in order to take advantage of Genet's expected arrival with new French commercial concessions, "to contrast the liberality of France with the restrictions of England." This appraisal was partly true, but

17See Setser, *Commercial Reciprocity*, 110–14; Malone, *Jefferson and Ordeal of Liberty*, 149–60.
18Jefferson to Washington, Feb. 16, to Ternant, Feb. 17, 1793, Ford, *Jefferson's Writings* VI, 179–82, 184, 188–89.

England's restrictions had already produced such tension between the two countries that Hammond thought it necessary to analyze for Grenville's benefit the "Consequences of war between the United States and Great Britain." His analysis is worth quoting, both for its contrast with the larger vision of Beckwith and for its arrogant assumption that Hamilton's fiscal system had placed the United States in Britain's power. Britain would be vulnerable through

> ... the attempt to wrest from her her American possessions—the annoyance of her navigation by privateers—a partial interruption of her commerce with this country—the insecurity of the debts owing to her subjects—and ... the lavish amount to which her capitalists have rashly speculated in the funds of the United States. With respect to the two former objects, the means of defence are as obvious as those of attack; in regard to two of the latter, they might be regretted as temporary inconveniences, but they could not essentially detract from the general national prosperity; in the last mentioned contingency the sufferers would have only to lament their own credulity and temerity.

> But the mischiefs, which this country would experience from a rupture with Great Britain, are immeasurable. Discontents prevail against its government and the individuals who administer it. Its navigation and commerce are as yet in their infancy, and the produce of its soil so far exceeds its consumption as to require an extraneous vent. The pressure of all these circumstances would be augmented by the operation of war. A very small portion of the British naval force directed against this country, exclusive of the alarm it would spread along its coasts, would be sufficient to block up all its ports and effectually prevent its importations and exportations. On duties levied upon the former (a small excise excepted) depend the whole of the funds applicable to the support of government and the payment of the public debt. Any partial or temporary obstruction in the sources that supply them, would effect their ruin, and ... the connexion between them and the government itself is so close as to render it more than probable that the destruction of the latter would not long be postponed after the subversion of the funds. In this common ruin the mercantile part of the community would be most immediately involved. The exportations being impeded, the excess of the produce would remain undisposed of, and the culti-

vators of the land would suffer not less than the merchants from the universal calamity.[19]

For several months after news of the outbreak of the Anglo-French war, Washington's administration was absorbed in the problems of formulating a policy of neutrality and of establishing it in the face of Genet's activities and the constant attempts of Britain to deny to France the benefits of American neutrality. Jefferson's report on commerce, however, was never lost sight of, and by the fall of 1793 the subject pressed for attention. At the outbreak of war, Britain had announced her determination to treat neutral powers according to the *Consolato del Mare*, rather than according to the newer principle of "free ships, free goods," which she had never recognized except in the now-moribund treaty of 1786 with France. Furthermore, she would insist on the observance of her own rules regarding contraband of war and blockades.

France passed the provision decree of May 9, 1793, partly in retaliation against English practice, and England made her regulations respecting neutral shipping even more restrictive by an order-in-council of June 8, directing the seizure by His Majesty's ships of all neutral vessels carrying corn, flour, or meal to any of the ports of France, or to any port occupied by the armies of France. The provisions were to be paid for and the vessels released with "a due allowance for freight." This measure, obviously intended to starve France into submission, was promptly attacked by Jefferson in instructions to Pinckney as an unwarranted extension of the rules governing contraband which would force America, if she were to accede to it, into a war she was striving to avoid.[20]

Excerpts from London newspapers which found their way

[19]Hammond to Grenville, Mar. 7, 1793, F. O. 5, 1. See Samuel F. Bemis, *John Quincy Adams and the Foundations of American Foreign Policy* (New York, 1949), 33.

[20]Grenville to Hammond, July 5, 1793, I. B. M., 40–42; Jefferson to Pinckney, Sept. 7, 1793, Ford, *Jefferson's Writings* VI, 412–16. Pinckney had hinted to Jefferson in March that such a measure was under contemplation. *Ibid.*, 243. See *ASP, FR* I, 240, for the text of the order.

into the columns of a Paris gazette reported that, from information received from a vessel returned from America at the beginning of September, "the people of America are almost to a man in favour of the French and so violent are they against the combined Powers that a war with the United States seems to be inevitable." American reaction to the provision order, the English sources continued, had caused alarm in the British ministry, and the American minister had been assured "that the American vessels should be amply indemnified for their freights, expenses and damages and that in future the American commence should not be impeded." The accounts concluded that, although America had no navy, "her situation renders her formidable against England on account of the English West India commerce." The reason for this condition, they explained, was that the trade winds forced that commerce to travel up the American coast before standing off for Europe, thus leaving it constantly exposed to capture.[21]

In preparing the foreign affairs section of the President's message to Congress, at the end of November 1793, Jefferson was careful to contrast the treatment of American commerce by France and by England. French officials, he wrote, had "manifested generally a friendly attachment to this country, have given advantages to our commerce and navigation, and have made overtures for placing these advantages on permanent ground." His first draft had continued: they "have given just and ready redress of the wrongs to our citizens and their property irregularly taken on the high seas, and carried into their ports." Information lately received from Pinckney and Morris, he explained to the President, had caused him to delete this last clause and to refer instead to the contradictory history of the French provision decree. The proceedings of Genet, which "have breathed nothing of the friendly spirit of the nation which sent him," were deplored, but, having thus differentiated between France and her obnoxious minister, the President was to assure Congress that

21AECPE-U, 38, 29vo–6o.

the effect of the unfortunate envoy's conduct had been counter-
acted by the exertions of the government.[22]

With regard to England, Jefferson made no such observations.
The British government, by orders given to the commanders of
its armed vessels, had undertaken to prevent American commerce in corn and other provisions with any ports but her own
and those of her allies. Discussions with the British on American
maritime grievances were now added to those concerning the inexecution of the treaty of peace of 1783. This was suggestive
enough, but Jefferson had not yet heard of the new Order-in-
Council of November 6! A few days later he defended what may
have seemed to Washington like partiality. "The motive too,"
Jefferson wrote, "of proving to the people the impartiality of
the Exec. between the two nations of France and England urges
strongly that while they are to see the disagreeable things which
have been going on as to France we should not conceal from them
what has been passing with England, and induce a belief that
nothing has been doing."[23]

Suggestions from Jefferson were not necessary, for less than
three weeks later he reported to his daughter that "the letting
loose the Algerines on us, which has been contrived by England,
has produced peculiar irritation." Congress, he thought, would
retaliate: ". . . if this should produce war tho' not wished for, it

22Jefferson to Washington, Nov. 30, 1793, Ford, *Jefferson's Writings* VI, 462.
The message is in James D. Richardson, ed., *Messages and Papers of the Presidents*
10 vols. (Washington, D. C., 1896–1907), I, 145–47.

23Dec. 2, 1793, Ford, *Jefferson's Writings* VI, 462. According to A. L. Burt, *The
United States, Great Britain, and British North America* (New Haven, 1940), 153:
"The order-in-council of November 6, 1793, headed Britain straight for war with
the United States." See also Ritcheson, *Aftermath*, 289–90, for a summary of the
events moving Britain and the U. S. "steadily, and apparently inevitably, toward
a second war . . . . The first major cause was Britain's roughshod and inept treatment of American shipping. The second cause was the design of Secretary Jefferson and the emerging Republican party to temper public indignation at the Genet
affair by drawing attention to the country's grievances against Britain." For
Ritcheson, therefore, "It is not the least significant condemnation of British policy
that it gave the Republicans a magnificent opportunity, seized immediately and
adroitly, to appear as champions of the nation against both an aggressive Britain
and a subservient minority at home, grasping for profits and power while sacrificing its self-respect and the nation's true interest."

seems not to be feared." To a friend he observed that the campaign against the Indians on the northwest frontier had ended unsuccessfully, owing to the failure of peace negotiations "which they protracted till the season for action was over." That was "a ray from the same centre." But,

> I believe we shall endeavour to do ourselves justice in a peaceful and rightful way. We wish to have nothing to do in the present war; but if it is to be forced upon us, I am happy to see in the countenances of all but our paper men a mind ready made up to meet it, unwillingly, indeed, but perfectly without fear. No nation has strove more than we have done to merit the peace of all by the most rigorous impartiality to all . . . .

Jefferson, who had striven most mightily, was the highest authority with regard to the truth of this last assertion. What more proof than that both Grenville and Robespierre agreed?[24]

Jefferson himself, having determined not to postpone his retirement beyond the end of 1793, decided to submit his report on commerce as one of his last official acts. Thanks to British arrogance in dealing with America, against which American opinion was presently reacting so violently and unanimously as a result of the Portuguese-Algerian truce and of the "provision" order of November 6, a more propitious time for the achievement of the objects of the report could hardly have been hoped for. The report, described by an appreciative Fauchet as "worthy of crowning the political career of this philosopher-minister," was transmitted to Congress on December 16, 1793.[25]

By instinct and conviction, Jefferson was a free trader. He heartily detested the restrictive navigaton policy which main-

24Jefferson to Martha Jefferson Randolph, Dec. 22, to Dr. Enoch Edwards, Dec. 30, 1793, Ford, *Jefferson's Writings* VI, 489, 495. George Canning paid Jefferson the perfect tribute a quarter-century later: "If I wished for a guide in a system of neutrality," the foreign secretary told the House of Commons in 1819, "I should take that laid down by America in the days of the presidency of Washington and the secretaryship of Jefferson, in 1793." Quoted in Thomas, *American Neutrality*, 13. John Quincy Adams later recorded a similar sentiment. See Dumas Malone, "The Relevance of Mr. Jefferson," *Virginia Quarterly Review* XXXVII (Summer 1961), 337.
25Fauchet to Minister of Foreign Affairs, May 17, 1794, C. F. M., 341. Jefferson's report is in *ASP, FR* I, 300–304, and in Ford, *Jefferson's Writings* VI, 470–84.

tained England's supremacy on the seas and directed world trade through artificial channels. He was realist enough, however, to know that England would never sacrifice her system to the power of persuasion alone, and he had long supported Madison's campaign for perfect reciprocity in commercial matters with all nations, reciprocal restrictions as well as favors. His report was designed to demonstrate the wisdom and even the necessity of this course.

The statistics contained in the report were admittedly old. They described the situation as it existed in the summer of 1792, "when things were in their settled order." They demonstrated clearly that American trade received generous and equitable treatment from France, Spain, and Portugal, but was severely circumscribed by Britain and, to a less degree, by Holland, also a principal reexporting nation.[26]

Aside from particular restrictions peculiar to British practice, Jefferson was most disturbed by the fact that, in addition to the restraints Britain employed against all foreign nations, the United States was forbidden to carry into British ports in its own bottoms even its own products. True, he admitted, the British executive had been given the power to suspend this act, which, in fact, was suspended from year to year by proclamation. But this practice was no substitute for a legal basis for that commerce, and the resulting insecurity, which Hammond had condescendingly referred to as "precarious indulgence," begot a condition intolerable to national pride.[27]

[26]Exports from the U. S. to England and her possessions amounted to $9,363,-416; to France and her possessions, $4,698,735; and to Spain and her possessions, $2,005,907. From these countries, respectively, the U. S. imported goods to the value of $15,285,428; $2,068,348; and $355,110. The U. S., therefore, had a favorable trade balance with France and Spain, who consumed at home what they imported, but not with England, which reexported about two-thirds, overall, of her American imports. American bottoms employed in commerce with those countries, moreover, showed the same tendency: with England, 43,580 tons; with France, 116,410 tons; and with Spain, 19,695 tons.

[27]Jefferson listed prohibitions against American salted fish and other salted provisions, except bacon, prohibitory duties against American bacon, whale oils, grains, meals, and breadstuffs, as principal items of discrimination, and also the prohibition against American shipping, even when purchased from and navigated by British subjects.

Jefferson's recommendations were disarmingly simple. The nation's navigation, he argued, deserved protection because industry and agriculture were dependent upon it. Protection was essential because, since the nation had little to fear from land attack, its merchant marine was a primary resource of defense. How, therefore, could it be adequately protected and encouraged? Two methods were possible: (1) "by friendly arrangements with the several nations with whom those restrictions exist"; (2) by retaliation to counteract their effects. Thus, when a nation refused to receive any other than American products in American vessels, the United States should do the same. When a nation refused to recognize as American any vessel not built in America, or refused the carriage of American products in American ships to any of her dominions, the same rule should apply. And so on, returning restriction for restriction, for "free commerce and navigation are not to be given in exchange for restrictions and vexations, nor are they likely to produce a relaxation of them."

James Madison, who had been urging exactly those remedies in the House of Representatives for years, was now to come into his own as the apostle of American economic independence. His previous efforts had always ended in failure, notably two years earlier when the Hamiltonians succeeded in shelving his resolutions. Now, however, the collaborators seemed assured of success: Jefferson's report had prepared the way, and on January 3, 1794, Madison rose in the House to offer a series of anti-British resolutions which would translate Jefferson's report into legislative action. Jefferson had just retired, leaving to his friend the direction of what may be termed the last great cabinet struggle between himself and Hamilton, who hastened to intervene.[28]

Ten days after Madison had introduced his resolutions, Hamilton counterattacked through William Smith of South Carolina. He had prepared a lengthy answer to Jefferson's report after Fisher Ames, his chief lieutenant in the House, secured a week's postponement of the question. Smith, in a speech which Jefferson

---

[28]Speech on discriminating duties, *Writings of Madison* VI, 203–208; Brant, *Madison: Father of Constitution*, 389–91.

recognized at once as "every tittle of it . . . Hamilton's except the introduction," derided the report on which Madison's resolutions were based as having minimized French measures unfavorable to American commerce, and exaggerated those of Britain. His chief contribution to the discussion, however, was the thinly veiled warning that the United States would be doomed to defeat in a commercial conflict with England, while the supposed chief beneficiary, France, would have to stand helplessly by, owing to her impotence at sea. Mr. Lodge, Hamilton's editor, asserts that this speech put "the question on business and commercial principles, and [lifted] it above national prejudices and resentments." He adds that "the effect of the argument was very great," but Jefferson, after reading it, assured Madison that "I find the Report . . . so fully justified, that the anxieties with which I left it are perfectly quieted. In this quarter, all espouse your propositions with ardor, & without a dissenting voice."[29]

The acrimonious debate in Congress between Madison and the defenders of England raged on into February, with every indication that the resolutions would carry; but in March, before final action could be taken, the discussions shifted to a more ominous plane. Britain's Order-in-Council of November 6, 1793, had directed British naval forces to seize any vessel carrying produce of the French colonies, or carrying supplies from elsewhere to those colonies. This order was not known in America until British cruisers suddenly swarmed about the French West India islands and seized almost three hundred American vessels.[30]

[29]Hamilton's draft of Smith's speech is in Henry Cabot Lodge, ed., *Works of Hamilton*. IV, 205–24. See especially, 219–20n. Apr. 3, 1794, Ford, *Jefferson's Writings* VI, 501–502. Hammond reported to Grenville on Dec. 19, 1791, that in "a very long and confidential conversation," Hamilton had hinted that France was offering the U. S. additional commercial advantages. Hamilton added, however, that he was preparing a report showing the "general aggregate advantages" of American commerce with Great Britain, which "decidedly preponderated" over those with France. F. O. 4, 11. Almost four months later, Hammond was still awaiting Jefferson's report, although he did not fear it, "as . . . Mr. Hamilton had prepared another of a very contrary tendency." Hammond to Grenville, Apr. 5, 1792, F. O. 4, 11.

[30]For a fuller discussion of the debate in Congress, see Brant, *Madison: Father of Constitution*, 391–94; Bowers, *Jefferson and Hamilton*, 240–43. The text of the

Meanwhile, despite the furious activity of some Federalists to head it off, popular opinion began to make itself felt in a flood of resolutions condemning Britain. These resolutions had already reached formidable proportions by the middle of March, and most insistent was the demand for an embargo against England. Commercial circles, however, still feared to offend the mistress of the seas, and a proposal for a thirty-day embargo was defeated in the House of Representatives on March 24 by the narrow margin of two votes. News of the West Indian seizures arrived the same day; and now the merchants, stricken on their most sensitive nerve, set up such a clamor that the embargo passed the House the next day by an overwhelming majority, the Senate concurring the day following. The Federalist ranks had broken, and merchants who had scorned Madison's campaign to win for them freedom and expanding commerical opportunities now lined up in support of retaliation against Britain's withdrawal of an indulgence they should have claimed as a right.

In something of an understatement, Lord Grenville had observed in a letter to Hammond on January 10 that, with respect to the order of November 6, "a considerable degree of dissatisfaction may have arisen in America." That he failed to see how very considerable the dissatisfaction in America was bound to become was an evidence of the arrogance which Grenville, and British officialdom in general, displayed in their relations with the United States. On the other hand, their callousness attests to their confidence in Hamilton, King, and William Smith, the main supporters of Britain's interest in America. Hammond was merely the channel of communication between the British ministry and Hamilton: the latter was Britain's effective agent. Dur-

Order-in-Council is in *ASP, FR* I, 430. According to the extract from a Boston gazette of Mar. 31 which Fauchet sent to his chief, 269 American ships were seized in the West Indies as a result of the November order, most of them being condemned while their cargoes were plundered. A Charleston paper one week earlier had estimated the seizures at 700 and accused Holland and Spain of connivance with Britain in war against the U. S. Aecpe-u, 40, 375–77vo. See Ritcheson, *Aftermath*, 299–310.

ing February, England's friends in America busily organized meetings of chambers of commerce in the coastal cities to draft resolutions for the purpose of counteracting those pouring in from the general mass of the citizenry condemning Britain and demanding retaliation.[31]

This political warfare grew so bitter as to threaten violence in the commercial centers, where merchants and their neighbors were stirred to peaks of exasperation against each other. Herman LeRoy, New York business associate of Senator Rufus King, confided to the Federalist leader at the end of February that he was to dine with his "Jacobin" neighbors, but "would almost as leave be whipped as go, yet it is disagreeable to be at variance with ones neighbors." England had at last overplayed her hand, however, for in March he expressed to King his irritation at American docility toward British condemnations. A few days later, thoroughly disgusted with Britain, LeRoy seized upon a piece of news indicating friction between Britain and her Spanish ally to "wish to God they would quarrel themselves into a general peace, that we may not be disturbed here . . . ." Other Federalist stalwarts saw not even this ray of hope. John Jay, second in influence among Federalists only to Hamilton, wanted to fortify the ports and place an embargo on exports for six to eight months. Demands for "putting the country in a state of defence" were not lost on Hamilton's closest lieutenant, Senator King.[32]

Simultaneously with the news of the West Indian seizures there arrived an account of an inflammatory speech delivered by Lord Dorchester, British governor general of Lower Canada, to a convocation of tribal chieftains of the Miamis. Though the meeting was secret, an Indian showed a friend in Montreal a copy of the speech, and on March 24 it appeared in the gazettes of New York. The message contained an exhortation to all the

[31]I. B. M., 47; Eugene P. Link, *Democratic-Republican Societies, 1790–1800* (New York, 1942), 49; William A. Williams, "Age of Mercantilism," 430–31.

[32]H. LeRoy to King, Feb. 28, 1794, Rufus King Papers, New-York Historical Society; LeRoy to King, Mar. 5, Jay to King, Mar. 19, 1794, King, *Life and Correspondence* I, 548–56.

Indian tribes on the fringes of the United States to join forces against the American intruders, and hinted that England would soon be at war with them herself. Close on the heels of this intelligence came reports of renewed Indian attacks on the frontiers, and thus the long-standing American resentment of British intrigue among the Indians, most unmistakably evidenced by the humiliating refusal of England to give up the frontier posts ceded by the treaty of peace, was joined to the wrathful indignation of Americans at England's provocative commercial policy.[33]

Now indeed "all the old spirit of 1776" was rekindled, and the United States hovered on the brink of a second war with England. Fauchet informed his government that the English commander in the West Indies openly acknowledged England's intent to attack the United States, and was keeping his forces in readiness for the commencement of hostilities. Hostile movements of Colonel John Graves Simcoe's forces from Upper Canada were reported in the American press, and Secretary Randolph, in a series of notes exchanged with Hammond over the Dorchester incident, warned the British minister that General Wayne had orders to meet any British violations of American territory with force. A Federalist correspondent of Secretary of War Knox wrote from Boston that "most of our cool good men think War inevitable," and an assembly of Carolinians gathered at Fayetteville to assure Congress of their support in a second war of independence, although they recognized that the war being forced upon them by Britain would involve "the ruin of our commerce and the suspension of our agriculture."[34]

[33]AECPE-U, 40, 80–81, 41, 9; Commissioners to Minister of Foreign Affairs, May 25, 1794, C. F. M., 351. Dorchester was later reprimanded by his government for this indiscretion. Grenville to Hammond, Aug. 8, 1794, I. B. M., 62. See Burt, *U. S., Great Britain, and British North America*, 133–35; Ritcheson, *Aftermath*, 309–13.

[34]Commissioners to Minister of Foreign Affairs, May 15, 1794, C. F. M., 351; AECPE-U, 40, 81–81vo, 84, 85, 403–405; *ASP, FR* I, 461–63; Henry Jackson to Knox, Mar. 1794, quoted in Channing, *History of U. S.* IV, 135n. That the French government was fully aware of the Anglo-American crisis is evident from an incident which took place toward the end of May. A packet of dispatches to Pinckney had been captured on an English vessel. Hearing of this, Morris asked that the bearer be released to continue his journey. "Considering the date of his departure from Philadelphia," the commissioner of external relations reported to the Committee

Amid all this talk of war, Madison kept his nonintercourse resolutions before Congress. They were not being pressed at this critical juncture because, as he explained to Jefferson, "the evils which they were to remedy . . . called for more active medicine." Still, he did not agree with those who believed that Britain meant to force war upon the United States.

> If she can destroy the branches of our commerce which are bene-
> ficial to her enemies, and continue to enjoy those which are bene-
> ficial to herself, things are in the best possible arrangement for
> her. War would turn the arrangement against her by breaking
> up the trade with her, and forcing that with her enemies. I con-
> clude therefore that she will push her aggressions just so far and
> no farther, than she imagines we will tolerate. I conclude also
> that the readiest expedient for stopping her career of depreda-
> tion on those parts of our trade which thwart her plans, will be
> to make her feel for those which she cannot do without.[35]

Jefferson agreed with his friend's analysis, which, indeed, had recently received support in the news of a British Order-in-Council of January 8, 1794, which relaxed that of November 6 more nearly into line with the British Rule of 1756. Jefferson, however, among his aroused Virginia neighbors, feared the experiment in commercial coercion might lose its opportunity. Rumors of a declaration of war, he told Madison, gratified "some other passions, and particularly of their ancient hatred to Gt. Britain. Still, I hope it will not come to that: but that the proposition will be carried, and justice be done ourselves in a peaceable way." Madison replied that accounts from the West Indies since the January order were favorable enough to alleviate the resentment of the merchants, "so that G. B. seems to have derived from the excess of her agressions a title to commit them in a less degree with impunity."[36]

---

of Public Safety, the dispatches must be "very important and contain the last overtures which will decide peace or war between the United States and England." The dispatches accordingly were hurried on their way. AECPE-U, 41, 76–76vo, 86.

[35]To Jefferson, Mar. 26, to Horatio Gates, Mzr. 24, 1794, *Writings of Madison* VI, 210–11, 208–209.

[36]Apr. 3, 1794, Ford, *Jefferson's Writings* VI, 212; Apr. 28, 1794, *Writings of Madison* VI, 212. The unilateral Rule of 1756 forbade all commerce with the

Jefferson took the occasion of a letter from Washington on the improvement of agriculture to propound to the President his thesis on dealing with British aggressions.

> Time, patience & perseverence must be the remedy; and the maxim of your letter, "slow & sure," is not less a good one in agriculture than in politics. I sincerely wish it may extricate us from the event of a war, if this can be done saving our faith and our rights. My opinion of the British govt is, that nothing will force them to do justice but the loud voice of their people, & that this can never be excited but by distressing their commerce . . . .[37]

But meanwhile drastic measures were pending. Abraham Clarke of Georgia introduced a resolution which passed the House on April 21 excluding all imports from England. Bills for the sequestration of British debts and for establishing liens on British imports were waiting their turn. The embargo was extended for another thirty days on April 25, but Madison's crucial nonimportation bill was defeated in the Senate three days later by the casting vote of Vice-President Adams, to whom Jefferson had just addressed an appeal for "some means . . . of reconciling our faith and honor with peace." The Hamiltonians, faced with the prospect of seeing the greatest part of the revenue on which Hamilton's elaborate tax structure was based dried up by nonimportation, had prevailed upon the President to send an emissary extraordinary to London to negotiate a settlement of American grievances. Jefferson, who ardently desired the passage of the nonimportation measure, was outraged to learn that Hamilton was proposed as the envoy, especially when such "a degrading measure" would amount to a vote of no confidence in the minister to England, Thomas Pinckney. This sharp reaction was common, for Madison wrote a few days later that Hamilton's

---

colonies of an enemy in time of war which had not been permitted during peace. This provision would have freed American commerce to the five French West Indian ports open to it before the war, but the laws on contraband and the blockade made the gain less substantial than it seemed.

[37] May 14, 1794, Ford, *Jefferson's Writings* VI, 510.

appointment "was likely to produce such a sensation that to his great mortification he was laid aside and Jay named in his place."[38]

The strategem of the Federalists had succeeded, and the appointment of Jay was only slightly less odious to the Republicans than that of Hamilton. The war crisis had passed with the rescission of the British November order, and the influence of Washington behind the Jay mission was enough to reassure the general public on that score. As Madison sadly wrote to Jefferson,

> the influence of the Executive on events, the use made of them, and the public confidence in the President are an overmatch for all the efforts Republicanism can make. The party of that sentiment in the Senate is completely wrecked; and in the House of Representatives in a much worse condition than at an earlier period of the session.

The embargo had been allowed to expire near the end of May, principally because Fauchet had exerted himself against its continuance in the conviction that it had proved more harmful to his own country than to England. He told his government that he had been forced to act to enable the provisions his mission had secured to be convoyed to France.[39]

Although Fauchet had been successful in regard to the embargo, he was frankly worried about the Jay mission. The war crisis had been surmounted by the appointment of special envoys to France and Spain, as well as to England, and Fauchet had nothing but praise for James Monroe, who was to succeed Morris at Paris. The duplication of ministers at London was overcome by naming Pinckney to negotiate the Mississippi question with Spain. The Jay nomination had served as an excuse for the abandonment of the entire discrimination program for at least this

[38] Jefferson to Adams, Apr. 25, to Tench Coxe, May 1, to Monroe, Apr. 24, 1794, *ibid.*, VI, 505, 507–508, 504; to Jefferson, Apr. 28, 1794, *Writings of Madison* VI, 212. Adams explained to his wife that the nonimportation bill had seemed to him "to involve nothing less than peace and war." Mar. 12, 1794, *Works of Adams* I, 467.

[39] May 25, 1794, *Writings of Madison* VI, 216–17; Commissioners to Minister of Foreign Affairs, May 29, 1794, C. F. M., 358–60.

session, although Fauchet was sure that "the American people want no more than we do to be subject any longer to the monopoly of the London shipowners, and to the arbitrary conditions of the Manchester bankers." Prophetically, he warned that "the most fatal blow which could be dealt [the American people] in the future, would be the conclusion of a treaty of commerce with England by Mr. Jay."[40]

This session of Congress ended, and its members adjourned to await Jay's success or failure in obtaining British respect for American neutrality. Within months, England had replaced France as the terrible threat to the peace and security of the United States. Genet's indiscretions were momentarily forgotten by all but the British fifth column of former Tories and Francophobes, as the arm of British sea power demonstrated England's powerful grip on America's economy.

But France's new policy of scrupulous regard for American sovereignty and neutrality had helped to redeem Girondist blunders, which had backfired dangerously. A new approach was indicated, and conciliation became the order of the day. Girondist internationalism gave way to Jacobin nationalism. French policy was now protectionist and restrictive, but it should be remembered that it nevertheless was expected to prove more advantageous to the United States than either the mixture of monopolies and privileges of the *ancien régime* or the vague liberalism of the Gironde.

French commercial policy under the Jacobins was based on the same nationalist considerations which motivated Jefferson and Madison in the United States. The latter and their supporters were theoretical free-traders, turned discriminationists as the only means of gaining economic independence and a real commercial reciprocity. Their great opportunity came when the arbiter of international commerce overplayed her hand and injured the group in America upon which she relied most for protection. The war crisis with Great Britain in the spring of 1794

[40]Fauchet to Minister of Foreign Affairs, May 17, 1794, C. F. M., 343.

was desperate. A decade of irritants of the most dangerous kind fused simultaneously. The British Orders-in-Council of June 8 and November 6, 1793, and the Dorchester speech, with the war-like activity on both sides of the Western frontier, taxed the Hamiltonian leadership to the utmost.

But the Republican leaders dreaded war no less than did the Federalists. Their methods of maintaining peace differed, the one demanding economic retaliation which would force just concessions from England, the others apparently willing to buy peace at any price—even neutrality. It was here that the prestige of Washington first was used for clearly partisan ends—his influence behind the special mission to London caused its general acceptance.

It seems clear that the Hamiltonian leadership of the Federalists—Hamilton's shock troops in Congress were the representatives of the New England merchants with close connections with mercantile correspondents in Britain—intended all along to preserve at any cost the intimate social and political correspondence with Britain through maintaining American economic dependence on the former mother country. These High-Federalists, however, could not carry with them moderate Federalists when, as the conservative Virginian, Edward Carrington, had told Hamilton, English attacks on American rights at sea made it necessary, "for the public honor, to resent the injury." About the same time, another Virginia Federalist had told Hamilton that "if we must either *fight*, or be kicked by G Britain; then, it will be found, that those who are now most averse to War, will be *first in the field*, and in the *front of the battle*."[41] The proposal of a special mission to England, therefore, was a desperate party stroke as well as a brilliant political maneuver.

As Madison pointed out in his rebuttal to Smith's distortions of Jefferson's report, the discrimination program he had proposed would foster not only commercial independence of Britain, but it would also give a great impetus to the development of

[41]Carrington to Hamilton, Apr. 26, Col. Heth to Hamilton, June 14, 1794, Hamilton Papers, Library of Congress, XIX, 2573-78, 2654-55.

American manufactures to supply the domestic market. It is ironic that Hamilton, usually regarded as the father of American industrialism, actually prevented America's industrial development as long as he exercised power; at the same time, Madison and Jefferson, traditionally cited as agrarian foes of industrialism, were contending for policies that would have forced industrial development almost a generation before it got fairly started. Had Hamilton in fact possessed the genius regarding economic affairs with which he is usually credited, he might easily have found means of replacing the government's lost revenues from commerce with Britain with income from other sources, especially through the expansion of trade with other nations.

Although Hamilton's effort to use the crisis for his favorite project of raising an army (he recommended to the President a program for fortifying the principal ports, "say one in each state," and raising ten regiments of auxiliary troops, at an estimated cost of $500,000) failed, Congress authorized the construction of six frigates, presumably for use against the Algerians. To raise additional revenue for this purpose, Hamilton's solution was characteristically political: new excise taxes, aimed at the agrarian South; and the proposal that the commerce of the rich in public securities and bank stock might also bear taxation was emphatically rejected. For the most part, Hamilton resorted to increased government borrowing abroad.[42]

It cannot be asserted that the Republican program would have saved the peace and won British respect for American rights, because it was never tried. It is evident, however, that the hat-in-hand approach Hamilton dictated gained the United States scant British consideration and respect, and the nation continued in a state of war alarm or of virtual war as long as the European conflict lasted. The history of the events leading to war with Britain in 1812, in particular the too-late rescission of the offending Orders-in-Council, is at least suggestive. At any rate, there is no

[42]"Thoughts submitted to the President March 8, 1794," *ibid.*, XXII, 3017; Williams, "Age of Mercantilism," 429–31; Brant, *Madison: Father of Constitution*, 398–99; John C. Miller, *Federalist Era*, 148–54.

reason to suppose that the Madison-Jefferson program of economic retaliation might not at least have gained more than Jay eventually brought back from London and thereby avoided later embroilments with France.

CHAPTER VII   The Shadow of
the Jay Mission,
1794–1795

> The American people want no more than we do
> to be subject any longer to the monopoly of the
> London shipowners, and to the arbitrary condi-
> tions of the Manchester bankers. The most fatal
> blow which could be dealt in the future, would be
> the conclusion of a treaty of commerce with Eng-
> land by Mr. Jay.
>
> FAUCHET TO FOREIGN MINISTER, MAY 17, 1794.

WHEN Fauchet arrived in Philadelphia on February 20, 1794, he was just thirty-three years old, and on the threshold of his first diplomatic mission. He was accompanied by the new consul general La Forest, a man twenty years his senior, who had previously served in the same capacity under both the Comte de Moustier and Ternant. Pétry, who arrived two days later with Le Blanc, had also had prior diplomatic experience in the United States. It required no great insight into probabilities to predict, as Gouverneur Morris did to Washington, that Fauchet, at least for a time, would be swayed by his more experienced colleagues.[1]

Under the favorable auspices which the outburst of anti-British sentiment in Congress and throughout the country presented, Fauchet began at once to repair the damage done by Genet and to improve the commercial relations which were so vital to his country. Two days after his arrival, he was presented to the Presi-

---

[1] C. F. M., 288n.; James, "French Diplomacy and American Politics," 154, 154n.; Morris to Washington, Nov. 12, 1793, *ASP, FR* I, 398.

154

dent by Secretary Randolph, who was so anxious to oblige the new minister that he called for him in his own carriage. Fauchet's reception by the President, he wrote to his government one month later, was "touching," and Washington was moved "almost to tears" by the action of the French government in sending a new minister. This was doubtless an exaggeration, but the President was pleased with the tone of the letter from the Committee of Public Safety and favorably impressed by its representative as well.[2]

Fauchet was so anxious to avoid Genet's associations, whom he characterized as having "more personal hatred for Washington than love for France," that he soon became something of a favorite among the Federalists. Senator King, less than one week after Fauchet's arrival, heard from his partner in New York, Herman LeRoy, that the latter was "very happy to learn that Mr. Fauchet is so much of a gentleman, that being the case he will not associate with the Jacobins as his predecessor did." One week later, LeRoy was still receiving pleasing accounts of Fauchet's conduct, while Monroe was informing Jefferson with disgust that "Fauchet was rec'd. with the most profound attention by the party heretofore opposed to his country & his cause." Monroe surmised: " 'Tis probable they might hope the fate of his predecessor wo'd. warn him to shun not only his errors but likewise the friends of France, upon the idea they wo'd. be the friends of Mr. Genet."[3]

Ignorant of the issues involved in the debates over Madison's resolutions, as Fauchet later explained, he relied upon the judgment of his experienced colleagues. They told him that Madison's project lacked "common sense," and that "its author deserved to be whipped." Confused, Fauchet kept himself apart from the controversy.[4]

2Commissioners to Minister of Foreign Affairs, Mar. 21, 1794, C. F. M., 308–309; Washington to R. H. Lee, Apr. 15, 1794, *Writings of Washington* XXXIII, 331.

3Commissioners to Minister of Foreign Affairs, Mar. 21, 1794, C. F. M., 314; LeRoy to King, Feb. 28, 1794, King Papers, New-York Historical Society; LeRoy to King, Mar. 5, 1794, King, *Life and Correspondence* I, 548; Monroe to Jefferson, Mar. 3, 1794, *Writings of Monroe* I, 284–85.

4Joseph Fauchet, "Mémoire sur les États-Unis d'Amérique," ed. by Carl Lokke, in *Annual Report of the American Historical Association, 1936* (1938), I, 105.

Fauchet was willing to accept the views of his colleagues on the proceedings in Congress the more readily because there were other matters of importance which required prompt attention. Randolph had hinted that the recruiting begun by Genet in Kentucky was causing concern, and Fauchet responded with a proclamation of March 6, forbidding all Frenchmen to violate the neutrality of the United States and revoking all commissions and authorizations which could compromise that neutrality.[5]

This proclamation was entirely in keeping with both the spirit and the letter of his instructions. It was rendered the more necessary by the fact that Genet, wild with anger at both the American government and at Robespierre, whom he considered an unprincipled usurper, had published his instructions in the United States just before the arrival of Fauchet. This rash display of passion had done serious injury to American friendship for France, not only because it outlined the aggressive intentions of Girondist zealots, but also because royalist policy before the French Revolution was so thoroughly castigated as faithless and deceitful. Genet gained nothing for himself by this act and further strengthened the determination of France's enemies in America, although Fauchet informed his superiors that this "impudence" had merely earned Genet "the scorn of honest men."[6]

Fauchet immediately broached the subject of Genet's arrest and was astonished at the objections raised by Randolph, who told him that the United States wanted only Genet's replacement and could not arrest him. The secretary also hinted that domestic violence might result from an attempt to seize him, and he ended

[5]Commissioners to Minister of Foreign Affairs, Mar. 21, 1794, C. F. M., 310; AECPE-U, 40, 147. Fauchet enclosed an extract from an American newspaper noting that "a storm dangerous to the peace of the United States rumbles on the banks of the Ohio." It attributed Clark's success in recruiting volunteers to the government's failure to obtain the right of navigation of the Mississippi. *Ibid.*, 40, 145–46vo.

[6]Commissioners to Minister of Foreign Affairs, Mar. 21, 1794, C. F. M., 315. See Fay, *Revolutionary Spirit in France and America*, 336–38. Reporting on Genet's publication of his instructions, Hammond observed: ". . . however intemperate reprehensible and unwarrantable his conduct may have been, he has not essentially exceeded the spirit of his instructions . . . ." Feb. 22, 1794, F. O. 5, 4.

the discussion with a request that Fauchet put his demand in writing. This Fauchet did on March 6, but Randolph never gave him a satisfactory answer.[7]

On his arrival, Fauchet faced that perennial embarrassment of French ministers since Moustier: lack of financial means. French credit was so shaky that American merchants refused to provision the vessel which had transported the commissioners to the United States, and letters of exchange received by American merchants from French officials were protested more often than not. Fauchet had to advance 12,000 francs of his personal funds to purchase supplies for the care of the one hundred and fifty sick sailors of the naval division which had escorted him across the Atlantic. But he could not hope to supply from such meager resources the needs of other ships of the Republic, scattered among the different ports of the United States, and also the needs of the refugees from Saint-Domingue who besieged him with demands for subsistence and for passage to France.[8]

In desperation, Fauchet did what Ternant and Genet had already done. At his first meeting with the President, he asked for further advances on the French debt to the amount of one million dollars, at which he estimated his minimum requirements for the next six months. After further discussions, the President agreed to advance half of the amount requested in two equal installments, the first payment to be made the following September, the second in November. Fauchet's request for the balance was referred to Congress. Although promising relief in the future, such distant payments offered no solution to problems of the present. For immediate expenses, therefore, the commissioners had to draw upon the five million livres entrusted to them by the Commission of Subsistences and Provisions for the purchase of flour and grain for France, while they attempted to negotiate better terms from the American government. Fauchet drew up a requested table of payments: twelve biweekly installments to

[7]Commissioners to Minister of Foreign Affairs, Mar. 21, 1794, C. F. M., 308–309; Fauchet to Randolph, Mar. 29, 1794, AECPE–U, 40, 354.
[8]Commissioners to Minister of Foreign Affairs, Mar. 21, 1794, C. F. M., 310–11.

begin May 15 and end November 1. This plan was rejected by Hamilton, who finally offered to facilitate the acceptance by the Bank of the United States of French drafts against the payments originally scheduled. This arrangement involved the loss of 1 percent on drafts thus negotiated, since the bank charged 6 percent interest and the United States paid only 5 percent on its loan, but Fauchet nevertheless accepted it as the best obtainable.[9]

The payments authorized by the President for the autumn of 1794 were simply those to become due on the debt at that time: according to Hamilton's records, there were no arrears outstanding on January 1, 1794. Fauchet never received any advances from the American treasury, and he even had to accept a loss on the $453,750 due for that year, since he had to draw against it through the Bank of the United States. The President did submit his request to Congress for the million dollars he wanted at once, but after it had passed the House of Representatives by a large majority, it failed in the Federalist-dominated Senate in June, as Madison had predicted to Jefferson.[10]

Besides these resources, the commissioners took over the treasury of Genet, which held a total of $8,673. Since the government had stopped the delivery of advances previously promised to Genet, the latter was able to secure funds only from the sale of the cargoes of French ships which had brought refugees from Saint-Domingue. But there remained in the United States Treasury $70,270 of two unpaid delegations to Genet, which had not been included in Fauchet's negotiations. On the President's authority, this was turned over to Fauchet.[11]

Fauchet's most pressing task, after mollifying the American government in regard to Genet, was to expedite the provisioning

[9]Washington to Senate and House of Representatives, Mar. 18, Fauchet to Randolph, Mar. 1 and 2, Randolph to Fauchet, Mar 12, Fauchet to Randolph, Mar. 12, Hamilton to Washington, Mar. 18, 1794, *ASP, FR* I, 427–28.

[10]Albert Aulard, "La Dette Américaine envers la France," *Revue de Paris* 32.5 (Mar. 1925), 544–45; June 1, 1794, *Writings of Madison* VI, 218.

[11]Commissioners to Minister of Foreign Affairs, May 7, 1794, c. f. m., 336, 338–39; to the Secretary of the Treasury, May 2, 1794, *Writings of Washington* XXXIII, 350.

of France from America. Britain's provision order of June 8, 1793, followed by the even more stringent one of November 6, rendered France's food supply precarious. As Morris wrote from Paris in the autumn of 1793: "The coming winter will be, I believe, dreadful, and the spring, should the war continue, must open with partial scarcities, if not general want."[12]

While the struggle over retaliation against Britain was raging in Congress, Fauchet was busy collecting a fleet of ships loaded with provisions for France. By March 18, the "innumerable difficulties" attending this task were almost resolved, and he took the strictest precautions to ensure that news of the convoy's sailing would reach Paris in time for a protective escort to be provided through the British blockade. Three days later he was able to announce that French merchant ships from Philadelphia, New York, Baltimore, Alexandria, and Norfolk had left those ports to rendezvous with Admiral Pierre-J. Vanstabel's division on the open sea between Sandy Hook and Cape Henlopen.[13]

By May 27, the commissioner of external relations (the new title of the foreign minister under the recent reorganization of the French government) had received news of the sailing of the convoy. Not until some time later, however, did Buchot receive Fauchet's dispatch with the news in detail, and he urged that protection be furnished immediately. Answering Fauchet on June 17, Buchot reversed the gloomy predictions of the previous autumn and expressed "great hopes of an abundant harvest," but Fauchet was nevertheless to redouble his efforts, for "we need all the provisions from America we can get." Before Buchot had closed his dispatch, the convoy had arrived at Brest. To his congratulations on the success of Fauchet's efforts, he added the information that its defense had occasioned "a very bloody battle." Buchot reported to the Committee of Public Safety on August 9 that "Fauchet's note announcing the sailing of this convoy has

12James, "French Diplomacy and American Politics," 155; Morris to Washington, Nov. 12, 1793, *ASP, FR* I, 398–99.
13C. F. M., 303–304, 319.

been responsible for the adoption of the measures which saved it."[14]

All the ships of the convoy were French, but under British maritime practice American ships would have been exposed to the same risk of capture. The destruction by Lord Richard Howe of the French covering fleet from Brest on June 1 demonstrated the extent of British determination to prevent provisions from reaching France and gave point to observations made by Fauchet in his dispatches of March 18 and 21. Because American ships were stopped on all the seas by British cruisers, he wrote, they could reach France only by the use of false papers, and the true ones usually had to be thrown overboard. As a result of increased British vigilance for this kind of deception, the only solution was for France to provide escorts for all American merchant ships with cargoes destined for France. France could count only upon her own strength, "and the Republic must protect a commerce which it needs." Two stout frigates and two corvettes, with five or six smaller vessels, he thought, would be regarded by American shipowners as sufficient protection for a score or more merchantmen. These warships would have to be sent over continually, if the stream of supplies was to continue. In addition, he had adopted the practice of sending a fast dispatch boat in advance of the convoy, in order that a naval division might be sent out of French ports to meet it as it approached the area of greatest danger off the French coast. All this, he added, with an eye on the debates in Congress, would become even more urgent if the United States failed to avoid war with England.[15]

Buchot approved the sending of dispatch boats but failed to mention anything about naval protection, probably because the dispatch on this subject, as late as July 22, had not reached him. He, too, was absorbed in the great question of war or peace between the United States and England, and he was most concerned

[14] AECPE–U, 41, 98, 196–97, 274. Palmer, *Twelve Who Ruled*, 342–50, recounts the battle and its significance.
[15] C. F. M., 304, 305n., 319–20.

that Fauchet had not sent more dispatches, for "lack of news leaves us in absolute ignorance of the measures Congress proposes to take to have its flag respected."[16]

While waiting for the arrival of French warships for convoy duty, Fauchet was doing the best he could with the means available. On July 7, a French ship arrived at Brest loaded with provisions and bearing the news that from fifty to sixty American ships were ready to depart from American ports but were awaiting convoy. Four or five had already departed, a corvette waited to convoy seven or eight more, and the rest would follow as soon as possible. Rather than wait longer for frigates from France, Fauchet was sending merchantmen to sea in small groups, with a single corvette as escort, whenever he could make one available. This procedure was very successful, for a dispatch from Paris dated July 22 mentioned that "great numbers of American ships" had reached French ports.[17]

Long before September the naval vessels available to Fauchet had all been dispatched, the last with a convoy of French merchantmen which finally left the United States on June 14. That convoy was met and dispersed by British men-of-war the day following its departure, but the commissioner did not receive an account of the disaster until August 18, when a French corsair brought the news. Fauchet wrote two lengthy reports of the fate of the convoy to emphasize the need for greater naval protection of merchant ships, but the truth was that France lacked the maritime forces to do more than protect her home ports. At length, Fauchet's request for regular dispatch boats was granted, but even the first of these did not reach America until November 7.[18]

Fauchet worked hard to fulfill the commercial requirements of his mission: purchasing and sending provisions to France, as

[16]Buchot to Commissioners, July 22, 1794, AECPE–U, 41, 196, 240.

[17]Representatives of Convention at Brest to Committee of Public Safety, July 7, Buchot to Commissioners, July 22, 1794, *ibid.*, 41, 228–29, 240.

[18]Buchot to Committee of Public Safety, Aug. 18, Commissioners to Department of Marine and Colonies, Aug. 30, 1794, *ibid.*, 41, 296–96vo. 330–31vo, 42, 176; Commissioners to Commissioner of Marine and Colonies, Sept. 1, 1794, C. F. M., 397–402.

well as masts for ships being built there (of wood that "is not too green, as in the last war," Deforgues had warned him); caring for Saint-Dominguan refugees; and a thousand and one other details. In addition, he had to audit the accounts of Genet, which he found in the wildest confusion, and of Ternant, which were relatively orderly. He also pursued the tedious negotiations with the Treasury Department for new advances. But despite all these demands upon his energies, political relations, after the first few weeks of feeling his way, absorbed the major share of his attention.[19]

The split between the commissioners, Fauchet and Le Blanc on one side, and La Forest and Pétry on the other, had developed early. Le Blanc wrote to his good friend Jean Nicholas Pache, the mayor of Paris, on March 19, 1794, denouncing his two colleagues as counterrevolutionaries. They insisted on seeing and knowing everything, he related, and their old friends were all either Royalists or members of the "Anglomaniac party." He and Fauchet were in constant fear that they would betray the Republic's interests, "or prevent them being served by us."[20]

Le Blanc certainly wrote without the approval, and probably without the knowledge, of Fauchet. As the latter explained in the *mémoire* which he wrote after his return to Paris, he had maintained an "ostensible neutrality" during the congressional debates over commercial retaliation against Britain. It was only toward the end, when an embargo was about to be imposed, that Senator Monroe came to visit him and made him realize how deeply involved were the interests of France. Monroe enlightened him, Fauchet continued, "on the composition of parties and told me that our friends saw with pain that I seemed to avoid them." It was after that enlightenment that Fauchet began a separate series of dispatches to his government, in violation of his instructions, in order to conceal his thoughts from his suspect colleagues.[21]

[19]Deforgues to Fauchet, Feb. 8, 1794, AECPE–U, 40, 79–79vo; Commissioners to Minister of Foreign Affairs, Apr. 13–June 8, 1794, C. F. M., 321–89 *passim*.

[20]AECPE–U, 40, 277vo–78.

[21]Fauchet, "Mémoire sur les États-Unis d'Amérique," 185.

About this time, according to Fauchet, he was visited by "many members of the Congress" who wanted to make sure that his provision fleet would sail for France before the embargo was put into effect. By March 21, when Fauchet reported these overtures, French vessels were weighing anchor in several different American ports, en route to a rendezvous at sea with Admiral Vanstabel's squadron. The embargo went into effect on March 26, but the Admiral's division did not set sail until almost three weeks later. Hammond, "as well as other agents of foreign powers," complained at once to Randolph against "this mark of preference," but the secretary seems to have ignored them. Perhaps Randolph, like Fauchet, thought the "torrent of public opinion" against "the vexations of the English" was the best answer to such representations.[22]

As the embargo's first month neared its end, Fauchet indicated no desires respecting its continuance. Daily expecting convoy vessels from France, he delayed a request that French ships be exempted, and as a result the embargo was renewed for an additional month. The second convoy for France would not be ready to depart within that time anyway, so there was no pressing reason for his intervention. As May 25 approached, however, the new convoy was about ready to sail, and a second renewal threatened to undo two months' work of collecting and loading supplies and ships. By that time Fauchet had decided that the embargo, although ordered originally in protest against British maritime practice, was actually hurting France more than her enemy. His choice, therefore, lay between accepting the continuance of a measure which inconvenienced Britain, but was very harmful to France, and trying to prevent its renewal. Fauchet worked among his Republican friends in the House of Representatives to such advantage that a motion for continuance was overwhelmingly defeated, although earlier tests on the measure had indicated the opposite result. Fauchet reported to his superiors that several of those who had reversed their positions had acknowledged pub-

[22]Commissioners to Minister of Foreign Affairs, Mar. 21, May 29, 1794, C. F. M., 316–17, 358; James, "French Diplomacy and American Politics," 156.

licly that the representations of the French minister had been responsible for changing their votes.[23]

Fauchet's first separate dispatch, dated May 5, 1794, carried the news of the appointment by the President of Senator Monroe to succeed Morris at Paris. Monroe's attributes, remarked Fauchet, "will endear him to the true friends of liberty," and his nomination had been made through the efforts of Randolph, another "entirely devoted" friend of France. The latter, Fauchet continued, could not be more cooperative: "we forewarn each other of the steps we are about to take by frank and friendly conversations," and those steps were always "compared and agreed upon in advance." Monroe sailed from Baltimore on June 18.[24]

Shortly after Monroe's appointment, Fauchet wrote to his government a dispatch which was later to cause Secretary Randolph untold trouble. Fauchet said that he had just come from a meeting with the secretary, at which Le Blanc had been present, when Randolph had spoken most frankly of men and parties in the American government. But Randolph, reported Fauchet, had been disturbed over the possibility of his confidences being shared with La Forest and Pétry, "who had continually manifested anti-republican opinions and who had intimate ties with members of the government and of the Senate . . . ." La Forest was especially accused of being an intimate of Hamilton and Knox, and Pétry, of Ralph Izard and William Smith, both members of Congress. Smith was identified by Fauchet as the same who had led the fight against Madison's resolutions. As for Madison himself, Fauchet had so far rejected the opinions of his colleagues that he characterized that "dearest friend of the new envoy to France" as "the Robespierre of the United States." Arriving shortly after the fall and execution of the Jacobin leader, this last must have proved interesting reading for Robespierre's Thermidorean executioners.[25]

[23]May 29, 1794, C. F. M., 358–59.
[24]Ibid., 333; Writings of Monroe I, 300, II, 10.
[25]June 4, 1794, C. F. M., 372–73. Randolph, in his Vindication, placed this inter-

Fauchet assured Randolph that La Forest and Pétry had long since ceased attending his conferences. He added, for the benefit of his superiors, that this was a "precaution which I had taken because I had the same opinion of them as the Secretary of State." A few days later, Fauchet, with Le Blanc's collaboration, presented further evidence against La Forest and Pétry. He had engaged two clerks in La Forest's office to watch the consul general's mail and to bring him one of his letters when the opportunity presented itself. This espionage was rewarded with the acquisition of a letter proving La Forest's correspondence with émigrés, some of whom had returned to France. This meager evidence was proof enough for the suspicious minister of La Forest's disloyalty, and the further discovery that Otto corresponded from Paris with the traitor was sufficient to clothe Otto, too, with suspicion. But Fauchet could not know that Otto had gone to prison already in the wake of Danton's downfall, or that he was soon to be released by the Thermidoreans.[26]

Before this intrigue was rewarded, it had been decided to send Le Blanc to Paris to enlighten the Committee of Public Safety on the state of American politics, especially in regard to Jay's mission to England, and also to denounce the two members of the commission suspected of aristocratic liaisons. To forestall any suspicions on the part of these gentlemen, Fauchet, in dispatches of June 3 and 8, gave the ostensible purpose of the mission. In the first, he reported that Le Blanc was to urge the need for regular packet service between France and America, which the commissioners, as well as American friends of France, had pleaded for

---

view in April, and Conway, *Edmund Randolph,* repeatedly insists on his subject's recollection. Neither substantiates his case, all the more necessary for Conway because his exoneration of Randolph depends on it. Fauchet gives every appearance of recording oral transactions shortly after their occurrence; it seems most likely, therefore, that the conversation took place at the end of May, or early in June. This conclusion does not necessarily weaken the real case for Secretary Randolph, but it does put in clearer sequence the development of the split among the French commissioners. Edmund Randolph, *A Vindication of Mr. Randolph's Resignation* (Philadelphia, 1795), 272n.; Conway, *Edmund Randolph,* 312n., 314.

[26]June 4, 1794, C. F. M., 372, 389–90; Masson, *Le Départment des Affaires Étrangères,* 320–21.

ever since their arrival. The second contained an answer to an order from the minister of marine for the purchase of 28-gun frigates: Le Blanc could enlarge upon the impossibility of fulfilling this commission, particularly since timber for this size vessel was not cut in America and because American neutrality prevented the arming of any French ships.[27]

By the time Le Blanc reached Paris, Thermidor had removed the Robespierrists, Buchot had replaced Deforgues, and the new order was taking inventory. The new regime was at a loss regarding American policy. As usual, the change of party produced a flood of reports and memoirs from ambitious citizens with programs to offer, most of whom doubtless aspired to carry them out. One which was unsigned, however, seems to have received more than the usual attention. It began with a statement that Denmark was making efforts in London to obtain American support for a new league of armed neutrality, but that Thomas Pinckney, though hostile to England, was powerless to offer satisfaction both because of a lack of instructions and "the absolute inability of the United States to wage offensive war."

America, the anonymous writer continued, was split into two parties, and the English, or aristocratic, party was making great efforts to bring on a war with England. This deduction, which would certainly have astonished Monroe and Fauchet, was based upon five suppositions which even those partisans would not have attributed to their opponents: (1) "because it is well known that the United States cannot win," (2) defeat would be blamed on too strong a connection with France, (3) "it would soon be necessary to conclude a disadvantageous peace with England and perhaps a treaty of commerce," (4) the taxes necessary to support the war would consolidate a financial system which already was crushing the people, (5) the very fear of war would force the opposing party to conclude a treaty of commerce with England rather than risk a new revolution.[28]

On the other hand, the author continued, the French party

[27]Le Blanc to Commissioner of Foreign Affairs, undated, c. f. m., 361, 388–89, 410.
[28]This reasoning was more ingenious than astute. Federalists and their English

rightly rejected all proposals for war, but wanted to avenge "the atrocities of the English" by the seizure of all English ships, cargoes, and funds, and by the sequestration of all English credits in the United States. These two measures, he thought, would have proved successful, but the executive, trying to steer a middle course between the two parties, had sent an ambassador to England to demand satisfaction before making a final decision. Since America was strong at home and could harass English commerce to that nation's great injury if provoked, the measures of the Republicans were unquestionably the best and deserved every encouragement from France.[29]

The reconstituted Committee of Public Safety lacked information on the mission of Fauchet. Only Fauchet's first dispatch had arrived, and this was condensed by Buchot on September 8: "the people of the United States are French and want war," but "the government is unprepared and wants to remain neutral," although "it leans toward France."[30]

That was slender information upon which to build a new policy, although it illustrated Britain's success in denying France the communication with her envoys abroad which so consistently hampered her relations with the United States throughout the war. By September, however, Le Blanc was on the scene, and Buchot had his letter explaining the purpose of his mission. This letter, giving only the headings of subjects Le Blanc wished to discuss, was very vague and, as Buchot explained to the Committee of Public Safety in October, "like his conversations with me, is full of generalities."[31]

---

correspondents alike regarded the prospect of war between the two countries with horror. A prominent New York Federalist, John Murray, wrote to Rufus King that "the consequences to us will be dreadful." He enclosed an extract of a letter from a friend in London rejoicing that impressions of British responsibility for turning loose the Algerines had been dispelled. "Had that report been true," he commented, "I should have blushed for my country." He assured Murray that Lord Chatham "was disposed to act a very friendly part towards America.'" John Murray to King, Apr. 25, 1794, King Papers, New-York Historical Society.

29Undated, but probably early July 1794, AECPE–U, 41, 150–52.

30To the Committee of Public Safety, *ibid.*, 41, 274–75.

31Undated, but probably Sept. 13, 1794, C. F. M., 410–11; Buchot to Committee of Public Safety, Sept. 13, 1794, AECPE-U, 41, 377–77vo.

Le Blanc wrote Buchot another letter on September 13 which was equally unsatisfactory, merely reiterating his plea to be allowed to address the committee. Buchot was still far from convinced that Le Blanc had anything worth the committee's time, but because "the situation in the United States must be getting more and more interesting," he finally asked the committee to hear him. The next day he was ordered to send Le Blanc to Philippe Antoine Merlin de Douai, who had been deputed to hear him. Nothing resulted from the interview which followed, and it seems certain that Merlin was no more impressed with Le Blanc's story than Buchot had been. Le Blanc appeared in the records of the Foreign Office more than one year later when, in response to his demand, the Committee of Public Safety ordered the commissioner of external relations to reimburse him for salary and expenses due at the time of his return to France.[32]

Small wonder that Le Blanc's story was confused. The ultra-Jacobin envoy apparently was not up to the task of altering a report intended for Robespierre to suit the unfriendly ears of the Thermidoreans. Fauchet himself had been under attack from the beginning of his mission—first, for his "connections with the Anglo-American party," and, after Robespierre's demise, for following "the plan of his patron Robespierre." These charges came to the Committee of Public Safety in a steady stream from General Donatien-Marie-Joseph de Vimeur, vicomte de Rochambeau, on parole in America after his capture by the English in the conquest of Martinique. A son of General Jean Baptiste Rochambeau, who had earned American gratitude as commander of the French army at Yorktown in 1781, he was angling for Fauchet's post some time before Fauchet himself decided that his commission should be recalled and Genet reinstated![33]

Before Fauchet had fully made up his own mind on American politics, he had begun to sound out Randolph on a new treaty

32C. F. M., 419; Committee of Public Safety to Buchot, Sept. 13, Decree of Committee of Public Safety, Oct. 10, 1795, AECPE-U, 41, 408–408vo, 44, 350.

33Rochambeau to Ministers of the Republic, Aug. 28, Oct. 10 and 16, Nov. 23 and 26, Dec. 3 and 4, 1794, Jan. 17, 1795, AECPE-U, 41, 328–29vo, 42, 103, 52–52vo, 259–60vo, 312–12vo, 322–22vo, 43, 87.

of alliance and commerce. The secretary, he reported on May 17, seemed disposed to receive his overtures, but Fauchet thought he detected "a little distrust and timidity" in regard to the proposed treaty of commerce as well as to the "political alliance." Since he was empowered to make only "the first advances," perhaps it would be better to treat with Monroe, if he carried the necessary powers. Monroe, he added, would be only too happy to take up the business in order to subvert Jay's mission to England, "concerning which he has very real fears which are only too well founded." Because Jefferson had earlier indicated a preference for the conclusion of a new treaty in America, his government could choose whether or not to send Fauchet more specific powers.[34]

Fauchet later declared that events in the United States, specifically those related to the so-called "Whiskey Rebellion" in western Pennsylvania, had conspired against the successful conduct of negotiations at Philadelphia. Everyone in America, he said, was persuaded that the continued success of French arms in Europe would contribute more to the contemplated negotiations than all the skill of the French minister. Fauchet was by then anxious to rationalize the failure of his mission, and he had decided to cast the principal blame on Randolph's alleged duplicity. Randolph, writing a few weeks later, instructed Monroe to refer the French government to its minister in America if the subject of a new treaty was broached: that was "a subject to be negociated with the government here" and "it has never been proposed to us by Mr. Fauchet." Perhaps the "timidity" was Fauchet's, for long afterwards, Wolcott, Hamilton's former assistant and successor, remembered "no overtures relative to a treaty of any kind" from Fauchet.[35]

Fauchet never again mentioned a new treaty in his dispatches. Already made suspicious of Jay's mission by Monroe, Fauchet devoted himself to the task of discovering its real purpose. Le Blanc

---

34C. F. M., 344.

35Fauchet, "Mémoire sur les États-Unis d'Amérique," 108; Monroe's instructions, dated June 10, 1794, *Writings of Monroe* II, 5–6; Oct. 6, 1795, C. F. M., 344n.

was already preparing to go to Paris when Fauchet described Jay's mission as "absolutely insignificant," undoubtedly for the purpose of concealing his fears from his fellow commissioners. Soon after, Fauchet reported the conversation he had just had with Randolph, in which the secretary unveiled for him "the mystery of the government" in order to reassure him as to the purposes of the Jay mission. In the course of the conversation, Randolph promised that the purpose was solely "to demand a solemn reparation of the spoliations which our commerce has experienced on the part of England" and "to enter into no negociations contrary to what we owe to France." Fauchet was given a scrap of paper with that part of Jay's instructions written in Randolph's hand, on condition that he burn it. Randolph had given this assurance with the approval of the President, but Fauchet was so little convinced by the secretary's confidences that he attached the note to his dispatch, describing it as "unimportant." Randolph did not suspect how completely he had failed to convince Fauchet and Le Blanc and did not know at the time that Fauchet's report of the conversation would be the beginning of his own downfall.[36]

Fauchet's attitude toward American politics had come full circle with his rejection of the assurances of Secretary Randolph. Arriving at Philadelphia in the critical spring of 1794, he had carried out at once his orders for the mollification of the American government. He did not realize the importance of the struggle in Congress until too late, and his ignorance of all things American was displayed in an early intimacy with the Hamiltonians which dismayed the real friends of France. Convinced by them of this error, he soon veered about to the other extreme, quarreling with his colleagues and disparaging Randolph, his only friend in the government.

Fauchet's accomplishments in getting provisions to France were important to his country, but his mission was a failure from a political standpoint. He, like Genet, gained only a superficial

[36]Commissioners to Minister of Foreign Affairs, May 27, June 4, 1794, C. F. M., 353, 373–75; Conway, *Edmund Randolph*, 314; James, "French Diplomacy and American Politics," 159–60.

understanding of Americans. The suspicions of Jay, which Monroe encouraged, could not be squared with Randolph's official explanations. Abandoned to the atmosphere of melodrama which anti-British zealots imparted to this Federalist maneuver, Fauchet could not accept the truth: that Jay's instructions were truthfully reported to him by Randolph, but that Jay later violated those instructions. Thus Randolph became doubly the victim of Jay's negotiations. Although Fauchet was right in his forebodings concerning the Jay mission, his dispatches misled his government. Before this mistake was apparent, he was too busy rationalizing his own failure to correct it.

It is doubtful whether any French minister could have changed the course of events at this stage. Nevertheless, Fauchet's clumsiness was to prove a major factor in accomplishing the very thing he dreaded—ratification of an Anglo-American treaty. While France and her minister presented no threat to American well-being whatever, the influence of England was quietly doing its work.

## CHAPTER VIII

Monroe's Mission to France

Being forced to send a republican character the admn. was reduc'd to the dilemna [*sic*] of selecting from among its enemies or rather those of opposite principles, a person who wod. be acceptable to that nation.

MONROE TO JEFFERSON, MAY 4, 1794.

W HEN James Monroe sailed from Baltimore, friendship and understanding between France and America were in greater danger than they had been since 1763. Relations between Secretary of State Randolph and Fauchet were no longer cordial; a tone of hostility had crept into the communications of the Frenchman, who tended increasingly to blame the hard-pressed secretary for the harassments and obstacles the course of events placed in his way. But more serious than maritime squabbles and the machinations of Hammond and his friends was the shadow of the Jay mission to England, which lay across the minds of the French minister and of American well-wishers of France like a dark cloud before a storm. Monroe himself, who had written a sharp protest to the President against the rumored appointment of Hamilton to London, had accepted the mission to Paris only to prevent its falling to someone less devoted to the French cause. On the advice of Madison and other friends, he told Jefferson, he had agreed to leave the Senate "upon the necessity of cultivating France."[1]

The uncertainty and suspicion surrounding the Jay mission provided the theme for the instructions delivered to Monroe.

1To Washington, Apr. 8, to Jefferson, May 27, 1794, *Writings of Monroe* I, 291–92, 300.

"The President," wrote Randolph, "has been an early and decided friend of the French Revolution" and is "persuaded that success will attend their efforts." France had been wise in not desiring American departure from neutrality. American ports, closed to prizes of Great Britain, were open to those of France, and supplies of grain could not well be shipped to France if the United States were a belligerent. True, the British Orders-in-Council made that commerce precarious, but it might be greatly facilitated "if the demands to be made upon Great Britain should succeed."

The neutrality of the United States was beneficial to France, and the President intended to pursue that policy "with faithfulness." With respect to Jay's mission, Randolph warned that "it is not improbable, that you will be obliged to encounter, on this head, suspicions of various kinds." To set these suspicions at rest, Monroe could say that Jay "is positively forbidden to weaken the engagements between this country and France" and that the objects of the mission were "to obtain immediate compensation for our plundered property, and restitution of the posts." Monroe could also argue that support of their government by the American people, "if war should be necessary . . . would be better secured by a manifestation, that every step had been taken to avoid it." This was "the path of prudence with respect to ourselves; and also with respect to France, since we are unable to give her aids of men or money."

Of less moment, by comparison, were other matters. Mention of the proposed treaty of commerce, so much alluded to both at Paris and at Philadelphia, was to be avoided: this was "a subject to be negociated with the government here." Thus was destroyed in advance Fauchet's best hope. What would have surprised Fauchet more, Monroe was instructed to dispel the impression presumably conveyed to Paris on the nature of American parties, the "mystery" of which had been unveiled to Fauchet by Randolph himself.[2]

2Fauchet to Minister of Foreign Affairs, June 4, 1794, C. F. M., 373.

The embargo in the United States, Randolph continued, might have "excited some uneasy sensations in the breast of the French minister." Monroe knew enough of "the history of this business, to declare, that the embargo was leveled against Great Britain . . . and also, that it was not continued, merely because it was reputed to be injurious to France." Monroe would then find it easy to present the American complaint against the Bordeaux embargo, and claims "for the captures and spoliations of our property, and injuries to the persons of our citizens, by French cruisers." Fauchet had already promised support of these claims.

In his conclusion, Randolph returned to the subject of Jay's mission. "You go . . . to France," he reminded Monroe, "to strengthen our friendship with that country," but "without betraying the most remote mark of undue complaisance." Specifically, "you will let it be seen, that in case of war, with any nation on earth, we shall consider France as our first and natural ally." America acknowledged gratitude for past services and for the recent intervention with Algiers, and Monroe was to avail himself of any future opportunity of invoking French assistance. This, explained Randolph, applied particularly to the event of a separate peace being negotiated between France and Spain, in which case "there may be an opening for France to become instrumental in securing to us the free navigation of the Mississippi." Monroe was to "contrive to have our mediation . . . solicited," if Spain fulfilled expectations and abandoned her British alliance.[3]

Monroe had written to Jefferson from Baltimore the day before he sailed, begging his friend and mentor for advice which might be useful "to the cause in which I am engaged, or to myself in advocation of it." When he reached Paris on August 2, 1794, he had need of better advice than either of his predecessors could give him, for Jefferson was removed from the scene by three thousand miles of ocean and had very incomplete knowledge of the internal strains of French politics, while Morris had virtually

[3]Instructions, June 10, 1794, *Writings of Monroe* II, 2–8.

suspended all communication with the government of the French Republic. If Jefferson was bewildered by French politics, as Edmund Randolph's biographer claims, what must have been the sensations of the new minister, who made his first entrance on that troubled stage during the confusion and recriminations following the demise of Robespierre?[4]

In a way, Monroe was fortunate. His reputation had preceded him, and the new government determined at once to receive him with *éclat*. Buchot drew up an elaborate ritual for his reception: "The Committee of Public Safety has all powers relative to foreign affairs, but the character of this minister from the United States demands that he be received by the representatives of the sovereign people." The reception of Monroe by the National Convention, he added, would also serve as an object lesson to Morris, who undoubtedly had attributed his cold reception to indifference to the United States, rather than "to our repugnance for his person and for his principles."[5]

Monroe was received "into the bosom of the Convention," on August 15. He read an address of his own and presented declarations of the Senate, the House of Representatives, and the President. As he later explained to Madison, "the effect surpassed my expectation," and the reference to the French Revolution, implied but not expressed in the speech, "was a gratification which overwhelmed them." The president of the Convention, Merlin de Douai, was so pleased with the sentiments of Monroe that he gave him the fraternal embrace and then delivered a reply more effusive than Monroe's. The Convention thereupon ordered extracts of the entire proceedings printed at public expense. A few days later, Monroe was offered the use of a house in possession of the government, which he tactfully declined, citing the constitutional prohibition against accepting foreign titles or presents. Two weeks later, he was able to return the compliment: having heard that the Convention had ordered the flag of the United

4June 17, 1794, *ibid.*, II, 9; Conway, *Edmund Randolph*, 196.
5Projet de Cérémonial, Thermidor, an 2 (July 18–Aug. 17, 1794), AECPE-U, 41, 280–81vo.

States hung in the hall of the Convention beside that of France, he donated an American flag for the purpose.[6]

Perhaps recalling the warning of Randolph's instructions against inclining "to any set of men" because of "the fluctuation and mutual destruction of parties," Monroe confided to Madison that he presumed that the tone of his address "will be scanned with unfriendly eyes by many in America." He was right, for Madison answered three months later that "the language of your address to the Convention was certainly very grating to the ears of many here." However, Madison added, publication of the letters of the President and of the secretary of state at the same time had effectively stifled criticism. But criticism had not been stifled, for two days earlier, on December 2, Randolph himself had written to Monroe expressly disapproving his speech, both on account of the place where it was delivered, and because "some expressions which were contained therein were liable to give offence to . . . G. Britain." Thus Monroe began his mission with the bad omen of having his first official act censured by his government.[7]

By September 3, one month after his arrival at Paris, the formalities pertaining to Monroe's reception had been completed. Actually, the new French government had acted with unheard-of speed, considering the derangement of public affairs incident to the overthrow of the old. Monroe discovered that the Genevan minister had already been waiting six weeks for official recognition and feared he might experience the same delay. American affairs loomed larger in the minds of the members of the Convention, apparently, than did those of Geneva: its minister was still waiting after Monroe's reception.[8]

[6]To Madison, Sept. 2, 1794, *Writings of Monroe* II, 11–12n., 15n., 40; Extract of Minutes of National Convention of Aug. 15 and 16, Commissioner of Foreign Relations to Monroe, Aug. 21, Monroe to Commissioner of Foreign Relations, Aug. 12, Monroe to President of National Convention, Sept. 10, 1794, AECPE-U, 41, 282–89vo, 312, 314, 400–400vo. Monroe's address and Merlin's reply are in *Writings of Monroe* II, 11–15, 33–34n.

[7]Monroe to Madison, Sept. 2, 1794, *Writings of Monroe* II, 40; Madison to Monroe, Dec. 4, 1794, *Writings of Madison* VI, 219–20; Conway, *Edmund Randolph*, 251.

[8]Monroe to Secretary of State, Aug. 25, 1794, *Writings of Monroe* II, 31. Monroe later explained the month's delay by inferring that the Committee of Public

Monroe knew little more than did Fauchet of the purpose of Jay's mission. His function was to obtain the reversal of policies which contravened the letter and spirit of the treaty of amity and commerce of 1778, and to soften the blow to France which must be contained in a successful result of the Jay negotiations. To the first part of this task, Monroe applied himself "like an apostle of the rights of man," but he was to regard himself, as well as France, deceived as to the second.[9]

A Committee of Public Safety shorn of the closest of Robespierre's followers served as the executive head of the French government during the interregnum between the fall of the Jacobins and the reorganization of the government under the Directory more than one year later. It was that body, after his dazzling reception by the Convention, which Monroe addressed on September 3, 1794. The objects of his mission which required immediate consideration, Monroe told the committee, were three: (1) "the departure on the part of France from the 23d and 24th articles of the treaty of commerce subsisting between the two Republics," (2) injuries resulting from the Bordeaux embargo, and (3) unpaid claims of American merchants for supplies furnished the colonial government at Saint-Domingue.

The committee had already authorized settlement of the Bordeaux claims, and Monroe announced his readiness to supply the evidence regarding Saint-Dominguan supplies to whatever board or tribunal should be appointed to consider it. The remaining object brought up once more the subject of the provision decree of May 9, 1793, the measure which had so long exasperated and disgusted Morris. Monroe could add little to the arguments previously advanced, but he reviewed them all as though for the first time, omitting any reference to the efforts of his predecessor in

---

Safety was originally hostile on account of the Jay mission. Monroe, *A View of the Conduct of the Executive* . . . (Philadelphia, 1797), vii–viii. Monroe cited Louis-Guillaume Otto, now undersecretary of foreign affairs, as authority for the committee's attitude. Stuart Gerry Brown, ed., *The Autobiography of James Monroe* (Syracuse, 1959), 60.

[9]Bemis, "Washington's Farewell Address," 254. Surprisingly, Monroe had not been shown Jay's instructions. Harry Ammon, *James Monroe* (New York, 1971), 115.

order to heighten the contrast between the two missions.[10]

Buchot forwarded Monroe's memorial to the committee the same day with a covering note. The only part susceptible to discussion, Buchot said, appeared to be that relating to entire freedom of navigation of commerce for American ships. "I would applaud sincerely," he continued, the exemption of Americans from the provision decree, if the committee thought that possible. If the decree was to be kept in force on grounds of absolute necessity, however, the commissioner proposed that it be waived in regard to direct commerce between Europe and America. This would deny to Americans the benefits of the European carrying trade but would leave their direct trade, more important to them and to France, unimpeded. Otherwise, Buchot feared, this and Monroe's other complaints would operate to discourage entirely direct American commerce to France, and importations from America would be limited to cargoes bought and shipped by the agents of the Republic in America.[11]

The Committee of Public Safety referred this correspondence to Merlin de Douai, its member responsible for foreign affairs, and Merlin in turn sent it to Otto, now restored to his position as chief of the first division of the Commission of External Relations, for study and report. Otto's superior, Buchot, thereupon devoted himself to more routine matters broached by Monroe, until he was superseded by Miot, an equally obscure civil servant.[12]

---

[10] *Writings of Monroe* II, 41–49; *Autobiography of Monroe*, 66.

[11] Sept. 3, 1794, AECPE-U, 41, 352–52vo.

[12] Masson, *Le Département des Affaires Étrangères*, 325. Buchot had succeeded to the head of the foreign office after Deforgues' expulsion in the wake of the fall of Danton, in Mar. 1794. Masson says that Deforgues had foreseen this event and had confided to Morris that he wanted to escape by going to the U. S. at the head of a new mission, which would include the indispensable Otto. Buchot had denounced Otto, Miot, and Miot's successor, Colchen, just before the Thermidorean revolution, but all were released shortly thereafter. Buchot was removed for incompetence early in Nov. 1794, but like his American counterpart, Timothy Pickering, a few years later, had to be removed bodily to make way for his successor. The Committee of Public Safety had first offered Buchot's place to Mangourit, Genet's old collaborator, but the former consul, in a letter remarkable for its modesty, declined on the ground that he lacked sufficient talent (*de lumières*). Miot retained the office until after completion of a peace treaty with Tuscany, the first

Monroe reported on February 12, 1795: "Upon my arrival here I found our affairs . . . in the worst possible situation. The Treaty between the two Republics was violated. Our Commerce was harassed in every quarter and in every article . . . ." He addressed Buchot on September 22 regarding the particularly troublesome cases of the *Mary* and the *Severn* but soon turned over all commercial complaints to Fulwar Skipwith, his trusted secretary of legation whom he had just appointed provisional consul general at Paris.[13]

Perhaps, aside from the burden of statistical labor involved, it seemed more appropriate for Monroe to confine his communications to the Committee of Public Safety, letting Fulwar Skipwith carry on commercial business with the commissioner of external relations, who was hardly more than the committee's clerk. But the cases of the *Mary* and the *Severn* must have aroused Monroe's particular interest, because they involved the seizure on American vessels of immigrants bound for his own country. They had been arrested and thrown into a prison ship at Brest because they were English citizens, but their captors had not bothered to find out that they were fleeing persecution in England because of their republican principles. The case not only represented a clear violation of ARTICLE XXIII of the Treaty of Commerce of 1778, but even worse, Monroe wrote Buchot, the interests of France and the United States were injured, while England actually profited. As Buchot told the Committee of Public Safety, repeating the arguments of Monroe, English gazettes had been lamenting this emigration for more than one year. The emigrants took much wealth with them and also could be counted upon to swell the ranks of England's enemies in America. The case was so plain to Buchot that he assured Monroe at once that every satisfaction

---

power of the Coalition detached by France, in Feb. 1795, whereupon he was sent there as ambassador. He was succeeded by Colchen. Otto had been imprisoned again on Nov. 2, following the return of Le Blanc from the U. S., but he was released and restored to his position once more the following month. *Ibid.*, 302–303, 321n., 323–25, 320–21, 348–49.
13To Randolph, *Writings of Monroe* II, 57–58; *Autobiography of Monroe*, 66; Monroe to Randolph, Dec. 2, 1794, *ASP, FR* I, 689.

would be granted, but it was three weeks before the committee answered.[14] Monroe was quickly learning that delays were inevitable, despite the real desire of the French government to extend every courtesy to him and to all known friends of its cause.

Otto's analysis of Monroe's original memorial was submitted to Merlin on October 3. The greater part naturally concerned the French provision decree, to which Monroe had objected as violating ARTICLES XXIII and XXIV of the Treaty of Commerce. Otto noted that exemptions in favor of the United States had several times been obtained, although finally the opinion of the Commission of Marine had prevailed. That opinion rested on the assumption that Americans had made no effort to force British observance of the principle of freedom for neutral commerce, an assumption which Otto now maintained was false, since the United States had "from the beginning made most vigorous remonstrances."

Actually, continued Otto, France gained very little from the decree's operation. The small number of England-bound American ships brought to France by French cruisers proved this fact, although it was also true that even the loss of these few vessels must inconvenience Britain by raising the price of provisions in her ports. But this advantage was probably outweighed by the fact that many American ships ostensibly bound for England were really destined for French ports: Americans, expecting English "brigandage" and French observance of treaty provisions, made a regular practice of purposely falsifying their papers.

Monroe had hinted that Jay's success in England would put her in the position of being more ready to honor American claims than France, but Otto did not expect any real success from Jay's negotiations, and everyone knew that it was the adoption of an illiberal system by England which had forced France to follow suit.

---

[14]Monroe to Commissioner of Foreign Relations, Sept. 22, 1794, *Writings of Monroe* II, 66–67; Buchot to Committee of Public Safety, Sept. 24, Buchot to Monroe, Sept. 27, Committee of Public Safety to Monroe, Oct. 21, 1794, AECPE-U, 41, 456–57, 466, 42, 80.

Otto listed the arguments against the provision decree in detail. Reciprocal needs, the interests of the merchants themselves, and better prices all combined to make trade with France more attractive to Americans, despite the tendency of the treaty to give England a monopoly of trade with America. The natural direction of American commerce under present conditions was toward France, and it would follow that course if the present obstacles were removed. Until then, arrival of provisions from America would be precarious, with promptness of supply depending upon freedom of commerce for neutral nations. Because of the greater profit in bringing provisions to France, Americans would continue to elude British cruisers by means of simulated destinations, and they would form connections and habits which would outlast the war.

Furthermore, said Otto, it was essential to deal justly with American merchants, because of their strength among all classes of society. That interest was not to be confused with the financial interest in America and was, in fact, "the basis of all operations of the American government as it was the principal cause of the Revolution." In short, Otto was once more urging the thesis that the commercial interest in the United States was more important than the financial, which leaned naturally toward Britain, and that the merchants could, with proper inducements, be led into closer lasting commercial relations with France.[15]

Otto therefore recommended that, although "it would be easy to get the American government to renounce some rights granted by the treaty of commerce which are at present unfavorable to us," France nevertheless had a greater interest "in loyally adhering to the strict execution of the treaty." First, such loyalty would discomfit the partisans of England and strengthen the hands of the friends of France in America. Secondly, the Americans were in no position to wage war, but they possessed a much better weapon against British commercial policy—the sequestration of British funds and the seizure of all English ships in their ports. Measures to accomplish these ends were being urged with energy

15 AECPE-U, 42, 18–29vo.

in America, and it was to France's advantage to hasten their adoption.[16] On October 5, Merlin sent Otto a letter from Monroe enclosing another memorandum, which he thought Otto might not have seen when he was drafting his report. His own marginal note to Otto contained the answer of the Committee of Public Safety: "it seems that freedom of commerce in provisions, claimed by the American minister, can be granted without any inconvenience."[17]

Events seemed to be conspiring in Monroe's favor, for Buchot now informed the committee that he had just received from one of the Republic's agents at Copenhagen news of the British revocation of the instructions of June 4 [June 8], 1793. Buchot could not know, or was not astute enough to perceive, that this order had been issued for the immediate purpose of smoothing Lord Grenville's negotiations with Jay. The new order's immediate effect, Buchot argued, would be to assure the free transport of provisions to France on neutral ships; it also proved that Britain was no longer interested in buying foreign grain. In accordance with ARTICLE 5 of the French decree, the whole measure should now be repealed by the National Convention. In a somewhat superfluous conclusion, Buchot remarked that "justice and wise policy require that France treat neutrals no worse than does England."[18]

The British order which so intrigued Buchot was dated August

16*Ibid.*, 42, 17–17vo.
17*Ibid.*, 42, 30.
18Oct. 5, 1794, *ibid.*, 42, 31. Burt, *U. S., Great Britain, and British North America*, 154, suggests that this order was owing to a good harvest in England, rather than to concern over aroused American opinion. Actually, it was one of two orders of Aug. 6, the other waiving part of the law restricting American appeals from the decisions of British prize courts in the West Indies. Regarding the latter, Professor Burt notes that American resentment at British practices had reached dangerous heights: "After Jay's arrival in England, Grenville quickly caught the point." Since one order was issued to placate America on Aug. 6, it would be at least a remarkable coincidence that another, even more conciliatory, was passed on the same day for an entirely different reason. The revoking order is printed in Josiah T. Newcomb, "New Light on Jay's Treaty," *American Journal of International Law* XVIII (Oct. 1934), 686. See also, Dora Mae Clark, "British Opinion of Franco-American Relations, 1775–1795," *W & M Quarterly*, 3d ser., IV (July 1947), 315; I. B. M., 66n.

6, 1794, indicating that French intelligence was not all that could have been desired. At last awakened to the danger of the anti-British ferment in America, George III's government belatedly determined on conciliating America. Its order rescinding the instructions to seize foodstuffs on neutral ships could hardly have been improved upon as a means toward this end, and it is highly significant that even so anti-American and doctrinaire a mercantilist as Lord Hawkesbury agreed on the necessity of concessions to the United States.[19] Indeed, if this new order, and the attitude it seemed to represent, stood, half of Jay's task was already successfully concluded and he had only to arrange for the payment of American claims and evacuation of the posts in the northwestern territory.

Of immediate concern to the British government was the intention of the United States toward the Scandinavian League of Armed Neutrality announced in April 1794. Anxiety on this subject had been frequently expressed in Lord Grenville's correspondence with Hammond, after the British Foreign Secretary had learned that Sweden, through Pinckney, had invited the United States to join. Since American acceptance would have ended all hope of an Anglo-American rapprochement and wrecked the negotiations with Jay, Hammond was exhorted to "exert yourself to the utmost to prevent the American government from acceding to the measure now proposed to them." Grenville even suggested, as an inducement to the American government, that American merchant ships bound for England might be permitted to sail under British convoy.[20]

Before Buchot received news of the British order, the cause of Grenville's concern had been removed by Hamilton's inexcusable disclosure to Hammond that the United States had already determined not to subscribe to the Swedish proposal. Further, according to Hammond's report to Grenville of April 17, Hamil-

19Bradford Perkins, ed., "Lord Hawkesbury and the Jay-Grenville Negotiations," *Mississippi Valley Historical Review* XL (1953–54), 291–304; Bradford Perkins, *The First Rapprochement* (Philadelphia, 1955), 3–4.

20Grenville to Hammond, May 10, June 5, 1794, I. B. M., 54–57, 58.

ton had even agreed that the United States would make no claims against Britain for seizures of American ships carrying French goods. Hamilton thus was surrendering the American maritime principle of "free ships, free goods" for which Jay was instructed to press in any commercial arrangement. But this was not new. When Hammond one year earlier had expounded Britain's contrary maritime policy to Hamilton, the latter had not only accepted it but had volunteered his personal guarantee that all the members of the government would do likewise. Hammond's argument undoubtedly coincided with Hamilton's reasoning:

> ... in every war powers that are neutral must expect to suffer some inconveniences; but that if ever those inconveniences should not be too nicely scrutinized, they certainly should not be in a war like the present, in which (as he had often agreed with me) all the dearest interests of society were involved, and which was a contest between government and disorder, virtue and vice, and religion and impiety—.[21]

Grenville's relief concerning the armed neutrality proposal was expressed in a dispatch to Hammond dated October 2, 1794. Thereafter, Britain was so little concerned over possible American retaliation against her maritime practices that, on April 25, 1795, she renewed the order of June 8, 1793, some five months after Jay had signed what Monroe, oblivious to proceedings in London at the time, later called a shameful document.[22]

---

[21]Hammond to Grenville, Aug. 23, Apr. 17, 1794, May 17, 1793, F. O. 5, 5, 4, 1. The instructions to Jay, signed by Secretary Randolph, are in *ASP, FR* I, 472, dated May 6, 1794. They are discussed at length by Professor Bemis, who is at pains "to show how thoroughly the ideas of Hamilton dominated the negotiation," in *Jay's Treaty*, 289–98. According to Professor Ritcheson: "Clearly, the envoy had come to Britain prepared to accept the principle of pre-emption, to leave unchallenged the Rule of '56, and to abandon the principle of 'free ships, free goods,' if Britain would only meet American expectations in other areas." *Aftermath*, 325. See also, Combs, *Jay Treaty*, 133–34.

[22]I. B. M., 67; Bemis, *Jay's Treaty*, 229, 246–48; Bemis, "Washington's Farewell Address," 255; Combs, *Jay Treaty*, 148. A contrary view is that of Professor Burt, who asserts that the Armed Neutrality presented no threat to Britain and that Grenville's efforts to forestall American adherence were "unnecessary." The article of Jay's instructions requiring him to cooperate with the Baltic powers was "abortive," according to Burt; because it had been inserted by "the francophile Ran-

Having no expectation of any incidental assistance from the British government, Monroe busied himself with his own campaign in the Committee of Public Safety. On October 17, 1794, Skipwith completed a lengthy report on the treatment of American commerce in French ports, which Monroe sent to the committee as supporting detail to his "more general exposition . . . of September 3." This memorial was forwarded to the committee with a commentary by Buchot, supporting, point by point, Skipwith's complaints.[23]

Almost certainly the Committee of Public Safety had already reached a new decision regarding America. Merlin now rejected Otto's recommendation that the 1778 treaty provision which permitted neutrals to carry noncontraband enemy goods be honored. The shipment of American goods in American ships was permitted by the decree of July 1, 1793; that law was repealed later in the same month only in regard to enemy goods, and was "a departure from the treaty Americans have no interest in objecting to, since the [provision] decree of May 9 assures payment." England, insisted Merlin, was bound to observe the principle of "free ships, free goods," even though she had no treaty with the United States. The United States was bound to resist British violations of that principle, and therefore Merlin proposed a decree "to show and to carry out in respect to Americans as well as toward other neutrals, the principles of justice and equity."[24]

The title page of Merlin's report bears the endorsement: "affair terminated by decree of 25 Brumaire, year 3 (November 15, 1794)." That decree followed Merlin's recommendations to the letter. Agents of the government were ordered to see to the speedy unloading of neutral ships, and their immediate release when their cargoes had been discharged. Property seized from neu-

---

dolph, it had not the backing of the American government, and Jay paid no attention to it." *U. S., Great Britain, and British North America*, 155n. An even more emphatic expression of this view is that of Ritcheson, *Aftermath*, 415–20; Perkins, *First Rappprochement*, 85–86.

23Skipwith to Monroe, Monroe to Committee of Public Safety, Oct. 18, 1794, *ASP, FR* I, 749–52, 683; AECPE-U, 42, 69–70vo.

24Undated, AECPE-U, 42, 186–211.

trals, if adjudged neutral in fact, was to be returned to the owners at once. The owners were to be allowed to sell their cargoes on the spot if they desired, and payment was to be made for freight, which could be used for the purchase of exportable French merchandise.[25]

Although this Merlin decree of November 15 specifically permitted French seizure of enemy goods on neutral ships, in violation of American treaty rights, Miot transmitted a copy to Monroe on November 23, hailing it as a "new proof of the desire of the government to maintain fraternity . . . with the United States." It represented a slight concession to American commerce, and Monroe had only a few weeks to wait for complete success. The National Convention resolved on January 2, 1795, that, since the provision decree of May 9, 1793, had been intended as a reprisal against England, it automatically became void after England changed her policy. France, therefore, henceforth would strictly observe her treaties, and all laws to the contrary were declared void. The Committee of Public Safety thereupon repealed that part of the Merlin decree which permitted the seizure of enemy goods.[26]

Monroe, quite naturally, was elated. The new decree, he wrote to the committee on January 4, was so important to the United States that extraordinary measures were warranted in transmitting the news to the American government. He proposed that Thomas Paine, who had been released from prison on October 31 at his request, be the courier: "he can explain the troubles France has come through and her present happy state . . . ." But since Paine was a member of the Convention, Monroe thought the committee's permission would be required. Also, since Paine "would be persecuted by England if captured," his departure would have to be secret. Monroe's hopes for success in this maneuver were so high that he had a ship waiting to take Paine aboard immediately, but the committee had no intention of let-

25*Ibid.*, 42, 212–14vo. The decree, with Miot's covering letter of Nov. 24, 1794, to Monroe, is in *ASP, FR* I, 689.
26AECPE-U, 42, 296, 43, 4–5vo.

ting the ex-Girondist out of the country. It saw "with satisfaction and without surprise" the interest Monroe attached to the decree's speedy transmittal to the United States. But as for Paine, "because of his position he cannot accept."[27]

The fate of the Paine proposal was an indication that Monroe's success was to be short lived, for unpleasant rumors had already reached France from England. One week before the passage of the decree which meant the success of Monroe's efforts, Merlin, for the Committee of Public Safety, had asked Monroe for an explanation of Jay's negotiations in London. "We are informed," wrote Merlin, "that a treaty of commerce and alliance has recently been concluded between the British Government and Jay . . . ." It was rumored, he continued, that Jay had forgotten France's "treaties with the American people and the sacrifices of the French people to set them free." The committee wanted to see Jay's treaty, since "that is the only way to let the French nation learn the truth concerning these rumors, which are injurious to the American government."[28]

But Jay had already precluded any possibility of an answer from Monroe. He had belatedly advised Monroe that a treaty had been signed on November 19. The treaty expressly recognized treaties of the United States with other nations, and therefore it could not affect those relations. Jay hoped that "the saving of our peace and our good understanding with this country will give umbrage to no other"; since the treaty was not yet ratified, however, it could not be made public. To Merlin, Monroe replied weakly that the hostile rumors must be unfounded, because "no American minister would ever forget the connections between the United States and France." Since he had to admit that he was "altogether ignorant of the particular stipulations of the Treaty," he could only repeat the assurances which had been contained in his instructions.[29]

[27]Committee of Public Safety to Monroe, Jan. 6, 1795, *ibid.*, 43, 6–6vo, 16. Monroe reported to Randolph on Nov. 7, 1794, that Paine was at liberty. *Writings of Monroe* II, 107–108.

[28]Dec. 27, 1795, AECPE-U, 42, 439–39vo.

[29]To the Committee of Public Safety, Dec. 27, Committee of Public Safety to

Monroe was understandably chagrined at what seemed to him
the probable sabotage of his mission by Jay's subservience to England. The suspicion had been growing on him for some time that
he was the dupe in a design of British devotees in the American
government "to cultivate Engl'd," as he hinted to both Madison
and Randolph. Jay was the perfect instrument in such a plot, to
Monroe's mind, and could be counted upon to put England's interests first.[30]

Although Jay was as experienced a diplomat as America then
boasted (the incomparable Franklin had died four years earlier),
he was, as a Virginia Republican remarked, "perfectly British in
his affections." A leading scion of New York's merchant aristocracy, he had the reverence for British society and institutions,
and the instinctive hatred of the French Revolution, of his class.
But his worst handicaps in diplomacy were those of his personality: his inflated vanity and rather pompous self-righteousness
were well known at Whitehall, which had been advised that "Mr.
Jay's weak side is Mr. Jay." Grenville, although considerably
younger, was shrewd enough to take every advantage of Jay's
weaknesses. Jay regularly reported from London to Hamilton
on the round of dinners and entertainments to which he was
treated by the highest officials. Although these apparently were
the sole cause of the "favorable appearances" Jay noted, mention
of them was omitted from his official reports to Randolph, because "they may be misinterpreted, tho' not by you."[31]

On the other hand, Monroe was a perfect cat's paw for Federalist foreign policy. He was something of a political blunderer,

---

Monroe, Dec. 27, Jay to Monroe, Nov. 24 and 25, 1794, Monroe to Jay, Jan. 17, 1795,
*Writings of Monroe* II, 162–63, 169–70n., 180. For Monroe's view of Jay's motives
in this exchange, see his dispatches to the Secretary of State of Mar. 17 and Apr.
14, 1795. *Ibid.*, II, 229–35, 238–44.

30Both dated Dec. 18, 1794, *ibid.* II, 154, 159.

31Bowman, "Jefferson, Hamilton and American Foreign Policy," 34–35; Harry
Ammon, "The Formation of the Republican Party in Virginia, 1789–1796," *Jour-
nal of Southern History* XIX (Aug. 1953), 306; DeConde, *Entangling Alliance*, 105;
Frank Monaghan, *John Jay, Defender of Liberty* (Indianapolis, 1935), 372; Jay to
Hamilton, July 10, Aug. 16, Sept. 11, 1794, Hamilton Papers, Library of Congress,
XXIII, 3131, 3178, 3185.

owing no doubt partly to his youth and to his unrestrained republican enthusiasm. Jefferson several years earlier had described him as a complete innocent: "turn his soul wrong side outwards, and there is not a speck on it." The conclusion that Monroe was sent to France "to mask [Jay's] mission" derives added support from the lack of Federalist opposition in the Senate to his nomination.[32]

Jay's reserve was the more ominous to Monroe because of military setbacks suffered by England on the Continent. French arms, in the fall and winter of 1794, were everywhere victorious. Expectations that Britain would be forced to sue for peace were high on both sides of the Atlantic. It seemed natural to Monroe that English reverses should greatly strengthen Jay's hand, and Madison agreed that French triumphs should bring success to his mission. Monroe, who had repeatedly assured the French that Jay was empowered only to adjust disputes between England and the United States, became so enthusiastic over the benefits which could accrue to his own country through British misfortunes that he asked Madison to urge on Congress a bold new course toward Britain. Despite the great French victories of recent weeks, he wrote on November 30, 1794, "the prospect is still more brilliant," a fact which "must strike terror into England & probably shake that government."

> The present is certainly the moment for our gov't to act with energy. They sho'd in my judgment put the British beyond the lakes & open the Mississippi, & by so doing we sho'd be courted into peace by those powers rather than threatened with war; and merely by negotiation we know we can do nothing, on the contrary we play the game that those powers wish us to play, for we give them time to try their fortune with France reserving to themselves the right of pressing us after that conflict shall be over, let the issue be as it may, even in case they sho'd be, as they certainly will be defeated.

If such a course should lead the United States into war with

---

[32]DeConde, *Entangling Alliance*, 344; Jefferson to Madison, Jan. 30, 1787, L & B, *Writings of Jefferson* VI, 72; Bemis, "Washington's Farewell Address," 254.

Britain and Spain, concluded Monroe, France would not make peace separately. This, he declared, would answer the wishes of the American people and put an end to their unrest.[33]

Monroe suggested the same program to Randolph. He was sure that Spain wanted peace with France, and he desired to secure French support for the claims of the United States in the impending negotiations. A memorandum on the navigation of the Mississippi he sent to the Committee of Public Safety on January 25, 1795, was received politely, but the committee was more immediately interested in the relations of the United States with England than with Spain. When Skipwith followed up Monroe's note one month later, Merlin answered that the ideas expressed were not new to him or to the committee and would receive "proper consideration." "However," he added bluntly, "that will depend largely on the conduct of the American government in relation to the treaty Jay took upon himself to conclude with England." The committee was not satisfied with Monroe's assurances without a copy of the treaty to substantiate them.[34]

Monroe was to fare badly in the controversy over that treaty, as he probably guessed by February 9, 1795, when he received Randolph's letter of December 2, 1794. The Secretary had taken Monroe to task for endangering American neutrality in the "unnecessary éclat" of his reception by the Convention, which might expose the United States "to the rancorous criticism of nations at war with France." Monroe defended himself vigorously, but henceforth must have felt himself embattled on two fronts. He entrusted his answer to Pierre Auguste Adet, the new French minister to the United States, whose career was to be more stormy and even less successful.[35]

[33]*Writings of Monroe* II, 135–36.

[34]Merlin to Skipwith, Feb. 22, 1795, *ibid.*, II, 182–86n., 218n.; "Observations of an American," undated, AECPE-U, 43, 215–15vo. Monroe was most tenacious with regard to the navigation of the Mississippi. He reiterated his plea for French intervention with Spain for the last time on Dec. 24, 1795, almost two months after Pinckney's successful conclusion of the matter in the Treaty of San Lorenzo. AECPE-U, 44, 555–55vo.

[35]Monroe to Randolph, Feb. 12, 1795, *Writings of Monroe* II, 193–205; Randolph to Monroe, Dec. 2, 1794, *ASP, FR* I, 689. According to Fauchet, Randolph told him

It was inevitable that the Thermidorean government should replace the Robespierrest Fauchet. The usual confusion and realignment of factions following a violent transfer of power delayed, in the summer of 1794, the reconstitution of the Republic's representation abroad until autumn. Fauchet's turn came on September 26, 1794, when the Committee of Public Safety revoked his powers, along with those of his fellow commissioners, at the same time designating a man named Oudart as his successor. Neither Buchot nor Miot took the trouble to recall Fauchet, who by December was complaining that rumors of his recall had ruined what credit he had left with the American government. On November 17, Miot sent official notification of the committee's action to Fauchet, but this was not delivered until the following June, when Adet arrived in Philadelphia with orders to arrest the three remaining commissioners "provisorily," for transportation back to France.[36]

Having decided to send a new minister, the committee began a study of French affairs in the United States. France was still interested in America primarily as a source of provisions. Fauchet's experience revealed that finances, on which those depended, were the greatest problem of the legation. Fauchet had been so besieged with claims for payment, many of them for preparations for Genet's abandoned projects, that his resources were exhausted before he could begin the purchase of provisions. The interest on the American debt and the one-million-dollar advance on the

---

in confidence that he was "delighted with the conduct of his friend M. Monroe," but he feared Monroe had gone beyond his instructions and would attract criticism. Fauchet to Minister of Foreign Relations, Dec. 1, 1794, C. F. M., 490. Randolph's fears were borne out in London in an unexpected way. Grenville wrote to Hammond that Randolph's "whole conduct . . . has given the greatest Dissatisfaction here," and that Randolph, rather than Monroe, was blamed for the minister's warmth in the hall of the Convention. Nov. 20, 1794. I. B. M., 72, 73–74.

36 AECPE-U, 42, 225, 224; Fauchet to Minister of Foreign Relations, Dec. 1 and 6, 1794, Instructions addressed to Oudart, dated Oct. 23, 1794, Adet to Committee of Public Safety, June 25, 1795, C. F. M., 491–92, 515, 734, 721. Le Blanc received more expeditious treatment: the committee ordered his dismissal on Jan. 18, 1795, and Miot wrote on Feb. 13 to inform him that the commission had been suppressed and that he was no longer employed as of Feb. 3. Possibly to forestall further communication with him, Miot added that the committee's action carried no taint to the good opinion of him or to its conviction of his patriotism. AECPE-U, 43, 89, 187.

debt requested of the American government would still not be enough. Specie had to be sent to America from France because, as there was no exchange between the two countries, the Republic's agents could not draw on the treasury at Paris. Besides this, the system whereby purchasing agents of the Commission of Subsistences bid separately in the American market was wasteful and unreliable; Fauchet had proposed commissioning one commercial house to act for the Republic under the supervision of the minister.[37]

Fauchet's suggestion was adopted by the committee, which gave the commercial house of Swan and Schweizer exclusive authority to purchase and send to France provisions from America. Joseph Philippe Létombe, newly appointed consul general with Oudart, was ordered to begin work on a project of instructions for the new mission with the commissioner of the marine.[38]

Since the Commission of Subsistences had placed a large sum of money in the hands of Swan and Schweizer, the new minister would not be called upon for payment for provisions. The legation, however, would need funds to buy provisions for the colonies and for French squadrons touching at American ports, and it would have to support hospitals and provide naval stores. Money for these purposes would have to be supplied by the Commission of the Marine; the American government could be

[37]"Situation of the French legation at Philadelphia according to the dispatches of March 14, 17, 20, and 21, 1794," dated Sept. 26, 1794, "Financial situation of the legation at Philadelphia according to the dispatches of April 13, May 7, and June 4, 1794," dated Oct. 20, 1794, AECPE-U, 42, 49–51vo, 76–78vo.

[38]Committee of Public Safety to Commissioner of Marine, Oct. 15, 1794, Report of Committee of Public Safety to Committee of Finances, Commerce, and Provisions, with "Observations of Committee of Commerce and Provisions," Nov. 3, 1794, ibid., 42, 48, 152. Létombe was described by the committee as the former consul at Boston who was recalled at the end of 1792 "after having usefully managed the consulate for 13 years." Ibid., 42, 440vo. Schweizer was the Swiss banker who had tried to buy the American debt for the house of Jeanneret and Schweizer four years earlier. James Swan had been seeking for one year to obtain the commercial agency for the French colonies, and then for France itself. Monroe wrote to Madison on Sept. 20, 1794, of Swan's agency for the French government and asked his friend "to be very attentive to him as he has been very obliging to us here." Two months later (Nov. 30), Monroe withdrew his recommendation of Swan, saying that "his character is better known to me now than it then was," and warned Madison to treat him with caution. Writings of Monroe II, 65, 139.

of no further help because of the extraordinary expenses it was incurring in the campaign against the Indians and in fortifying the ports. The committee recognized that "the debt of the United States is considerably reduced," and could produce no significant revenue in any case. It desired from the new minister, however, "exact and precise information on the present state of the Republic's credit in the United States."[39]

The instructions drawn up for Oudart were dated October 23, 1794. Like his predecessors, Oudart was particularly instructed to see to the execution of the several treaties between France and the United States, particularly ARTICLES XVII, XXI, and XXII of the Treaty of Commerce. These provisions had been violated consistently since the outbreak of war with England, and he was to use every means to force a reconsideration of its position upon the American government.[40]

American complaints regarding French violation of the provisions of ARTICLE XXIII were largely eliminated by the decree of November 15. But France was far from reconciled to the old bogey, the American tonnage duty. The minister was empowered to discuss the bases of new treaties, whose object should be the establishment of the commercial relations of the two republics "on stipulations reciprocally more advantageous and more clearly enunciated" than before. The only *sine qua non* was that insisted upon ever since Congress enacted the first tonnage duty in 1789: exemption in favor of French vessels.

In all his relations with Americans, Oudart was to be guided by ARTICLE 119 of the French constitution, by which "the Republic promises not to interfere in the management by other nations of their own affairs." This article followed the customary form, but the committee apparently decided to drop this pre-

39"Note on the pecuniary needs of the French legation at Philadelphia," Oct. 25, 1794, AECPE-U, 42, 105–106vo; Instructions for Oudart, Oct. 23, 1794, C. F. M., 721–28.

40Oudart was to cite, as an example worthy of American imitation, the case of Denmark, which allowed the sale of French prizes on condition that the proceeds be impounded by the Danish treasury until the peace. Behind this legal façade the Danes connived in turning over the money, but whether the French government thought the British were deceived is not clear.

tense, because a draft of supplemental instructions completely reversed this restrained approach and outlined the provocative course that Adet subsequently adopted.

Ignorance of American conditions was characteristic of each of the successive French revolutionary governments, but that of Merlin and his Thermidorean colleagues was unequalled. The advice of those who had some knowledge of America was either rejected, as in the case of Otto, or not even listened to, as in Le Blanc's case. Perhaps their unexpected success against the Puritanical dictatorship of Robespierre, and the apparent invincibility of the French armies, made it seem to them unnecessary to do more than consult their preconceptions. Whatever the explanation, the political supplement is an astonishing document; small wonder that Adet was misled.

Congress, according to this supplement, was divided into two parties, one favoring France, and the other, England. The minister was to ally himself closely with the French party, but without antagonizing the other. Although his conduct toward all domestic concerns of the partisans of France must be cautious, he should never forget that he "must cherish one party and direct it without exposing himself to the risk of becoming its instrument." In the last session of Congress, the partisans of England, "or rather of her commerce," proposed great armaments which the United States would have been absolutely unable to support. Their aim was to involve their country in a disastrous war with Britain which would result in a treaty of peace and of commerce with that nation. The course proposed by the friends of France, and which the minister was to support, was the sequestration of all British property and the seizure of all British merchantmen in American ports. But if "the arrogant conduct of England finally forced the United States to undertake reprisals," the impression that France desired their participation "in this war of liberty against despotism" was to be avoided, and there would be no assurance whatsoever of French assistance if war should result.

The future of Franco-American political relations toward the end of 1794 was becoming more and more uncertain because of suspicions engendered by Jay's protracted stay in London. Monroe informed Madison on November 30 that Jay's tarrying caused him increasing embarrassment, because the French were convinced that the special envoy must be seeking more than mere reparations. A few days before the Anglo-American treaty was actually signed, the Committee of Public Safety had decided that there was little chance of gaining a new Franco-American treaty in view of Pitt's probable success with Jay. It was suggested that the new minister be given full powers nevertheless, to be used as a means of disrupting the negotiations in London, or the fruit of those negotiations.[41] Oudart, however, never went to Philadelphia. A member of the committee forced his resignation on November 26, for unspecified reasons, and on the same day Pierre Auguste Adet, then resident of the French Republic at Geneva, was appointed in his stead.[42]

Adet inherited the instructions for Oudart. With the war against Spain apparently approaching an end, the committee was interested in Spain's American possessions. The astonishing progress of the western parts of the United States, wrote the committee, indicated "that their growing strength will soon threaten the great but feeble possessions of their Spanish neighbor." The committee wanted all the information possible on them and on the attitude of Congress toward them, and especially on the "revolutions which must be brewing in the English and Spanish colonies due to the progress of agriculture, industry, and, especially, liberty."[43]

As the campaigns of 1794 drew to a close and the first coalition seemed to be disintegrating under the weight of French victories, the Committee of Public Safety cast about for resources to continue the war. Politely brushing aside Monroe's discreet offer of American mediation between Britain and France, the committee

41 *Writings of Monroe* II, 136–37; "Note on a new treaty of commerce with the United States," dated Nov. 15, 1794, AECPE-U, 42, 216–17.

42 AECPE-U, 308–309.

43 "Nota," undated, C. F. M., 728–30; Circular letter from Committee of Public Safety to all new agents to the U. S., Nov. 2, 1794, AECPE-U, 42, 141–42.

informed him that their purpose was to prolong the conflict until their archenemy should be forced to sue for peace. But they were, as usual, embarrassed for funds, and they sounded him out on the possibility of floating a loan in the United States, to be guaranteed by the national lands. Monroe told the committee that there were three possible sources from which a considerable sum might be raised: "the general government, the state governments and from individuals." Writing to Madison, he "most sincerely" hoped the money might be provided, but in reporting the exchange to Randolph he emphasized the value of such a service in winning a French guarantee of the claims of the United States against Britain and Spain.[44]

In accordance with Monroe's suggestion, Adet was given authority to negotiate a loan of thirty million livres in the United States. In support of this project, he could urge the obvious connection between the destinies of France and the United States. England and Spain were doubtless in collusion in keeping the western posts, in denying the use of the Mississippi, and in stirring up the Indians against the United States. In the negotiations which were sure to follow the inevitable French victory, it would be in the power of France to adjust all these matters to the satisfaction of the United States. By lending money to ensure French success, the United States would no longer have to husband funds for use in its own defense. Finally, the loan would add to American prosperity because it would be spent in the United States, benefiting agriculture and increasing the activity of commerce.[45]

Létombe left Paris on February 22, 1795, but because preparations at Rochefort were not complete as late as April 5, the committee ordered him to proceed to Bordeaux at once to embark on the first American vessel to leave. Adet remained at

---

[44]To the Secretary of State, Dec. 2, Nov. 20, "Observations Submitted to the Consideration of the Diplomatic Members of the Committee of Public Safety," Nov. 30, to Madison, Nov. 30, 1794, *Writings of Monroe* II, 146, 121, 124–27, 138.
   [45]C. F. M., 729–30.

Rochefort while the committee berated the port authorities, finally setting sail on April 15.[46]

Adet sailed into the American storm over Jay's treaty, while Monroe remained to bear the brunt of its effects in Paris. In accordance with his instructions, Monroe had spared no efforts to restore friendship and confidence between France and America. But Merlin's ominous inquiry about Jay warned Monroe that his gains might prove temporary, and Randolph's censure made it clear that the support of his own government was not to be counted upon.

[46]Note dated Feb. 22, Commissioner of Foreign Relations to Commissioner of Marine and Colonies, Mar. 31, Committee of Public Safety to Létombe, Apr. 5, National Agent of District of Rochefort to Commissioner of Foreign Relations, Apr. 15, 1795, AECPE-U, 43, 217vo, 364, 390–92, 417.

## CHAPTER IX

Ratifying Jay's Treaty

> I explicitly gave it as my opinion to Mr. Jay, En-
> voy to Great Britain, that *"unless an adjustment*
> *of the differences with her could be effected on*
> *solid terms, it would be better to do nothing."*
>
> ALEXANDER HAMILTON, 1800.

O N March 5, 1795, Fauchet reviewed the accomplishments of the session of Congress just ended. The popular temper at the end of the session was much calmer than it had been at the beginning. The so-called "Whiskey Rebellion" in western Pennsylvania had petered out with less violence than expected, and the President's rebuke of "certain self-created societies" in his message to Congress had lost its novelty. The frontiers had remained relatively peaceful ever since General Anthony Wayne's pacification of the Indians in the Northwest the previous August, and it was announced that all the tribes wanted to make a general and definitive peace during the following June.[1]

The real author of Washington's attack on the Republicans, Alexander Hamilton, had retired from office on January 31, removing the principal storm center of American politics of the Washington era. Hammond lamented Hamilton's departure, "which deprives me of the advantages I derived, from the confidential and friendly intercourse, that I have uniformly had with him, when the most influential member of this administration." But Hammond noted that the large Republican majority

---

[1] C. F. M., 594–600; Sixth Annual Address, Nov. 19, 1794, *Messages and Papers of the Presidents* I, 162–67.

in the new House of Representatives would have lessened Hamilton's influence anyway.[2]

It was only from the other side of the Atlantic that trouble threatened the public tranquillity. The government was being forced to ease the laws against the exportation of munitions because the Algerine pirates would accept ransom for American captives in no other form. American worry over becoming involved in the European war was evident in the proposed amendment banning the exportation of those arms to the possessions of the belligerent powers. This attitude was symptomatic of the general state of expectation with which all America awaited the treaty with England, and already the two parties were engaged in preliminary skirmishes over it.

The treaty arrived at Baltimore as Fauchet penned his dispatch. It reached Philadelphia on March 7, and the President immediately summoned the Senate into special session. Fauchet was in a most difficult position. He knew from Randolph only that Jay had been instructed to agree to nothing contrary to America's obligations to France, but persistent rumors indicated that Jay had effected a comprehensive rapprochement—a treaty of navigation, of friendship, and of commerce—with England. Heretofore, Fauchet had avoided any move which would announce his lack of the detailed information and instructions which should have been expected from his government, but he had never played that game successfully: Randolph knew at least one month earlier of the Oudart and Adet appointments. Fauchet now decided that inactivity would ensure ratification of the treaty. He tried to obtain a copy, but Randolph replied that, much as he wanted to, he could not oblige him before the Senate was assembled. Only the President and he had seen the agreement, but he would assert most emphatically that it contained nothing contrary to the interests of the French Republic nor anything which could raise the shadow of such a suspicion.

To Fauchet, these were "tortuous dissimulations and protes-

2Hammond to Grenville, Jan. 5, 1795, F. O. 5, 8.

tations whose aim I had learned to recognize." All reasonable assumptions belied Randolph's assurances. If the treaty gave France no cause for complaint, why so much mystery? And if the United States had not weakened its engagements to France, why was there a treaty of commerce at all? The United States had nothing to offer in exchange for the favors "and even the Justice" it sought. Britain already dominated American commerce through the indebtedness of American merchants to her, as well as American industry and finance through her monopoly of investment capital. Any maritime concessions she might make would be forced upon her by French military successes. Unwilling to, or incapable of, granting justice, the British ministry meant to delay, and to lull the Americans by flattering them with a treaty containing mere promises.[3]

Fauchet began by redoubling his complaints against American interpretations of the treaties with France and British infractions of them. He knew that his efforts would be useless since the weakness of the American government forced it to temporize, sacrificing present violations to the hope of solid permanent arrangements. Lest silence give the impression of indifference, Fauchet kept up the correspondence, contrasting the treatment of the United States by France and by Britain and observing that despite the record the government still seemed to have a predilection toward the new treaty with the old enemy.[4]

Fauchet found some encouragement in the knowledge that the last elections promised a majority of Republicans in the next House of Representatives. He initiated discussions with several of these and with some members of the Senate, which, scarcely affected by the election, would be about evenly divided. But "the British party and the English minister at its head" had been busy preparing public opinion for months, "with a profusion of pamphlets designed solely to ridicule our Revolution, exaggerate our misfortunes, blacken our character, rejoice over our catastrophes,

[3]Commissioners to Committee of Public Safety, Mar. 8 and 16, 1795, C. F. M., 601, 603–609; Fauchet, "Mémoire sur les États-Unis d'Amérique," 108.
[4]Mar. 21, Apr. 19, May 11, May 23, 1795, C. F. M., 609, 649, 686, 700.

accuse us of devising, with the Jacobins of America whom we keep under our wing, anarchical and disruptive plans." British agents and their allies were too shrewd not to attend to the members of the body most immediately concerned; they had weighed the attitudes of the senators and they knew which ones weakness or cupidity rendered pliant. Because he feared committing Adet to a course on which he might not be instructed, and because of the prohibitions contained in his own instructions against meddling in domestic affairs, Fauchet hesitated resorting to the bribery which he alleged Hammond was already practicing. He devoted his energies to writing a protest against the treaty to Randolph which sounded so much like a popular manifesto that the latter cautioned him against reverting to the tactics of Genet. By the time Randolph's reply was ready, Adet had arrived and the note was delivered to him.[5]

The Senate convened on June 8. After consulting Fauchet, the opponents of the treaty decided to move for its publication at once. This move to force the treaty into public view was defeated, and it was only that circumstance, Fauchet later averred, which decided him to embark on a program of corruption. For, reasoned Fauchet, the transformation of an evenly divided house into one with a clear majority for "the British interest" could only have been made with British gold. This was not supposition, insisted Fauchet, he had proof; and, needing only eleven members to defeat the treaty, against twenty for ratification, he could do the same.[6]

Fauchet had asked, on the opening day of the session, that the Senate's vote be suspended until Adet should arrive and announce his instructions regarding the treaty, but the President saw no reason for complying. Adet reached Philadelphia on

[5]Fauchet, "Mémoire sur les États-Unis d'Amérique," 110; Commissioners to Committee of Public Safety, June 9, 13, 1795, C. F. M., 708–709, 714; Fauchet to Randolph, June 8, Randolph to Fauchet, June 13, 1795, ASP, FR I, 614–20; Conway, Edmund Randolph, 247–48; James, "French Diplomacy and American Politics," 162.

[6]Commissioners to Committee of Public Safety, June 9, 1795, C. F. M., 707–708; Fauchet, "Mémoire sur les États-Unis d'Amérique," 110–11.

June 13, to the great relief of Fauchet, who feared the votes were lacking to defeat the treaty. Fauchet remembered six months later that one week after Adet's arrival, Henry Tazewell, Monroe's successor to the Senate from Virginia, came to see him in a state of great anxiety. Only six senators could be counted upon against the treaty; "several timid men" dared not, by voting against the treaty, accept the responsibility before their constituents of a rupture with England while there was no assurance of French support. Two of these, Fauchet quoted Tazewell, could be enlisted by means of "pecuniary advances." Busy arranging his affairs in preparation for his return to France, and no longer possessed of official status, Fauchet could only accompany Tazewell to Adet. The latter wrote the same evening that the affair was arranged and that "we can count upon complete success."[7]

Next day in the Senate so strong a shift of sentiment was apparent that Randolph was stirred to action—Fauchet wrongly insisted that the secretary was the most ardent proponent of the treaty—and Hammond came hurrying back from the country. Three days later, on June 24, the treaty passed the Senate. In Fauchet's patent defense of the failure of his mission, he said

[7]Fauchet, "Mémoire sur les États-Unis d'Amérique," 112, 110–11; Conway, *Edmund Randolph*, 248. This account was written after Fauchet had returned to Paris, when he was doing his best to explain away the evident failure of his mission to a political faction which had bloodily removed his sponsors. Although he himself used the word *advances*, the whole implication of his story is that bribes were required. This was doubtless deliberate—to jibe with his earlier indictment of America: "How long will this Government last, if it has so soon become rotten. Such, Citizen, is the evident consequence of the financial System conceived by Mr. Hamilton. It has made of the entire nation a stock-jobbing, speculating, self-seeking People. Only wealth commands respect here, and since no one wants to be looked down upon, everyone pursues it." Fauchet to Commissioner of Foreign Relations, Oct. 31, 1794; Irving Brant, "Edmund Randolph, Not Guilty!" *W & M Quarterly* 3d ser., VII (Apr. 1950), 192. Although this incident was not mentioned elsewhere by either Fauchet or Adet, there is no reason to believe it was entirely fabricated. The most logical explanation is that Tazewell was suggesting that Fauchet advance payments due two senators who had already fulfilled provisions contracts for France, in order to free them from the threat of persecution by credit and banking sources which were solidly behind the Jay Treaty. The blackmail methods of the treaty's champions made such threats anything but idle. They, rather than the bribery Fauchet accused Hammond of, were the Federalist weapons—more sophisticated and therefore harder to combat. See Brant, "Edmund Randolph, Not Guilty!" 195, 197.

that he learned later that Adet's converts were given only promises, while Hammond subsequently reached them with *"Res non
verba."*[8]

Adet had left his post at Geneva with the greatest reluctance,
and his distaste for the mission to the United States increased
with every moment on American soil. He wrote to the Committee of Public Safety from New York that he had been forced to
land at Newport and proceed overland to Philadelphia because
English ships were lying offshore in the expectation of capturing
him. Britain had so little respect for American territory, he said,
that his legation was safe only on land. He had discovered that
supporters of France "are not in the majority everywhere," and
he had been told in Boston that the American government
"seems completely dominated by the cabinet of St. James." From
Philadelphia two days after his arrival there, and after discussions with Fauchet, Adet wrote even more to the point. It was a
fatal mischance that Fauchet's dispatches concerning the conduct
of the American government toward France and the Jay negotiations had not arrived before his departure, so that the committee could have given him appropriate instructions. All that
he could do under the circumstances was to try to prevent ratification of the British treaty, and the strength of the British influence was such that he doubted his success.[9]

Having failed to influence the vote of the Senate on the treaty,
Adet decided to exert what pressure he could on the executive.
On June 30 he sent to Randolph an extract from his instructions
on the subject of a new consular convention and treaty of commerce, with assurance to the President that he would be happy
thus to contribute to strengthening the ties between the two re-

[8]Fauchet, "Mémoire sur les États-Unis d'Amérique," 111.

[9]Adet to Committee of Public Safety, June 15, 1795, AECPE-U, 44, 57–57vo; Adet
to Committee of Public Safety, June 25, 1795, C. F. M., 734–39. Otto wrote in 1797
that Adet accepted with repugnance "a place where there were so many mistakes to
repair and where he was destined to add still more." Adet wrote a letter to some
friends in Geneva before his departure which conveyed the idea that the Americans were barbarians in comparison with the cultivated Genevans, and that "he
deplored being obliged to live among them and being deprived of a society as interesting as that which he had just left." Otto, "Considérations," 28.

publics. Randolph answered the following day that he would be glad to discuss the bases of a new treaty, but he did not think Adet's instructions included full powers. Randolph wanted to know whether he was correct, but Adet, rather than admit that he was, accepted the reply as intentionally evasive and dropped the subject. Adet had already put into the hands of Benjamin Franklin Bache, editor of the *Aurora*, an unofficial copy of Jay's treaty, and its publication on June 29 had aroused the hoped-for public respense. He then began a correspondence with Randolph on France's objections to it, but Randolph's office was soon in the hands of Timothy Pickering, and Adet himself was embroiled in the British intrigue which resulted in Randolph's downfall.[10]

The Senate had approved the treaty with Great Britain by a vote of twenty to ten, but only on condition that ARTICLE XII, which granted a limited trade with the British West Indies, be suspended. This article had been most objectionable to Alexander Hamilton who, practicing law in New York after his retirement from the Treasury at the beginning of 1795, had "not entirely lost my appetite for a little politics." That was an understatement, for Hamilton, for several years after his official

[10]Adet to Randolph, June 30, Randolph to Adet, July 1, 1795, AECPE-U, 44, 87–87vo; Adet to Randolph, June 30, Randolph to Adet, July 6, 1795, *ASP, FR* I, 594–96; July 3, 1795, C. F. M., 741–43. Adet says that he had had the treaty sent to Franklin's grandson, "without his being able to suspect it came from me." The *Aurora* received it from Senator Stevens Thomson Mason. The treaty appeared in the *Aurora* the day before Randolph obtained President Washington's permission to give Adet an official copy. See Conway, *Edmund Randolph*, 261; Brant, *Madison: Father of Constitution*, 426; Charles, *Origins of American Party System*, 105. In view of the innuendo which has pursued Senator Mason for his part in making the treaty public for the benefit of Americans, it is noteworthy that Hamilton's successor, Oliver Wolcott, found it necessary to inform Hammond in detail of the Senate's action the same evening it was taken. Hammond to Grenville, June 25, 1795, F. O. 5, 9. In addition, a number of senators called upon British Consul General Bond immediately after the Senate adjourned, so that within 24 hours Bond was able to describe in detail the transactions of the special secret session of the Senate in a private letter to Grenville. Since no minutes were kept during the session, Bond's letter remains the only account of the proceedings. Joanne L. Neel, *Phineas Bond* (Philadelphia, 1968), 125. Hamilton, however, opposed the efforts of the pro-British clique in the Senate to keep the treaty secret after it had been approved. To Wolcott, June 26 and 30, 1795, *Works of Hamilton* X, 106–107.

withdrawal, continued to exercise a powerful influence in the administration. This influence was especially true in regard to the British treaty. As early as May he laid down the line to William Bradford, then attorney general: the treaty's ratification should contain a clause nullifying the twelfth article. Although his had been the guiding hand in the accord with England, Hamilton was even willing to risk a British rejection of such a ratification. He did not, of course, think that the risk was very great, adding, to Rufus King, that it would save time by eliminating the necessity of negotiating anew. "I do not see that if the ratifications be exchanged with this saving, there can be any doubt of the matter operating as intended." It did so operate, giving further point to Professor Bemis' remark that Jay's treaty was really Hamilton's treaty.[11]

But Randolph was less certain than Hamilton about the procedure entailed by the Senate's conditional approval. Aside from the very real constitutional problems involved in such an unprecedented course, Randolph had been turned against immediate ratification by unofficial news that Britain had renewed the Provision Order of June 8, 1793. He wrote to Monroe on July 2 that the President had not yet made up his mind in regard to the treaty; a few days later his arguments against ratification were adopted by the President, despite the contrary opinions of his colleagues in the cabinet, Oliver Wolcott, Timothy Pickering, and William Bradford. Randolph was authorized to inform Hammond that the treaty would not be ratified while the obnoxious order remained in force. At the same time, Randolph was instructed to prepare the form of ratification and instructions for the emissary who would be charged with the exchange of ratifications in London.[12]

The course advocated by Randolph had a powerful ally in Hamilton as far as its aim, if not its method, was concerned.

[11]*Treaties and Other International Acts of the United States* **II**, 271–72; Hamilton to Bradford, May –, to King, June 11, 1795, *Works of Hamilton* X, 99–100, 101–102; Bemis, *Jay's Treaty*, 373.

[12]Conway, *Edmund Randolph*, 267; Carroll & Ashworth, *Washington: First in Peace*, 260–62, 262n.

Wolcott was favored with the suggestions of his mentor on August 10, and the President, who had asked Hamilton for a "dispassionate" analysis of the treaty, had already received similar advice. Randolph had been instructed by his chief on July 31 to draw up a memorial for the British cabinet which would make repeal of the Order-in-Council a positive condition of ratification. Two weeks later the storm broke around Randolph, and the President ratified the treaty, completely disregarding his previous determination.[13]

Although Fauchet would not have dreamed it, Grenville had foreseen difficulty over the treaty with Randolph, whom he regarded as motivated by "a Spirit of Hostility towards Great Britain and a desire of turning to that Object every Event which has occurred." At the end of a long letter to Hammond of November 20, 1794, Grenville wrote:

It will therefore be absolutely necessary that without making

13 *Works of Hamilton* X, 113–14; Washington to Hamilton, July 3, 13, 14, 29, 1795, *Writings of Washington* XXXIV, 226–28, 237–40, 241–42, 262–64; Conway, *Edmund Randolph*, 268–69. The mystery of the secret provision order was not cleared up until 1934, by Josiah T. Newcomb, "New Light on Jay's Treaty." Grenville, alarmed at the reaction in the U. S. to the resumption of provision-ship seizures, of which he was made aware by Hammond's dispatches and by the strong representations of William Deas, U. S. chargé d'affaires at London (Jay had returned home and Pinckney was in Madrid negotiating with Spain), got the order repealed in September but did not send notification of the original order to his chargé in Philadelphia until Nov. 4, 1795. (Hammond had been recalled by Grenville on Dec. 10, 1794, pursuant to a suggestion from Jay, and took formal leave Aug. 14, 1795.) Bond informed Pickering of the April order but apparently did not transmit a copy of it. Grenville himself compounded the misunderstanding by not explaining to Deas that the order authorized the confiscation of enemy property only, as was permitted under ART. 17 of the treaty. Deas, and presumably all Americans, continued to believe that it had the same scope of the much broader order of June 8, 1793. Pickering wrote to Deas on Sept. 15, 1795, approving his representations to Grenville, which were "certainly well judged, as a protest against the instructions for capturing American vessels laden with provisions and bound to France; although a revocation of the instructions was not expected as a consequence of your representation." I. B. M., 97n., 88n., 93n., 89n. See Ritcheson, *Aftermath*, 354. The repeal of an order clearly warranted by the treaty demonstrates the extraordinary value that Grenville placed upon ratification of the instrument. At the same time, President Washington's reversal of his stated determination concerning the treaty shows how powerfully Randolph's undoing contributed to control of the situation by the partisans of England.

any Ministerial Remonstrances on what is passed, you should converse confidentially on this Subject with those Persons in America who are Friends to a System of amicable Intercourse between the two Countries, in the view that some Step may be taken in respect to the Affair so as either to convince Mr. Randolph of the necessity of his adopting a different Language and Conduct, or at least, to place him in a Situation where his personal Sentiments may not endanger the Peace of Two Countries between whom I trust a permanent Union is now established.

Grenville realized that Randolph would have to be treated with caution, no doubt because, as Hammond had recently reported, ". . . the President seems to be more attached to him than he has ever yet been to any minister whom he has employed." But Hammond needed no hints from Grenville. On April 28, 1795, he reported that Randolph was now openly anti-British and, "in terms of arrogance and menace," had suggested that unless Britain altered its policy the treaty might not be ratified; or, if ratified, it might fail through a refusal of the House of Representatives to adopt measures necessary to carry it into effect. Hammond thought Randolph had been influenced by the popular rejoicing over French successes in Europe, "or from his being improperly influenced by the french agents here (a circumstance which from private confidential information I have long had reason to suspect and which the pecuniary embarrassments and general character of Mr. Randolph render far from improbable) . . . ."[14]

In view of this, the interesting dispatches of Fauchet picked up by the British vessel which captured the Frenchman, *Jean Bart*, must have seemed made to order. Grenville hastened to send a précis of their contents to Hammond on May 9, and promised to send "by a future conveyance" the originals, "the Communication of some of which to well disposed Persons in America may possibly be usefull to the King's Service." On June 5, Grenville sent "the Original of the Dispatches from the different Ministers and Agents of the French Convention in America . . . with the

14I. B. M., 73–75; June 9, 1794, F. O. 5, 5.

view that you should communicate such Parts of them as you may deem expedient to well disposed Persons in America."[15]

Hammond received the dispatches on July 22, with a duplicate of the May instruction and the précis. The original précis did not arrive until July 27, when Hammond outlined its contents to Secretary of the Treasury Wolcott, turning over to him the dispatches themselves the following day. Grenville and Hammond knew their man: Wolcott immediately put to use the one dispatch which appeared to reflect on Randolph's integrity, but withheld the others, which explained the first and would have dispelled the impression of guilt.[16]

Fauchet's dispatch No. 10 was written on October 31, 1794. Jay and Lord Grenville were to sign their treaty nineteen days later, but this would not be known in America for almost three months. The subject of the dispatch was the "Whiskey Rebellion," a widespread but disorganized demonstration against col-

---

[15] I. B. M., 83, 85; Perkins, *First Rapprochement*, 36. Hammond and Bond, according to the latter's biographer, had begun to despair of the treaty's ratification. "Still there remained one, last move to which Bond and Hammond pinned their hopes: Fauchet's dispatch number ten." Neel, *Phineas Bond*, 133. In all the discussion occasioned by Fauchet's dispatches, it seems to have surprised almost no one that they were written in clear language. Otto said later that it was Fauchet's duty to encipher such material, or at least to entrust it to a reliable courier. In view of the results of his failure to take minimum precautions, Fauchet was certainly chargeable with gross negligence. Otto, "Considérations," 28.

[16] Hammond immediately reported to Grenville his receipt of the dispatches, "... of which I shall endeavour to make such an use, as will I hope be productive of the most beneficial effects to the general interests of His Majesty's service. The originals ... are peculiarly interesting, and will, I am persuaded, if properly treated, tend to effect an essential change in the public sentiment...." July 27, 1795, F. O. 5, 9. See Brant, "Edmund Randolph, Not Guilty!" 183–84n.; Brant, *Madison: Father of Constitution*, 426. Hammond was proud of his part in the affair, which may have earned him the undersecretaryship he assumed upon his return to England. In Dec. 1795, he tried to draw out John Quincy Adams, who had been called away from his post at The Hague to handle arrangements relative to the official exchange of treaty ratifications in London. He told Adams that he had no doubt that Randolph was bribed by the French and, probably to increase Randolph's difficulties in any defense he might attempt, added that "he had better be quiet on that score; for if he presumed to deny it, other proof, amounting to demonstration, would be produced." Allan Nevins, ed., *Diary of John Quincy Adams* (New York, 1951), 11–12. At Philadelphia, however, Bond was "very nearly unnerved" at what Randolph might reveal of questionable British activities in connection with the treaty by way of defending himself. Neel, *Phineas Bond*, 135.

lection of the excise tax on distilled spirits which broke out in several counties of western Pennsylvania in the summer and autumn of 1794. In the belief that "to limit the present crisis to the simple question of the excise is to miss its real significance," Fauchet attempted a history of the origins of parties in America, and he referred to some "valuable disclosures" (*précieuses confessions*) of Secretary Randolph which he had reported in his dispatch No. 3 of June 4. He knew that an army of 15,000 men was marching into western Pennsylvania, under the personal command of the President, with the secretary of the treasury in attendance, and he expected "a general explosion which has been building up in the public mind for a long time." This great force had been raised at Hamilton's instigation for purposes of repression. Fauchet continued: "This was undoubtedly what Mr. Randolph meant when he told me that *under pretext of giving energy to the Government it was intended to introduce absolute power and lead the President astray into paths which would make him unpopular.*" (Fauchet's italics.) The path of repression having been decided upon with the raising of the army, according to Fauchet, it was necessary to find collaborators with Republican credentials to influence public opinion in the government's favor: among the governors, only Thomas Mifflin of Pennsylvania was known to oppose "the Secretary of the Treasury & his Systems"; and the secretary of state of Pennsylvania, Alexander J. Dallas, had influence with the Republican societies, and he could be useful. Then came the sentences which appeared to incriminate Randolph in some sinister design:

> It seemed, therefore, that these men, with others whom I don't know, doubtless with Randolph at their head, were weighing decisions on a course of action. Two or three days before the proclamation was published and the Cabinet had ordered measures to execute it, Mr. Randolph came to see me in a state of great anxiety, and made me the overtures which I reported in my No. 6. Thus with a few thousand dollars the Republic would have decided on Civil War or Peace here! Thus the consciences of the pretended Patriots in America already have their price![17]

[17]C. F. M., 444–51; Brant, "Edmund Randolph, Not Guilty!" 182–84. The stan-

The extravagance of Fauchet's language can doubtless be explained in several ways: he was frustrated at his own impotence; he desired to justify his failure to manage events in a country he despised; he wanted to shift the blame for his failures to others; and perhaps he was also carried away by the drama of the situation. He was now evidently disenchanted with Secretary Randolph (he went on to say that there were still some "Patriots" whom he respected, and he named Monroe, Madison, and Jefferson), and the charge he seemed to be making against the secretary was that of demanding pay to continue resistance to repressive measures of the government.[18]

To any reasonable person, the answer to the "overtures" Fauchet mentioned lay in his dispatch No. 6, as the "valuable disclosures" had to be explained by No. 3. So it seemed to President Washington, who immediately asked Wolcott and Pickering if it would not be proper to ask Fauchet's newly arrived successor, Adet, for copies of the relevant parts of the dispatches. "These might condemn, or acquit, unequivocally and if innocent whether R will not apply for them if I do not?" The secretaries opposed an application to Adet and, inexplicably, the President did not press the matter. When John Marshall was gathering materials for his biography of Washington in 1806, he asked Wolcott about the Randolph affair. Wolcott reproduced the President's questions from "his handwriting which he delivered to me and which has constantly remained in my possession," and then answered thus:

> After mature consideration it was considered to be improper to make any application to Mr. Adet; that it was improbable that Mr. Adet would permit his records to be inspected; that neither Fauchet's dispatch nor any certificate of the French Minister could be regarded as conclusive evidence in favour of or against Mr. Randolph. That Mr. Randolph's conduct at the time an explanation was required would probably furnish the best means

---

dard work on the Whiskey Rebellion is Leland D. Baldwin, *The Whiskey Rebels* (Pittsburgh, 1939). See also, Carroll & Ashworth, *Washington: First in Peace*, 180–217; Mitchell, *Alexander Hamilton* II, 308–28.

18C. F. M., 451–52.

of discovering his true situation and of duly estimating the defence he might make.[19]

It seems evident that Wolcott and Pickering wanted to take no chance on Randolph's acquittal, and they may have feared that Fauchet's Nos. 3 and 6 might do that. Knowing Randolph, they could be reasonably sure that his reaction to being suddenly confronted with so ambiguous, yet potentially grave, a charge would not be sufficiently lucid and precise so as to dispel the presumption of guilt. Randolph did later ask for and promptly receive from Adet the relevant paragraphs of Nos. 3 and 6. Considering the adamancy of the two secretaries regarding ratification of the British treaty and their hatred of Randolph for opposing them, one may conclude that their aim was not to prove Randolph's guilt but to destroy Washington's trust in him.

Reading Fauchet's No. 3 could only have made them, if possible, more determined. Fauchet quoted Randolph:

> The President of the United States is the mortal enemy of England, and the friend of France, I can swear this on my honor; but he has often been the dupe of the dark maneuvers of Mr. Hamilton, who manipulates him in a hundred ways to drag him into actions which will cause him to lose his popularity: under pretext of giving energy to the Government; they want absolutely to make him a monarch, they deceive him on the true temper of the people as well as on the affairs of France.[20]

These were the "valuable disclosures"; they were indiscreet, of course, coming from the secretary of state and the President's most trusted subordinate, but Fauchet read the same thing every day in the Republican press and heard it from his Republican

[19]To the Secretaries of Treasury and War (Aug. 12–18, 1795), *Writings of Washington* XXXIV, 275–76; George Gibbs, *Memoirs of the Administrations of Washington and John Adams, Edited from the Papers of Oliver Wolcott, Secretary of the Treasury* 2 vols. (New York, 1846), I, 243–44. Brant, "Edmund Randolph, Not Guilty!" 190, 190–91n. Mr. Brant presents persuasive evidence that Wolcott and Pickering actually had Fauchet's No. 6, and perhaps No. 3 as well, in their possession and purposely concealed the fact. *Ibid.*, 191n., 194n. Combs, *Jay Treaty*, 196, however, points out that the précis of the French dispatches sent by Grenville to Hammond does not list Fauchet's Nos. 3 and 6 and concludes they were not received.

[20]June 4, 1794, C. F. M., 373–74.

friends. If they were valuable disclosures, they were valuable only in the sense that they indicated that Fauchet had gained the confidence of the President's chief lieutenant, who assured him that the President was faithful to France. The conclusion seems inescapable that Fauchet intended primarily to impress his superiors at Paris with his own worth. But these were the very sentiments which, as far as Wolcott and Pickering were concerned, damned Randolph.

Fauchet's No. 6 was a different matter. By September 5, 1794, the Whiskey Rebellion had reached the crisis stage; Randolph had lost his fight to send commissioners instead of bayonets to deal with the rebels; he saw civil war, an opportunity for England and her Indian allies to detach the West from the nation; and the overthrow of republican government in favor of a despotism. "Scarcely was the explosion known," wrote Fauchet,

> when the Secretary of State came to my house; his whole countenance showed grief; he asked for a private interview; it's come to this, he said to me, civil war is going to ravage our unhappy country. Four men by their talent, their influence and their energy can Save it but they are indebted to merchants and at the slightest step they take they will be thrown into jail. Can you lend them for the time being funds sufficient to protect them from English persecution?[21]

No. 6 was almost as cryptic as No. 10. Fauchet had begun by reporting rumors in the American press that England was on the verge of suing for peace and might request the mediation of the United States, with Jay as the mediator. Fauchet did not know whether there was any basis to the rumor, but it proved to him one thing: that the American government wanted at any cost to play a role among the European powers; not, said Fauchet, out of a desire to assure the liberty of a friendly people, but out of a vainglorious ambition to be regarded as a power. He went on to denounce Jay as "a man sold to England and the mortal enemy of the Republic," touched on the humiliations the American government cravenly submitted to at the hands of the

21Sept. 5, 1794, *ibid.*, 414.

English, and expatiated on the oppressive plans of the government against the virtuous and brave farmers of the West before abruptly injecting the reference to Randolph's visit.[22]

When confronted with Fauchet's No. 10 by the President and his cabinet, Randolph supplied from memory the context of his application to Fauchet, and both he and Fauchet later explained it in detail. These accounts agreed that Fauchet had protested to Randolph that there had been a meeting at New York, attended by the ministers of both Britain and Spain, Hammond and Jaudenes, aiming at discrediting friends of France, including Governor George Clinton of New York and Randolph himself. Randolph answered that he feared that the British were seeking to foment civil war in the West in order to detach that region from the United States. Could Fauchet obtain proof of this conspiracy, asked Randolph? Yes, he thought he could, said Fauchet, and Randolph suggested that he use three or four men who were prominent among the merchants supplying flour for the account of France to uncover such an English plot in Pennsylvania. These men, however, were likely to be in debt to British merchants and therefore open to reprisal by their creditors; could Fauchet offer them for the time being advance payments on their flour contracts?[23]

Reporting Randolph's explanation of Fauchet's No. 10, Wolcott wrote to Hamilton that "This foolish story could make no impression. . . . the whole is idle nonsense." It may have been nonsense to Wolcott, but it probably was not to Hamilton, and certainly not to Washington. The President should have recalled that, on the very day of Randolph's visit to Fauchet, he and Randolph, with Governor Mifflin and others, had conferred on measures to be taken against the Whiskey Rebels. Randolph and Mifflin had both urged the view that the rebels might be victims of British intrigue. Mifflin had already written to the President of "ground for suspecting that the British government has already, insidiously and unjustly attempted to seduce the

22*Ibid.*, 411–14.
23Brant, "Edmund Randolph, Not Guilty!" 186, 187; *Oliver Wolcott* I, 265–66.

citizens on our western frontier from their duty," and soon after Randolph suggested to the President the awful consequences "If the intelligence of the overtures of the British to the western countries be true": the destruction of General Wayne's army; the secession of that territory from the United States; and war with England.[24]

Awed for once, perhaps, by the implacable certainty of Wolcott and Pickering, seconded by Attorney General Bradford, Washington did not recall either these discussions or Lord Dorchester's speech to the Indians, or the rankling issue of British retention of the western posts, or the Indian War which had ended with General Wayne's victory at Fallen Timbers on August 20, 1794, barely two weeks after Randolph's expression of concern. The suspicions conjured up by Fauchet's No. 10 crowded out everything else.

That Wolcott and Pickering were prepared to resort to any game, no matter how desperate, to overcome the President's stubbornness concerning the treaty can scarcely be doubted. Characteristically, Wolcott at once apprised Hamilton, who had supported a conditional ratification of the treaty, of the windfall from Hammond. Two days later, on July 30, Wolcott announced to Hamilton, with heavy irony: "I shall take immediate measures with two of my Colleagues this very day—they are firm & honest men. We will if possible, to use a French phrase *save our Country*."[25] Fauchet's dispatch No. 10 turned out to be as "usefull to

24*Oliver Wolcott* I, 266; Randolph, *Vindication*, 62–63; Brant, "Edmund Randolph, Not Guilty!" 184. In his letter to Hamilton, Wolcott did not report that Randolph had said the suspected New York conspiracy was directed against France through those supposed to be its friends, but he did say that subsequent reports "change the complexion of this first declaration of Randolph's, and represent the conspiracy as one to ruin France." Wolcott then neatly turned the conspiracy charge inside out to fit his preconceived story of Randolph's treason: "What could have been the footing of these men when they could familiarly talk about the subversion of the government, and inviting the French to aid the insurrection with money." *Oliver Wolcott*, 266. Either Wolcott's malevolence had made him deaf to anything which did not support Randolph's guilt, or he feared to reveal awkward details to Hamilton.

25Wolcott to Hamilton, July 28 and 30, 1795, *Oliver Wolcott* I, 219, 219–20; Hamilton Papers, Library of Congress, XXV, 3405–3406. Hamilton later told Washington: "I have seen the intercepted Letter, which I presume led to his

the King's Service" as either Grenville or Hammond could have wished: Randolph was ruined, the treaty was ratified. This result was accomplished by, in the words of James Madison's biographer, Irving Brant, "two of the most malevolent men who ever decorated a presidential cabinet—Timothy Pickering and Oliver Wolcott."[26]

Fauchet left Philadelphia on June 26 for Newport, R. I., where he was to board the French frigate *Medusa* for the voyage home. His packet-boat was forced by contrary winds to put into Stonington, Conn., en route, and while waiting to resume his journey he learned from French Vice-consul Arcambal at Newport that the British warship *Africa* was lying offshore to intercept him. Fauchet thereupon determined to continue by land, taking all his papers with him. He arrived at Newport to find that the *Peggy* had indeed been stopped and a search made for him and his papers. This violation of United States sovereignty in American territorial waters was immediately protested by Adet to the American government and by the latter to the British minister. But the *Africa* remained in the vicinity of Newport, mooring at night in the harbor entrance, until six weeks later, when a dense fog permitted the *Medusa* to slip out to sea with Fauchet aboard.[27]

Meanwhile, Pickering and Wolcott had prevailed upon Randolph to summon back to Philadelphia the President, who had gone to Mt. Vernon to await the result of his ultimatum to Hammond regarding the provision order. Washington returned to Philadelphia August 11 and on the following day, at the end of

---

resignation—I read it with regret, but without much surprise—for I never had confidence in Mr. Randolph, and I thought there were very suspicious appearances about him on the occasion to which the letter particularly refers." Oct. 16, 1795, *Works of Hamilton* X, 123–24.

26Brant, "Edmund Randolph, Not Guilty!" 180. See the comments on Wolcott and Pickering in Carroll & Ashworth, *Washington: First in Peace*, on the unnumbered page facing their portraits, between pp. 287 and 288.

27Fauchet to Commissioner of Foreign Relations, Oct. 26, 1795, Adet to Committee of Public Safety, Aug. 25, 1795, C. F. M., 718–19, 772–73; McMaster, *History of the People of the United States* II, 234. The correspondence regarding the *Africa* affair is printed in *ASP, FR* I, 662–67.

a cabinet meeting, announced that he would ratify the treaty with England. The signing took place on August 14, but the stunned Randolph was required to deliver a memorial to Hammond, stating that ratification implied no acquiescence in the provision order. Hammond noted with pleasure that the secretary had not attempted to conceal his chagrin and had confessed that his opinion on the ratification had been overruled. Five days later, Randolph stood accused of corruption, with the strong implication of treason as well, before a Star Chamber court presided over by the President, whose perspective had been vitiated by the venom of the jurors, Pickering and Wolcott.[28]

After that humiliation, Randolph sent his resignation to the President. He appeared, at five o'clock the next morning, at the residence of the French minister, whose aid he sought in obtaining proofs of his innocence. The outraged man unburdened himself to Adet: his plight was the fruit of the machinations of Hamilton and "his creatures Wolcott and Pickering," who were carrying out the vow of Great Britain to punish him for his opposition to ratification of the treaty. This analysis, accurate as it concerned Wolcott and Pickering, was a tribute to Randolph's intuition, for he could not have possessed the existing proofs. Randolph told Adet that he had tried to open the President's eyes to British intrigues and that, if his advice had been followed, "the United States would not today be under the yoke of Great Britain." His views had not prevailed because the President was already favorable to England, from which Adet somehow inferred that "the President detested France and her revolution." Because France's interests were involved, "and because Mr. Randolph has assured me that if we furnish him the means of clearing himself, the House of Representatives would oppose execution of the treaty," Adet agreed to enlist the aid of Fauchet.[29]

Adet, hostile toward the United States even before entering upon his mission, began his at the point where both Genet and

28Conway, *Edmund Randolph*, 282–88; Hammond to Grenville, Aug. 14, 1795, F. O. 5, 9; Brant, "Edmund Randolph, Not Guilty!" 185.
29Adet to Committee of Public Safety, Aug. 26, 1795, C. F. M., 774–76.

Fauchet had ended theirs. He jumped to the unwarranted conclusion that Washington personally despised France and immediately attributed all the troubles of his country's agents to the animus of the President. He must nevertheless have known that his predecessors had regularly assured their superiors of Washington's sympathy for their cause, only turning on him finally with the charge that he had permitted himself to become the captive of the British faction. But Adet sensed at once what his predecessors had learned through painful experience: the enormous prestige of the President was more than sufficient to command the support of his countrymen against no matter how serious a charge made by a foreign minister.

Adet therefore seized on Randolph's desperaton as the means of destroying the British party, including the President, and the treaty as well. He agreed to accompany Randolph to Newport for an interview with Fauchet, but on second thought abandoned the plan as inimical to his object. He sent his brother with a forceful appeal to Fauchet to give Randolph complete satisfaction: the fate of France was in Fauchet's hand, as well, perhaps, as the liberty of America. If Fauchet could give Randolph a certificate which satisfactorily explained the *"précieuses confessions"* of his dispatch No. 10—translated by Pickering as "precious confessions"—then "all the little English maneuvers will fail and we will see this country free, united more closely with France."[30]

[30]For the mistranslations of Pickering and others, see Brant, "Edmund Randolph, Not Guilty!" 190ff. Adet's letter of Aug. 20 to Fauchet is in AECPE-U, 44, 265–65vo. It is almost incredible that the case against Randolph could have hinged on so vague and indefinite a phrase; yet "precious confessions" quickly became a partisan byword and passed, for a time, into the vocabulary of politics. Alexander DeConde treats the Randolph affair briefly, concluding: "From the Federalist viewpoint, Randolph's disgrace is understandable; it was essential in saving the Hamiltonian system and perhaps in countering French influence in the United States." *Entangling Alliance*, 125. Bradford Perkins refers even more briefly to what he calls "this disagreeable affair," but some of his facts are misstated. *First Rapprochement*, 36–37. John C. Miller, *Federalist Era*, 169–71, pronounces Brant's analysis "exhaustive" and refers to "Randolph's alleged conniving with the French minister," but he concludes: "The truth is, Randolph's actions convinced the President that French influence was rife even in the highest councils of the government and that unless a settlement was made with Great Britain the United

Randolph hurried to Newport armed with another letter from Adet and talked to Fauchet on the eve of his departure. Fauchet agreed to supply the certificate requested, but before he had finished writing it a dense fog closed in and the captain of the *Medusa* seized the opportunity to elude the *Africa*. The French vessel slipped out of the harbor and set sail for France as Fauchet completed his statement, which was delivered to the pilot, addressed to Adet. The latter turned it over to Randolph in Philadelphia, together with the pertinent paragraphs of Fauchet's dispatches numbered 3 and 6, referred to in No. 10.[31]

Fauchet's statement from memory was a complete and accurate exoneration of the unhappy Randolph, who published it in full in the *Vindication* he put through the press three months later. Meanwhile, the episode had become merely a part of the nationwide controversy over the Jay Treaty, and a party issue which had no chance at all of being judged on its own merits. Randolph's memory turned out to be less reliable than Fauchet's, and to the confusion this imparted to his *Vindicaton* he added a comprehensive condemnation of Washington for his conduct in regard to the treaty and to himself. Adet thought that the campaign against "the American Idol" was going well and wrote to the Committee of Public Safety at the end of September: "One can conclude from this and perhaps with some basis, that the Reign of Washington is past."[32]

On the contrary, Washington's enormous prestige was once

States stood in grave danger of being converted into a French satellite." Lycan likewise cites Brant, but he offers Wolcott's "first-hand account" apparently in rebuttal and his conclusion is hostile to Randolph: "The evidence against him was not conclusive, and treason was apparently too strong a word for describing his actions and intentions; but he was clearly not working in harmony with the administration." *Hamilton & American Foreign Policy*, 248. Ritcheson, *Aftermath*, omits mention of the intrigue and Randolph's disgrace altogether. On the other hand, Combs, *Jay Treaty*, devotes a brief appendix (pp. 193–96) to the affair, but his conclusion is ambiguous, appearing to acquit all concerned of any deliberate misconduct.

[31]Adet to Committee of Public Safety, Sept. 30, 1795, C. F. M., 783–84; Brant, "Edmund Randolph, Not Guilty!" 186–87.

[32]Randolph, *Vindication*, 7–10; Conway, *Edmund Randolph*, 319–21; Brant, "Edmund Randolph, Not Guilty!" 187–88; C. F. M., 783–84.

more working its accustomed magic. On July 27, Hammond reported that the ferment against the treaty had "considerably increased": mobs had burned copies of the treaty in front of his
house and that of Consul General Phineas Bond in Philadelphia.
Hammond departed for home on August 14, the day he wrote his
last dispatch to Grenville: there was still no secure channel by
which he could send information, and he would soon be able to
report orally. Bond, who became chargé d'affaires on Hammond's
departure, perceived almost immediately, "with great Pleasure,
the sudden Effects produced upon the Minds of the People in
Consequence of the President's" acceptance of the treaty. This
factor, and the addresses being procured from merchants' associations thanking the President for ratifying the treaty, Bond
continued, "will I trust, completely suppress that Spirit of Faction and Turbulence, which has, of late, been excited without
cause, for mere Party Purposes." By the following March, according to the eminent physician Benjamin Rush, a complete revolution in popular sentiment concerning the treaty had been
effected, owing largely to President Washington, "in whose integrity all *confide* and in whose *wisdom* a great majority of our
citizens have still the most unlimited confidence."[33]

The ratification of the Jay Treaty ended the first phase of
the American struggle for neutrality. President Washington's
administration, now clearly a partisan Federalist one, had compromised the neutral rights it had previously championed.[34] Acquiescence in Britain's maritime practices meant that the United
States accepted absorption into the British economic sphere and
the role of at least a passive ally of Britain in her life and death
struggle with France. Jay's treaty accomplished what Hamilton
had tried to effect through Washington's Proclamation of Neu-

[33]F. O. 5, 9; Bond to Grenville, Aug. 16, 1795, *ibid.*, 10; Rush to Samuel Bayard,
Mar. 1, 1796, Lyman H. Butterfield, ed., *Letters of Benjamin Rush* 2 vols. (Princeton, 1951), II, 768–69n.
[34]Bemis, *Jay's Treaty*, 365–67. In the judgment of Felix Gilbert: "In the light
of later developments, the value of the Jay Treaty for the preservation of a neutral course in American foreign policy must be regarded as doubtful." *Farewell
Address*, 118.

trality, the "shuffling off" of the Franco-American treaties of 1778. By giving Britain the same privileges in American ports enjoyed by France by virtue of her treaties and her past services to American independence, the United States defied France.

Historians have generally accepted Federalist claims that Jay's treaty was the only alternative to a disastrous war with Britain.[35] The logical corollary of that thesis, however, that acceptance of the treaty might lead to war with France, has received less attention, partly because the Republicans made less use of it, and partly because war with France seemed less frightening, or less credible, than war with England. The Federalists had gained a tactical political advantage by raising fears of a British war, and the Republicans were placed on the defensive and concentrated their polemics against what they considered a red herring. Although undeclared war with France did in fact follow later, Republicans probably expected that France would be patient and generous enough, if the treaty were enforced, to await the Federalists' removal from power and a reorientation of American foreign policy.

The Federalists did not insist that war would follow immedi-

[35]Few, however, have gone as far as Ritcheson, *Aftermath*, 357, whose view is almost identical to that of the British government: "The Treaty was a fair, honorable, and reasonable settlement . . . ." Two ministerial papers in London noted the signing of the treaty: ". . . the most fair, candid and honourable transaction that ever took place between two States . . . ." *True Briton*, Nov. 22, *Sun*, Nov. 25, 1794, quoted in Perkins, *First Rapprochement*, 5. Perkins believes that "the agreement settled, or at least moderated, controversies which might have led to armed conflict . . . ." *Ibid.*, 6. DeConde reverses the proposition: while the treaty "may not have saved the country from war with England, it did at least remove the threat of such a war . . . ." *Entangling Alliance*, 140. Similarly Gilbert, *Farewell Address*, 119: the treaty "removed the risk of sudden explosion." Two historians of the treaty agree that its rejection would have meant war: Bemis, *Jay's Treaty*, 372, says that the treaty "served to postpone hostilities to another remove and to give the United States in the meantime an opportunity to develop in population and resources, and above all in consciousness of nationality . . ."; and Combs, *Jay Treaty*, 183, believes that "it is certain that rejection of the treaty would not have brought an immediate declaration of war from Britain [but] it is difficult to conceive that peace could have been maintained . . . ." Less ambiguous than these on the question of war's inevitability are John C. Miller, *Federalist Era*, 227, who says that the treaty was the sacrifice necessary "in order to preserve peace," and Charles, *Origins of American Party System*, 118–20, who argues that war probably would not have come.

ately, only that Britain would hold on to the Northwest posts and encourage the Indians to set the frontier aflame again, renew depredations against American commerce, and resume the impressment of American seamen. The Republicans responded that London was not likely to abandon its Indian allies even if it did evacuate the posts, and there had been no concessions regarding British maritime principles or impressment. Since the treaty deprived the United States of peaceable means of retaliation—levying discriminatory duties and sequestering debts were specifically prohibited—the United States would be able in the future to defend its interests only by war.[36]

In any case, Republicans argued, Britain was in no position to pick a quarrel with the United States. The anti-French coalition had disintegrated: Holland had deserted Britain and joined her enemy; Spain and Russia had withdrawn from the struggle, and Spain was about to follow Holland's example; Austria was hard-pressed, and the young General Bonaparte would soon impose upon her a victor's peace. Britain herself was near exhaustion and sentiment for peace was so strong that the King had to promise publicly to negotiate with France if occasion offered; rumor even cast John Jay in the role of mediator in England's behalf. At home, England suffered from bad harvests and had been forced to adopt a system of outdoor relief, her funds had dropped to their lowest level in almost twenty years, and ministers were not sure how much longer they could find the resources to continue the war. As John Quincy Adams was soon to write from his post in Holland to his father: despite "that deep rooted malignity towards us which governs the [British] cabinet . . . they

[36]Talleyrand, the peripatetic French aristocrat and former bishop, was in exile in America in the winter of 1794–95, having had to flee France as a suspected royalist and then been expelled from England on suspicion of being a French Republican agent. To him, the question of whether an American rejection of Jay's treaty would have meant war or not was irrelevant, because England was already waging war against America: ". . . a frank and declared war could not have been much more efficient than the measures of your government, and would have been less treacherous," he wrote to his English friend, Lord Lansdowne, on Feb. 1, 1795. Charles Maurice de Talleyrand-Perigord, "Les États-Unis et l'Angleterre en 1795," *Revue d'Histoire Diplomatique* III (1889), 64–77.

have however so much at present upon their hands that they will not quarrel with us."[37]

There were still other considerations. America was indispensable to Britain, not only because the two countries were each other's best customers and the Anglo-American trade produced a huge favorable trade balance for England, but because debts and investments in American funds made Britain America's largest creditor. Indeed, debts owed to British merchants had been the greatest single grievance of Britain against the United States since the Peace of 1783, and they were a primary object of Grenville in his negotiations with Jay. On the other hand, though the Federalists understandably did not press the point, uninterrupted commercial intercourse with Britain was indispensable to Hamilton's fiscal system; loss of the revenue derived from that commerce, he had told Washington, "would cut up credit by the roots."[38]

Nevertheless, although Hamilton dominated the Jay Treaty from its inception to its implementation, he did not necessarily believe that war would follow its rejection. In his famous pamphlet assailing John Adams during the presidential canvass of 1800, he wrote: "I explicitly gave it as my opinion to Mr. Jay, Envoy to Great Britain, that *'unless an adjustment of the differences with her could be effected on solid terms, it would be better to do nothing.'*" (Hamilton's italics.) Hamilton was among the first to see that these conditions had not been met, as his opposition to ARTICLE XII on the West Indian trade and his support of Randolph's effort to force repeal of the supposed new British provision order attest. He probably did characterize the treaty as an "execrable one" made by "an old woman," as was reported to Jefferson.[39]

---

[37]The debates were over the question of whether the House of Representatives should vote funds to carry the treaty into effect. They are in *Annals of Congress* V (4 Cong., 1 sess.). See DeConde, *Entangling Alliance*, 134–39; Combs, *Jay Treaty*, 181–86; Charles, *Origins of American Party System*, 118–19; and Perkins, *First Rapprochement*, 38–42. John Quincy Adams to John Adams, Feb. 10, 1796, Adams Papers, Massachusetts Historical Society, vol. 381.

[38]Apr. 14, 1794, *Works of Hamilton* V, 109.

[39]*Ibid.*, VII, 359; "Anas," Aug. 24, (1797), L & B, *Writings of Jefferson* I, 416.

Not only did Hamilton afterwards view the treaty as less than perfect, but he would not have regarded the absence of a British treaty as an unmitigated disaster. In fact, he explained the heart of the matter to Senator Rufus King on June 20, 1795, four days before the Senate approved the treaty. "The common opinion among men of business of all descriptions," he wrote from New York, "is that a disagreement to the treaty would greatly shock and stagnate pecuniary plans and operations in general . . . endangering the stability of our present beneficial . . . situation."[40] Not a calamitous war with the mistress of the seas, but an interruption of normal business and its profits would have followed rejection of the treaty. How severely this interruption would have damaged American prosperity at the time is debatable, but it is relevant to recall that the Republicans, and particularly Madison, had for years been attempting to bring about such an interruption as a means of providing a much greater prosperity for the nation. It was no accident that the most unequivocal provisions of the treaty were those which prohibited the very measures encompassed by Madison's discrimination program. American merchants generally had consistently shown a preference for safe and sure profits, compared to the risks that went with exploiting new opportunities.

However unenthusiastic Hamilton was over the treaty (he probably would have agreed with Sir Winston Churchill, that Grenville was "considerably aided by Jay's ineptitude in negotiation"), his masterly defense of it under the pseudonym "Camillus" ably seconded the crucial influence of Washington in reconciling a majority of Americans to its acceptance. In thus

---

See John C. Miller, *Hamilton*, 422–23; Bowers, *Jefferson and Hamilton*, 271–72. As late as Aug. 10, 1795, Hamilton was insisting that ratification of the treaty be delayed until Britain revoked its provision order. The U. S. could never, said Hamilton, give even an implied sanction to a British claim of the right to seize provisions on neutral ships; ratification while the order was in force would "give color to an abusive construction of the eighteenth article of the treaty, as though it admitted the seizure of provisions"; and ratification without revocation of the order would "give cause of *umbrage* to France." To Wolcott, *Works of Hamilton* X, 113–14.
[40]*Ibid.*, X, 103.

lending once more his prodigious polemical talents, he quickly made his peace with the extremist New England leadership of his party which had insisted on an accommodation with Britain at any price. Such New England High Federalists as Christopher Gore, Theodore Sedgwick, Fisher Ames, and Stephen Higginson were decidedly impatient with quibbles over the British provision order. Privately, they were so obdurate as to talk of disowning Washington, and their influence gave even Wolcott and Pickering enough courage, in effect, to defy Hamilton. As has been noted, Wolcott was not particularly impressed with Hamilton's warning against a ratification of the treaty which might imply sanction of a British right to seize provisions on neutral vessels; Wolcott and the High Federalists were probably no more interested in Hamilton's concern that everything be done to quiet French fears regarding the treaty. Still devoted to peace with France as well as with Britain, Hamilton had told Wolcott: "It is well to guard our peace on all sides, as far as shall consist with dignity." As far as this New England merchant clique was concerned, there was only one side to worry about—the British side.[41]

Despite his efforts in behalf of Jay's treaty, Hamilton was not content that America should be a mere satellite of Britain. As the Republicans had foreseen, the treaty did not eliminate conflicts of interests between the two countries. Three years after the struggle over the treaty, Hamilton penned sentiments which could have come from either Jefferson or Madison:

> ... it is of the true policy as well as of the dignity of our government, to act with spirit and energy as well toward Great Britain as France. I would *mete* the same measure to both of them, though it should ever furnish the extraordinary spectacle of a nation at war with two nations at war with each other. One of them will quickly court us, and by this course of conduct our

41Winston S. Churchill, *A History of the English-Speaking Peoples* 3 vols. (New York, 1957), III, 345; Charles, *Origins of American Party System*, 106–107; June 26, 1795, *Works of Hamilton* X, 106.

citizens will be enthusiastically united to the government. It will evince that we are neither *Greeks* nor *Trojans*. In very critical cases bold expedients are often necessary.[42]

Hamilton was brought into line by the *fait accompli* of unconditional ratification (save the deletion of ARTICLE XII), a result of the wretched intrigue which destroyed Randolph. Washington could rationalize his actions, as he did in a letter to Charles Carroll:

> Twenty years peace with such an increase of population and resources as we have a right to expect; added to our remote situation from the jarring power, will in all probability enable us in a just cause, to bid defiance to any power on earth.[43]

Washington's confidence of the future was ultimately justified. His greatest error, however, was his inability to understand the reality of political parties, an inability attributable to a congenital belief that opposition to republican government was merely factional, and to the advancing age and mental debility which were already diminishing his powers, as Jefferson, Madison, and he himself recognized. His biographers, more concerned to palliate than to understand his manipulation by Wolcott and Pick-

---

[42]Hamilton to Pickering, June 8, 1798, *Works of Hamilton* X, 294.

[43]May 1, 1796, *Writings of Washington* XXXV, 30–31; Combs, *Jay Treaty*, 187. The President thus justified his erratic course in regard to the treaty with an appeal to the future. His influence over succeeding generations has been as great, or greater, than that over his own, which helps explain why historians have been so gingerly in their treatment of him. See Dumas Malone, "Hamilton on Balance," *Proceedings of the American Philosophical Society* 102 (Apr. 1958), 132. Not even hostile contemporaries questioned his integrity, though doubtless many felt as did Jefferson, to whom Washington was "the only honest man who has assented to" the treaty: "I wish that his honesty and his political errors may not furnish a second occasion to exclaim 'curse on his virtues, they have undone his country'." To Madison, Mar. 27, 1796, L & B, *Writings of Jefferson* IX, 331. A French purchasing agent in America reported at the time that Randolph, on account of his opposition to the treaty, was the victim of a frame-up in which Washington was the dupe. Although the President signed the treaty because of the Fauchet dispatch, he regretted it after Fauchet cleared Randolph, but it was too late. Charles Reinhard (French minister to the Hanseatic cities) to Committee of Public Safety, quoting Lecomte, Nov. 8, 1795, AECPE-U, 44, 375–78vo.

ering, have missed the point that at last Washington proved to be human: if, indeed, to err is human.[44]

The treaty had become a party necessity, as both Federalists and Republicans recognized.[45] Those Federalists who saw an identity of interest between their country and Britain, or between their control of government and British opposition to the "disorganizing principles" of the French, had made it the keystone of American foreign policy. They came close to achieving the "economic partnership and a common foreign policy" a recent historian of British policy says Pitt wanted.[46]

Republicanism was gaining rapidly in America, as the midterm elections of 1794 showed, and strong measures were required; Jefferson and Madison could not be discredited, but Randolph was vulnerable.[47]

Despite their success in the Randolph conspiracy, the demogogic appeals to fear of war and their threats to tie the fate of the popular Pinckney treaty with Spain to that of the British treaty, the Federalists could not ultimately prevail. The struggle over the treaty contributed enormously to the eventual creation of a Republican majority in America. The treaty failed in the long

[44]Malone, "Hamilton on Balance," 132; Bowman, "Jefferson, Hamilton and American Foreign Policy," 38.

[45]Jefferson explained to Madison: ". . . a bolder party-stroke was never struck." And, as in previous times of political crisis, he urged the Republicans' ablest advocate: "For god's sake take up your pen, and give a fundamental reply to Curtius & Camillus." Sept. 21, 1795, Ford, *Jefferson's Writings* VII, 31–33. Samuel Bayard, a moderate Federalist resident in London, emphatically opposed the treaty and deeply suspected British designs until after news of ratification arrived. David L. Sterling, "A Federalist Opposes the Jay Treaty: The Letters of Samuel Bayard," *W & M Quarterly* 3d ser., XVIII (July 1961), 408–24.

[46]Perkins, *First Rapprochement*, 59; J. Steven Watson, *The Reign of George III, 1760–1815* (Oxford, 1960), 471.

[47]Charles, *Origins of American Party System*, 46–47. Randolph brought his troubles upon himself through his habitual vacillation, though it was ironic that his fall was the result of taking for once a firm stand. Madison's judgment was just: "His greatest enemies will not easily persuade themselves that he was under a corrupt influence of France, and his best friend can't save him from the self-condemnation of his political career, as explained by himself" (in his *Vindication*). Madison to Jefferson, Apr. 23, 1795, to Monroe, Jan. 26, 1796, quoted in Brant, "Edmund Randolph, Not Guilty!" 197.

run: as Churchill has written, "The atmosphere was charged afresh with distrust, and the seeds were sown for another war between Britain and the United States." In the meantime, there was the French reaction to deal with.[48]

[48]Churchill, *History of English-Speaking Peoples* III, 346. It doubtless is true, as some recent writers assert, that Federalist and Republican attitudes toward Jay's treaty were at least partly determined by contrasting views of American power. Of course Republicans were more sanguine about American ability to coerce Britain than were the Federalists, but America was not as helpless as Federalists seemed to believe. The point is not whether the U. S. was important enough to Britain to win meaningful concessions, but what the consequences of not trying were. The struggle over the treaty eventually doomed the Federalists, and two wars followed instead of the one they feared. See Combs, *Jay Treaty*, ix, 187–88; Paul A. Varg, *Foreign Policies of the Founding Fathers* (Lansing, Mich., 1963; Baltimore, 1970), 114; Richard Hofstadter, *Idea of a Party System* (Berkeley, 1969), 180.

## CHAPTER X

France Reacts
to Jay's Treaty

> The United States . . . have sacrificed, *knowingly* and *evidently*, their connexion with the republic; and the rights, the most essential and least contested, of neutrality.
>
> DELACROIX TO MONROE, MARCH 11, 1795.

I N the early months of 1795 the Thermidorean Committee of Public Safety seemed willing to await the fate of Jay's negotiation before reconsidering its American policy. It continued to cooperate with the American minister in removing American maritime grievances, while at the same time it tried to bolster the financial position of the new French minister at Philadelphia, Pierre Auguste Adet. Its solution to the financial problem was to sever the one official bond which served as a concrete reminder of the French contribution to American independence. The transferral of the United States debt to France to the American merchant-speculator James Swan was only the first of a series of steps toward a Franco-American estrangement.[1]

On January 25, 1795, the Committee of Public Safety designated Swan as sole commercial agent of the French Republic in America and placed at his disposition the whole remaining French credit on the United States. When Adet reached Philadelphia on June 13 to find an empty legation treasury, Swan was winding up his negotiations with the Treasury Department. It was only Swan's advance of two million livres to support his mis-

[1] Committee of Public Safety to Monroe, Jan. 7, Decree of Committee of Public Safety, Jan. 17, 1795, AECPE-U, 43, 26, 88.

sion, Adet stated later, which saved French credit at this time. He soon found it impossible to obtain the loan he was instructed to float; the government's resources had been exhausted by the late western expedition against the Indians and money could be borrowed only from the banks, which required a government guarantee. Only Congress could make such a guarantee; although the composition of the House promised approval, the Federalist Senate was certain to veto such a commitment.[2]

No one in Paris seemed to know how much remained of France's credit on the United States, but the Committee of Public Safety and Swan, when the latter left Paris with authority to arrange the liquidation of the debt, apparently had settled on a figure of about twenty-two million livres. At Philadelphia, Swan went over the records of the legation with Fauchet, and finally arrived at the figure of 19,914,627 livres, 16 sols, 2 deniers, which he used as a basis for negotiation. Treasury records, however, yielded only 14,388,913 livres, 19 sols, 7 deniers, a difference of more than five and one-half million livres. In order to avoid the delay of a long disputation, a compromise was necessary.[3]

Before any negotiation to convert the debt could begin, congressional authorization was required. This authorization was granted in an act signed by the President on March 3, 1795, transforming the foreign debt into a domestic one, the debt to Holland as well as that to France. Under the law, a loan was opened to stand until December 31, 1796, to draw interest at .5 percent more than the interest of the foreign loans. Sums subscribed to the loan were to be payable and receivable up to the amount of the foreign debt.[4]

Owing, one suspects, to Hamilton's and Wolcott's distrust of Swan, negotiations were not begun until May 5, 1795, when the Treasury announced that it owed only 10,341,915 livres, 16 sols,

[2] Adet to Minister of Foreign Relations, Mar. 21, 1796, to Committee of Public Safety, July 17, Oct. 4, 1795, C. F. M., 893, 750–51, 788.

[3] Aulard, "La Dette Américaine envers la France," 547; "Report on the Debt of the United States towards the French Republic," dated Mar. 5, 1795, AECPE-U, 43, 304–11vo.

[4] Annals, LV, 1519ff.; Aulard, "La Dette Américaine envers la France," 546.

and 4 deniers. This was accounted for by deduction of two and one-half million livres, payment of which had already been arranged for September and November following, and 980,957 livres advanced for purchases made by the French marine. Agreement was finally reached on June 15, 1795, on the sum of 11,156,-473 livres, 16 sols, 7 deniers, through a compromise in which the United States surrendered the interest on its advances and France gave up the claim to compensation for payments in depreciated assignats. In United States currency, this came to $2,024,900, of which $1,848,900 was converted into bonds at 5.5 percent, and the remaining $176,000, into stock at 4.5 percent. Swan was given certificates for the greater amount at 5 percent interest and for the rest at 4 percent, the interest to commence the first of the next year. In consequence of this, Secretary Wolcott was able to state that "the debt as due under former contracts to the Republic of France may be considered as discharged."[5]

Phineas Bond, the British chargé, naturally watched these proceedings carefully and reported fully to Grenville. One intriguing aspect of the transaction which he noted was that some $800,000 to $1,000,000 worth of the new stock had immediately been sent to England for sale by English bankers. "In whatever Shape the Certificates of this Stock may appear, it can be considered in no other Light than as the Property of the present Rulers of France...."[6]

Whether or not London was prepared to interfere with the operations of international finance at this point, the Committee of Public Safety, like Monroe, had had second thoughts about Swan. On February 21 it sent Adet orders to stop Swan and verify his accounts, but by the time Adet received this word it was too late to do anything but institute a thorough investigation. The investigation resulted in a report, dated June 29, 1796, which praised Swan's efforts but criticized his large expenses. During

[5] *Works of Hamilton* X, 105; Aulard, "La Dette Américaine envers la France," 547-48; *American State Papers, Finances* I, 671; U. S., Treasury Department, "Loans and Subsidies Granted by France to the United States during and immediately following the Revolutionary War" (Nov. 8, 1923), 2-3.

[6] Aug. 16, 1795, F. O. 5, 10.

the intervening year, Adet enthusiastically supported Swan, noting finally that the delays and difficulties which had accompanied requests for credit by French representatives had ceased as soon as Swan presented evidence of the debt's assignment.[7]

Thus the debt, on which French governments and their agents had relied so much, was extinguished, and the French legation thereafter was dependent on Swan. The financial results, from Adet's point of view, were undoubtedly beneficient. As Otto had warned years before, however, and as Adet himself once agreed, the American debt was the only practical obligation which bound the United States to France.[8]

By March 1795, consular reports from America made it apparent that Monroe's success at Paris had not inspired the reciprocal easing of restrictions France hoped for, and the suspicion grew that American merchants were using double sets of papers principally to avoid French condemnation of goods destined for Britain. This suspicion was strengthened by Consul General Fulwar Skipwith's claims that great shipments of provisions preparing in the United States for France were threatened by the Portuguese truce with Algiers. Skipwith wanted France to intercede with the dey.[9]

A report to the Committee on Skipwith's request illustrated how deep French suspicion had become. It pointed out that American ships destined for France were forced by winds and tide to follow a northerly route far from the Algerines' sphere of operations and hence American ships coming into that zone were really bound for Spain or Portugal. France's interest lay only in protecting American vessels going home from French ports, since the same elements prescribed a southerly route on the homeward voyage. The Committee of Public Safety did not inform Monroe

[7]Aulard, "La Dette Américaine envers la France," 548–49; Adet to Minister of Foreign Relations, Mar. 21, 1796, C. F. M., 874.

[8]Adet to Committee of Public Safety, July 17, 1795, to Minister of Foreign Relations, Mar. 21, 1796, C. F. M., 750–51, 874; Margaret M. O'Dwyer, "A French Diplomat's View of Congress, 1790," *W & M Quarterly* 3d ser., XXI (July 1964), 419.

[9]Commissioner of Marine and Colonies (Dalbarade) to Committee of Public Safety, Mar. 6, Skipwith to Committee of Public Safety, May 7, 1795, AECPE-U, 43, 312, 484–87.

of its conclusion, however, even after the minister, on July 5, asked its support of David Humphreys, who had come to Paris for French aid in negotiations with Algiers. A treaty was signed on September 5 between the United States and the dey, which cost the United States about one million dollars, but France had no part in it at all.[10]

During all these months, Monroe heard no word from the committee concerning the Anglo-American treaty. On October 25 he wrote to Pickering, Randolph's successor, that the government of the Directory, the executive body under the new constitution, was to be installed two days hence, and that he expected some action then, anticipating that "if Mr. Jay's treaty is ratified, it will excite great discontent here."[11]

The committee had meanwhile been laying the groundwork for a reconsideration of American policy. In the middle of July, Monroe's memorandum of the previous September was pulled out for study in the committee, and one week later a list of maritime grievances entertained by France since the beginning of the war was presented to Monroe. Not knowing exactly what was coming, Monroe asked for further details so that he would be able to give a "most frank and prompt explanation of the conduct of our government towards our allies." Two months later the committee had a report from its diplomatic section on French rights in the United States under her treaties, with a commentary on how they were observed.[12]

But the committee was about to pass out of existence. It addressed a valedictory to Adet on October 25, 1795, announcing that the new constitutional government was about to take over. Relations with the United States, it began, have long demanded "a profound labor of which we have only laid the foundations."

10*Ibid.*, 43, 488–89; Monroe to Committee of Public Safety, July 5, to Randolph, Aug. 1, to Pickering, Oct. 4, 1795, *Writings of Monroe* II, 315–17, 333–34, 370–71.

11*Ibid.*, II, 398–401.

12French translation of Monroe's letter of Sept. 3, 1794, Committee of Public Safety to Monroe, July 24, Monroe to Committee of Public Safety, July 28, 1795, "Validity of French pretensions assured by treaties of the United States with European Powers," dated "toward the year IV" (late Sept. 1795), AECPE-U, 44, 131–35vo, 137–37vo, 160, 290–98vo.

The confident aspect her recent triumphs had given to France's external situation was the source from which Adet was to "reanimate the zeal of our friends." Despair had redoubled the efforts of France's enemies to revitalize "the infernal spirit of factions," but firmness and wisdom had triumphed over all those plots. France's success should give "our friends . . . new strength to destroy the maneuvers of the English party." France's rapprochement with Spain should suggest pleasing rewards from French friendship, but Adet was also to hint that the American government's connections with the British cabinet "will require explanations one day."[13]

In the United States, sentiment in regard to the British treaty, especially after its abrupt ratification by the President, was far beyond the explanation stage. A public controversy whose bitterness has rarely, if ever, been surpassed in American history raged through the second half of 1795 and on into 1796. Northern merchants had been disappointed by the treaty, but were forced to defend it against the violent attacks of its Republican opponents. Bulwarks of Southern Federalism like Charles Pinckney, former governor of South Carolina and cousin to Charles Cotesworth Pinckney and Thomas Pinckney, went over to the Republicans, and party lines solidified to a degree undreamed of in 1787. The war of the memorials drew on the best talents of the most gifted pamphleteers of the day. The contest was reported in detail by Adet, who emphasized his own distaste for everything American by forwarding about the same time a review of the cultural accomplishments of Frenchmen in America, with the observation that Americans had contributed nothing worth mention because they were so completely absorbed in money-chasing.[14]

Adet fired his first broadside against the treaty in a note of September 28, 1795, to Pickering, and a little later the new French government asked for complete files on all officials of

13*Ibid.*, 44, 366–68vo.
14Charles Pinckney's report on Jay's Treaty to the citizens of Charleston, July 22, 1795, AECPE-U, 44, 229; *DAB* XIV, 612; C. F. M., 447–881 *passim*: Delauney (French consul at Philadelphia) to Commissioner of External Relations, Nov. 21, 1795, AECPE-U, 44, 395–96.

the American government. The Directory was beginning the "profound labor" of working out a policy toward America. The preface of the first note which came to hand was an indication of the frame of mind of the directors as they approached their task —"the government of the United States has added the full measure of perfidy towards the French Republic, its most faithful ally." Jay's "shameful" treaty, the writer concluded, really nullified the treaties of 1778 and was actually an act of hostility against France. This conclusion corresponded with those being received from Adet, who thought France faced the choice of either submitting to England's domination of America or of declaring war on her late ally.[15]

Fauchet had returned to Paris and on December 15, 1795, he sent to Charles Delacroix, first minister of external relations in the government of the directors, a *mémoire* on the United States. In an accompanying letter to Delacroix, Fauchet condemned the policies of all previous French governments toward the United States; the worst was that which had sent him to America with "the most absurd or the most perfidious instructions." He had warned his superiors of their false illusions regarding the United States, and now the misfortunes he had warned of had arrived. France should speak out firmly; her minister should have authority to make the United States hear "the voice of France thundering against the treaty and demanding justice."[16]

Fauchet complained to the minister of his difficulties in getting a hearing. He had spent hours waiting outside committee rooms since his arrival in Paris. Despite Monroe's impression of an attentive reception accorded Fauchet, the former minister was destined to cool his heels for some time longer. Almost two months later, on February 5, 1796, Delacroix answered Fauchet that the disorder of the ministry and accumulated business had prevented

15 *ASP, FR* I, 643–44; Minister of External Affairs to all French agents abroad, Nov. 18, 1795, "Note comparing treaties of France with the United States in 1778, and of the United States with England in 1795," undated, AECPE-U, 44, 385–85vo, 43, 13–15; Adet to Committee of Public Safety, Oct. 1, June 25, 1795, C. F. M., 786–87, 737.
16 AECPE-U, 44, 450–52vo.

his reading his *mémoire*. He was now going to study it and would be glad to discuss the subject if Fauchet cared to spend a day at his office. Fauchet confessed that he had given up hope of seeing the minister and therefore had not written the other reports he had planned. He promised to get busy on these at once, since he thought he saw an excellent opportunity to destroy England's commerce and also to bring about the overthrow of the present American government.[17]

Delacroix had in fact been busy with "accumulated business," but that busines was American policy and it was worked out and formulated without the benefit of Fauchet's advice. Delacroix had begun his task by trying to attend to isolated incidents pertaining to French interests in America but was almost immediately forced to reconsider the bases of Franco-American relations in the light of the Jay Treaty. He instructed Adet to press the matter of the *Cassius*, a French corvette seized and condemned at Philadelphia, but one week later, December 20, 1795, he deplored the difficulties preventing greater speed and regularity in trans-Atlantic communication and contented himself with urging the minister to redouble his efforts in combatting British-inspired propaganda.[18]

It was not to the agents of Robespierre, but to those of the Gironde that the Directory turned for advice on America. Early in 1795, when the rough and able Jean François Reubell was running foreign affairs for the Committee of Public Safety, he had been impressed by a memorandum from Mangourit. The former consul at Charleston had condemned American policy but suggested retaliation by "political and insidious means," since war would be too injurious to France. Mangourit specifically recommended a secret alliance with the Creek Indians on the

---

[17]AECPE-U, 45, 129, 172–73. Monroe wrote to Pickering on Nov. 5, 1795: "Mr. Fauchet has lately arrived, and as he appears to be extremely dissatisfied with Mr. Jay's treaty with G. Britain, and is apparently well received by his government, I doubt not his communications on that head will be attended to." *Writings of Monroe* II, 410.

[18]AECPE-U, 44, 444–44vo, 534–34vo. The correspondence relating to the *Cassius* is in *ASP, FR* I, 629–39.

southern border of the United States. This would "hold in check this ungrateful nation at little expense," and would also limit "the insatiable territorial ambitions of the United States." France would thus gain the same preponderance in the South which similar methods had won for England in the North.[19]

By the end of 1795, Reubell was one of the five directors, and he had arrogated the direction of foreign policy to himself once more. Perhaps recalling Mangourit's earlier proposals, he asked him to submit his ideas to Delacroix, and Mangourit obliged on December 24, 1795. The English treaty, said Mangourit, violated those of the United States with France, and the American government had ratified it in spite of the opposition of three-fourths of its citizens. But the coming November elections could not guarantee the repudiation of the treaty because two-thirds of the Senate would remain Federalist. Fear of England had produced the treaty; let a counterfear destroy it. This could be accomplished by creating the prospect of war with France without the necessity of actually waging it. Simply withdraw all the agents of France except for a commercial chargé d'affaires and a few purchasing agents, giving no explanation and allowing the people and the government to make their own deductions. Within six months, predicted Mangourit, France's political representatives would be recalled "by the vote of America."[20]

Delacroix thought Mangourit's proposal too abrupt and presented a report of his own to the Directory on January 16, 1796. The report was later greatly expanded in length and resubmitted on March 28 to Reubell and his fellow-director and faithful supported, Louis Marie La Revellière-lépeaux. The expanded version was, as Delacroix observed, "perhaps more complete" than the original, but it contained nothing more of significance.[21]

19Unsigned and undated, but internal evidence suggests Mangourit was the author, AECPE-U, 43, 9–10.

20Ibid., 44, 554–54vo.

21Ibid., 45, 41–53, 323. The extended version is in ibid., 45, 323–51vo. It has been maintained that Fauchet's much longer essay formed the basis for the Directory's policy toward the U. S., but Delacroix's neglect of Fauchet suggests otherwise. See E. Wilson Lyon, "The Directory and the United States," American Historical Review XLIII (Apr. 1938), 514. Dr. Lokke, editor of Fauchet's mémoire,

After reviewing France's causes for complaint against the American treaty with Britain, Delacroix got down to a discussion of future French policy. It had to be recognized, he said, that France was already in a state of war with the American government—"but only with the government"—because its actions, culminating in a virtual alliance with France's mortal enemy, constituted nothing less. But if France declared war she would only bind the United States more tightly to England, "that new Carthage"; invite the loss of what remained of her West Indian islands; and destroy entirely her commerce with America. These disadvantages far outweighed the relatively small benefits to be acquired.

Rather than break openly with the United States, argued Delacroix, it was more than ever necessary for France to "negotiate," and he explained what he meant in paragraphs drawn almost verbatim from the dispatches of Adet. The negotiation was to be with the American people; France must exert all the influence she possessed in order to save them from the English servitude being forced on them by their government. France had to detach the United States from its English connection and eventually cause a rupture between those unnatural allies.

Delacroix was obviously dazzled with the unlimited possibilities Adet had conjured up. The United States at war with England! France's enemies deprived of the resources of America, which would serve France and her allies exclusively! The United States could regain Canada for France, forcing England to divide her forces and costing her the superiority at sea which was her greatest strength. France would then be able to provide sufficient escort vessels to ensure the regular delivery of the provisions she badly needed; and the United States, deprived of English manufactures, would take French products in exchange, thus promoting French industry and commerce. Since the position of the

---

correctly says it "fell on deaf ears. His bid for attention from the Directory in December 1795 had no more effect than his dispatches from Philadelphia to the committee of public safety." Fauchet, "Mémoire sur les États-Unis d'Amérique," 86–87.

United States destined it to become one of the world's greatest maritime powers, the future benefits of this commerce would be incalculable. Thus crippled, England would be deserted by her allies and the time would be ripe even for an invasion of Ireland.

How was this brilliant prospect to be realized? The means, according to Delacroix, "belong less to diplomacy than to political events and to the popular movements which seem to be pushing the United States to a declaration of war against England." The subservience of the American government to the British cabinet must be swept away, and Washington must be replaced by a friend of France. Adet thought that "popular discontent and insurrectional movements" would force Washington to resign, but it was dangerous to count too much on the continuance of popular agitation. "There is the delicate point": to sustain the discontent and to excite continual agitation, a dangerous task but one which could be accomplished by a sufficiently adroit agent. Adet was that man, concluded Delacroix: let him have the authority to use every means in his power to effect "the happy revolution."

Delacroix and others argued for what was essentially a policy of temporization, but the Directory at first decided upon a more active course, closer to that proposed by Mangourit. On February 15, 1796, Monroe called upon Delacroix on routine business, but before he could broach it, the minister informed him that the Directory had made up its mind regarding the British treaty. The alliance between France and the United States was considered as ended from the moment of that treaty's ratification and the Directory "had or would appoint an Envoy Extraordinary, to attend and represent the same to our Government," and his commission would expire on completion of his particular assignment. Adet had requested and obtained his recall, but Monroe could not discover whether a successor was to be appointed, although it was rumored that one would be. Delacroix further told Monroe that the Jay treaty was considered as "throwing us into the scale of the Coalesced powers," and he added, Monroe told Madison, that

France would rather have an open enemy than a perfidious friend.[22]

Monroe was stunned, but the shock turned to alarm after he left the ministry. In a conference with Delacroix the following day, he urged strongly the harmful effects such a mission would produce, the dismay with which the friends of France would receive it, and the rejoicing among her enemies. The minister promised to carry Monroe's objections to the Directory, but the next day, February 17, a decree was published appointing "Citizen Vincent, Director of Fortifications for the Colony of Saint-Domingue," envoy extraordinary to the United States to fulfill a temporary mission. By the same decree, Adet, "at his request," was recalled.[23]

Panic now seized Monroe and he hastened to Delacroix to unburden himself. Delacroix was too correct to let Monroe know that he agreed with him, but he wrote at once to the Directory that the American minister was "so frank on the internal affairs of his countrymen and on the measures of his government, as to make one suspicious that this friendliness to the point of imprudence might be a calculated policy intended to lull us into inactivity by apparent frankness." Nevertheless, Delacroix thought the Directory would profit from Monroe's advice. He noted that Monroe's view—that a special embassy would force matters to extremities—"coincides perfectly with the notes that I have sent to the Directory on that subject." As Monroe said, the affairs of the United States were approaching a climax in which precipitation would redound to France's disadvantage and ensure an unfavorable result of the election. But, "as for the danger from the intervention of a foreign hand on which Mr. Monroe much insists; the danger exists only when the hand betrays itself." With

[22]Monroe to Secretary of State, Feb. 16, to Madison, Feb. 27, 1796, *Writings of Monroe* II, 454–56, 461.

[23]Monroe to Secretary of State, Feb. 20, 1796, *ibid.*, II, 456–60; AECPE-U, 45, 197, 150. French historians have almost invariably accepted the Directory's view of the effect of the Jay Treaty on Franco-American relations. For a recent example, see Jacques Godechot, *France and the Atlantic Revolution*, trans. by Herbert H. Rowen (New York, 1965), 232.

"ingenuity," much could be done in the intervening six months, and "we can always return to our system of rigor after the crisis expected this year . . . ."[24]

The directors conceded Delacroix a partial victory, and he blandly wrote Monroe on February 19 that the Directory was surprised at his fears. Adet had asked for his recall; the sending of a successor, instead of causing the results Monroe feared, would do the opposite in demonstrating that the two countries still carried on friendly relations. That the United States had not contributed to this end as it should have caused the Directory to feel "more the chagrin which regrets the missteps of a friend than discontent leading to a rupture."[25]

Monroe had just before this received the long note on the "multiplied wrongs of the government of the United States against the French Republic" which Delacroix had promised two weeks earlier. The Directory had ordered him to break the silence heretofore maintained on this subject because "it feels that too long indulgence changes generosity into weakness." Weakness could never be attributed to the French government, which had the power to make its enemies fear it and its false friends respect it. The United States had not reciprocated France's "marks of sincerest friendship; on the contrary, they had forgotten their duties to their allies and betrayed their own best interests." The misrepresentation of the rights of friendship, the disregard of the mutual conventions of the alliance, the selling of France's commerce to her enemies and the protection of enemy attacks on France's maritime forces even in the ports of the United States, the severe treatment of Frenchmen in American courts, the evasion or indifference with which the representations of the French minister were received—all these grievances had culminated in the treaty with England, "the gravest of our

---

24Monroe to Delacroix, Feb. 17, 1796, "Observations on the letter of Mr. Monroe to the Minister of External Relations," undated, AECPE-U, 45, 146–47vo, 148–49. The account of this conversation which Monroe sent to Pickering was much less frank than that to Madison, sketchy as was the latter. To Secretary of State, Feb. 20, to Madison, Feb. 27, 1796, *Writings of Monroe* II, 456–60, 460–62.

25AECPE-U, 45, 160–61.

injuries." But the Directory was convinced that the intrigues of Britain had seduced the American government and it was resolved to use every means of conciliation. Justice was demanded, "so our old friendship will not be entirely broken by the influence of England, our common enemy."[26]

Meanwhile, the Directory was busy drafting instructions for Vincent. The mission was to be temporary; Vincent was to demand reparations for what France regarded as violations of her treaties with the United States and he was to insist on the strict execution of France's treaty rights. He was to inform the American executive that France regarded the Jay Treaty as "the equivalent of an intimate alliance with our cruelest enemy," and as the abandonment of the "new principles of public law," contained in American treaties with France, Holland, Sweden, Prussia, and most recently, Spain. The British treaty must be annulled, or at least neutralized: to help effect this the Directory would send an imposing maritime contingent to the United States which would give the American government "the pretext of fear" and also "inspire it with a salutory anxiety."[27]

The House of Representatives, Vincent was told, held the key to his conduct. If that body showed opposition to the British treaty, and the President nevertheless tried to prevent the treaty's annulment, as expected, Vincent, by an "adroit, prudent, and cautious" conduct, could encourage France's friends in the House while offering a new treaty of alliance to the executive. Such a treaty would "consecrate" the chief features of the treaties of 1778 in one pact, but purely commercial relations would be left for regulation at "a more opportune time." Since the lack of powers in this respect had been the radical vice of previous missions, Vincent would receive full powers, so that the federal government would have no pretext for inaction.

The Directory expected, however, that Vincent's overtures would be rejected. In that case, his mission would be ended and

26Delacroix to Monroe, Feb. 17, 1796, *ibid.*, 45, 153–59.
27"Memorandum to serve as Instructions to Citizen Vincent, Minister Plenipotentiary of the French Republic," dated Mar. 6, 1796, *ibid.*, 45, 182–91.

he would resume his former functions at Saint-Domingue, leaving the papers of the legation in the hands of the first secretary, who would remain as chargé d'affaires. The chargé would represent the minister's withdrawal as proof of his government's displeasure, but he would assure the American government that it did not constitute a breaking off of relations. It would then be the task of the chargé to arouse the American people, whose "voice . . . will surely be heard in a decisive manner," while at the same time he redoubled his attentions to the government so as to give no cause for resentment. Everything depends, continued the Directory, on the replacement of Washington by Jefferson, "who is more disposed in our favor," but circumspection was essential to avoid being compromised. In cultivating the House of Representatives, he would "concert with all prudence and secrecy possible with Madison and others on their course of action," but would solemnly declare that "we reject with horror" any idea of directly influencing the domestic affairs of the United States. Far from desiring to create anarchy, France wanted only to strengthen the Constitution of the United States and to regain the position her alliance and her services gave her a right to expect.

The Directory planned to second the efforts of the chargé "with vigorous measures, to cause a reaction against the Jay treaty, and to diminish the disadvantage in which it places us." These measures would not fail to be considered reprisals justified by the conduct of the American government. The chargé would reply evasively to demands for explanations, pretending ignorance of the causes or even of the existence of particular measures, but he would defend them on the assumption that they were authorized and would promise justice from his government. Finally the chargé would himself open the subject of a new treaty, but if the American government's attitude showed no improvement, he would await further instructions.

The Directory's policy toward the United States was outlined in February and early in March 1796. It was revised, but not changed by subsequent events. Monroe asked for and got an interview with the Directory on March 8. On the basis of that conversation, he claimed that his efforts for the abandonment of the special mission had succeeded, but the Directory's spokesman, Reubell, was in fact only interested in impressing upon him the extent of the government's discontent regarding America's treaty with Britain. Thereafter, on instructions from the Directory, Delacroix opened a correspondence with Monroe dealing with France's objections to the treaty in detail.[28]

After the Monroe interview the Directory began considering the implementation of the "vigorous measures" of Vincent's instructions. The new rules which were to govern Franco-American commercial relations were contained in a projected decree dated "Pluviose (mid-January to mid-February). Because "the United States have abandoned the strict line of neutrality, in sacrificing to England the modern maxims of public law," France would treat America exactly as the United States permitted itself to be treated by England. French warships and privateers would be ordered to bring into French ports all American vessels loaded with provisions for England; but the cargoes and the expenses of detention would be paid for, and the ships would be released as quickly as possible. But English property would be confiscated; naval stores and construction materials were added to the list of contraband; and the Directory's colonial agents were to proclaim England's colonies in a state of seige, thereby subjecting American ships captured in violation of the blockade edict to seizure and condemnation without recompense.[29]

Unfortunately, this decree was lost, and the one which was issued on July 2, 1796, merely provided that neutral vessels would henceforth be treated by France "in the same manner as they shall suffer the English to treat them." The Pluviose *projet*

[28]Monroe to Secretary of State, Mar. 10, 1796, *ASP, FR* I, 731. The Monroe-Delacroix correspondence on the treaty is in *ibid.*, I, 732–35.

[29]AECPE-U, 45, 275–76. A supplementary decree was originally intended ordering the minister of external relations to (1) notify the Barbary regencies that France would suspend its good offices in behalf of the U. S., and (2) invite Spain and Holland to join France in representations to the U. S. against the Jay Treaty. *Ibid.*, 45, 277.

at least had the merit of being reasonably specific; the Messidor decree was so broad and undefined that, inevitably, it created the greatest confusion and was followed by general abuses. An explanatory decree of March 2, 1797, restored some system to the Directory's commercial policy, but it was more stringent than the one projected one year earlier, and meanwhile French privateers were compiling a record of high-handed actions.[30]

Vincent, whose mission was to be supported by such measures, was unable to leave Paris. On March 9, one month after his appointment, he had not received official notification of it. He wrote to Delacroix of his impatience, adding that he had already taken the liberty of communicating to the Directory his opinion that he should be sent to America merely as Adet's successor rather than an envoy extraordinary. At the same time he was indiscreet enough to recommend for another diplomatic mission two men whose names he personally had expunged from the list of émigrés. That affair served as a convenient pretext for dispensing with Vincent's services. The would-be minister burst into a frenzy of activity in refutation of the "grave accusations" which had been put forward anonymously, and he asked Delacroix's intercession with the Directory, which he understood to have been irritated with some expressions he had addressed to it. Almost certainly, Vincent was too bumptious for the Directory, to say nothing of the suspicion of royalist sympathies. Whatever the cause, his fate was settled before March 21, when Delacroix urged the Directory to hurry the nomination of a new minister to the United States.[31]

In Delacroix's view, the prospect for the success in America of the policy he championed was greatly enhanced by the generally expected retirement of President Washington. Jefferson would succeed him, and that would increase the possibility that the House of Representatives would "veto" the Jay Treaty, especially

[30] *ASP, FR* I, 577.
[31] Vincent to Delacroix, Mar. 9, to Directory, Mar. 18, 1796, to Minister of War, Oct. 27, 1794, to Delacroix, Mar. 18 and 20, "Report to Directory on the necessity of deciding on the nomination of a minister to the United States," dated Mar. 21, 1796, AECPE-U, 45, 222–22VO, 251–56, 262.

if Americans were informed of the views of France. The Directory was even then negotiating with Spain for the retrocession of Louisiana and West Florida and this, if successful, would provide another lever for influencing the United States. All signs, said Delacroix, pointed to a change in American policy. England realized this and had just sent a new minister with a distinguished reputation, Robert Liston, to combat any veering toward France, which must not be left unrepresented at such a crucial time. As for Adet, the hope of hearing each day of the appointment of a successor had caused the department to suspend its correspondence with him; practically abandoned by his government, Adet's credit was very low in the United States, even with those Americans predisposed toward France. In this state of affairs, Delacroix begged his masters, either name a new minister or give him authority to send instructions to guide Adet.[32]

But Adet had decided that he should stay after all, and wrote the news to a friend in the Department of the Marine. A few days later, on April 22, word of his imminent replacement reached the United States, destroying for a time what remained of his authority. It was not until the middle of June that the Directory issued a decree rescinding Vincent's appointment. Adet, having withdrawn his resignation, it ordered further, would be retained, and Delacroix was to revise the instructions prepared for Vincent and resubmit them to the Directory before sending them to Adet.[33]

Doubtless, Monroe deserved some credit for forestalling the Vincent mission,[34] but he owed something to the indiscretions of Vincent himself. In accordance with the Directory's promise to Monroe, Delacroix drew up an *Exposé Sommaire* of France's grievances, but he could not have regarded it as other than an

[32]Mar. 21, 1796, *ibid.*, 45, 262–63vo.

[33]Bourdon to Delacroix, June 12, 1796, *ibid.*, 46, 36–37. The decree of June 15 is in *ibid.*, 45, 41. Adet to Minister of Foreign Relations, Apr. 23, 1796, C. F. M., 896.

[34]Forwarding to Washington a letter from Gouverneur Morris reporting the Directory's intention of sending a new envoy and a fleet to America with an ultimatum, Hamilton predicted that "a war will probably be the consequence. The British will be glad of this." May 5, 1795 [1796], Hamilton Papers, Library of Congress, XXIV, 3330–31.

exercise to keep Monroe busy while the Directory awaited news from America. The representations presented to Monroe by Delacroix came under three heads: (1) the inexecution of treaties, (2) the outrage committed upon Fauchet by the *Africa*, (3) the Jay Treaty.

In detail, the first was a collection of old complaints. American courts took cognizance of prizes brought in by French privateers. English warships were admitted into American ports after having taken French prizes. French consuls were denied jurisdiction over French citizens in disputes among themselves, and American judges presented obstacles to the consuls' exercise of their right to arrest deserters from French ships. Finally, in the case of the *Cassius,* American courts had assumed jurisdiction over acts committed by French officers on the high seas.

The complaint about the *Africa* incident was merely for the record, but that concerning the Jay Treaty was real: it was that treaty which was almost wholly responsible for the situation in which Monroe found himself. France was chagrined that her ally had made a treaty with her own bitterest enemy during a war between them, but most important were the provisions which promised incalculable harm to France's ability to continue that war. The surrender of the "free ships, free goods" principle and the acceptance of the extension of contraband to include provisions proved that the "United States . . . have sacrificed, *knowingly* and *evidently*, their connexion with the republic; and the rights, the most essential and least contested, of neutrality."[35]

Monroe, in a paper three times as long as that of the minister, took up each point in order. In answer to the contention that American courts wrongly claimed jurisdiction over French prizes, Monroe claimed two exceptions. If the vessel which brought in the prize had been fitted out in the United States in violation of American laws, or if the capture took place in American territorial waters, then it was necessary and proper for American courts to assume jurisdiction. The treaty with France prohibited enemy warships from entering the ports of the two

[35]Delacroix to Monroe, Mar. 11, 1796, *ASP, FR* I, 732–33.

countries only if accompanying their prizes. Even this provision was difficult to enforce in all cases because of the length of the American coastline and the lack of a navy. As for the alleged violations of the consular convention, since no particular case was presented, it was difficult to answer. Consular jurisdiction in so large a country, however, was extremely hard to arrange, but the courts had always assisted the consuls in the apprehension of deserters. Finally, in regard to the *Cassius*, the captain had been released, and the case turned actually upon whether or not the vessel had been armed in Philadelphia. That was a judicial problem which admitted of no diplomatic interference.[36]

Proceeding to the second complaint, Monroe remarked that the British consul involved in the *Africa* affair had lost his exequatur, and that the American minister at London was instructed to complain formally to the British government. As to the Jay Treay, Monroe did the best he could. England had never recognized the liberal principle contended for by the Armed Neutrality in the late war: how compel her adherence now when many powers leagued against her then were on the opposite side? America's inability to gain such recognition was regrettable, but certainly not culpable, and conditions were at least no worse than they had been. This applied with equal force to the objection concerning contraband, regarding which the United States had actually won a concession, since England bound herself by the treaty to pay for any provisions seized, which otherwise would simply have been subject to confiscation. Concerning the charge that the United States had abandoned her connection with France and showed a striking "condescension" toward England, Monroe was silent. His defense of the Jay Treaty throughout was weak, but it was probably as strong as the facts permitted. And it was wiser to ignore charges which, from his point of view, were irrefutable.[37]

[36]Monroe to Delacroix, Mar. 15, 1796, *ibid.* I, 734-35.

[37]Monroe to Pickering, Mar. 25, 1796, *ibid.* I, 734-35; Beverly W. Bond, Jr., "The Monroe Mission to France, 1794-1796," *Johns Hopkins University Studies in History and Political Science, 1907* XXV, 60-61.

As far as the French government was concerned, it made little difference what Monroe said in any event. An analysis of Monroe's defense dated May 9, 1796, stated as much, after labeling his various arguments as incorrect or as vain excuses. Of the old complaints, the most exceptionable answer was Monroe's insistence upon the American interpretation of ARTICLE XVII of the Treaty of Commerce of 1778. If the American contention that only enemy vessels "entering with prizes" could be excluded from the ports of the two nations, instead of "all vessels having taken prizes" (and hence all armed vessels belonging to the enemy), were allowed to stand, then, in the opinion of the analyst, the treaty might as well be torn up. But Monroe's defense of Jay's Treaty, the "most specious" part of his paper, drew the sharpest comment. His arguments either "passed much too lightly" over specific points or enunciated "hateful doctrine." The concessions made by the United States would have been contrary to American honor and interests in time of peace; in time of war they were "open violations of neutrality," a conclusion which "no arguments could destroy."[38]

The writer recommended, however, in view of the situation of France's affairs at Philadelphia, that Monroe's paper be answered, primarily for the benefit of the American government. By May 25, Monroe had heard nothing further on the subject, and thought he probably would hear no more. It was June 25 before his hopeful calm was broken by a curt note from Delacroix. The newspapers reported, began the minister, that the House of Representatives had agreed by a vote of 51 to 48 to support the British treaty. If true, that would fully implement the treaty and "the state of affairs which must result from it deserves all our consideration." Was the report true? Not only America was "a tip-toe" over the treaty's fate in the House, as Jefferson wrote Monroe, but so was France.[39]

[38] AECPE-U, 45, 419–22vo. The author was probably Caille, then secretary in the American department of the foreign ministry.

[39] Monroe to Pickering, May 25, 1796, *ASP, FR* I, 736–37; AECPE-U, 46, 68–68vo; *Writings of Monroe* III, 9n. Delacroix's information was correct: the House so voted on Apr. 7, 1796. Ford, *Jefferson's Writings* VII, 67.

248

Monroe answered at once that he had no more information in that regard than had the minister. As to how Delacroix should view the report if true, Monroe could add nothing to his previous replies, which, since they had not been answered, he had supposed were satisfactory. The Directory issued the broad decree of July 2 ordering the treatment by France of all neutral powers in the same manner that they were treated by England, but the decree was not published and was not communicated to Monroe. Delacroix sent it to Adet on July 5, hailing it as another reason for "redoubled zeal in your functions." He was busy preparing new instructions to send in accordance with the decision just taken by the Directory.[40]

Then Delacroix wrote again to Monroe. The daily expectation of seeing Adet's successor depart, he said, had prevented his answering sooner Monroe's defense of American policy. "Time . . . has sufficiently ripened the points that were then in discussion, and, far from being enfeebled, our complaints against that treaty have acquired since, in our estimation, new force." The Directory, he continued, had never wavered in the opinion that the treaty constituted a breach of friendship and an abandonment of the agreements which had united the two countries since 1778. Therefore, it was compelled to regard "as altered and suspended" the provisions of the treaties of 1778 respecting neutrality, and "it would fail in its duty if it did not modify a state of affairs which would never have been consented to, but upon the condition of the most strict reciprocity."[41]

Monroe had written to Pickering of Delacroix's request for positive information on the decision of the House of Representatives, but he had thought that inquiry proceeded solely from the hostility of the minister. He was forced to admit to the secretary of state late in July that he had failed to distract the Directory from the treaty. Monroe's attitude now seemed to have changed as much as had that of the French government. Despite a convincing paper he drew up to show that the House of Representa-

[40]*Writings of Monroe* III, 9n.; AECPE-U, 46, 73–73vo, 78.
[41]Delacroix to Monroe, July 7, 1796, *ASP, FR* I, 739.

tives was required, on account of political reasons, to accept the treaty, Monroe, like Delacroix and his mentor, Reubell, undoubtedly hoped the House would resist. The retreat from his earlier wishful optimism which Monroe made after receiving Delacroix's latest note was eloquently illustrated in a dispatch to Pickering.

> I sincerely wish it were now in my power to say that this affair was ended, and that neither of us would ever hear of it again; but this I cannot say: for so deep founded has their discontent appeared to be, and so vehement their desire to give some signal proof of it, that it is impossible, even at this moment, to determine in what scale their councils will ultimately settle in regard to us.[42]

The "signal proof" contemplated by the Directory was a variation of the idea behind the abortive Vincent mission, with Adet playing the principal role. But who was to play the supporting role of the eventual chargé d'affaires? Létombe had been consul general, but that office had been discontinued for reasons of economy, though most of its work was still performed by Létombe as consul for Pennsylvania. He was the logical choice until the embarrassments created at Madrid by a protégé of Reubell presented another. This was Mangourit again, the first secretary of legation and former consul at Charleston before and during the time of Genet. Mangourit's customary excess of revolutionary zeal so hampered the French ambassador, Dominique-Catherine, marquis de Pérignon, in the delicate negotiations with Spain for the retrocession of Louisiana, that the latter, seconded by Manuel de Godoy, the Spanish foreign minister, insisted upon his recall. That Godoy took advantage of the split in the French mission to fortify his determination to hold Louisiana, at least for the present, is probable. At any rate, Mangourit was detached from the Madrid embassy and, on July 26, nominated chargé d'affaires of the Republic at Philadelphia.[43]

42Monroe to Pickering, July 21, 1796, *ibid.*, I, 738.
43AECPE-U, 46, 142; Raymond Guyot, *Le Directoire et la Paix de l'Europe* (Paris, 1912), 240–41; Robert R. Palmer, "A Revolutionary Republican: M. A. B. Mangourit," *W & M Quarterly*, 3d ser., IX (Oct. 1952), 489–90; Decree of the Directory,

The Directory probably had before it Adet's dispatch No. 17 of April 22, which summarized the propaganda of fear employed by the proponents of the British treaty against their Republican adversaries, who preferred, he thought, "war to the peace of slavery." In his dispatch, and in an enclosure accompanying it, Adet placed much stress upon the motion to reject laws to put the treaty into effect, and he forwarded a note containing constitutional amendments proposed by the Virginia House of Delegates. The substance of the amendments was that the House of Representatives should hold a veto over treaties, the power to try impeachments should be taken away from the Senate, and the term of office of senators should be reduced to three years. Also, the peripatetic American soldier of fortune now in the service of the French Republic, General Eustace, had recently delivered to Delacroix a printed pamphlet containing the text of the treaty "as finally ratified by the American legislature," with a compendium of published American expressions for and against it and a "fraternal project" for French merchants, pointing out ways to compensate for losses caused by American laws resulting from the treaty's adoption.[44]

On the basis of such information, Mangourit might have appeared just the man to help Adet revive popular enthusiasm for France and to keep it burning after Adet's retirement from the scene. According to the custom of the time, Mangourit drafted his own instructions for the approval of the Directory, instructions which, in view of their authorship, were surprisingly restrained. He would watch carefully the effects produced in the United States by the substitution of a chargé for the minister, and he would explain frankly the causes of France's discontent.

July 26, 1796, AECPE-U, 46, 92. Pérignon's negotiations resulted in the Treaty of San Ildefonso, signed Aug. 20, 1796, whereby Spain became France's ally, but France had to forego the retrocession of Louisiana for the time being.

44C. F. M., 892–96; AECPE-U, 45, 384–85vo, 387–87vo, 42, 261–94vo. The struggle in the House and in the U. S. generally over the implementation of the treaty can be traced in *Benton's Abridgement of the Debates of Congress* (New York, 1857), I, 639–754. See also Brant, *Madison: Father of Constitution*, 434–39; Henry Adams, *Life of Albert Gallatin*, reprint ed. (New York, 1943), 159–66; and Charles, *Origins of American Party System*, 108–16.

Pre-eminently, that discontent proceeded from the Jay Treaty, in which, "in spite of the dexterity of the negotiators in respecting the letter of our prior treaties, the Directory has seen . . . the equivalent of an intimate alliance with our cruelest enemy" and the abandonment of "that rigorous neutrality that the United States have appeared so jealous of maintaining."

The frank representations of the chargé would be more productive if, as hoped, Jefferson were elected President at the end of the year, but he would evade a discussion of the bases of a new treaty of commerce by hinting that a renewal of the Treaty of Alliance would have to come first. In regard to Louisiana, the Americans should be kept in uncertainty about French designs, and Mangourit would encourage separatist feeling in the western parts of the United States bordering Louisiana and Canada, while at the same time fostering projects for an American invasion of Canada. But Mangourit would have to conduct himself with the utmost caution in order not to compromise himself or to betray French hopes for Washington's retirement. Mangourit knew "what advantage our enemies have drawn from the phantom of our pretended influence in pushing the United States towards England . . . ."[45]

Mangourit set to work with his usual energy to enlighten the Directory on what had really been happening in America. He presented a *mémoire* on August 29, explaining how England had actually profited from American independence; by regaining the profits of America's trade, England had virtually recovered her old colonial relationship, without having the expenses of administration and protection of her satellite. France's greatest mistake, insisted Mangourit, was in her agents' blindness regarding Washington. The Chevalier Anne César de la Luzerne and Ternant had seconded American idolatry of the Revolutionary hero who had forgotten that he had been a rebel, to the later embarrassment of Genet, whose legitimate activities outraged the President's counterrevolutionary sympathies. It was inexplicable to

[45]Mangourit's instructions are in c. f. m., 930–43. See also Palmer, "Mangourit," 490–91.

Mangourit that Genet and his consuls (himself included, of course) could have been recalled through fear of Washington's displeasure. Fauchet, who had undone all their work in accordance with his instructions, soon realized how wrong his government had been, and his removal was effected by Randolph. By the time Adet arrived, he saw that his mission could not succeed and asked to be recalled.

Through all these errors, France had lost the certain conquest, or at least the independence, of Canada, Louisiana, and the Floridas, and her treaties with the United States had become valueless. The American government had sent a "most violent aristocrat" to treat in London while sending to France "a patriot with powers as insignificant as his republican virtues are great." The only remedy Mangourit saw for this deplorable situation was the election of a new President—either Jefferson, "by conviction and by inclination" a republican, or General (Governor George) Clinton would adopt a policy favorable to France. John Adams, on the other hand, would act more wisely and more cautiously than Washington, but had even less sympathy for France. His task, therefore, would be to work for the election of Jefferson.[46]

The Directory, or rather Reubell and his Minister Delacroix, certainly shared Mangourit's views, however inapplicable to an assignment in the United States. But Mangourit's bad luck was pressing him closely and he was not sent to the United States after all. Monroe, whom he had praised so highly, heard of his appointment and hurried at once to Delacroix to protest. According to the American minister, Delacroix was unmoved by his arguments, but at length promised to lay them before the Directory. Monroe also found an occasion to sound out his friend Carnot, the only director who had been on the Jacobin Committee of Public Safety, who also promised to present his objections. A few days later, Lazare N. M. Carnot told him that Mangourit's appointment had been canceled. Monroe's guarded optimism for the future returned as a result of this success; but two weeks

46AECPE-U, 46, 123–24vo.

later, near the end of August, it went into eclipse again when he heard that Adet was to be recalled without any successor and after having announced that normal relations between the two countries were to cease.[47]

The Directory on August 23 ordered Adet to suspend his functions and carry out steps to be prescribed for him. Létombe was to assume the post of consul general once more and retain it indefinitely. These measures, as well as the retaliatory decree of July 2, were to be kept secret from Monroe until after the departure of the packet boat which was to carry Adet's instructions to the United States.[48]

Reubell had dictated notes to Delacroix on August 14 which were to provide the heads of Adet's new instructions. The result was approved by each of the directors on August 23 and addressed to Adet the following day. The instructions began with the Directory's resolution to suspend regular diplomatic relations with the United States. Before announcing that, however, Adet was to "develop" all the grievances of France to the American government. The assumption by American courts of jurisdiction over French prizes, on whatever pretext, was the first. France regarded as reasonable the procedure proposed by Jefferson to Genet in June 1793: in cases where the prize was of doubtful validity, the government, through the governors of the states, would request the French minister, or the consul in ports other than Philadelphia, to detain the vessel on his authority till an investigation could be made. In all other cases, French vessels were to be permitted to enter or depart freely. Adet, therefore, was to demand the cessation of all seizures and the repeal of all acts giving any authority over French prizes.[49]

47Monroe to Pickering, Aug. 4, 15, and 27, 1796, *ASP, FR* I, 741, 742. Apparently, Mangourit was never officially notified of his abrupt dismissal. He used his new title in a letter to Delacroix of Sept. 9 and again on Oct. 24, when he reported that the botanist André Michaux had just arrived in Holland from the U. S. with a treasure of botanical specimens. AECPE-U, 46, 169–69vo, 288–89vo.

48Decree of Directory, Delacroix to Directory, Aug. 23, Delacroix to Minister of Marine, Aug. 26, 1796, AECPE-U, 46, 135, 142–42vo, 153–53vo.

49*Ibid.*, 46, 236–36vo, 137–40vo. For the letter of Jefferson to Genet, June 25, 1793, see *ASP, FR* I, 160.

The second complaint regarded the sale of French prizes. France did not regard as legitimate Randolph's distinction of May 1795, excluding prizes made by the enemy on France but permitting their captors to enter American ports freely. These were advantages France counted upon as a result of having brought about American independence. The third and last grievance was the Jay Treaty, which was "the equivalent of an alliance with their former oppressor, and their most implacable enemy, against a faithful ally, and a generous liberator." That treaty combined all that made American neutrality profitable to England and disadvantageous to France.[50]

After transmitting these grievances, Adet was to announce the suspension of his functions and also the order commanding the French marine to treat American vessels as the Jay Treaty allowed them to be treated by England. But he was to explain that this act of reprisal merely constituted execution of the "most-favored-nation" clause of the Treaty of Commerce of 1778. He should also explain that complaints against this measure would most properly be addressed to those who had contributed to its cause.

The American government, *"and the American people,"* would be assured by Adet that these measures did not constitute a declaration of war, but a mark of discontent, to last until the American government returned "to sentiments and measures more comfortable to the true interests of the United States, to the alliance, and to the friendship sworn between the two nations." At the same time Adet would contrast "the conduct of the French republic with that of the republic of the United States," offering reflections to "all the American friends of liberty" on "the strange change which has just produced the union of North America, and of England, during a war which the latter has waged against us with so much fury, in order to gain revenge for the independence of the United States, which was our work." The Directory desired that this declaration be written "with the

[50]For Randolph's letter to Fauchet, May 29, 1795, see *ASP, FR* I, 609–14.

energy which characterizes a powerful government which sees itself outraged; but all of it must be precise, well-formulated, full of force, and of moderation." In all this, Adet was to use the tone of offended friendship, rather than that of threat.

Delacroix informed Adet that his declaration to the American government "must produce a great effect." He was to remain in America as long after his mission ended as would be useful. Delacroix wanted to be informed of the results, especially of the election, but Adet was to come home as soon as his presence ceased to carry any advantage. He assured Adet that the Directory was completely satisfied with his conduct and with his work to obtain a more favorable result during the last Congress.[51]

Monroe caught glimpses of these proceedings and tried to draw out the directors in an interview, but without success. Carnot refused to volunteer any information, so Monroe was forced to await the communication of the Directory's decree on relations with America, to be transmitted by Delacroix, who was doing his best to keep Monroe in the dark. By September 21 he still had no word, and four days later he tried a direct approach, inquiring of Delacroix if it were true that orders had been given for seizing enemy property in neutral vessels. Delacroix refused to accept the bait, however, and on October 4 demanded of Monroe whether the United States had placed an embargo on French ships, a report which Monroe immediately denied.[52]

Monroe's anxiety was relieved on October 7. Delacroix, after receiving word of the sailing of the dispatch boat from the minister of the marine, forwarded the decrees relating to the suspension of Adet's functions and to the maritime reprisals. These reprisals had been adopted, he explained to Monroe, because of grievances already outlined: "The federal government is too enlightened not to have foreseen all the results of the [Jay] treaty."[53]

Monroe replied a few days later in a tone of sorrowful resigna-

---

[51]Delacroix to Adet, Aug. 24 and 28, 1796, AECPE-U, 46, 144–45, 160.

[52]Monroe to Delacroix, Sept. 2, 25, Oct. 5, 1796, *ibid.*, 46, 167, 190, 218–18vo, 220.

[53]*Ibid.*, 46, 230, 231–32.

tion. He had read Delacroix's letter with "real concern" because he had presumed that his earlier explanations had been satisfactory. The subject was before his government, and he could do nothing but await its orders. He thanked the minister for his attention to the communications "in which I tried to divert you from any measure of this kind," and to assure him of his "most grateful remembrance" for the generous sentiments expressed toward him.[54]

Monroe already suspected that his sojourn in Paris was about to end. Early in September he received a letter from Secretary of State Pickering dated June 13, in which the latter cast all the blame for France's dissatisfaction over the Jay Treaty on Monroe, because he had not removed the complaints with early explanations. Monroe decided at first not to answer Pickering's aspersions, which he told Madison were addressed to him "as from an overseer on the farm to one of his gang . . . ," but on September 10 he wrote a long refutation of a charge "not more unjust and unexpected than the testimony by which you support it is inapplicable and inconclusive." He pointed out with much heat that, to answer complaints, they had first to be made, and it had been his primary object from the first to prevent their being made at all.[55] Monroe thought he saw the hand of Hamilton in "these little Connecticut Jockey [Wolcott] tricks," and knew that he, like Randolph one year before, had been marked by partisan malice for disgrace. In November he received without surprise, therefore, Pickering's accusing letter announcing his recall and the appointment of General Charles Cotesworth Pinckney as his successor.[56]

---

[54] Monroe to Delacroix, Oct. 12, 1796, *ibid.*, 46, 237–37vo.

[55] *ASP, FR* I, 742–43. Monroe told Madison that "I have detained them seven months from doing what they ought to have done at once." Sept. 1, 1796, *Writings of Monroe* III, 53.

[56] Monroe to Madison, Sept. 1, 1796, *Writings of Monroe* III, 53–54; Pickering to Monroe, Aug. 22, 1796, *ASP, FR* I, 741–42. Wolcott actually was the prime mover in Monroe's recall. He urged his view on Hamilton with the declaration that ". . . we must stop the channels by which foreign poison is introduced into the country, or suffer the government to be overturned." June 17, 1796, *Oliver Wolcott* I, 361. As in the Randolph episode, an intercepted letter was used to destroy Mon-

Delacroix had heard of Monroe's ouster by November 2, when he told Adet that he hoped "deference for [public] opinion" would cause the sending of a successor "not like Bingham, more suited to foment new occasions of distrust than to calm those which exist." He heard of it again on December 1 from Tom Paine, who had just learned of Pinckney's arrival at Bordeaux. To a friend in the American section of Delacroix's department, Paine suggested that Pinckney's appointment was unconstitutional, since it had not received senatorial confirmation and was made by a President about to go out of office. Washington should have left such an appointment to his successor—Jefferson would undoubtedly keep Monroe at Paris—and opposition to Pinckney in the Senate was sure. Therefore, the change could only be intended as an insult to France and to Monroe. The best way to handle the situation, advised Paine, was to treat Pinckney as a private citizen awaiting ministerial powers from his government. This would make "ridiculous and laughable the crafty policy of Mr. Washington" without at all offending the American people or the Congress.[57]

Delacroix was sufficiently interested in Paine's idea to have Caille investigate its validity. The latter replied that Paine was wrong; Pinckney's appointment was perfectly legal, and his powers would be in proper order. The French government was too powerful to stoop to such petty means in any case, even if Pinckney would not be able to make the government look ridiculous in disproving such arguments. But, said Caille, "if we want to refuse Mr. Pinkney [sic] we have several other good reasons to

---

roe's credit with President Washington. Again, Wolcott and Pickering were the hatchetmen, now supported by James McHenry, a Hamilton sycophant and secretary of war. Monroe's dismissal was noteworthy in that it removed the last Republican from high office in the national government. Stephen G. Kurtz, *The Presidency of John Adams* (Philadelphia, 1957), 119–22. Perhaps encouraged by their success in blackening the character of the hapless Randolph, Wolcott and Pickering spread reports that Monroe had misappropriated government funds for speculation in Paris and he was actually charged by the Treasury Department with a shortage in his legation accounts. See Brant, *Madison: Father of Constitution*, 443. For Monroe's consequent tribulations, see Lucius Wilmerding, *James Monroe, Public Claimant* (New Brunswick, N. J., 1960).

57 AECPE-U, 46, 355, 425–26vo.

give, which will all be supported by true and incontestable relations between these governments, without giving examples of subtleties that could one day be twisted around to our disadvantage." Delacroix had already informed Monroe of the formalities to be observed on the arrival of Pinckney and asked for his letters of recall. Monroe responded that he would be glad to have Pinckney forward his credentials as soon as he arrived, as well as his own letter of recall, which the secretary of state, announcing "only the fact that I was recalled," said would be delivered by his successor.[58]

On December 6, Monroe told Delacroix that Pinckney had arrived and desired an interview. Three days later the minister received them, and the next day Monroe sent his letter of recall —the President had written that he had found it "expedient to grant Mr. Monroe permission to return to the United States"— and Pinckney's credentials to the Directory. A report accompanying these documents suggested that constitutional objections regarding Pinckney's powers could be raised. Delacroix had discovered a clause overlooked by Paine and Caille; the President could fill a position become vacant during the Senate's absence, but the post at Paris was not vacant. These suggestions were submitted only "incidentally," however; if the Directory wanted to refuse to accept Pinckney, it would not want to become involved in useless constitutional arguments.[59]

The Directory had already made up its mind not to receive Pinckney. When Delacroix presented his report, he was instructed to inform Monroe "that the Directory will no longer recognize or receive a Minister plenipotentiary or other Political agent of the United States, until after the redress of grievances demanded of the American government, and which the French Republic has a right to expect of it." This message was forwarded to Monroe on December 11 and communicated by him to Pinck-

---

[58]"Observations on Paine's note concerning Pinckney," Dec. 6, 1796, *ibid.*, 46, 427–28; Monroe to Delacroix, Dec. 3, 1796, *ASP, FR* I, 746.

[59]*ASP, FR* I, 746; AECPE-U, 46, 170, 171–71vo, 436–36vo. President Washington's letter to the Directory, as well as Pinckney's credentials, was dated Sept. 9, 1796.

ney, after which Monroe asked Delacroix for an appointment to take formal leave of the Directory without delay, in accordance with the orders of his government. Delacroix answered, December 27, that the Directory would receive him on December 30, and that he himself would have the honor of escorting him there.[60]

Although Delacroix had told Monroe that his would be a private audience, its proceedings appeared in the Directory's official gazette, *Le Redacteur*, on Sunday, January 1, 1797. Monroe had made a brief address to the directors in which he testified his own devotion to the principles of their revolution, which he believed to be the same as those of his own country, and he expressed the earnest desire that harmony between the two nations might be perpetual. In reply, the President of the Directory, Paul F. N. Barras, castigated the American government for its subservience to "its ancient tyrants." The American people, he continued, "will weigh in their wisdom the magnanimous friendship of the French people, with the crafty caresses of perfidious men, who meditate to bring them again under their former yoke." Monroe was to assure them "that, like them, we adore liberty; that they will always possess our esteem, and find in the French people that republican generosity which knows how to grant peace, as well as how to cause its sovereignty to be respected." As for Monroe:

> You have fought for principles; you have known the true interests of your country—depart with our regret. We restore, in you, a representative to America; and we preserve the remembrance of the citizen whose personal qualities did honor to that title.[61]

Monroe has frequently been criticized for not by this time having acquired the sense of a distinct American nationality, and with it an awareness of American interests separate from those of every other nation. Frenchmen in influential positions did not suspect that Monroe, although whole-heartedly devoted to the extension of republican principles in Europe through the instru-

[60] AECPE-U, 46, 437; *ASP, FR* I, 746–47, 747
[61] *ASP, FR* I, 747; AECPE-U, 47, 3–3vo.

mentality of France, was, like Americans in general, attached, not to England or to France, but to the United States. They would have been as bitterly disillusioned at discovering this as was Adet, who at this very time was writing that Jefferson himself, France's white hope in America, was not "a man entirely devoted to our interests."[62]

Probably no one but Monroe could have kept the French government for almost one year from reacting violently against the United States on account of the Jay Treaty. President Washington had sent to England no greater a partisan than he had sent to France, and it was impossible for his government simultaneously to enjoy the good wishes of the two giants of Europe, engaged in a remorseless struggle for survival, and with both of whom the United States had close political and economic connections. Jay's treaty had strengthened American ties to England and weakened, if not ruptured, those with France. President Washington's role in this had been decisive, and the French government naturally blamed him. Monroe's recall was another evidence of the President's pro-British policy; as far as Delacroix was concerned, this was "only a maneuver of General Washington, who wants to throw on the ex-minister and on the party to which he is supposed to belong in America the odium of the present state of affairs."[63]

[62] Adet to Minister of Foreign Relations, Dec. 31, 1796, c. f. m., 983. Adet continued: "Mr. Jefferson loves us, because he detests England; he wants to draw close to us again, because he fears us less than Great Britain; but he would change his mind perhaps tomorrow in regard to us, if tomorrow Great Britain ceased to inspire him with fear. Jefferson, although the friend of liberty and of science, although an admirer of the efforts that we have made to break our bonds and to dissipate the cloud of ignorance which weighs down the human race, Jefferson, I say, is an American and, on this account, he cannot sincerely be our friend. An American is the born enemy of all European peoples." Monroe told Madison that "It is impossible to forsee [sic] the consequences of this measure [the suspension of Adet's functions] which I sincerely regret, but here no change can be expected and of course if the same councils prevail in America the alliance is at an end not to count the other injuries we shall receive from the loss of this nation so preponderant as it is with such valuable possessions in our seas." Sept. 1, 1796, *Writings of Monroe* III, 53. See Carnot's testimony on Monroe's passionate devotion to the French cause and his avidity for a French hegemony over all of Europe. H. Carnot, *Mémoires sur Carnot* (Paris, 1863), II, 133.
[63] Delacroix to Adet, Jan. 3, 1797, AECPE-U, 47, 5–6.

CHAPTER XI    The Directory, Hamilton, and the Election of 1796

> A war with France & an alliance with G. B., enter both into print and conversation; and no doubt can be entertained that a push will be made to screw up the P. to that point before he quits the office.
>
> MADISON TO JEFFERSON, JANUARY 29, 1797.

> A little clandestine war, like England made on America for three years, would produce a constructive effect.
>
> LOUIS-ANDRÉ PICHON, VENDÉMIAIRE, AN 5.

OTTO, then living in temporary retirement at Lesches, called Monroe's recall "the most unpardonable . . . of all the many political blunders, made on both sides the Atlantic these six years past." Pinckney, a moderate Federalist who was genuinely concerned for a restoration of amicable relations between France and the United States, could not be received for fear of indirectly aiding in the discrediting of Monroe, but he did not deserve the harsh treatment he received. After he first was introduced to Delacroix by Monroe, he never saw the minister again. He wrote to remonstrate against the decision of the Directory, and to inquire what its intentions were in regard to him, but Delacroix refused to answer. He sent the secretary-general of his department around to tell Pinckney that, being a private citizen as far as the French government was concerned, he would have to conform to the laws governing aliens. In other words, since there was no intention of granting him a permit to remain, he would have to quit the territories of the Republic.[1]

On January 23, 1797, the Directory ordered Pinckney out of France at once, and Pinckney shortly withdrew to Amsterdam, where he kept abreast of developments in Paris through his legation's secretary, James C. Mountflorence, while he awaited new instructions from Philadelphia. The Directory had realized the effect Pinckney's rejection would have in the United States. Delacroix wrote to Adet on January 3 to explain that, since the partisans of England would make much of the incident, it was up to Adet to "destroy the effect of these calumnies." Since the new administration would not take office until March, Adet would still have intercourse with Washington or with Pickering—he could tell them that France had been forced to reject Pinckney because of his government's conduct.[2]

Delacroix again referred to Pinckney in a letter he wrote to Adet on March 21. The Directory's refusal to fall into Washington's trap in regard to Monroe was a further way of showing its irritation with his government. Adet should explain this to France's friends in the Congress, and also that "we still mean to avoid the extremes which have made our acts unpopular and our partisans with them." The retirement of Washington was known through the public press, but no word had been received of his successor, nor of the important activities that should have engaged Adet during the previous October.[3]

At the end of March 1797, Delacroix received a batch of Adet's dispatches which testified to the minister's industry. Late in Au-

---

[1] Lyon, "The Directory and the United States," 517; Delacroix to Adet, Jan. 3, 1797, Report of the secretary general of the Department of External Relations on his interview with Pinckney, to Delacroix, Dec. 15, 1796, AECPE-U, 47, 5–6, 46, 444–45vo; Pinckney to Pickering, Dec. 20, 1796. Pinckney's first mission to France is discussed in Zahniser, *Charles Cotesworth Pinckney*, 137–49.

[2] AECPE-U, 47, 38, 46, 461–61vo, 47, 5–6. Pinckney's correspondence is in *ASP, FR* II, 5–18 *passim*.

[3] AECPE-U, 47, 181–83. Delacroix's dispatch of Jan. 3 stated that no word had been received from Adet since his No. 34 of June 21, 1796. *Ibid.*, 47, 6.

gust 1796, Adet had made a trip to Boston, where he had found the Republicans so discouraged at having heard nothing from France that they were almost ready to see Adams win the election by default. The rumor of Washington's retirement had not yet been substantiated, but Adet set to work and "reanimated their hopes" for the election of Jefferson. Shortly after his return to Philadelphia, Adet learned of the appointment of Pinckney to succeed Monroe. He had thought that self-respect and good policy would prevent Washington from yielding to the evident desire of "the Britannic faction" for the sacrifice of Monroe, but "Hamilton and his party" had succeeded in replacing him with "a blind instrument" of "the Federal administration to which he is absolutely devoted." Adet was right in believing that the Directory would not accept such an envoy, but the Directory had made its decision long before it received, on November 2, 1797, Adet's bitter diatribe against the American government.[4]

Adet's spectacular public disputation with Pickering in the fall of 1796 began on October 27, 1796, when he addressed to Pickering a long note giving a summary review of the reasons which had caused France to issue the order of July 2, 1796, which he enclosed. Adet immediately had his letter published, as Pickering caustically noted in his answer of November 1, "to awaken the public attention" at the time of the choosing of electors to select a new President. Pickering's reply rejected Adet's contention that the United States was bound to defend the "free ships, free goods" principle and defended his failure to answer a previous note from Adet on British treatment of American commerce on the grounds that, even if the subject had not been already exhausted, it was still repugnant to him to answer letters full of unpleasant and unwarranted insinuations. Then Pickering challenged Adet by questioning the authenticity of the announced decree. As Adet informed Delacroix, news of the decree had in fact already reached the United States through English

4*Ibid.*, 47, 221; Adet to Minister of Foreign Relations, Sept. 24, Oct. 3, 1796, C. F. M., 947–48, 950–52.

newspapers, but the alarm thus caused had been quieted by a letter from Rufus King in London saying that the Directory had assured Monroe in August that it would not order the seizure of American vessels. In this situation, Pickering wanted to know, what was the policy of France to be, and what orders had been given, "and what, if they exist, are the precise terms of these orders?"[5]

Adet acknowledged receipt of Pickering's answer, "which was delivered to me last night, and which I find this morning in the newspapers," two days later. He expected to furnish in a few days "more ample information," but now he merely wanted to point out that the decree he had communicated bore no resemblance to the supposed order of the King letter.[6] He reported that this exchange had been received with confidence by both parties. The Federalists thought that, "nonplussed by the arguments of Mr. Pickering, I would be forced to ask for pardon and that his impertinence which they took for firmness, would so over-awe me that I would no longer dare to appear in the arena." The Republicans impatiently awaited his reply, "certain beforehand that the stupidity of the Secretary of State would be easily exposed to the public censure." What the result would be, Adet did not know; those who were supposed to be friends of France were stimulated most by hatred of Washington. And while they all thought the Directory right, "they are not equally satisfied to see it speak to the American [government] in language that they would rather were used only to other peoples." Americans could not forgive the Directory for destroying their illusion that they were "the first people of the earth," if it had not at the same time given them "the means of avenging themselves on Washington and of fighting with stronger weapons the Britannic faction."[7]

Adet let loose his promised barrage against the American government in a letter to Pickering dated November 15, which took

[5] *ASP, FR* I, 576–77, 578; Adet to Minister of Foreign Relations, no date, C. F. M., 969–70.

[6] Adet to Pickering, Nov. 3, 1796, *ASP, FR* I, 579.

[7] C. F. M., 970–71.

up ninety-four columns of *Claypool's Gazette* on November 21.[8] Following Delacroix's outline, Adet reviewed French complaints dating back to 1793 against alleged American violations of the French treaties. He insisted that France had been denied the advantages belonging to her by virtue of the treaties of 1778: not only had England been permitted to share privileges reserved by the treaties to France, but it was found necessary to give them a treaty basis. That negotiation, "covered with the veil of dissimulation," resulted in a treaty which deprived France of all the benefits of her antecedent treaties and at the same time agreed to commercial provisions which wreaked serious injury on France to the great advantage of England. As a result of this deliberate betrayal of France, by what amounted to an alliance with England, Adet was ordered "to suspend, from this moment, his ministerial functions with the Federal Government." But, "notwithstanding the wrongs of its Government . . . the executive directory did not wish to break with a people whom they fondly regard as friends," and the suspension of his functions was to be regarded not as a rupture, but "as a mark of discontent, which is to last until the Government of the United States returns to sentiments, and to measures, more comfortable to the interests of the alliance, and the sworn friendship between the two nations." Adet concluded his note with a long, passionate appeal to gratitude and to ancient friendship: "Let your Government return to itself, and you will still find in Frenchmen faithful friends and generous allies."[9]

Two days later, Adet turned over his office to Létombe, who as consul general would avoid any political intercourse with the American government. He was not to be a chargé d'affaires: if correspondence on a particular matter with the secretary of state were absolutely necessary, it should be conducted verbally. Adet himself would remain in the United States as long as he could be

8Washington to Hamilton, Nov. 21, 1796, *Writings of Washington* XXXV, 288. Claypool published the entire note on authority of the government because Bache had already printed a summary of it in his *Aurora*.

9*ASP, FR* I, 579–83.

useful in maintaining contact with his friends in Congress, but only as a private citizen.[10]

The acrimonious public debate between Adet and Pickering was partly owing to the Directory's orders to Adet and partly the product of the anti-French frenzy of Pickering.[11] But the political climate in which it took place had been prepared by President Washington's Farewell Address. Though usually described in such terms as "ever since a polestar of American foreign policy," the famous pronouncement was at the time recognized for what it was, at least in considerable part, an electioneering maneuver of Hamilton attacking France and the Republicans through the awesome prestige of George Washington. The New England High Federalist Fisher Ames characterized it "as a signal, like dropping a hat, for the party racers to start."[12]

Both the timing and much of the wording of Washington's famous valedictory were really Hamilton's. When the President had determined to retire in 1792, he had asked Madison to sketch an address of farewell to public life. Reluctantly, he had bowed to the pleas of Jefferson and Hamilton, among others, that he accept a second term, but by 1796 he could not be dissuaded and turned, this time, to Hamilton. The latter not only thoroughly revised the Madison draft Washington sent him, but he included precise advice on the timing of Washington's message: "The proper period now for your declaration seems to be *Two Months* before the time for the Meeting of the Electors. This will be

10 Adet to Létombe, Nov. 19, 1796, AECPE-U, 46, 374–8ovo.

11 Pickering was ruled by his hatreds and was constitutionally incapable of playing a diplomatic role. Earlier, according to Hammond, he had exhibited "a most blind and indistinguishing hatred of Great Britain," and Canada's Governor Simcoe called him "in principle a Jacobin." Subsequently, Hammond's successor said he was "one of the most [violent] Antigallicans I ever met with." Hammond to Grenville, Jan. 5, 1795, Simcoe to Duke of Portland, Dec. 22, 1794, Liston to Grenville, April 18, 1797, I. B. M., 83n., 129n.

12 Bemis, "Washington's Farewell Address," 262–63; Ames to Wolcott, Sept. 26, 1796, *Oliver Wolcott* I, 384–85; DeConde, "Washington's Farewell, the French Alliance, and the Election of 1796," 648–52; Brant, *Madison: Father of Constitution*, 441–42. See Arthur A. Markowitz, "Washington's Farewell and the Historians: A Critical Review," *Pennsylvania Magazine of History and Biography* XLIV (Apr. 1970), 173–91.

sufficient. The parties will in the meantime electioneer conditionally, that is to say, *if you decline*; for a serious opposition to you will I think hardly be risked." Madison scarcely recognized the address Washington published on September 19, 1796. It was a partisan manifesto aimed at destroying the Republican party and also the French alliance, a measure in keeping with Hamilton's policy from the Neutrality Proclamation of 1793 through the Jay Treaty of 1795. It was a defense of past policy rather than a "Great Rule" for the future.[13]

Adet mistakenly thought the address would cause American opinion to react in favor of France. He sent a copy to Delacroix on October 12, 1796, with this exasperated comment:

> It would be useless to speak to you about it. You will have seen the lies it contains, the tone of insolence which governs it; immorality characterizes it. You will have no difficulty in recognizing the author of a piece where ingratitude is extolled, where it is presented as a virtue necessary to the happiness of the States, where interest is presented as the only compass governments should follow in their negotiations putting aside honor and glory. You will have recognized at once the doctrine of the former Secretary of the Treasury Hamilton, and the principles of loyalty which have always directed the Philadelphia Cabinet.

Washington's Farewell was not a plea for "non-entanglement," and the best commentary on the situation which it precipitated came from the author of that term. "Our countrymen," Jefferson wrote to Elbridge Gerry on June 21, 1797, "have divided

13Washington to Hamilton, May 15 (containing Madison's draft), June 26, 1796, *Writings of Washington* XXXV, 50–61, 103–104; Hamilton to Washington, July 5, 1796, *Works of Hamilton* VIII, 408–409. The address is in *Writings of Washington* XXXV, 214–38. Brant, *Madison: Father of Constitution*, 442; DeConde, "Washington's Farewell, the French Alliance, and the Election of 1796," 649; DeConde, *Entangling Alliance*, 465–71; Charles, *Origins of American Party System*, 48. See also Albert K. Weinberg, "Washington's 'Great Rule' in its Historical Evolution," in Eric F. Goldman, ed., *Historiography and Urbanization* (Baltimore, 1941) and Victor H. Paltsits, ed., *Washington's Farewell Address* (New York, 1935). A recent commentator suggests that the long central section of the address, that devoted to "party," went far beyond Washington's thinking but gave the address "its real weight." Gilbert, *Farewell Address*, 129. Richard Hofstadter, however, says that the subject of "party" reflected "a nagging concern of [Washington's] remaining years." *Idea of a Party System*, 96.

themselves by such strong affections to the French and the English that nothing will secure us internally but a divorce from both nations."[14]

Reaction to Adet's own farewell was surprisingly unanimous—both Federalist and Republican leaders disliked and feared it. Following so closely upon Washington's Farewell Address, it seemed a prime example of "the insidious wiles of foreign influence" against which the President had warned. Madison, who thought Adet had acted with great tact during the House debate over Jay's treaty, wrote Jefferson that

> Adet's note . . . is working all the evil with which it is pregnant. Those who rejoice at its indiscretions, and are taking advantage of them, have the impudence to pretend that [it] is an electioneering manoeuvre, and that the French Govt have been led to it by the opponents of the British Treaty. Unless the unhappy effect of it here, and cause of it in France, be speedily obviated by wise councils and healing measures, the crisis will unquestionably be perverted into a perpetual alienation of the two Countries by the secret enemies of both.[15]

Oliver Wolcott, on the other side of the political fence, was just as fearful. He sounded the alarm at once to Hamilton: "Measures to prevent any panic or depression of the public opinion are necessary." To his father, the governor of Connecticut, Wolcott confided doubts of the success of the Federalist ticket after "the publication of Mr. Adet's note . . . . If Mr. Jefferson is elected it will be owing entirely to the influence of this paper." Hamilton agreed that the situation was most serious and proceeded to take charge, as usual. First, he told Wolcott, he had not been pleased with the "hardness and epigrammatic sharpness" of Pickering's reply to Adet's previous note, and Pickering had been wrong in at least one particular. Then, because "I am very anxious that our government should do right in the present occasion," Hamilton proposed that an answer to Adet's valedictory be transmitted, not to Adet, since his functions were suspended, but

[14]C. F. M., 954; L & B, *Writings of Jefferson* IX, 405–406.
[15]*Writings of Madison* VI, 300–301; Dec. 5, 1796, U. S., Congress, *Letters and Other Writings of James Madison* (Philadelphia, 1865), II, 107.

through Pinckney to the Directory. To make sure Pickering's compostion had "steady resolution more than feeling," Hamilton added a complete outline of the proper form and content of the note. He had already suggested the same steps to Washington, and had included for the President's Message to Congress a paragraph which "contemplates a full future communication of our situation with France." Thereupon, Hamilton leaped into the dispute himself, writing a series of papers in answer to Adet for the *Minerva*, under the pseudonym "Americanus."[16]

About two weeks from the date of Hamilton's letter, Wolcott reported that the business was proceeding according to his plan. But Wolcott's own best energies, and those of most other political leaders, were devoted to the "plots and counterplots" of the presidential contest. Adams and Thomas Pinckney, for the Federalists, were generally the pawns, Hamilton doing his best to put in Pinckney over Adams, as likely to be more tractable, and New England standing fast by its man. Both Federalist groups, however, agreed with Wolcott: "the electon of Mr. Jefferson . . . [would be] fatal to our independence, now that the interference of a foreign nation in our affairs is no longer disguised." Fear of war, which only recently had saved the Jay Treaty for the Federalists, now was working for the Republicans. Many of the supposed "friends to the government" in Philadelphia, Wolcott reported angrily, had deserted the Federal Party on the grounds "THAT THE ELECTION OF MR. JEFFERSON WAS NECESSARY TO PREVENT A RUPTURE WITH FRANCE!!!"[17]

The ostensible villain of the piece kept himself aloof from the political jobbery, while trying to forestall those whom he felt were bent on war. As soon as the results of the election were known (with seventy-one votes Adams became president-elect,

[16]Wolcott to Hamilton, Nov. 17, to Wolcott, Sr., Nov. 19, 1796, *Oliver Wolcott* I, 395–96; Hamilton to Wolcott, Nov. 22, to Washington, Nov. 19, 1796, *Works of Hamilton* X, 209–13. The "Americanus" papers are in *Works of Hamilton* VI, 206–59. For Washington's dependence on Hamilton, and for Hamilton's lack of confidence in Pickering, see Kurtz, *Presidency of Adams*, 129, 271–72.

[17]Wolcott to Hamilton, Dec. 8, to Wolcott, Sr., Nov. 19 and 27, 1796, *Oliver Wolcott* I, 407, 397, 401. Manning J. Dauer deals in detail with election politics in *The Adams Federalists* (Baltimore, 1953), 92–112.

while Jefferson, with three less, won second place; Pinckney and Burr were out of the running with fifty-nine and thirty votes, respectively), Jefferson wrote his congratulations to his old friend, expressing the devout wish that "you may be able to shun for us this war by which our agriculture, commerce & credit will be destroyed." Because of certain expressions in the letter which he feared might worsen the present good relations between Adams and Jefferson, Madison, to whose approval Jefferson had submitted the letter, advised that it not be sent. The new Vice-President did congratulate Adams, but he advised Archibald Stuart against offering antiwar advice to Washington, whom he believed sincere in desiring to avoid war anyway. To other correspondents he tirelessly urged peace in the face of the hue and cry over foreign influence. "Those who have no wish but for the peace of their country, & its independence of all foreign influence," he told General Horatio Gates, "have a hard struggle indeed, overwhelmed by a cry as loud & imposing as if it were true, of being under French influence, & this raised by a faction composed of English subjects residing among us, or such as are English in all their relations & sentiments . . . ."[18]

In President Washington's Annual Message to Congress on December 7, 1796, all reference to France was omitted until the very end of the address when, after stating that American commerce was receiving extensive injuries under French maritime decrees, and that further dangers were expected, it was announced that a special message would subsequently be delivered on the subject. Meanwhile members not privy to the secret had been sittting on the edges of their seats. They were kept waiting, for the special message had not been presented by January 15, when Madison wrote Jefferson that he understood it would be "extremely voluminous"; but, from the moderate tone of the President's reply to the address of the House, he hoped it would

18Jefferson to Adams, Dec. 28, 1796, to Madison, Jan. 1, to Stuart, Jan. 4, to Gates, May 30, 1797, Ford, *Jefferson's Writings* VII, 95–97, 101–104, 130–31; Madison to Jefferson, Jan. 15, 1797, *Writings of Madison* VI, 302–305; Brant, *Madison: Father of Constitution*, 446–47. For the significance of Jefferson's unsent letter to Adams in Republican political strategy, see Kurtz, *Presidency of Adams*, 214–16.

be "calculated rather to heal than to irritate the wounded friendship of the two countries." But one of Madison's Federalist opponents who thought that "our country must get over its love sickness for France" ran much less chance of disappointment.[19]

The message on France was delivered to Congress on January 19, with a prefatory note by the President which was the only conciliatory part of it. Madison thought Pickering's report calculated to turn "the wounded friendship" of the two countries "into an incurable gangrene." The die was cast. "The British party since this overt patronage of their cause, no longer wear the mask .... A war with France & an alliance with G.B., enter both into print and conversation; and no doubt can be entertained that a push will be made to screw up the P. to that point before he quits the office." Madison had little confidence that Adams's succession would improve or alter the train of events, but Jefferson still hoped war could be avoided. Adams, he thought, would not "truckle to England as servilely as has been done .... If he assumes this front at once, and shews that he means to attend to self-respect & national dignity with both the nations, perhaps the depredations of both on our commerce may be amicably arrested." Jefferson, it should be noted, was far from the scene of these doings in the repose of Monticello.[20]

Pickering's counter-manifesto was transparent in purpose, as far as Adet was concerned. "You will see," he wrote to Paris on February 3,

that M. Pickering has not attacked a single one of the proofs by which I supported my case; he has not refuted one of my reasons; he has garbled the facts, has wandered off in vague discussions, and finally has replied to nothing .... It will be seen further-

[19]*Messages and Papers of the Presidents* I, 199–204, 209–10; *Writings of Madison* VI, 304–305; Chauncey Goodrich to Wolcott, Sr., Jan. 18, 1797, *Oliver Wolcott* I, 436–37.

[20]*ASP, FR* I, 559–76; Madison to Jefferson, Jan. 22, 1797, *Letters and Other Writings of James Madison* II, 114; Madison to Jefferson, Jan. 29, 1797, *Writings of Madison* VI, 307; Jefferson to Madison, Jan. 22, 1797, Ford, *Jefferson's Writings* VII, 107–10. For a favorable view of Pickering's note, see Bemis, "Washington's Farewell Address," 265–66, and Octavius Pickering and Charles W. Upham, *The Life of Timothy Pickering* 3 vols. (Boston, 1873), III, 359–64.

more that this response, full of bad faith and of sophisms, is the consequence of the plan long since formed by the Executive to break with us. Everything is calculated to irritate the French Government and Nation and to push them to hostile measures against the United States . . . .

In short, the Federalist government hoped to force France to declare war as a means of rallying all Americans to its party and to consummate the treaty of alliance with England "of which Jay's Treaty is only the introduction." But the Directory was too wise to fall into this trap: it knew that a rupture with the United States would deprive its colonies of provisions and perhaps subject them to invasion, that thirty thousand sailors would be added to the British marine, and that Louisiana and the Floridas would soon fall into American hands and probably Mexico into British. By limiting itself to measures already taken and assuming the attitude of awaiting explanations, France could foil the plans of the British faction. The American government would not dare declare war itself since that would lead to civil war. It would have no choice but to negotiate with France and to offer just reparations.[21]

Hamilton had already anticipated Adet. He told the President on January 22 that Pickering's letter was, "in the main, a substantial and satisfactory paper," which would, "in all probability, do considerable good in enlightening public opinion at home . . . ." But it lacked "that management of expression and *suaviter in modo* which a man more used to diplomatic communications could have given it, and which would have been happy if united with its other merits." This faint praise for Pickering was only a preface to the real matter. Hamilton wanted, as he had written Washington just three days earlier, "a solemn and final appeal to the justice and interest of France, and if this will not do, measures of self-defence." Expanding upon this idea, the

[21] C. F. M., 986–88. Pinckney never had the opportunity to deliver Pickering's note. Adet sent a translation of it to Paris on Jan. 23, 1797, but it did not arrive until the following Nov. 2. Another copy arrived sooner, since the foreign office had a synopsis of it dated Apr. 8, 1797, but little attention was paid to either one. AECPE-U, 47, 51–108vo, 233–36vo.

similarity of the present situation with that which prevailed when Jay was sent to England suggested at once an extraordinary mission, and he proposed that Madison and George Cabot be joined to Pinckney, already on the scene, to negotiate a new treaty. He thought Madison would have "the confidence of the French and of the opposition"; Pinckney would have it to a less degree, and Cabot, "without being able to prevent their doing what is right, will be a salutary check upon too much Gallicism, and his *real* commercial knowledge will supply their want of it." These commissioners might be safely entrusted with a revision of "the *political* and *commerical relations* of the two countries . . . ," but of course they would have to be restrained by precise instructions from doing anything inconsistent with the Jay Treaty.[22]

This was the plan adopted by President Adams three months later, but under altered circumstances. Washington in January had already withdrawn almost completely from public affairs, and Hamilton soon devoted his attentions to the friends of Adams. In the middle of March news arrived of the Directory's treatment of Pinckney, and some of Hamilton's hotheaded New England friends threatened to get out of hand in their enthusiasm for war. The party chieftain renewed his exertions, outlining to Pickering his previous plan, slightly revised. First, Hamilton thought it would be "politically useful" to "appoint a day of humiliation and prayer," and then Congress should be convened as soon as possible. The President should appoint "a commission extraordinary" (Madison, Cabot, and Pinckney, though Jefferson would do in place of Madison) and urge the adoption of "defensive measures"—an embargo against France, "additional revenue

---

22 *Works of Hamilton* X, 233–35, 229–30. Elbridge Gerry expressed to his friend the President-elect his concern that Pickering's manifesto was needlessly irritating to France, but he had deduced from internal evidence that it was Hamilton's work. Allusions by Gerry to other Hamiltonian intrigues, particularly the plot to put Thomas Pinckney into the presidency over Adams' head, caused Adams to reply that ". . . Pickering and all his colleagues are so much attached to me as I desire . . . . I have no jealousies from that quarter." Gerry to Adams, Feb. 3, Adams to Gerry, Feb. 13, 1797, *Works of Adams* VIII, 520–22, 522–25.

for additional expenses," the creation of a naval force and of a "provisional" army, and the arming of merchant vessels.[23]

The French government, meanwhile, awaited the first moves of the Adams administration. Delacroix was reminded in the fall of 1796 that the Directory intended to take no further action toward the United States until after official news of the election's results had been received. Although France then still expected Washington to be a candidate once more, the President's withdrawal had no influence upon that resolution, and the contest between Adams and Jefferson was followed closely by the Directory and the Department of Exterior Relations.[24]

French merchants, especially those interested in privateering, were not content to wait. One such company had addressed complaints to Delacroix in regard to the decree of July 2, 1796, which made American ships again subject to French seizure. Since American vessels were still exempted, regulations were needed to make the Americans feel the sting of French displeasure for their treachery. As a matter of fact, the situation resulting from the July decree required clarification, especially in the French colonies, where shipowners and captains followed their own interpretations until the government's commissioners, in both the Windward and the Leeward islands, decided to enact regulations of their own.[25]

For various reasons, therefore, the Directory issued a new decree on March 2, 1797. But since the new constitution reserved legislation to the Council of Five Hundred, the Directory

[23]Uriah Tracy to Wolcott, Sr., Jan. 24, 1797, *Oliver Wolcott* I, 439, 474–82; Hamilton to Sedgwick, Feb. 26, to Pickering, Mar. 22, 1797, *Works of Hamilton* X, 239–41, 243–46. The same program was urged simultaneously on Secretary of War McHenry. Mar. 22, 1797, *Works of Hamilton* X, 241–43.

[24]"Note for the Minister (Delacroix)," dated "brumaire, an 5" (Oct. 21–Nov. 20, 1796), "Notes on the United States," Jan. 14, 1797, AECPE-U, 46, 292–92vo, 47, 32–33vo. From information received up to the middle of January, a political analyst in his department predicted to Delacroix that the vote would be Adams, 65, Jefferson, 75.

[25]Tiesses Fils et Compagnie to Delacroix, Dec. 22, Decree of Commissioners of the Windward Islands, Dec. 24, Decree of the Commissioners of the Leeward Islands, Dec. 26, 1796, AECPE-U, 46, 489–89vo, 491–93, 495.

pointed in the decree's preamble to the provision decree of May 9, 1793, and the various laws which confirmed or expanded it, for the present decree's authority. This precedent was to assume importance not long after, when the Directory would find itself accused of usurpation of the prerogatives of the Five Hundred. Having thus established the legal position that these decrees required reiteration, the Directory proceeded to announce its own maritime policy in detail. ARTICLE I of the new decree warned the commissioners of the Directory in the ports to see that no judgment on prize cases contrary to the provision law of May 9, 1793, was rendered without prior consultation with the minister of justice. In other words, enemy property found on neutral ships was considered good prize.[26]

ARTICLE III explained that the treaty of 1778 with the United States had been modified by the American treaty with Great Britain of November 19, 1794, since the Franco-American treaty guaranteed complete reciprocity. Therefore, all enemy property found on American ships was to be confiscated, the ships themselves to be released at once. The list of contraband was extended to include all materials used in the arming or equipping of ships, unwrought iron and fir planks excepted, to correspond with ARTICLE XXIV of the Jay Treaty. And in conformity with ARTICLE XXI of that treaty, any American holding a commission from France's enemies, or serving on any enemy vessel, whether his service was obtained by force or otherwise, was to be treated as a pirate.

What followed next was to cause the most trouble and was apparently conceived with malice aforethought. Previous laws stipulating the procedure for ascertaining the ownership of property in neutral vessels were to be fully executed: "every American ship shall, therefore, be a good prize, which shall not have on board a list of the crew in proper form; such as is prescribed by the model annexed to the treaty of the 6th of February, 1778,

26This decree is in AECPE-U, 47, 143–44 and in *ASP, FR* II, 12 and 30. It was printed in *Le Redacteur* No. 447, Mar. 7, 1797.

the observance of which is required by the 25th and 27th articles of the same treaty." French maritime tribunals were ordered to deal severely with any American or other neutral vessel discovered practicing fraud by means of blank sea-papers, double passports, and the like.

The decree of March 2, 1797, thus was designed to inflict the greatest damage possible on American commerce without necessarily serving as a prelude to formal hostilities. It was what Louis André Pichon, former secretary of Fauchet's legation, who had returned on the *Medusa* one year earlier, had proposed: "An open war would reunite the parties [in America]. A little clandestine war, like England made on America for three years, would produce a constructive effect."[27]

The situation looked quite promising to Delacroix, when he wrote on April 1 to Adet. The minister's public declarations, according to his own account, had produced "almost the effect we wanted." That, and the reprisals ordered by the Directory, were responsible for a "new spirit of accommodation" in the American government. There was no longer any doubt that Adams was President, and "the system of his administration" would soon be clear. From Adams's known jealousy of Washington, continued Delacroix, and because of the caution which his narrow majority should have imposed upon him, "we should await a favorable event." He explained the decree of March 2, which was "a development of that of 14 Messidor (July 2, 1796)." The Directory would adhere to this policy "until the federal government furnishes sufficient motives for a change." Adet knew the position of the United States too well "to fear on their part any act of vigor which might have the character of hostilities"; he was to watch their activities closely, but "in no case suggest a means of lessening [our] present coldness." The American government would have to take the first steps toward a reconciliation.[28]

---

[27]"Notes on our position towards the United States and the measures to be adopted towards them," dated Vendémiaire, an 5 (Sept. 21–Oct. 20, 1796), AECPE-U, 46, 223–28.

[28]*Ibid.*, 47, 221–23.

Adams was preparing to do just what Delacroix expected, but that minister's stringent policy would shortly be under attack from within his own government, and his master in the Directory would be forced to sacrifice him before the arrival of a new American mission.

CHAPTER XII   Politics at Philadelphia
and Paris, 1797

> Our agents have only wanted to see in the United
> States two political parties, the French party and
> the English party. But there is a middle party
> much more numerous composed of the most es-
> timable men of the other two parties. This party
> ... is the American party which loves its country
> above all and for whom prejudices either for
> France or for England are only accessory and
> often passing affections.
>
> LOUIS-GUILLAUME OTTO, JUNE 1797.

PRESIDENT Adams's Inaugural Address, March 4, 1797, announced "an inflexible determination to maintain peace and in-
violable faith with all nations," as well as an intention of seeking
a solution of the dispute with France through amicable negotiation. The tone of the speech was highly gratifying to such moderate Federalists as Adams's old friend, Henry Knox, who wrote
to suggest that Jefferson go to Paris to negotiate a settlement.
According to Hamilton, however, some Federalists "lamented it
as temporizing."[1]

Adet was sufficiently heartened by the message to call and
reassure Adams on French designs in the American West, and
he reported to his government that Adams was friendly and
appeared to be honestly convinced by his explanations. The
President, Adet concluded, was sincerely desirous of reaching an

[1]*Messages and Papers of the Presidents* I, 231; Knox to Adams, Mar. 19, 1797,
*Works of Adams* VIII, 533–34, 533n. See Dauer, *Adams Federalists*, 114–21; *Presidency of Adams*, 224–27.

accommodation with France for the restoration of harmony and friendship.[2]

Hamilton's program for handling the French imbroglio probably first reached Adams through Fisher Ames, who called on the new President the day after his inauguration. As Adams remembered it long afterwards, the subject of a special envoy had already occupied his attention for some time, and he was considering several names, including that of George Cabot, whom Ames specifically recommended. The new President first called upon Jefferson, who agreed that someone should go to France but reinforced the President's own doubts of the propriety of sending the Vice-President. As Adams reported to Knox and to Gerry, Jefferson was also personally averse to a European journey. In that case, Adams had told Jefferson, he would join Gerry and Madison to Pinckney, who was awaiting instructions in Holland. These would form a commission "which by its dignity should satisfy France, and . . . all parts of the United States." Jefferson agreed to consult Madison.[3]

Madison likewise declined the mission, but before Jefferson could relay this information to the President, Adams had a conversation with Wolcott which effectually ended that part of the business. At the mention of Madison's name, Wolcott assumed an air of profound gloom and intimated that the entire cabinet would resign if the President should persist in his intention. Adams missed his best chance of maintaining peace abroad and harmony in his official household by not accepting Wolcott's offer. Wolcott opposed sending any mission at all right up to the end, despite some strong language from Hamilton, who warned

2Adet to Minister of Foreign Relations, Mar. 26, 1797, C. F. M., 1001.

3"Letters to the Boston Patriot," 1809, Adams to Knox, Mar. 30, to Gerry, Apr. 6, 1797, *Works of Adams* IX, 282–85, VIII, 535–36, 538–40; "Anas," Mar. 2, 1797, L & B, *Writings of Jefferson* I, 413–15. Apparently Hamilton's first suggestion of a special mission to France was in a letter to President Washington of Jan. 19, 1797. In reply, Washington noted that the idea had appeared "in some of the Gazettes, and in conversation also," and he asked Hamilton to elaborate. Hamilton then proposed that Madison, Pinckney, and Cabot constitute the mission. Hamilton to Washington, Jan. 19 and 22, 1797, *Works of Hamilton* X, 229–30, 233–35; Washington to Hamilton, Jan. 22, 1797, *Writings of Washington* XXXV, 372–73.

him that "a suspicion begins to dawn among the friends of the government that the *actual* administration is not averse from war with France." Hamilton feared "lest the *strength* of your feelings . . . should prevent that pliancy to circumstances which is sometimes indispensable," and advised Wolcott to "watch yourself on this score." Pickering likewise received a check from Hamilton and was cautioned "to avoid unofficial publications of official matter," because they were "fuel" for the charge that "the *actual* administration are endeavoring to provoke a war."[4]

Madison wrote to his father, shortly after the new President had taken office, that "the last accounts from Paris respecting negotiation for peace & the temper of France toward this country, are not favorable." He referred to the news of Pinckney's expulsion, which he attributed to "the British Treaty, which many of its zealous advocates begin now to acknowledge was an unwise & unfortunate measure." But Adams intended to try a new negotiation nevertheless, and he called an extra session of Congress to convene on May 15. Since he had adopted the system, as well as the cabinet, of his predecessor, he next addressed a list of questions on the administration's policy toward France to the members of his administration. The first question asked whether "a fresh mission to Paris" would be proper, but the remaining thirteen questions were all predicated on an affirmative assumption. They were designed to elicit opinions as to what powers, and what instructions, should be given the envoys, and as to whether the Senate should be consulted upon those subjects.[5]

In his answer, Wolcott labored hard to prove that no mission should be sent, then that no envoy friendly to France should be

[4]"Letters to the Boston Patriot," *Works of Adams* IX, 285–86; "Anas," Mar. 2, 1797, L & B, *Writings of Jefferson* I, 415; Hamilton to Wolcott, Mar. 30, Apr. 5, to Pickering, Apr. 1, Mar. 19, 1797, *Works of Hamilton* X, 248–49, 251–53, 250, 246–48. A Virginia representative, approached by Attorney General Charles Lee on the subject of General Marshall's acceptability, had suggested that Madison was preferable. "The answer was, 'Nobody of Mr. Madison's way of thinking will be appointed.'" Jefferson to Madison, June 1, 1797, Ford, *Jefferson's Writings* VII, 131–32.

[5]Mar. 12, 1797, *Writings of Madison* VI, 307–309; Mar. 25, 1797, *Messages and Papers of the Presidents* I, 232–33; To the Heads of Department, Apr. 14, 1797, *Works of Adams* VIII, 540–41.

included, and finally proposed conditions on the mission which would have doomed it to failure in short order. Pickering reluctantly approved the mission, because the country demanded it, but would concede nothing to French views. Attorney General Lee provided a strong contrast with the New England men in being decidedly in favor of a new negotiation and of equalizing the commercial footing of Britain and France. The Secretary of War from Maryland, James McHenry, sent Adams's questions at once to Hamilton for answer, and his own moderate reply, according to his biographer, "is interesting . . . as showing the measure of the secretary's reliance upon Hamilton." McHenry's loyalty to his idol was not tinctured with the uncompromising Francophobia of his New England colleagues.[6]

The President addressed the special session of Congress on May 16. After reviewing the history of the Pinckney mission, he referred to Barras' speech to Monroe, which disclosed, he said, "sentiments more alarming than the refusal of a minister, because more dangerous to our independence and union, and at the same time studiously marked with indignities toward the Government of the United States." Nevertheless, he continued, "I shall institute a fresh attempt at negotiation, and shall not fail to promote and accelerate an accommodation on terms compatible with the rights, duties, interests, and honor of the nation." But France had passed a decree on March 2 "contravening in part the treaty of amity and commerce of 1778, injurious to our lawful commerce and endangering the lives of our citizens." Therefore,

> While we are endeavoring to adjust all our differences with France by amicable negotiation, the progress of the war in Europe, the depredations on our commerce, the personal injuries to our citizens, and the general complexion of affairs render it my indispensable duty to recommend to your consideration effectual measures of defense.[7]

[6] *Works of Adams* VIII, 541–43n.; To the President, Apr. 25, 1797, *Oliver Wolcott* I, 502–17; Bernard C. Steiner, *Life and Correspondence of James McHenry* (Cleveland, 1907), 213–22; Pickering & Upham, *Pickering* III, 364.
[7] *Messages and Papers of the Presidents* I, 233–39.

The Federalist extremists did not dare work openly against the new mission to France while there seemed a prospect of a general peace resulting from Lord Malmesbury's negotiations with France at Lille, but information received from Europe before Congress convened indicated that the peace talks had collapsed. On the heels of this intelligence came news of the failure of the Bank of England, which caused the greatest alarm in financial circles and carried losses estimated at ten million dollars to merchants operating on British credit. Still, the British ministry had already been able to raise on its own terms the sums necessary for another year of war, and it probably could have had more for the asking. France's ineptitude at sea had caused a complete fiasco in the attempt of December 1796 to invade Ireland under the leadership of General Louis Lazare Hoche and the Irish nationalist, Theobald Wolfe Tone.[8]

Although the President knew vastly more of Europe's affairs than his secretary of state ever learned, such momentous intelligence strengthened his determination to show, as he wrote to his son at The Hague, that "America is not SCARED . . . ," a defiance which seemed to be borne out by the answers to the President of the two houses. Hamilton, while approving "the course of Executive conduct," was irritated at the "hard words" of the answer of the House of Representatives. Jay and others, he told Wolcott, agreed with him in wanting the answer toned down: "*Real firmness* is good for every thing . . . . *Strut* is good for nothing."[9]

Adamant in his determination to negotiate, Adams nominated three envoys to France on May 31, but his cabinet had succeeded in limiting the mission to reliable Federalists. John Marshall of Virginia and Chief Justice of Massachusetts Francis Dana were to join Pinckney. Although already approved by the Senate, Dana

[8]Uriah Tracy to Wolcott, Sr., Mar. 15, Rufus King to Wolcott, Mar. 6, 1797, Dec. 12, 1796, *Oliver Wolcott* I, 474–75, 524–25, 473–74; John Quincy Adams to John Adams, Dec. 30, 1796, Feb. 3, 1797, Worthington C. Ford, ed., *Writings of John Quincy Adams* 7 vols. (New York, 1913–17), II, 66–70, 101–106; Jefferson to Madison, June 1, 1797, Ford, *Jefferson's Writings* VII, 124–27.

[9]Mar. 31, 1797, *Works of Adams* VIII, 537; June 8, 1797, Ford, *Jefferson's Writings* VII, 138–39; June 7, 1797, *Works of Hamilton* X, 268.

declined, whereupon Adams sent in the name of Elbridge Gerry. The cabinet, which had already expressed itself unanimously against Gerry, was not consulted again, and Adams told his friend he would have appointed him in the first place, "if I had not been over-ruled by the opinions of many gentlemen . . . ."[10]

The reappointment of Pinckney was well received, although Adams himself had fleeting doubts of its wisdom. Marshall was generally respected, Adams told Gerry: "a plain man, very sensible, cautious, and learned in the law of nations." The President neglected to add, however, that Marshall had already earned the title of Virginia's most ardent Federalist by his vigorous defense of Jay's treaty. Marshall two years earlier had rejected Washington's offer of the attorney generalship but displayed his intense partisan sentiments by recommending in his stead the aging Patrick Henry because, as a friend explained it, "we are fully persuaded that a more deadly blow could not be given to the Faction [Republican Party] in Virginia, & perhaps elsewhere, than that Gentleman's acceptance . . . ."[11]

Gerry was distrusted by many Republicans because he had voted for his old friend Adams in the last election. Jefferson, however, was delighted with the appointment, feeling that Gerry shared his wish ". . . that there were an ocean of fire between us and the old world . . . that we could take our stand on a ground perfectly neutral & independent towards all nations." Gerry's inclusion, he said, ". . . gave me certain assurance that there would be a preponderance in the mission, sincerely disposed to be at peace with the Fr. govt & nation."[12]

10 *Messages and Papers of the Presidents* I, 245; Létombe to Delacroix, June 5, 1797, C. F. M., 1027; Adams to Gerry, June 20, 1797, *Works of Adams* VIII, 546. Adams wrote a few years later that he appointed Gerry "against the advice of all my ministers, to the furious provocation of Pickering, and against the advice of all the Senators whom he could influence." Quoted in *Oliver Wolcott* I, 471.

11 July 17, 1797, *Works of Adams* VIII, 549; Albert J. Beveridge, *Life of John Marshall* 4 vols. (Boston, 1916), II, 133, 125. Henry's conversion to federalism was explained to Washington by another Virginia Federalist, Edward Carrington, on Oct. 13, 1796: ". . . he is improving his fortune fast, which must additionally attach him to the existing government & order." Beveridge, *Marshall* II, 125–26.

12 Jefferson to Gerry, May 13, June 21, 1797, Ford, *Jefferson's Writings* VII, 121–23, 149.

The cause of Jefferson's optimism remains a mystery. Here was no mission with a preponderance sincerely disposed toward peace with France, as Adams's original choice of Madison, Gerry, and Pinckney would have been. Marshall, who was known to Americans in Paris as "one of the declaiming apostles of Jay's treaty," was motivated by a violently partisan hostility to Republicans both in his own country and in France. Before the American Revolution, Pinckney had been educated at Oxford and later at a French royal military academy, and his earlier rejection by the French tinged his orthodox Federalist antipathy toward Republican France with personal bitterness. Such considerations not surprisingly led the French government to suspect that the mission was really destined for the court of Louis XVIII rather than the Directory.[13]

Marshall and Gerry prepared to sail for Europe, while ominous portents multiplied on both sides of the Atlantic. The victories of Hoche and Jean Victor Moreau on the Rhine and of Bonaparte in Italy, the latter resulting in the preliminary peace of Loeben detaching Austria from the anti-French coalition, presaged a new arrogance on the part of the Directory. Although Lord Malmesbury was back at Lille, Jefferson reported to Madison the opinion of the French scholar C. F. Volney that "France will not make peace with England, because it is such an opportunity for sinking her as she never had & may not have again." A French invasion of England itself was to be attempted, and Jefferson had also heard that the Directory had asked the Council of Ancients for a declaration of war against the United States, which the Council had refused.[14]

The House of Representatives reacted to the events of Europe by trying to write instructions to the envoys into its answer to the President's message. A move to strike out a suggestion favor-

[13]Fulwar Skipwith to Jefferson, Mar. 17, 1798, *Oliver Wolcott* II, 160. This was one of several letters which their bearer turned over to Wolcott. See below, ch. 14, n. 7.

[14]Jefferson to Madison, June 15, to Aaron Burr, June 17, 1797, Ford, *Jefferson's Writings* VII, 142–44, 149.

ing the placing of France on an equal commercial footing with other nations (i.e., England) was defeated by one vote, a failure which led to an unsuccessful attempt to make compensation for spoliations a *sine qua non* of the negotiation. The Federalist extremists finally decided not to "force that nail but . . . leave more offensive measures to issue of negocn or their own next meeting . . . ." The House then concentrated on passing bills for completing the construction of three frigates, speeding the erection of coastal fortifications, and creating a provisional army.[15]

The author of the instructions to the three commissioners cannot be determined. The lack of "offensive expressions" and other internal evidence, according to one writer, points to the authorship of Marshall,[16] and the occasional practice of letting envoys draft their own instructions adds some support to his theory. Marshall's biographer, however, makes no such claim, but remarks that, "a circumstance which may or may not have been significant," Hamilton was in Philadelphia in early July.[17] Most likely, Marshall and Hamilton collaborated.

The instructions stipulated a revision of the treaties of 1778 to place France upon the same footing Britain enjoyed as a result of the Jay Treaty. Five *desiderata* were listed:

> 1. Conscious integrity authorizes the Government to insist, that no blame or censure be directly, or indirectly, imputed to the United States. But, on the other hand, however exceptionable in the view of our own Government, and in the eyes of an impartial world, may have been the conduct of France, yet she may be unwilling to acknowledge any aggressions, and we do not wish to wound her feelings, or to excite resentment. It will therefore be best to adopt, on this point, the principle of the British treaty, and "terminate our difference in such manner, as, without referring to the merits of our respective complaints and preten-

15Jefferson to Madison, June 1 and 8, 1797, *ibid.*, VII, 132, 140–41. Wolcott nevertheless lamented to Washington: "Congress will do but little this session; as the danger increases, a disposition to inaction appears, unfortunately, to prevail." June 15, 1797, *Oliver Wolcott* I, 547.

16Henry J. Ford, "Timothy Pickering," in Samuel F. Bemis, ed., *American Secretaries of State* II, 217.

17Beveridge, *Marshall* II, 218.

sions, may be the best calculated to produce mutual satisfaction and good understanding."

2. That no aid to France during the present war be stipulated.

3. That no engagement inconsistent with the obligations of any prior treaty be made.

4. That no restraint on our lawful commerce with any other nation be admitted.

5. That no stipulation be made, under color of which tribunals can be established within our jurisdiction, or personal privileges claimed by French citizens incompatible with the complete sovereignty and independence of the United States, in matters of policy, commerce, and government.[18]

The terms of the Adams administration for a reconciliation with France amounted to, in effect, the surrender of the privileges of the 1778 treaties and the acceptance of the priority of the Jay Treaty with England. Other than peace, however, with the continuance of whatever commerce could elude the British navy, the United States could offer nothing to a haughty and all-conquering France. Nevertheless, the implied offer to arbitrate spoliation claims, with the conciliatory tone of the instructions, might have provided a basis for negotiation, given a sincere desire for accommodation on the part of the commissioners. After all, Jay had carried no less explicit instructions to England, and he had experienced no great difficulty in overcoming them. But Jay in England was one thing; a mission to France dominated by Marshall would be another. Contrary to the original intent of President Adams, the stacking of the mission with a majority the French assumed to be hostile made that sincerity suspect.

While the High Federalists represented by Pickering and Wolcott appeared intent on conceding nothing to France, instead offering provocation, Hamilton insisted upon caution. In a memorandum he prepared for the use of William Smith in overcoming Federalist objections to sending the mission, he warned that it was absolutely necessary to avoid any idea among the American people that the Federalists were intent on war.

18 *ASP, FR* II, 153–57. The instructions are dated July 15, 1797.

"Hence it is all important to avoid war if we can—if we cannot to strengthen as much as possible the opinion that it proceeds from the Unreasonableness of France . . . ."[19]

Ideally, from Hamilton's point of view, France would acquiesce in the treaty with England and in the consequent loss of her advantages under the 1778 treaties with the United States. With apparent justice the Federalists would then claim that their foreign policy was correct and that Republican criticism stemmed from soft-headedness or a disloyal preference for France. The presence of Jefferson or Madison on the commission, in Hamilton's original scheme, would merely emphasize Federalist concern for peace and involve the Republican leadership in responsibility for Federalist foreign policy. Jefferson and Madison doubtless understood this: Jefferson would not have gone in any case, and Madison probably saw no possible benefit to the United States, to France, or to the Republican Party in lending himself to Federalist purposes. Madison never received a letter from Thomas Paine predicting his reception in France: "Individually as Mr. Madison you will be welcome; but as the French government now know that Mr. Monroe was sent with a lie in his mouth they will suspect that this is a second trick of the same kind . . . they will send you away."[20]

France, with her continental enemies crushed, rejecting peace overtures from England and preparing an invasion for the final conquest of that proud island, could hardly be expected to accept dictation from the United States. The commission appointed, then, was doomed to failure, as the High Federalist irreconcilables intended and as a more realistic Hamilton would have foreseen. But Hamilton's main concern, to throw the onus, if a rupture occurred, on French intractability, was vindicated in the end. When informed of the mission's result, he promptly

---

[19]Hamilton to William L. Smith, Apr. 10, 1797, quoted in Charles, *Origins of American Party System*, 125–26.

[20]Paine to Madison, Apr. 27, 1797, quoted in Brant, *Madison: Father of Constitution*, 450–51.

answered Pickering: "I have this moment received your two favors of the 25th. I am delighted with their contents . . . ."[21]

Marshall arrived at The Hague at the beginning of September 1797, his vessel having three times been boarded by British men-of-war. Adet had sailed for France more than two months before, after announcing through Swan that he expected no war and that all misunderstandings would be cleared away upon his arrival at Paris, if not before. He left a *mémoire* to serve as instructions for Létombe, the burden of which was that the federal government wanted war, but the Directory did not. Létombe's task, therefore, was to prevent a rupture. Adams, Adet believed, sincerely wanted peace, both because it was necessary to the prosperity of his country, and because of his enmity for Hamilton, who Adet said was the head of the war party. Also, Adet believed, Adams knew that by bringing about a reconciliation between France and America he would earn the confidence and gratitude of the country, which would "assure in his hands the exercise of a power of which he is jealous."[22]

Létombe, despite Adet's confidence, and especially after the President's message to the special session of Congress, disagreed with his departed chief. On the day that message was delivered, he wrote to Delacroix that Adams was the same uncompromising, suspicious, and stubborn man Comte Charles Gravier Vergennes had described in 1782. Jefferson, with whom Létombe had had a frank conversation, was still friendly, but his passive

[21]Hamilton to Pickering, Mar. 27, 1798, *Works of Hamilton* X, 280; Charles, *Origins of American Party System*, 126. Perhaps to restrain once more the impetuousness of his High Federalist friends, Hamilton quickly added: "I am against going immediately into alliance with Great Britain."

[22]Beveridge, *Marshall* II, 229; George Cabot to Wolcott, Apr. 22, 1797, *Oliver Wolcott* I, 496; Létombe to Minister of Foreign Relations, May 16 and 5, 1797, C. F. M., 1017, 1010–16. Marshall carried with him the commission and instructions of John Quincy Adams, who had been appointed by his father to Prussia instead of Lisbon, "where there will be little to do, that I can foresee, besides sleeping *siestas*." In the same letter, Adams reacted to Pickering's recent conduct: "I wish you to continue your practice of writing freely to me, and cautiously to the office of State." The President had already informed his son that William Vans Murray, "your old friend, with whom you formed your first acquaintance at the Hague," was to succeed him there. June 2, Mar. 31, 1797, *Works of Adams* VIII 545, 537.

role prevented him from influencing policy. Furthermore, Pinckney's rejection at Paris had alienated many friends of France in the Southern states. Jefferson insisted that Pinckney had been "attached to the interests of France for twenty years, and that he could have conciliated the differences." Victor Dupont, consul at Charleston, confirmed the fact that Southern members of Congress had turned against France, whose friends in the Eastern states were also disaffected, although principally because of the depredations on American commerce encouraged by French colonial administrators. England, Létombe concluded, "pushes the United States with all her strength to an open rupture with France."[23]

Two weeks later, Létombe returned to his theme: England was behind all the intrigues through which Americans were being manipulated into war. Adams was England's tool, and "I continue to see the President, whose face reflects the designs which his Secretary of State has the clumsiness to parade," as could be seen in Pickering's official letters. The correct policy for France, then, was "to stall, to temporize," to invade England (a project Jefferson repeatedly described as practicable) and reduce her to a second-rate power, and to contain the United States by seizing the Floridas, Louisiana, and Canada. Marking time was most important—the Directory should "imitate the wisdom of Fabius."[24]

These views were reinforced in part by an interview granted Létombe by Vice-President Jefferson on June 5. France, said

[23]Létombe to Minister of Foreign Relations, May 16, 1797, C. F. M., 1017-18. A British friend in Edinburgh wrote to Rufus King in Jan. 1797 that he was certain, "when I heard of the hostile menaces of the French Directory against your government," that his country would support the U. S. "It is too consonant to the common policy of European states to think it improbable, that they will endeavour to widen the breach betwixt America and France, to foment, if possible, into actual hostilities, their present differences." King Papers, New-York Historical Society. Grenville at the same time authorized Liston to offer "a naval Protection to the commerce of the United States against the attacks of the Common Enemy" in case of actual war. Jan. 27, 1797, I. B. M., 129.

[24]Létombe to Delacroix, May 30, 1797, C. F. M., 1024-25. Jefferson urged an invasion of England on France, through Létombe, as he wrote to Edmund Randolph, because "nothing can establish firmly the republican principles of our government but an establishment of them in England. France will be the apostle for this." June 24, 1797, L & B, Writings of Jefferson IX, 412.

Jefferson, could expect no good from Adams, who was "vain, suspicious, obstinate and of excessive conceit, taking advice from no one . . . ." But he would be President only five (*sic*) years: "The system of the United States will change with him." The present resentment occasioned by the great injuries of French cruisers, from the West Indies in particular, to American industry and navigation would not last long. The bonds uniting the two republics were relaxed but not broken: "It is up to France, great, generous, at the summit of her glory to equivocate, to be patient, to precipitate nothing and everything will return to normal." Jefferson thought that the Directory should receive the new envoys and hear them; it should "drag out . . . the negotiation and mollify them by the urbanity of its behavior." War would separate America and France forever, and the conjunction of British and American power would be enormously dangerous to France's position in Europe.[25]

This Jefferson-Létombe advice was seconded emphatically by Hauterive, the former consul under Genet, who had arranged a pseudonymous, secret correspondence with Adet. Recalling the calamitous consequences of the intercepted Fauchet letter, Hauterive told Adet that "I will have sent to the minister by indirect and obscure routes . . ." letters on American affairs. As good as his word, Hauterive sent voluminous reports to Paris during June and July, but the letters which followed the first, dated June 7, merely amplified ideas already expressed.

The French party, Hauterive announced, was temporarily crushed. Adams, despite his ineptitude, was sincere and very much wanted the commissioners to succeed in order to "add to his glory at home and diminish his unpopularity and that of his party." If the negotiation failed, added Hauterive prophetically, "it is hoped that dispatches, drafted according to the method of Malmesbury and of Pinckney, will strike a great blow at the popularity of the French cause, discrediting the chiefs of the minority, and creating a favorable atmosphere for the great work of

25Létombe to Delacroix, June 7, 1797, C. F. M., 1029-30.

the English alliance . . . ." The Directory could easily discover "these ambitious and criminal views."

> If the conduct and the offers of the negotiators do not satisfy France, the negotiation can be either broken off or neglected and postponed without danger, provided that by prudent forms the government give carefully pronounced regard to American public opinion, to the national pride, and to the influence of the party which cherishes the French alliance.

And even if the Directory intended to effect "a real and final reconciliation," the same rule should be observed. In either case, "the consequences will be as salutary as the practice of it is simple." Hauterive regarded war with the United States as unthinkable. He was aware of the High Federalist state of mind and agreed with Jefferson and Létombe on how to thwart it.[26]

Writing during the last half of June, Jefferson regarded it as obvious that the convocation of Congress had been decided with war in mind. The communications of the executive had been so incendiary that "nothing less than such miraculous events as have been pouring in on us from the first of our convening could have assuaged the fermentation produced in men's minds." The French successes and the British difficulties and, "above all, the warning voice, as is said, of Mr. King, to abandon all thought of connection with Great Britain, that she is going down irrecoverably, and will sink us also, if we do not clear ourselves, have brought over several to the pacific party, so as, at present, to give majorities against all threatening measures." By the end of June, Congress was rejecting one by one the measures loudly supported in May, and "what was the majority at first, is by degrees become

26 AECPE-U, 47, 340, 344–44vo, 393–97. This remarkable correspondence is treated at length in Frances S. Childs, "A Secret Agent's Advice on America, 1797," in Edward M. Earle, ed., *Nationalism and Internationalism* (New York, 1950), 18–44. Hauterive was called by his biographer "one of the most celebrated political consultants of the 18th century." E. Angot, "Talleyrand et le Comte d'Hauterive," *Revue des Questions Historiques* 93 (1913), 485. Talleyrand's estimate of Hauterive's worth is attested by the fact that he received, in the spring of 1798, 5,000 livres for "secret work in the United States." Guyot, *Le Directoire et la Paix de l'Europe*, 550n.

the minority, so that we may say that in the Representatives moderation will govern." Liston, the British minister, was disgusted, and Hauterive reported with characteristic scorn that, while a few weeks earlier, Congress had talked "like a nation of Hercules, they act today like a nation of pigmies."[27]

Pickering did what he could to stem the tide running against war measures. On June 22, the President transmitted the report on depredations on American commerce requested by the House of Representatives twelve days earlier. Before the House had asked for such a report, Pickering had thoughtfully begun culling news of seizures of American vessels by French cruisers from the *Gazette of the United States* and the *Philadelphia Gazette*, two newspapers notable for the intensity of their devotion to Federalism and of their hatred of "Jacobinism." This had been necessary, he explained, because "official papers to prove the very numerous depredations on our commerce, and the atrocities and abuses attending the capture and condemnation of our vessels and cargoes, by French cruisers and tribunals, not having been publicly called for, few have been received." There had probably been "a number of captures by Spanish cruisers" as well, but "captures and losses by British cruisers, the Secretary presumes have not been numerous . . . ." Pickering asserted that, although the list of French captures was not at all complete, "yet the number collected exceeds three hundred, of which but few escape condemnation." This, he explained, was because officers and seamen were bribed and threatened to swear falsely and thus provide the justification for condemnation: "but it was reserved to these times," Pickering concluded in a tone of horror, "when offered bribes were refused and threats despised, to endeavor to accomplish the object by TORTURE." He then repeated the celebrated story of Captain William Martin's thumb-screwing, quoting

27Jefferson to Madison, June 15 and 22, to Aaron Burr, June 17, to Edward Rutledge, June 24, to Edmund Randolph, June 27, 1797, L & B, *Writings of Jefferson* IX, 397–400, 407–408, 400–404, 408–11, 411–12; Liston to Grenville, June 26, Aug. 31, 1797, F. O. 5, 18; Hauterive to Adet, July 1, 1797, AECPE-U, 48, 3. See Col. John Trumbull to Wolcott, Apr. 9, Rufus King to Wolcott, Apr. 14, 1797, *Oliver Wolcott* I, 549–50, 550–51.

Rufus King to the effect that "the marks of the torturing screws will go with him to his grave." Pickering neglected to add, as King had been careful to do: "It is impossible that these barbarous outrages should be authorized; indeed, the concealment observed by the perpetrators of them, who refused to tell their names, or the port of their equipment, evince that they are not so."[28]

Fulwar Skipwith in Paris was kept busy carrying on a futile argument with Delacroix over the article of the March 2 decree requiring the *rôle d'équipage*. American ships brought into French ports were being condemned for the sole reason that they lacked it. Since there had been no period of grace granted for the procurement of a paper which American vessels had not been accustomed to carrying, capture was tantamount to condemnation. Although nominally in conformity with the treaty of 1778, Skipwith objected that the treaty itself nowhere mentioned that the simple roster of the crew and passengers had to be countersigned by a public official of the United States. Delacroix disagreed and quoted the treaty in answer, but his conclusion proved the real motive of the measure: ". . . it is notorious that almost all English commerce with the United States is carried on during the war under the American flag." Therefore, he continued, "we have no guarantee against this perfidious collusion but in the execution of our treaties." In answer, Skipwith repeated that the *"lettres de mer, ou passeports"* of the treaty could not be construed as the *"rôle d'équipage"* of the decree, and he repelled the charge of fraud with the explanation that English merchants required that their shipments be paid for and ownership transferred before the goods left England, so that the Americans would have to assume all shipping risks for their import as well as their export trade. Delacroix refused to continue the discussion and Merlin, the minister of justice, whom Skipwith addressed next, was no more responsive. Skipwith continued to present periodic

---

28King to Pickering, Apr. 12, 1797, *ASP, FR* II, 28–29, 64. Despite Pickering's attempt to exonerate Britain, he had long been complaining vigorously to Liston against British impressment of Americans. By August this practice, Pickering told Liston, ". . . *is past enduring.*" Liston to Grenville, May 12, Aug. 30, 1797, F. O. 5, 18.

complaints to Delacroix, but by the middle of June he reported that more than twenty-five American vessels had been seized in the past three months.[29]

The Directory was sure that, despite the severity of its retaliatory measures, the United States would not declare war. One of those who was beginning to think that France was going too far toward driving America into the arms of England was Ducher, the author of the protectionist policy signalized by the provision decree of May 9, 1793. Ducher wanted the decrees of February and March 1793, which granted full freedom of navigation among France's colonies to American ships, restored; and he thought it wrong to use the reciprocity clause of the treaty of 1778 as the basis for reprisals. The Jay Treaty itself was sufficient grounds for retaliation, he claimed, because it violated American neutrality; but he much preferred a policy of wooing the United States away from England by commercial privileges and the offer of England's American possessions.[30]

Asked by the Directory to comment, Delacroix belittled Ducher's fears. Ducher feared most a war with the United States, said Delacroix, but, "for us who have demonstrated the futility of his fear," the resolution of the problem lay in present policy. America had to be "circumspect," he continued, both because of England's precarious military situation and because of "her interior situation." Eventually the United States would realize that it was France's natural ally, and Ducher's wish for an intimate alliance would come true.

[29]Delacroix to Skipwith, Mar. 9, Skipwith to Delacroix, Mar. 13, Skipwith to Minister of Justice, Apr. 4, Minister of Justice to Skipwith, Apr. 23 (published in *Le Redacteur* of May 6), Skipwith to Delacroix, June 15, 1797, AECPE-U, 47, 149–50vo, 169–71, 230–30vo, 275–75vo, 375–75vo. The merits of this dispute were of scant practical importance. Skipwith had more of the right on his side, but Delacroix had little difficulty in twisting the ambiguous wording of the treaty to suit his purpose. The "Form of the Passports and Letters, etc." attached to the treaty stated that "the Marine Ordinances and regulations" were to be kept on board ship, but that the master should also "enter in the proper Office a List signed and witnessed containing the Names and Sirnames ... of the Crew of his ship ...." *Treaties and Other International Acts of the United States* II, 23–24, 28–29.

[30]"Observations on some proposals of Ducher," from the Directory to Delacroix, dated Apr. 19, 1797, AECPE-U, 47, 247–53.

THE STRUGGLE FOR NEUTRALITY

Delacroix's self-confidence was undisturbed when he wrote to Létombe on June 15. According to Adet's last letters before his departure, the Directory's actions had aroused a ferment in the United States. Delacroix knew that France's enemies would try constantly to increase it, but he had no doubt "that Adams and Jefferson oppose a vigorous resistance to these plots, and that they appreciate perfectly their aim."

The results of the special session of Congress were expected momentarily; Delacroix hoped that these results would be "as the principles binding the two nations, and the essential interest of the Americans would desire." Létombe could assure Adams that the Directory entertained the most flattering hopes from his promotion to the presidency, "and that it expects from him a conduct which may realize them." Adams was too intelligent not to know that "the United States cannot, without danger, isolate themselves thus from France for long, and that a rupture would be, for America, the signal for the most grievous events." The motives of those who sought to carry matters to extremes could be appreciated for what they were, and the Directory, for its part, rejected every thought of breaking relations with the United States. The measures it had been forced to take "will cease as soon as the government, by sending a man who can inspire confidence, will have given guarantees of a change of system," and it was ready to give in return "unequivocal marks of good will." Létombe knew, said Delacroix, saving till last the reason for his optimism, that England had just reopened peace negotiations under circumstances which presaged a greater chance of success than before.[31]

Adet did not share Delacroix's complacency. He wrote on June 16 from Le Havre, where he had just arrived after a thirty-five day passage, that despite ill health he was hurrying to Paris to report on conditions in America. Delacroix had just received Adet's dispatch of March 21, which recounted the outburst of resentment in the United States against the "arbitrary and tyrannical manner" in which the colonial agents were executing the

31*Ibid.*, 47, 383–84.

"badly interpreted decree of the Directory." This was serious, said Adet, because that conduct, especially the mistreatment of American seamen, had antagonized "that part of the people which was devoted to us." Now alarmed, Delacroix sent Adet's letter to the minister of marine, asking him to investigate and regulate the conduct of the colonial commissaries, and he also requested that the Directory take the "direct measures it might think suitable." But then, on June 20, a battle against the Directory's provocative policy opened in the Council of the Five Hundred and led to another political convulsion and the coup d'état of 18 Fructidor (September 4, 1797).[32]

It is to this domestic contest that Otto's remarkable essay, "Considérations sur la Conduite du Gouvernement des États Unis envers la France, depuis 1789 jusqu'en 1797," belongs. The paper is endorsed "Messidor an 5"; but from its position in the archives it must have been presented on June 1, 1797. The fact that it contained carefully blunted but nonetheless telling jabs at Delacroix and at the Directory indicates Otto's correspondence with the moderate, conservative party led by his old colleague in America, François Barbé-Marbois; by Claude E. J. P. Pastoret; and others of the old lesser nobility. Indeed, Otto's whole life and career would now have dictated his allegiance to the anti-directorial party in any case.[33]

Otto began with the declaration that "I will speak the cold language of Reason, convinced that my readers will prefer this language to that mistaken eloquence, which since the beginning of the Revolution has misrepresented and distorted the most palpable truths." He condemned successive ministers to the United States vigorously, with the exception of Ternant, whose recall in 1792, despite his relative inertia, "must be considered as a calamity," and La Luzerne, who with Barbé-Marbois had

[32] Adet to Delacroix, June 16, Delacroix to Minister of Marine, June 17, Delacroix to Directory, June 19, 1797, *ibid.*, 47, 381, 386, 399–400; Adet to Minister of Foreign Relations, Mar. 21, 1797, C. F. M., 999.

[33] Otto's "Considérations" is in AECPE-U, 47, 401–18vo. Gilbert Chinard's edition is taken from Otto's personal papers and contains in italics part of the work omitted in the final draft.

won American affection for France. Moustier was a supercilious aristocrat who hated Americans and their government for not according him the deference he believed his due, and he left behind him profound prejudices against the French government.

Genet, Fauchet, and Adet were all upstarts, whose ignorance and lack of understanding of America were primarily responsible for the present desperate state of Franco-American relations; Genet was the worst because he was the ablest and most energetic of the three. It was "the absurd and arrogant pretensions of these agents, of a nation that Monroe never ceased to represent as sincerely attached to America," that finally caused Washington to recall Monroe. Through the influence of the worst of the lieutenants of these agents, Mangourit and Le Blanc, Delacroix persisted in their error. How, asked Otto, could the French government always assume that most of the American people were devoted to France and only the government was sympathetic toward England, in a country which had the freest elections in the world? The cardinal error was always the assumption that the American government did not represent the American people. The truth could be easily read in the long dispatch of Jefferson, "always considered as the friend of France," demanding the recall of Genet. Otto continued:

> Our agents have only wanted to see in the United States two political parties, the French party and the English party. But there is a middle party much more numerous composed of the most estimable men of the two other parties. This party, whose existence we had not even suspected, is the American party which loves its country above all and for whom prejudices either for France or for England are only accessory and often passing affections. It is in this party that the people repeatedly choose their Representatives and their Magistrates, fully convinced that patriotism will triumph over every foreign political opinion.

Otto denounced as "UNJUST AND IMPOLITIC" the Directory's harsh policy toward the United States. Now that the American government was sending another embassy to resolve the differences between the two countries—"a new proof of its invariable desire to maintain a good understanding with the French Republic"—the mistake of the Pinckney dismissal must not be repeated. "Let us throw away fatal preconceptions," concluded Otto; "let us believe that two nations equally interested in resisting the usurpations of Great Britain will reunite for their common good, will make a commerce founded on reciprocal needs flourish and will give to Europe the impressive spectacle of a durable friendship recently cemented by the adoption of political and social institutions similar to those of the United States."

It is doubtful that Delacroix gave much attention to Otto's advice, although certainly his successor, Talleyrand, did. Delacroix was too busy parrying the thrusts against his masters in the domestic political arena. That struggle had become acute because of the moderate and royalist—that is to say, anti-Jacobin—victory in the spring of 1797, in the first elections under the constitution of the year III. One-third of the Council of Five Hundred was replaced; and one of the Directors was replaced by the election of François Barthélemy, a former noble who had spent the entire period of the Revolution outside France on diplomatic missions. Barthélemy at once became the favorite director of the majority in the legislative bodies. He was soon joined by Carnot, whose insistence on consolidating a revolution he regarded as completed naturally placed him in opposition to the militant La Revellière-lépeaux and to Reubell, the one real Jacobin of the Directory.[34]

[34]Georges Lefebvre, *The Directory* (New York, 1967), 91–105; Albert Soboul, *La Ire République* (Paris, 1968), 225–50; Crane Brinton, *The Lives of Talleyrand* (New York, 1936), 99. See also G. Pariset, *La Révolution, 1792–1799* (Paris, 1920), 335–50, and G. Lefebvre, R. Guyot, and P. Sagnac, *La Révolution Française* 2d ed. (Paris, 1938), Bk. III, ch. 3. M. Pariset's chapter title, "Échec de la Conspiration Anglo-Royaliste," indicates his view of the subject. Guyot concurs, and his *Le Directoire et la Paix de l'Europe,* 431ff. uncovers diplomatic intrigues which support that view. Albert Sorel, *L'Europe et la Révolution Française* (Paris, 1903), V, 170–225, however, sees the conflict as one between a "peace" faction—"the former boundaries"—and a "war" faction—"the natural boundaries." President Adams related to Pickering in Oct. 1797 that his youngest son, Thomas Boylston Adams, was in Paris at the time of the drawing for the retiring director. "Instead of being ordered out of France, as our Jacobinic papers boasted," young Adams had been invited to dine with Carnot, "by whom he was civilly treated, and urged to endeavor to reconcile the two countries." The visitor was then invited to attend the ceremony which determined Le Tourneur's retirement from the Directory. *Works of Adams* VIII, 557.

Whatever may be said concerning the European aims of the Directory's majority, particularly in relation to peace with England, the government's aggressive policy toward the United States provided the opposition with a convenient club with which to belabor Reubell and Company. Pastoret delivered the indictment before the Five Hundred on June 20, in a speech entitled "On the present state of our political and commercial relations with the United States of North America." He began by attacking the Directory for issuing "decrees which make real aggressions" against the United States, without obtaining the sanction of the legislative body. Those constituted, he asserted, usurpation of the latter's constitutional prerogative on questions of war and peace, to say nothing of the executive's assumption of legislative functions.[35]

Pastoret then proceeded to a consideration of the treaty of 1778 and the new provision decree of March 2, 1797. That decree could not pretend to be in execution of the provision law of May 9, 1793, he pointed out, because that law had been repealed twice and re-enacted once in the same year. As for the 1797 decree itself, the "barbarism" of the piracy clause was entirely unjustified, and the *rôle d'équipage* requirement was based on an error: the treaty did not specify such a paper except as a basis for issuing a passport, and such a thing had never been demanded of Americans before.

But Pastoret approved "fierce jealousy" in government for the interests of France, and he agreed that the American government deserved the resentment of France for treating with the old enemy without consulting its ancient ally. "However, let us also remember: France no longer had a marine which could protect the commerce of the United States; the English dominated all the oceans; anarchy was devouring our unhappy country at the time of the treaty, and the Americans still did not know that 9 Thermidor had at last dethroned crime." The United States had been sorely tried by the inexcusable conduct of Genet and Fauchet, and France was now out-doing Britain in "maritime ruthless-

35 AECPE-U, 47, 419–31VO.

ness." The Americans had violated propriety and friendship, but they had usurped no right nor broken any engagement. In making the Jay Treaty, they exercised "the universal prerogative of nations, of contracting when and as they wish." "Are we then the sovereigns of the world?" demanded Pastoret. "Are then our allies only our subjects?"

One of the targets of the anti-Jacobin alliance was Merlin, whom Pastoret attacked for his published reply to Skipwith in defense of the 1797 decree. The Directory itself came in for abuse because of its rude treatment of Pinckney, whom Pastoret called "a firm and profound friend of peace and of France." The Directory's agents in the Leeward Islands received the severest castigation: they had armed eighty-seven cruisers on their own responsibility to prey on American commerce, and in three months they had brought their administration from bankruptcy to solvency and made favored individuals wealthy. They had no decree for excuse, and they defended their acts by vilifying the United States. This was, according to Pastoret, "brigandage justified by egoism and calumny," and was boasted of in an incredible letter— it "makes one think he is dreaming"—to the minister of marine.

The Directory, insisted Pastoret, was serving England by antagonizing the United States. Instead, France should accept the United States as being allied to both belligerents! In between, they would necessarily be neutral and France would benefit from "their great facilities for navigation and commerce." Peace not only with America, but universal peace was what France wanted. Pastoret wanted all the Directory's American decrees turned over to a committee to decide what should be done about the Directory's violation of the constitution. In the meantime, the Directory should submit a report on relations with the United States, and a committee should be set up to study a new organic law.[36]

This aspect of the quarrel was of concern to French merchants, and they were quick to make themselves heard. A shipowner of St. Malo wrote to Delacroix defending the 1797 decree against

[36]Lefebvre, *Directory*, 91, suggests that Pastoret used the U. S. as a stalking horse for England.

Pastoret's denunciation, complaining at the same time that the tribunal at Le Havre refused to condemn an American ship he had seized under that decree. The "Merchants, Ship-owners and Sailors" of the commune of Nantes sent a memorial to the Five Hundred supporting Pastoret's plea for a general peace, but disagreed with him on the 1797 decree, of which they approved. "Pacific negotiations . . . have just opened," they remarked, and they wanted the Five Hundred to avoid a rupture with the United States, and "to fix in a positive manner the political and commercial relations which exist between France and the United States." Delacroix sent another memorial, which had already appeared in an opposition newspaper, to the Directory. The 1797 decree, it charged, was an infraction of treaties, a virtual declaration of war; and furthermore it was unjust, impolitic, and unconstitutional. The writer, Delacroix said, did not know what he was talking about. But at the end of a long analysis of the public objections of other critics, including Skipwith, Delacroix suggested: "If political considerations and some other motives can make the executive Directory fear that its decree of 12 Ventose last has some dangerous consequences," the proper procedure would be to propose that the legislative body amend it.[37]

Three days after Pastoret's act of defiance, the Rightists began an oratorical attack against the Directory's most successful Jacobin general, Bonaparte. Next came a demand for the dismissal of the Jacobin ministers, among them Delacroix. Barras, who without principle was always ready to sacrifice whatever was necessary for his personal security, shifted with the wind to the side of the Jacobin directors and their popular generals. But Barras detested Delacroix, whom he thought "too ultra-republican and too submissive to Reubell," and he exacted his replacement

[37]Thomas the elder of St. Malo to Delacroix, June 28, 1797, Memorial of Merchants, Shipowners and Sailors of the Commune of Nantes to the Council of the Five Hundred, undated, Report to Directory, unsigned and undated, Report to Directory by Delacroix on complaints against the 1797 decree, undated, AECPE-U, 47, 474–75vo, 440–44, 456–58, 448–55. The St. Malo correspondent gained his end by methods reminiscent of the intrigues which followed the decree of May 9, 1793. On appeal from the tribunal of Le Havre, the civil court of the Department of Seine Inférieure reversed the previous decision. *Ibid.*, 48, 165, 166–69vo.

by Talleyrand as the price of his loyalty. The "triumvirs" then replaced the moderate ministers with Jacobins, retaining Merlin and Dominique Vincent Ramel-Nogaret, the two ministers most hated by the Five Hundred's majority. The coup d'état of 18 Fructidor resulted in the complete victory of the directorial party. Carnot and Barthélemy were expelled from the Directory, and Pastoret had precipitated the destruction of his own party.[38]

One of Delacroix's last services to the Directory was the composition of a paper defending it against the charges of Pastoret. "It is at the time," he said, "when the executive Directory has just sent assurances to the new President of the United States, that it will avoid with the greatest care anything which could bring about a rupture between the two nations, that it is accused of violating treaties and the laws." He defended the 1797 decree, insisting that it was not that which had caused the coldness between the two nations but the grievances against the American government which had accumulated during three years of useless representations, and the Jay Treaty, "which destroys the effect of our treaty of 1778, and violates the neutrality of the Americans." If, however, the legislative body found the laws enforced by the Directory too severe, it could repeal them, but they would be executed until that was done.[39]

The day following this report, Delacroix communicated to the Directory the latest news from America. Discontent at Pinckney's treatment, he noted, and the Directory's farewell to Monroe, had brought about an almost even balance in Congress between the friends and enemies of France. But sentiment for peaceful negotiation had prevailed. France had even received in advance the bases of the American commission's instructions, in the congressional resolutions to put France on the same footing with England and to demand indemnities for infractions against the

[38]Lefebvre, Guyot, and Sagnac, La Révolution Française, 355. An anti-Jacobin bias is evident in the belittlement of Delacroix's abilities by Masson, Le Département des Affaires Étrangères, 390–93. Carnot, Mémoires sur Carnot II, 144, thought Delacroix inadequate, but Guyot, Le Directoire et la Paix de l'Europe, 68–70, emphatically disagrees.
[39]June 25, 1797, AECPE-U, 47, 445–47.

rights of the United States as a neutral nation. The first would produce the complete annihilation of American commerce, which could only mean, Delacroix thought, that the United States intended to try to get England to recognize the "free ships, free goods" principle. If the same wording was used by the commissioners as in the second resolution, it could not embarrass the government: there would be a thousand ways to quibble over the meaning of the "rights of the United States as a neutral nation," and the Directory's moderation would determine how valuable those were.[40]

Delacroix thought the situation serious nevertheless. Information from various sources that England was preparing an invasion of Louisiana from Canada prompted him to urge the Directory to alert Spain, and to "activate our negotiations for the retrocession of Louisiana, in progress for two years," because General Victor Collot's military survey proved that Spain could not hold it. It would be natural for the British to try to use the Mississippi River for the invasion. Delacroix, suspicious of secret cooperation between England and the American government, instructed Létombe to tell Adams of France's pleasure that the United States had not yielded its interests by letting British forces cross its soil to invade Louisiana. By the middle of July, in his last week in office, Delacroix received Adams's message to Congress. Despite Adams's tone and that of the House of Representatives, he told Létombe, he still hoped that the President did not want "to come to extremes." The situation demanded prompt information, however, and Hauterive should be able to keep on intimate terms with representatives friendly to France, without compromising them. But the Directory's concern with America was best illustrated by the fact that Adet was summoned to an audience with the Directory immediately upon his arrival in Paris on June 28. Even if the Directory had been intent on war with the United States, which it was not, such a war begin-

---

[40]June 26, 1797, *ibid.*, 47, 459–60. Madison agreed that putting France on the same maritime footing as England would mean the destruction of American commerce. Brant, *Madison: Father of Constitution*, 455.

ning by miscalculation would be disastrous to the Directory, and would probably ensure the crushing of the executive arm of the government by the Five Hundred and the Ancients.[41]

[41]"Note for the Directory," June 26, Delacroix to Létombe, July 3 and 13, 1797, AECPE-U, 47, 461–63, 48, 10–11vo, 41–42. Adet had sent General Collot on a secret mission to Louisiana in 1796. See Durand Echeverria, "General Collot's Plan for a Reconnaissance of the Ohio and Mississippi Valleys, 1796," *W & M Quarterly*, 3d ser., IX (Oct. 1952), 512–20, and George W. Kyte, "A Spy on the Western Waters: The Military Intelligence Mission of General Collot in 1796," *Mississippi Valley Historical Review* XXXIV (Dec. 1947), 427–42.

## CHAPTER XIII

"The X. Y. Z. Dish"

> The Americans, who, since their treaty of alliance and commerce with Great Britain, make amends every day for the crime of having vanquished liberty.
>
> RIOU IN COUNCIL OF FIVE HUNDRED, SEPTEMBER 15, 1797.

> The question of war & peace depends now on a toss of cross & pile.
>
> JEFFERSON TO MADISON, MARCH 29, 1798.

CHARLES Maurice de Talleyrand-Périgord, who assumed the portfolio of exterior relations on July 18, 1797, was an ex-noble and a former bishop, and on those two counts was heartily despised by the Jacobin directors.[1] They distrusted him also because, like Gouverneur Morris, who had once shared Talleyrand's mistress, he was a citizen of that international community of finance which Professor Nussbaum called "the Sixth Great Power," and because of his lurid reputation in both private and public affairs; but they were obliged to accept him for the sake of Barras' support. He had only recently returned from America, where he had been lionized by "the most respectable and liberal of our society" under the patronage of Rufus King, Hamilton, and others. When his appointment became known in America, Oliver Wolcott foresaw difficulties for the lately departed envoys from Talleyrand's supposed vindictiveness at not

---

[1] Barras years later made much of his mistaken agency in securing Talleyrand's appointment. George Duruy, ed., *Memoirs of Barras* (London, 1895) II, ch. 30.

being received by President Washington. Adams thought him too reasonable for that, because "he received a great deal of cordial hospitality in this country, and had not the smallest reason to complain . . . ." Although the Republicans must have had reservations concerning Talleyrand, Skipwith wrote on July 20 to congratulate the new minister. He hoped, he told Talleyrand, that the new envoys could fulfill their mission "with the more facility, that no one can appreciate better than you the true dispositions of the government and people of the United States, and their attachment to the French Republic."[2]

Talleyrand unquestionably regarded a reconciliation with the United States as an immediate necessity, and his zeal in preparing the ground for it led him almost at once to challenge Reubell. Delacroix had earlier recommended that Isaac Barnet, of New Jersey, whom President Washington had appointed consul of the United States at Brest, be granted his exequatur, but Reubell vetoed the proposal. Talleyrand resurrected the matter and easily refuted Reubell's objections in a report to the Directory at the end of July. But Reubell held firm, despite Talleyrand's continued needling.[3]

In a letter to Létombe early in August, Talleyrand wrote that he had nothing to add to Delacroix's instructions. He was disturbed by the "sharpness" of the latest gazettes from America and feared that "thoughts of a rupture are cherished by certain persons as a means of bringing the United States and England much closer together." The Directory, he assured Létombe, would do nothing to further such schemes: "If . . . the American commissioners come furnished with powers which permit them

[2]Lefebvre, Guyot, and Sagnac, *La Révolution Française*, 355; Huth and Pugh, trans. and eds., "Talleyrand in America as a Financial Promoter, 1794-1796," v; King to John Langdon, July 13, Christopher Gore to King, Aug. 5, 1794, King, *Life and Correspondence* I, 569, 571. The phrase is Gore's. Wolcott to the President, Oct. 24, 1797, *Oliver Wolcott* I, 571; Adams to Wolcott, Oct. 27, 1797, *Works of Adams* VIII, 558-59; AECPE-U, 48, 117-17vo. Talleyrand was disliked by all the Directors, including Barras, who nevertheless hoped to use him. Carnot considered him depraved and "too obsequious." *Mémoires sur Carnot* II, 116-17.

[3]Talleyrand to the Directory, July 29, "Note," Aug. 10, 1797, AECPE-U, 48, 137-38, 162-64.

to negotiate on bases suitable to the dignity of the Republic and to its interest, the differences will soon be terminated." He was "not a little astonished," however, at the idea in Adams's Message to Congress that France wanted "an unlimited ascendancy in America." Létombe could dispel this misconception in interviews with Adams, "whom I believe more disposed to appreciate [our views] than Mr. Pickering; the published letter of the latter to Mr. Pinckney proves to us, either that he lets himself be influenced by men who shrink at nothing to gratify their hatred towards us, or else that he is himself carried away by an enmity no less blind." "Such sentiments," he concluded, "are scarcely proper to reassure us on the sincerity of the negotiations which are about to begin."[4]

On April 8, 1797, the Directory had decreed that American passports would no longer be recognized in France. Mountflorence, the only American diplomatic representative in Paris since the departure of Monroe and then Pinckney, was afraid that this would prevent the new American mission from being admitted into the country. He explained his concern to Talleyrand, who at once issued instructions to all the ports of France ordering that the Americans be spared any hindrance. Talleyrand told Létombe that, "although Mr. Adams, in appointing Mr. Pinckney again, has not given a great proof of a spirit of conciliation, we will do all in our power, when the commissioners arrive to make perfectly clear our pacific intentions." As far as Pinckney was concerned, his previous rejection had not been on his personal account, "and the incident can be repaired." It was "truly unfortunate," however, that it had annoyed the Southern states: the French government had only wanted "to show the American government our discontent in dramatic fashion."[5]

---

4Aug. 4, 1797, *ibid.*, 48, 152–53. One month later, Talleyrand frankly did not know what to think of Pickering's manner and suggested to Létombe that "he would not take so high a tone if Great Britain were not making many advances and promises." Sept. 1, 1797, *ibid.*, 48, 215vo. Later still, he thought Pickering's conduct made "inconceivable Mr. Adams' obstinacy in keeping him in his position." To Dupont, Nov. 15, 1797, *ibid.*, 48, 360–62vo.

5July 29, 31, Sept. 1, 1797, *ibid.*, 48, 139, 140, 214–15vo.

While the domestic political situation grew more tense as the inevitable showdown between the respective majorities of the councils and of the Directory neared, Talleyrand had a mass of American news to ponder. American vessels were being stopped on the high seas by the English and told that their government had declared war on France; and the minister of marine thought there was something suspicious in a group of American ships awaiting convoy at Malaga, on Spain's southern coast near British Gibraltar. Boston papers in August were busy spreading rumors that Frenchmen were being sent from San Domingo to burn American towns, while George Rogers Clark wrote that war, "due to the machinations of the English faction," was inevitable, and offered his services to the Directory. The internal contests on both sides of the Atlantic were fused when Bache printed in his *Aurora* a pamphlet by Fauchet returning Pastoret's attack and accusing Pastoret of intentionally putting the Directory at a disadvantage on the eve of negotiations with the United States. Fauchet had claimed that royalists in France and America were acting in concert, and Bache agreed "that Messrs. Pickering & Co. carry on the same intrigues in other countries, for which they so vehemently blame (without any proofs) the French agents here." In an ingratiating letter to Talleyrand, Fauchet stated that his opinion that America was on the way to becoming a British colony again had gained him the hatred of the English faction, but he concluded with a plea that both countries forget past animosities and restore harmony for their mutual benefit.[6]

[6]Extract from the journal of the *Ontram* of June 8, enclosed in Minister of Marine to Talleyrand, Aug. 4, Extract from Boston newspaper of Aug. 31, Clark to Samuel Fulton, June 3, Fauchet, "Sketch of the Present State of the Political Relations with the United States of North America," Sept. 1, 1797, *ibid.*, 48, 147, 146, 254-55, 131-31vo, 216-31. Though Clark probably never knew it, Consul General Bond had suggested employing him for a British attack on Spanish Louisiana and had even drawn up a report on the Spanish defenses. Bond to Grenville, Jan. 2, May 3, 1796, F. O. 5, 13. Liston later burned his fingers by being implicated in the so-called Blount conspiracy to seize Florida. Liston to Grenville, Jan. 2 and 5, Feb. 13, Mar. 16, May 10, June 24, July 8 and 12, 1797, Liston to Hammond (Private), Mar. 16, 1797. Most of these letters are in Frederick J. Turner, ed., "Documents on the Blount Conspiracy, 1795-1797," *American Historical Review* X (Apr. 1905), 574-606.

Talleyrand asked Adet for a report on his mission as a matter of course, but before Adet could answer, the convulsion of 18 Fructidor (September 4, 1797) destroyed the opposition to the triumvirate and ushered in the period of the second Directory. The support of the Jacobin directors by the armies was decisive: during the night of 17–18 Fructidor, troops which had been brought into Paris, in violation of the laws, seized the legislative leaders of the opposition. Carnot escaped by fleeing; and Barthélemy, who refused to follow suit, was arrested. Reubell was then able to effect the abolition of the opposition's power in the Five Hundred by declaring vacant one hundred and seventy-seven seats on both councils, and the vacancies were increased by the resignations of some moderates who had escaped arrest, notably Dupont de Nemours. Sixty-five men were condemned to exile and almost certain death in the colony of Guiana on the coast of South America; but only eighteen, among them Barthélemy, Jean Charles Pichegru, the Five Hundred's president whose treasonable correspondence with British agents had been discovered, and Pastoret, were actually deported.[7]

The power of the legislative body had not been great and it was now negligible, the purged Directory having substantially increased its authority as a result of the coup d'état. The old Jacobin laws against émigrés and priests were restored and the Jacobin clubs reopened, but the press was placed under close censorship. The purge was extended to the administrative and judicial services, with the Directory exercising the prerogative of filling vacancies, a most important step in the consolidation of its actual dictatorship. In foreign affairs the new Directory assumed a more arrogant tone than before. The Jacobin triumph had implicitly committed France to new wars and to the constant dependence on the armies which led directly to Bonaparte's advent to power. Protégés of Reubell replaced the negotiators at Lille and delivered to the English an ultimatum which achieved its purpose of breaking off the peace talks. Reubell brooked no

7Adet to Talleyrand, Sept. 22, 1797, AECPE-U, 48, 258. See Lefebvre, Guyot, and Sagnac, *La Révolution Française*, 367–72, and Lefebvre, *Directory*, ch. 7.

interference with his high-handed diplomacy, and Talleyrand had to submit quietly to carrying out his orders.[8]

On September 15, the purged Council of the Five Hundred adopted a resolution celebrating the Directory's triumph over "royalism." The "royalist conspirators," declaimed Riou, the resolution's author, had cherished England and "the Americans, who, since their treaty of alliance and commerce with Great Britain, make amends every day for the crime of having vanquished liberty." Pastoret, he continued, was a traitor and the provision decree of March 2 deserved praise. Anyway, the constitution made the Directory an independent authority in foreign affairs and the Five Hundred had no jurisdiction. On Joseph F. M. Riou's motion, Pastoret's resolution was repealed.[9]

Since Reubell was the leading proponent of a punitive American policy, Talleyrand was understandably a little less optimistic about settling Franco-American differences after Fructidor. Like Monroe in 1794, Marshall and Pinckney arrived in France in the wake of a political upheaval, but the new Thermidoreans were the losers this time. The Americans reached Paris on September 27, 1797, and the following day Talleyrand wrote to Létombe that "the negotiations will not be long in opening on the subject of their mission." It was impossible to foresee their result, he continued, but he would neglect nothing to reestablish harmony. He hoped that the envoys carried "very broad powers and instructions drafted in a spirit of conciliation."[10]

This supposition corresponded with advice Adet was including in the report Talleyrand had asked for. The American government, Adet thought, would like the three commissioners to receive the same treatment as Pinckney: that would provide an

[8]See Sorel, *L'Europe et la Révolution Française* IV, 255, and Lefebvre, *Directory*, 102.

[9]Extract from the *Gazette National ou le Moniteur*, 1 Vendémiaire an 6 (Sept. 22, 1797), AECPE-U, 48, 244–46vo.

[10]Sept. 28, 1797, AECPE-U, 48, 269–70. Létombe hastened to impart the contents of this letter to Jefferson. Jefferson to Madison, Jan. 2, 1798, Ford, *Jefferson's Writings* VII, 185–86. Talleyrand's previous dispatch had ordered Létombe to keep in close touch with the Vice-President, but without giving offense to the jealous Adams. Sept. 1, 1797, AECPE-U, 48, 214–15vo.

excuse for breaking with France. To frustrate this ploy, France's friends in America hoped that the Directory would receive the envoys and deal justly with them, and Adet agreed that frank negotiation was "the means of ending differences it is not our interest to prolong."[11]

In the meantime, Talleyrand was working on an agenda for negotiations in which the Directory seemed to have little or no interest. He traced his own ideas on how they would proceed in a paper dated October 2. He thought the American envoys would have broad powers and, despite the arrogant tone of Pickering, which he attributed to "the personal malevolence of the Minister," Adams's "precarious situation" would ensure in the instructions a conciliatory spirit. The two resolutions of the House of Representatives in their answer to the President's message probably formed the bases of those instructions. Therefore, Talleyrand reasoned, the negotiations would turn on three points: a "cessation of the apparent state of war," indemnities for prizes captured by French vessels, and "permanent arrangements on objects which require new stipulations, or clarification of old ones." The Americans, of course, would want to discuss indemnities first and would not be much interested in permanent arrangements. Talleyrand thought that it was most important to France to prepare for the future rather than to "conciliate the interests of the moment." This opportunity should be used "to repair the vices or omissions of the old treaties" and to get rid of the concessions granted by the "excessive generosity" of the former government.[12]

As far as ending hostilities was concerned, Talleyrand knew that the provision decree of March 2 could not be given up, but he thought that the requirement for the *rôle d'équipage* might be suspended or modified. That would lead naturally to a discussion of indemnities, which the Americans would claim for all ships seized. The government would have to become involved in discussions of many kinds of property, or it could agree to hear

11Adet to Talleyrand, Sept. 22, 1797, AECPE-U, 48, 258–64vo.
12*Ibid.*, 48, 278–83vo.

only claims arising from the *rôle d'équipage*; but, whatever
claims were consented to, there would be "many ways of reducing their extent, and finally of eluding the payments." For example, France could claim damages for prizes taken from French
corsairs in American ports and then agree to the creation of
claims commissions like those provided by Jay's treaty for the
arbitration of the claims of both nations. There were innumerable ways in which such arrangements necessarily operated to the
advantage of the debtor and forced on the plaintiff the acceptance of whatever was offered. But better than that procedure,
suggested Talleyrand, France could make the United States drop
their claims "in just compensation for the guarantee of our colonies," a maneuver which would humiliate both England and
the American government. The success of this last stratagem
would depend upon circumstances, but "we should be able to
carry it."

As to "permanent arrangements," should France, asked Talleyrand, require the United States to abrogate the Jay Treaty? He
thought not, because of the great sacrifice of national dignity that
would be involved. Besides, he continued, France's complaint
was not the treaty itself so much as the time at which it was concluded. France had never denied the right of the United States
"to make even a shameful treaty with England, so long as their
obligations to us were not impaired." France really had no great
interest in the actual annulment of the treaty. She could propose
stipulations in a new treaty which would amount to that and still
would not give England an excuse for immediate revenge. But
it was up to the Americans to suggest means of rectifying the
conditions stemming from Jay's treaty. On a basis of "justice and
firmness," France should insist, he concluded, not only in ending
existing differences, but in establishing, "in an unequivocal and
clearly defined manner," the future political and commercial
relations of the two nations.[13]

13Talleyrand's view of the Jay Treaty as necessary to the U. S. had not changed
since he explained its advantages to financial correspondents in Jan. 1795. "However favorable is the opinion conceived in this country of Mr. Jay's negotiation,

Talleyrand, then, had every expectation of effecting a reconciliation with the United States. He was prepared to use all of his influence and skill to steer toward that objective a Directory whose attitude toward America was more punitive than ever. His program was simple: the Directory should receive the American envoys and permit a frank negotiation which would dispel the mutual suspicions resulting from past injuries. France should surrender the most objectionable features of her commercial policy, admitting American claims arising from the *rôle d'équipage* provision. These could be balanced by French counterclaims or minimized through the establishment of a mixed claims commission, so that no great loss would result to the French treasury.

Of greater importance to Talleyrand was an end to the unofficial hostilities and the establishment of a permanent understanding with the United States. The instructions of the Americans, he thought, would be sufficiently conciliatory to allow the settlement of the important points in a manner satisfactory to France. He realized that President Adams and his moderate followers would welcome a negotiation which would grant French acquiescence in the new American neutrality. Some concessions on the part of the United States would be in order, but he knew that the Federalist party's war faction would be eager to take advantage of any seeming French intransigence.

Pinckney and Marshall arrived at Paris one week before being joined by Gerry, and the three envoys were received by Talleyrand on October 8, 1797. They were told "that the Directory had

---

there is no doubt that at the moment when these hopes change to reality a rise [in American funds] will be the consequence. I believe that this business is actually decided in England and I await news of it at any moment. The treaty with England will fix the price of American funds and will preserve them from the variations which always result from a precarious existence. That of America is assured by the peace and by the tranquillity of its commerce, to which neutrality procures immense advantages." "Talleyrand in America as a Financial Promoter, 1794–1796," 92. Talleyrand had long believed, as he wrote to Lord Lansdowne from America on Feb. 1, 1795, that America's economic interest bound the U. S. to England because of the latter's commercial and industrial primacy and willingness to extend long-term credit. "Les États-Unis et l'Angleterre en 1795," 64–77.

required [Talleyrand] to make a report relative to the situation
of the United States with regard to France, which he was then
about, and which would be finished in a few days, when he would
let us know what steps were to follow." Talleyrand at once ordered courtesy cards delivered to the envoys, putting them under
the protection of the government during their sojourn in Paris.[14]

Talleyrand was convinced that an accommodation could be
worked out with the Americans, and he lacked only the Directory's authorization to initiate negotiations. In an effort to turn
its attention to the United States, he followed up his report of
October 2 with a note suggesting that Spain be invited to join
in the discussions. This would please France's new ally, who had
made common cause at Philadelphia in representations against
the Jay Treaty. More important, it would emphasize the need for
reestablishing the liberal commercial principles of the treaty of
1778—principles which had been incorporated in Spain's recent
treaty with the United States. With a keen eye for France's stra-
tegic requirements, Talleyrand was insistent on this point long
before Bonaparte demonstrated its utility three years later.[15]

Talleyrand had already requested the minister of marine to
furnish information on American prizes taken by French ships,
because "negotiations with the United States [are] on the point
of opening." But the Directory was not interested in the United
States, and it ignored its minister. Eighteen Fructidor had
doomed the negotiations with England at Lille, and the Directory was immersed in plans for the final destruction of France's
archenemy. Lord Malmesbury quit Lille on October 15, and two
days later Bonaparte's Treaty of Campo Formio dismembered
the anti-French coalition and isolated England. With revolutionary ardor now at high pitch, the Directory decreed the formation of an Army of England to prepare for a cross-channel
assault; on October 19, all Frenchmen were summoned to a cru-

[14]Envoys to Secretary of State, Oct. 22, 1797, *ASP, FR* II, 158. Beveridge, *Mar-shall* II, chs. 6–8, is the most detailed account of this mission, although the author's bias in Marshall's favor is extreme.
[15]"Note," Oct. 4, 1797, AECPE-U, 48, 287–48.

sade whose end would be the dictation of peace in London under the bayonets of "the Great Nation."[16]

In this situation, the directors probably preferred that their ministers concentrate upon replenishing a national treasury hopelessly inadequate, as usual, to their grand designs. The means had already been found. France had imposed upon her helpless Dutch ally a forced loan of twelve million guilders the previous July. Portugal had recently been forced to buy a peace with France, and part of the obligations she had undertaken in the treaty consisted of a large loan to France. As Talleyrand turned from the Portuguese minister with whom he had been closeted to greet the American envoys on October 8, ideas of similarly smoothing the path of negotiation must have occurred to him as a matter of course.[17]

That path would require smoothing. Reubell and La Revellière regarded the United States as a treacherous appendage of England and hated Adams as the epitome of aristocracy and Anglomania. Barras was indifferent, as always, to all save what contributed to his own personal fortunes; and the two new directors, Merlin, former minister of justice, and François de Neufchateau, poet and recent minister of the interior, palely reflected the views of Reubell and La Revellière. The attitude of the Directory at this time was probably expressed by the minister of marine, Admiral Georges-Réné Pléville le Pelley, whom Talleyrand asked for a frank opinion on what to do about the American emissaries. The admiral supposed that the Americans were instructed to raise "preliminaries" concerning the conduct of French corsairs. If so, they could not be heard, because the Directory would expect reparations for the conduct of the United States. If without such instructions, "they can work with us—but as that is not prob-

16Sept. 30, 1797, *ibid.*, 48, 271; Lefebvre, Guyot, and Sagnac, *La Révolution Française*, 387.

17Adams to Murray, July 7, 1797, *Writings of John Quincy Adams* II, 187; July 7, 1797, Worthington C. Ford, ed., "Letters of William Vans Murray to John Quincy Adams, 1797–1803," *Annual Report of the American Historical Association, 1912* (1914), 357; King to Secretary of State, Nov. 18, 1797, King, *Life and Correspondence* II, 243; Beveridge, *Marshall* II, 248, 251.

able, I foresee war." America's weight in the scales with England would prolong the general war, and he hoped that there would be found a way "to avoid for humanity all the subsequent evils," but he was not optimistic. Pléville's advice to the Americans would be: if they had not been admitted to an audience of the Directory, they should go home, "and their withdrawal will mean a declaration of war."[18]

The minister of marine knew that Talleyrand was already feeling out the American envoys on certain "preliminaries" of his own devising, and thought that "you have the proper man in the honest and informed citizen intermediating between us and the American deputies." Talleyrand had sent Lucien Hauteval, "a French gentleman of respectable character," according to the Americans, and an interpreter and general utility man in Talleyrand's department, to sound out the envoys on their attitude toward the financial arrangements the Directory was sure to require. Of all the assorted personages who took a hand in the "intermediation," only Hauteval ("Z") was a bona fide *citoyen*: Jean Conrad Hottinguer and Bellamy, the Messrs. "X" and "Y" of the envoys' dispatches, were Hamburg bankers, members of the international financial community to which Talleyrand himself belonged, and Madame de Villette, who exercised great charm upon Marshall and Pinckney, was the lady in whose home Marshall and Gerry had rented apartments.[19]

The first intimation that all would not be speedily settled came to Marshall, who was the recipient of information intended for

[18]Georgia Robinson, *Revellière-lépeaux: Citizen Director, 1753–1824* (New York, 1938), 218; Nov. 4, 1797, AECPE-U, 48, 343–44. Barras was also hostile towards America, "weary, it seems, at hearing the American virtues too much praised." Faÿ, *Revolutionary Spirit in France and America*, 403.

[19]Envoys to Pickering, Oct. 27, 1797, *ASP, FR* II, 162; Guyot, *Le Directoire et la Paix de l'Europe*, 560; Beveridge, *Marshall* II, 290–92; Samuel E. Morison, "Elbridge Gerry, Gentleman-Democrat," *New England Quarterly* II (1929), 24–25. "W" was Pierre Augustin Caron de Beaumarchais, whose claims against Virginia for supplies furnished during the American Revolution had been handled by Marshall. Later, Pinckney was approached by three other mediaries of Talleyrand in turn: Sainte-Foix, Montrond, and André d'Arbelles. All three had been involved in intrigues with Malmesbury for England's purchase of peace from the Directory. Guyot, *Le Directoire et la Paix de l'Europe*, 561–62n.

Gerry that the present was a most unfavorable time for the prosecution of their business and that they had better bide their time, else "all would probably be lost." This was friendly advice, but it was lost on Marshall, who thought it not worth reporting in the voluminous dispatches written to his government. When the envoys learned that Mountflorence had been told by Talleyrand's chief assistant that the Directory was incensed at some references to France in Adams's message to the special session of the Congress, they were prepared for the unraveling of some sinister plot.[20]

Talleyrand had apparently hit upon the Adams speech as the most plausible means of testing the Americans' instructions. He drafted a letter to the envoys asking for an explanation of certain passages of the speech. Whose "depredations" was the President thinking of? Against whom were the "effectual measures for your defence" to be directed? Against France? The Directory, he said, required an explanation of these points before notifying the envoys of its intentions. For his part, Talleyrand earnestly hoped that "your answer will satisfy the Directory."[21]

This was the letter displayed by Bellamy in his efforts to get the Americans to propose financial arrangements to the Directory as a preliminary to the negotiations upon their actual business. Hauteval had already suggested what Talleyrand had in mind: a douceur of twelve hundred thousand livres for "the pocket of the Directory and ministers"; and a loan by the United States to France, perhaps in the form of American purchase of thirty-two million florins of a depreciated Dutch bond issue, in which, incidentally, both Hottinguer and Bellamy had a personal interest. Probably Talleyrand would expect the Americans to appreciate the irony of demands for money from what he had often derided as a nation of bourgeois moneygrubbers.[22]

20Beveridge, *Marshall* II, 254; Envoys to Secretary of State, Oct. 22, 1797, *ASP, FR* II, 158.

21Talleyrand to Envoys, undated, not sent, AECPE-U, 48, 353–54.

22Envoys to Pickering, Nov. 3, 1797, *ASP, FR* II, 164–65; Channing, *History of U. S.* IV, 187–88. Talleyrand undoubtedly intended to benefit personally from the "douceur" demanded of the Americans, but he was probably more concerned, as

While these informal advances were going on, Talleyrand wrote on November 15 to Dupont, now consul at Philadelphia, that "the negotiation with the American commissioners at Paris has made no progress." At about this time, Hauterive finally reached Paris, after having been kept under arrest at Bordeaux as an émigré since the end of September. Hauterive's first report since leaving America informed Talleyrand that there was a temporary truce between the political parties and a general impatience for the result of the negotiation. The Republicans, he said, had forebodings on account of the prejudices of the commissioners: they approved Gerry's political opinions but distrusted him as being easily swayed and somewhat unpredictable. Hauterive thought that some influential Republican would soon arrive "to watch over the mission, in which Adams's partiality prevented them from participating." Aaron Burr had decided to come but had changed his mind, "but whoever it is will not be personally as unknown as the President's commissioners." This would influence the course of the negotiations and "it will prove that there is a party in the United States sincerely devoted to the Gallo-American cause."[23]

Merlin, whom Talleyrand's emissaries had repeatedly represented as most adamant on the subject of the United States, especially in regard to the *rôle d'équipage*, on which he "had written

---

Hauteval suggested, with the means of purchasing the support of the Directors, Barras and Merlin, for example, for an accommodation with the U. S. As Georges Lacour-Gayet noted, Talleyrand's new position afforded "exceptional facilities, either in permitting speculation in public funds with a sure touch, or in having his signature to a treaty bought by a gift of money." *Talleyrand* 4 vols. (Paris, 1928–34), I, 236. Lacour-Gayet details Talleyrand's corrupt gains, but his evidence is for the most part hearsay, and he relies strongly on the spiteful accusations of Barras. *Ibid.*, I, 236–38. It was not the suggested bribes, however, but the demand for a loan that made the American envoys indignant, because they feared it would antagonize Britain. Kurtz, *Presidency of Adams*, 298. In fact, Americans previously had not supposed that loans by a neutral to a belligerent necessarily contravened neutrality; and they could cite Vattel, the eighteenth century's preeminent authority on international law, to the effect that such loans were permissible if in the best interest of the lender. The crux of the matter was that Republican France would benefit. Hyneman, "The First American Neutrality," 40–41.

[23]AECPE-U, 48, 360–62vo, Hauterive to Talleyrand, Sept. 22, Nov. 19, 1797, *ibid.*, 48, 265–66vo, 369–70.

a treatise," finally broke the directorial silence in regard to the American commission. He had seen in the gazette *Bien-Informé* a translation of President Adams's First Annual Address at the opening of the Congress in November. He at once tore it out and sent it to Talleyrand with a curt note scratched in the margin: "sent to the Minister of Exterior Relations for prompt report, 3 pluviose an 6 [January 22, 1798]." One week later, there arrived the exhaustive memorial on matters in dispute between France and the United States over which Marshall had labored all month. It was with difficulty that Marshall, exasperated by European diplomacy's un-American indirectness, had obtained Gerry's reluctant acquiescence to this final step. Marshall had been urging it since early in January, after it became apparent that the request to the Directory to be received, which he had also inspired, was to be ignored. The force of Marshall's personality was responsible for the fact that he and Pinckney acted in unison, although the stubborn Gerry refused to abandon peace to the younger Virginian's sense of propriety, despite the exhortations of King in London, who knew Gerry better than did his Republican friends. King's anxiety for an accommodation with France lessened in proportion as England demonstrated the strength to continue the war and repel the expected French invasion.[24]

Twice, before Merlin belatedly showed interest in American affairs, had the Directory taken steps which affected America. On December 24, 1797, it ordered Talleyrand orally "to confer with the envoys of America and of Hamburg for the purchase of Batavian rescriptions at par." One month later, on January 18, 1798, the Directory pushed through the councils a decree which made any neutral ship good prize which had on board any article produced either in England or in her colonies, and in addition forbade foreign vessels to enter French ports if they had touched at any British port en route. The oral order was sufficient to show

24*Ibid.*, 48, 377–79, 49, 10–63vo. The Marshall memorial was dated Jan. 27, 1798. It is also in *ASP, FR* II, 169–82. Beveridge, *Marshall* II, 296–309, discusses it but concludes that it "remained unread." *Ibid.*, 310. King to Pinckney, Marshall, and Gerry, Nov. 15 and 24, Dec. 9 and 23, to Pinckney, Dec. 24, to Gerry, Dec. 24, 1797, Feb. 20, 1798, King, *Life and Correspondence* II, 242–43, 245, 247–48, 262–65, 282.

in what light the United States was considered by the Directory; its effect upon the sensitive dignity of the Americans, had they known of it, can be imagined. The maritime law was an extension of the economic war against England, but its unprecedented rigor operated only for the benefit of privateersmen and redounded to the great harm of French industry and commerce without really effecting its purpose. It was the "continental blockade" of Napoleon, but it was premature.[25]

The whole business of the American negotiation had obviously reached a crisis by the end of January. Talleyrand had a "substance of a memoir sent by the American ministers" prepared at once, and he used this as a starting point to cover the whole ground in a report to the Directory. As a result of the envoy's memoir, he began, "it becomes indispensable to take a part on the conduct that we will follow in regard to them." He noted that he had outlined the general situation almost five months earlier, when he had concluded that there were "real risks and nothing to gain in not hearing the envoys." He had proposed then that, "after punishing the United States as hard as we could, we should terminate in a lasting manner the differences which divide the two republics."[26]

France's grievances, continued Talleyrand, had been amply avenged by the retaliatory measures of the last two years "which the law of nations, our treaties, and even common sense authorized us to take," and "which today put the United States at our knees." It was necessary now to undertake "seriously pacific negotiations" in order to foil the British faction at Philadelphia which wanted war. The armaments lately proposed by Adams were intended only to prepare the public mind for an alliance with England, which France had to prevent or "lose our power to injure American commerce and unite the Americans under a British-dominated cabinet."

[25]Guyot, *Le Directoire et la Paix de l'Europe*, 559; *ASP, FR* II, 182; Lefebvre, *Directory*, 126–27; Bemis, *John Quincy Adams and Foundations of American Foreign Policy*, 92.

[26]AECPE-U, 49, 139–43vo, 174–87vo. Talleyrand's "substance of a memoir" and his report are dated "Pluviose an 6" (Jan. 20–Feb. 19).

America had claims on France for debts contracted by the Republic and by its colonial agents with American citizens. These debts had not been paid because of the financial derangement caused by the war, but had long been recognized. Claims based on the decrees of the Directory presented more difficulty but, since the Americans recognized "the reality of the cause of our displeasure" and wanted "to rectify the inconveniences which would result for us" from the Jay Treaty, that obstacle was not insuperable and "we can satisfy the Americans without, for the moment, any sacrifice of the public treasury." As for French maritime claims on the United States, it would be best to consider the satisfaction retaliation had brought as suitable reparation.

Talleyrand had already proposed to demand of the American commissioners "a solemn reparation" for Adams's speech, but there were difficulties in the usual forms. The envoys' powers would not be sufficient and before they could receive new ones a rupture would occur, or the President would use the demand as an excuse for war. It would be "more useful and surer to substitute for this reparation a pecuniary loan—such as the purchase at par of our Batavian bonds and the purchase of a few issues of our loan against England." Political injuries had been compensated by monetary concessions before, and this would have a double advantage. It would provide immediate capital for the prosecution of the war against England in the first place, but its purpose would be not so much to raise additional funds as "to compromise the United States vis-à-vis Great Britain."

"I have operated on the principle that the Directory did not wish to carry matters to extremities," concluded Talleyrand: it was France's interest to prevent a war which would permanently estrange America and throw her into the arms of England. Let him be authorized to begin a negotiation on these bases, but let him first get rid of the two Federalists. Pinckney had been sent back only "to defy us," but Gerry had shown himself to be truly conciliatory ever since his arrival and could guarantee "the disappearance of all obstacles of personal malevolence." Since the commissioners had been appointed "jointly and severally," such a plan was proper. Talleyrand had not forgotten Merlin's demand, and he had discussed Adams's November speech at length in a separate report, but he did not think it wise to add anything more to the negotiation he proposed. He had already written to Dupont that the speech "breathes intentions not at all pacific."[27]

Having adopted the Directory's demand for disguised reparations—the Batavian notes—Talleyrand thought that he had at last found a way to bring together the Directory and the Americans; but he reckoned without Marshall. By February 19, Marshall could no longer restrain his impatience to learn of the effect of his memorial, and he persuaded his colleagues to send Pinckney's secretary, Major Henry Rutledge, to inquire. The Directory had not yet reached a decision, answered Talleyrand. Despite now acrimonious relations with Gerry, Marshall was able to gain his consent to a demand for a joint interview with Talleyrand, but two conversations, on March 2 and 6, failed to produce anything new. Talleyrand's earlier report to the Directory bears a notation to the effect that it was adopted as of March 18, which was the date on which he addressed a memorial to the Americans in answer to theirs of six weeks earlier. Without attempting to answer Marshall, he denounced the American government for the Jay Treaty, for the "invectives and calumnies" against France in the newspapers of America, which he asserted were in the pay of England and under the control of the federal government, and for sending to France "persons whose opinions and connexions are too well known to hope from them dispositions sincerely conciliatory." This last he contrasted with the sending of Jay to London, and ended with an offer "to treat with that one of the three, whose opinions, presumed to be more impartial, promise, in the course of the explanations, more of that reciprocal confidence which is indispensable." This note was dispatched to Létombe a few days later with instructions to give it all possible

[27]Report on the President's speech, Jan. 24, 1798, Talleyrand to Dupont, no date, *ibid.*, 49, 188–95, 215vo.

publicity in America. It was intended as much for the American people as for their representatives in the first place.[28]

Again, Marshall undertook to answer for his colleagues, having gained their consent that "I should state that no one of the ministers could consent to remain on a business committed to all three." This was done, and the reply, after a bitter squabble between Pinckney and Gerry, was sent to Talleyrand on April 3. It dealt in detail with Talleyrand's complaints, passing over a defense of Jay's treaty, which had been the principal subject of the January memorial. It ended with the assertion that no one of the commissioners was empowered to negotiate without the other two, and a clear invitation, in case the prejudices against the ministers had not been removed, to send them their passports and letters of safe conduct to protect them from French corsairs.[29]

There followed a few days' jockeying over passports with Talleyrand while Marshall, whom Talleyrand now openly blamed for trying "to produce a rupture in such a manner as to throw the whole blame on France," prepared to depart for home. Marshall mistakenly thought that Talleyrand's personal spleen had made the envoys' position more uncomfortable than his orders required, and he was glad to hurry to Bordeaux, after his passport arrived, whence he sailed on April 24.[30]

Pinckney received his passport with Marshall's on April 13, but decided to visit the mineral waters in the south of France for his daughter's health. He obtained the necessary permits and

---

28*Ibid.*, 49, 235–40vo; *ASP, FR* II, 188–91. Talleyrand's opinions concerning Marshall and Pinckney suggest the influence of Hauterive, who was now firmly established in the minister's confidence. He had written from America that the envoys "are only the instruments of England's instruments in this country," although to everyone "they represent a friendly nation interesting in its present state and great in its future destinies." He had been sure that the French government would "take measures adapted to the double aspect of their position." Hauterive to Adet, Aug. 1, 1797, AECPE-U, 48, 143vo.

29Beveridge, *Marshall* II, 326, 328; *ASP, FR* II, 191–99.

30Beveridge, *Marshall* II, 332–33; Marshall to Talleyrand, Apr. 13, 1798, AECPE-U, 49, 323. Perhaps the most perceptive criticism of Talleyrand is the general one of Pieter Geyl: Talleyrand's "notorious venality" was not his worst fault; he was a "time-serving opportunist . . . never prepared to risk his office for his convictions." *Debates with Historians* (New York, 1958), 231.

left Paris, after roundly upbraiding Gerry, who determined to stay in the belief that war would follow his departure. Neither Marshall nor Pinckney bothered to say good-bye to Gerry. Murray at The Hague was sorry to hear that Gerry's "oppression of spirits" was very great, because he thought him "infinitely too good for the bed which in a moment of indecision he has made for himself." He heard also that Gerry intended soon to send his secretary, the nephew of Republican Senator Tazewell of Virginia, to Philadelphia with dispatches, and to follow himself in a few weeks.[31]

While Marshall was sailing homeward, his adventures in Paris were the cause of an enormous outburst of patriotic sentiment in America. Owing to the slow abatement of the yellow fever in Philadelphia—an epidemic which Létombe told Talleyrand was more frightful than that of 1793—Congress was slow in assembling for the opening of the session that was to have begun on November 13. The minds of the members, as they gradually returned, were fixed on France and the fate of the negotiations entrusted to the three commissioners, and little business was transacted from day to day. In the absence of reliable information, conjecture was rife. General Washington, in retirement at Mount Vernon, wondered, in a letter to Wolcott, if Fauchet and Adet could have been appointed to negotiate for France. Madison was alarmed at "the rash measures of our hot-headed Executive" and thought only public opinion was preventing Adams from rushing the country into war, notwithstanding his mission to France. Madison was beginning to share Jefferson's suspicion that news from the envoys was being "hushed up," though Jefferson adopted an air of unconcern in assuring General Gates that "this is one of the cases where no news is good news."[32]

The refusal of Congress to enact provocative measures recommended by the administration infuriated Wolcott, who ex-

[31]Beveridge, *Marshall* II, 333; May 18, 1798, "Letters of Murray to J. Q. Adams," 407.
[32]Dec. 21, 1797, C. F. M., 1087; Dec. 17, 1797, *Oliver Wolcott* II, 8; Madison to Jefferson, Feb. ?, 1798, *Writings of Madison* VI, 309–10; Jefferson to Madison, Jan. 25, to Horatio Gates, Feb. 21, 1798, Ford, *Jefferson's Writings* VII, 191–92, 203–206.

pressed his chagrin in a mournful sentence: "My hopes respecting the present government are almost extinguished." Wolcott's despair stemmed from the failure to put through Congress a bill for the arming of merchant vessels, despite the delivery by Adams of "an inflammatory message" on the subject on the day the bill came up for discussion. Nothing having been heard from France, Wolcott's gloom was probably deepened by his belief that "the ministers, after being treated with insult and indignity, will be received."[33]

Neither Wolcott nor Pickering took the trouble to answer a long query from the President which was based on a different conclusion. Adams had believed right along that France, while she did not desire war, nevertheless had no interest in a peaceful settlement of the differences between the two countries. As he had told Pickering in October, neither Talleyrand nor "even the Triumvirate, as they begin to be called in France, will be for a measure so decided . . . . A continued appearance of umbrage, and continued depredations on a weak, defenceless commerce, will be much more convenient for their views."[34]

Passions taut from the prolonged disappointment of awaiting news from France which did not arrive erupted sporadically in the disgraceful fight between Republican Matthew Lyon of Vermont and Connecticut Federalist Roger Griswold in the House, and in the slanderous recriminations following the publication of Monroe's defense of his mission to France—*A View of the Conduct of the Executive*. Adams broke the tension on March 5 by sending to Congress a terse message announcing the receipt of dispatches from the commissioners. Being voluminous, they would take some days to decipher, but he thought it his duty to transmit a particular letter, written in the clear, which announced the Directory's decree of January 18, and concluded: "We can only repeat that there exists no hope of our being offi-

[33]To Frederick Wolcott, Feb. 27, 1798, *Oliver Wolcott* II, 13; Jefferson to Madison, Feb. 8, 1798, Ford, *Jefferson's Writings* VII, 97–98.

[34]From the President, Jan. 24, 1798, *Oliver Wolcott* II, 10; To the Heads of Department, Jan. 24, 1798, to Pickering, Oct. 31, 1797, *Works of Adams* VIII, 561–62, 559–60.

cially received by this Government, or that the objects of our mission will be in any way accomplished."[35]

This message was followed two weeks later by another containing the President's conclusion from the now digested dispatches: "I perceive no ground of expectation that the objects of their mission can be accomplished on terms compatible with the safety, the honor, or the essential interests of the nation." Adams therefore demanded action:

> Under these circumstances I cannot forbear to reiterate the recommendations which have been formerly made, and to exhort you to adopt, with promptitude, decision, and unanimity, such measures as the ample resources of the country afford, for the protection of our seafaring and commercial citizens; for the defence of any exposed portions of our territory; for replenishing our arsenals, establishing foundries, and military manufactures; and to provide such efficient revenue as will be necessary to defray extraordinary expenses, and supply the deficiencies which may be occasioned by depredations on our commerce.

He had also, he informed the Congress, revoked the executive prohibition against the arming of merchant vessels, because "I no longer conceive myself justifiable in continuing them."[36]

The "insane message," Jefferson told Madison, had produced a great change in "our political atmosphere"—"exultation on the one side, & a certainty of victory; while the other is petrified with astonishment." The House could now count a bare majority of one (53 to 52) for peace. Jefferson hoped that that majority could be used to override the President's invitation to arm by passing a legislative prohibition, and to maneuver an adjournment to consult the people, since "to do nothing & to gain time is everything with us." One week later the Vice-President was very despondent. The executive, supported by two-thirds of the Senate and half of the House, was too much for the other half of the latter: "The question of war & peace depends now on a toss of cross & pile."[37]

Two days after this, Talleyrand received Létombe's dispatch

35 *ASP, FR* II, 150–51.
36 Message to Congress, Mar. 19, 1798, *ibid.* II, 152.
37 Mar. 21 and 29, 1798, Ford, *Jefferson's Writings* VII, 218–21, 224–27.

of December 28, informing him that "the Republican party is gaining ground in America." But the worst was still to come. Distrusting Adams, the Republicans decided to demand the submission of the envoys' dispatches, and the Federalists, who already had been advised to do this by Hamilton, were glad to oblige. Adams sent the dispatches, with the instructions to the commissioners, to both houses of Congress on April 3, with an injunction to secrecy "until the members of Congress are fully possessed of their contents, and shall have had opportunity to deliberate on the consequences of their publication; after which time I submit them to your wisdom." That wisdom was devoted first to the consideration of how many thousands of copies of the dispatches should be printed but, that decided, the war party proceeded to carry everything before it. No one, apparently, paused to note the contrast between Adams's complaisance and Washington's adamancy regarding the correspondence relative to the Jay negotiation in England.[38]

Jefferson, while admitting that "the first impressions from them are very disagreeable and confused," was inclined to place the principal blame for the envoys' failure on the President. Madison agreed, but he thought that "the conduct of Talleyrand is so extraordinary as to be scarcely credible.... Its unparalleled stupidity is what fills one with astonishment." On April 12, Jefferson reported that "the public mind appears still in a state of astonishment"; and one week later, "the impressions first made by those communications continue strong and prejudicial here." By May 3, "the impressions" were such that the survival of the Republican party was clearly threatened:

> The spirit kindled up in the towns is wonderful. These and N. Jersey are pouring in their addresses, offering life and fortune. Even these addresses are not the worst things. For indiscreet declarations and expressions of passion may be pardoned to a

38 C. F. M., 1095; *ASP, FR* II, 153; Hamilton to Pickering, Mar. 17, 1798, *Works of Hamilton* X, 275–78. This letter contained a seven-point program for arming merchant ships, enlarging the army and navy, fortifying the ports, imposing new taxes, and suspending the treaties with France, all of which was quickly enacted by the Congress.

multitude acting from the impulse of the moment. But we cannot expect a foreign nation to shew that apathy to the answers of the President, which are more thrasonic than the addresses. Whatever chance for peace might have been left us after the publication of the dispatches, is completely lost by these answers. Nor is it France alone, but his own fellow citizens, against whom his threats are uttered . . . .

Truly, "the X. Y. Z. dish cooked up by Marshall" had set America on fire, with the citizens of Philadelphia, the front line in this war of declamation, the most heated of all. But there was an important exception, and Joseph Hopkinson reported to Wolcott from New York: "It is a mortifying fact, my dear sir, that the federal spirit of this city is not worth a farthing . . . . It is entirely unlike that which animates us in Philadelphia . . . ." Hopkinson would like to have had "the whole city to undergo the Turkish ceremony of the bastinado."[39]

On May 4, Adams transmitted to Congress another letter from the commissioners, enclosing Marshall's memorial of January 27. After reading it, Madison wrote to Jefferson that

It is evidently more in the forensic than the Diplomatic stile, and more likely in some of its reasonings to satisfy an American Jury than the French Government. The defence of the provision article is the most shallow that has appeared on that subject. In some instances the reasoning is good, but so tedious and tautologous as to insult the understanding as well as patience of the Directory, if really intended for them, and not for the partial ear of the American public.

But the Federalists were delighted with "Marshall's superb memorial to Talleyrand [which was] another blow to Republican hopes." Successive installments of the dispatches from Paris were communicated almost as soon as they arrived, each one serving to rekindle and to raise higher the popular pulse. On June 5 and 18, Adams sent messages to Congress, and on June 21 he an-

[39]Jefferson to Madison, Apr. 6 and 12, May 3, 1798, to Edmund Pendleton, Jan. 29, 1799, Ford, *Jefferson's Writings* VII, 234–36, 237–38, 246–48, 336–39; Madison to Jefferson, Apr. 15, 1798, *Writings of Madison* VI, 315–19; May 17, 1798, *Oliver Wolcott* II, 49. Hopkinson had just made a stirring contribution to the right spirit in his popular song, "Hail Columbia." Beveridge, *Marshall* II, 339.

329

nounced that "I will never send another minister to France without assurances that he will be received, respected, and honored, as the representative of a great, free, powerful, and independent nation."[40]

This prefaced the communication of a letter of Gerry to Adams in which the former explained that the Directory refused to permit him to leave France, and that he was convinced that to defy their wish would cause a declaration of war. Assuring the President that Talleyrand wanted to negotiate, Gerry asked his friend to extricate him from his anomalous position by appointing new commissioners. But Adams's answer had already been given in the final enclosure in the message—Pickering's peremptory letter of March 23 ordering the entire commission home.[41]

A slogan-loving people was loudly chanting "Millions for defence but not one cent for tribute!" when Marshall landed at New York in the middle of June, from a ship whose name— *Alexander Hamilton*—doubtless caused considerable Republican comment. Unexpected, he accepted only the briefest Federalist hospitality before hurrying on to Philadelphia, where he was greeted on June 18 by extravagant official and private demonstrations unsurpassed in that city's history. Edward Livingston, a Republican representative from New York, accompanied Marshall on the journey to Philadelphia and was told that "they had no idea in France of a war with us," but the contrary idea

40*ASP, FR* II, 169–82, 185–89, 199; May 20, 1798, *Writings of Madison* VI, 320–22; Beveridge, *Marshall* II, 339.

41*ASP, FR* II, 199–201. By way of contrast to the public disgrace prepared for Gerry, Irving Brant describes the metamorphosis of John Marshall from debt-ridden lawyer to affluent hero thus: "Two years later the Fairfax notes impelled Marshall to accept President Adams' offer of a special mission to Europe. He guessed correctly that the financial reward would exceed his four-or-five-thousand-dollar income as leader of the Virginia bar. It did. His exposure of the bribe-soliciting XYZ papers electrified the country. He came home a national hero. A Federalist and generous Congress allowed him $19,963.75—'the greatest Godsend,' Jefferson wrote, 'that ever could have befallen a man.' This sum, as Beveridge points out, exceeded Marshall's actual expenses by $15,000 and gave him a year's income almost equal to the combined salaries of the President and his entire cabinet." "John Marshall and the Lawyers and Politicians," in W. Melville Jones, ed., *Chief Justice John Marshall* (Ithaca, 1956), 44. Beveridge, *Marshall* II, 373, supplies the conclusion: "Thus, for the time being, the Fairfax estate was saved."

was firmly fixed in Congress, and generally in Federalist circles elsewhere. New England in particular was straining for "open and deadly war with France," a course at last appearing practical to her Federalist war-hawks, now that "the yeomanry are not only united but spirited."[42]

Rejoicing in the state of affairs which "the useful profligacy of the French has produced for us," the Federalist majority in Congress translated into law in rapid succession the several war measures dictated by Hamilton from his New York office.[43] National warships were authorized to capture French armed vessels, and commercial intercourse between the United States and France and her possessions was suspended. This last stipulation was superfluous as far as France was concerned, because mercantile groups in the larger ports were already refusing to ensure cargoes destined for that country, but it served notice of an intention to starve into submission for the benefit of England France's West Indian colonies. On July 7, 1798, the Franco-American treaties were formally abrogated by the unilateral action of Congress, but this interment of a corpse long dead was an empty sacrifice to Federalist fury, and a most gratuitous insult to France.

A few days earlier, Livingston had proposed in the House that the President authorize Gerry to negotiate alone in Paris, whereupon the Federalists pushed through the infamous Alien and Sedition acts, determined to crush not only all sympathy for "Gallicism" but every trace of opposition to themselves as well. "If we hesitate or pause now," Stephen Higginson wrote to Wolcott from Boston, "the faction will revive, and all the avenues for French poison and intrigue be again opened . . . . Nothing but an open war can save us, and the more inveterate and deadly it shall be, the better will be our chance for security in future." Higginson, like most Federalists, looked upon the interests of his country and his party as identical; more than that, the inter-

[42]Beveridge, *Marshall* II, ch. 9; Jefferson to Madison, June 21, 1798, Ford, *Jefferson's Writings* VII, 272–75; Samuel E. Morison, *Life and Letters of Harrison Gray Otis, Federalist, 1765–1848* 2 vols. (Boston, 1913), I, 96; McMaster, *History of the People of the United States* II, 374ff.
[43]Ames to Wolcott, June 8, 1798, *Oliver Wolcott* II, 51.

est of country and self were synonymous, as Higginson and his friends were demonstrating in patriotically subscribing to a fund they were raising to be loaned to their government at only 6 percent interest! [44]

Létombe told Talleyrand that the Alien Bill was one of proscription against Frenchmen as well as Irish immigrants. Many Frenchmen, including the scientist Volney and Victor Dupont, to whom the ailing Létombe had tried to turn over his office because of ill health, chartered a ship and sailed to France, leaving twenty thousand of their compatriots behind in daily fear of arrest. Létombe, against whom a suit by American creditors of France was pending, expected to be jailed after the cancellation of the treaties had removed that protection, and Rozier in New York expected that all France's commercial agents would soon be expelled, an expectation borne out in part when Pickering, on July 13, revoked the exequaturs of all French consular officials. [45]

The Alien Bill was, according to Madison, "a monster that must forever disgrace its parents," but the Sedition Act made it seem gentle by comparison. Hamilton, who repeatedly was forced to check his hotheaded lieutenants, and who a few weeks earlier had told Wolcott to tone down the President's language because "we must make no mistakes," was greatly alarmed. "Let us not

[44]Létombe to Talleyrand, July 3, 1798, AECPE-U, 50, 5–5vo; Higginson to Wolcott, June 29, July 11, 1798, *Oliver Wolcott* II, 69, 71. Heretofore the U. S. had been able to borrow money abroad at 5-percent interest, but even 6 percent turned out to be generous. Higginson thought that "a douceur of some kind may be given to induce monied men to exert themselves to procure and to furnish money." The patriotic Federalist "monied men" were finally persuaded to lend $5,000,000 at 8 percent to support the army and navy for which they were clamoring! Higginson to Wolcott, Dec. 13, 1798, *Oliver Wolcott* II, 177–78.

[45]Létombe to Talleyrand, May 8, Apr. 14, 1798, Rozier to Talleyrand, June 30, 1798, Létombe to Talleyrand, July 10, 1798, Pickering to Létombe, July 13, 1798, AECPE-U, 49, 359–59vo, 328vo, 464–66vo, 50, 25–25vo, 55–56vo; Jefferson to Madison, May 31, 1798, Ford, *Jefferson's Writings* VII, 262. Dupont had been transferred from Charleston to the Philadelphia consulate. He and Létombe arranged his succession to the consul generalship, but President Adams refused to grant him an exequatur. This situation was unknown in France, where the Directory had just authorized Dupont to remain in the U. S. to assist his father, Dupont de Nemours, on his projected scientific expedition. Decree of the Directory, May 15, 1798, AECPE-U, 49, 366. It was the elder Dupont who prompted Adams's famous remark about French philosophers who "have disorganized the world, and are incompatible with social order." To Pickering, Sept. 16, 1798, *Works of Adams* VIII, 596.

establish a tyranny," he wrote. "Energy is a very different thing from violence . . . . If we make no false step, we shall be essentially united, but if we push things to an extreme, we shall then give to faction *body* and solidity." The stakes were too large to risk building up a reaction through precipitation: Hamilton was already dreaming of himself as conqueror of a hemisphere, a return on Bellamy's twelve hundred thousand livres demand worthy of the imagination of a Bonaparte![46]

Hamilton's political instinct in regard to the Sedition Act was true in the end; but in the spring and summer of 1798, the "X. Y. Z. fever" was such that Republican congressmen who had been on friendly terms with Létombe avoided him, and he reported helplessly to Talleyrand that "on the other side the Quakers desire the conversation of peace between the two republics." Repeated assertions that there were two parties in the United States, assertions which kept appearing in the French press, Létombe was told, were responsible for the frenzy of "the Torys." The Republicans, he wrote, wanted such talk stopped, because their own fate depended on successfully combatting the Federalist line that their loyalty was only to France. The Federalists would overreach themselves if the Directory were wise enough to avoid their trap—both Madison and Jefferson saw proof of this fact in the Alien and Sedition laws. By the middle of October, Jefferson could say that the anti-French delirium was subsiding, and that "the alien and sedition laws are working hard," but it was still strong enough to return the Federalists' largest majority ever to Congress in the elections of 1798.[47]

[46]To Jefferson, May 20, 1798, *Writings of Madison* VI, 320; Hamilton to Wolcott, June 5 and 29, to King, Aug. 22, to Francisco Miranda, Aug. 22, 1798, *Works of Hamilton* X, 288, 295, 314–15, 315–16. Hamilton, now Washington's deputy commander of the new army, told Miranda that he hoped the project for the Anglo-American campaign against Spain's American empire would mature before winter, "and an effectual co-operation by the United States may take place. In this case I shall be happy, in my official station, to be an instrument of so good a work. The plan in my opinion ought to be: A fleet of Great Britain, an army of the United States, a government for the liberated territory agreeable to both co-operators, about which there will be no difficulty . . . ."

[47]Létombe to Talleyrand, Apr. 11 and 14, May 8, 1798, AECPE-U, 49, 316vo, 328–29vo, 359–59vo; Brant, *Madison: Father of Constitution*, 457; to Mason, Oct. 11, 1798, Ford, *Jefferson's Writings* VII, 282–83.

## CHAPTER XIV

Talleyrand and
Reconciliation
with America

Nothing but an open war can save us, and the
more inveterate and deadly it shall be, the better
will be our chance for security in future.

HIGGINSON TO WOLCOTT, JUNE 29, 1798.


The influential mass wants only to defend America's honor and otherwise avoid at any price the
mixing in Europe's quarrels.

PICHON TO TALLEYRAND, AUGUST 1, 1798.


An entirely different scene had been unfolding in France.
Having got rid of Marshall and Pinckney, Talleyrand planned to
adopt the maxim of Machiavelli—*nil repentè*—recommended to
him through Létombe by Jefferson. He wrote to Gerry on April
3, 1798, inviting him to call the following day in order to "resume our reciprocal communications upon the interests of the
French republic and the United States of America." But Gerry
answered that he could only "confer informally and unaccredited," since he had no authority to do more as an individual.
Talleyrand did not answer, content with Gerry's implicit assurance that he would remain in Paris. By April 20, Gerry was becoming impatient and wrote to complain of "the most painful
situation" in which the departure of his colleagues had left him.
He had not gone away then because of the threat of war, but he
had expected that "propositions for terminating all differences"

would be made by the Directory, which he would be able to deliver to his government. Still no answer from the minister, who privately professed to disagree with Gerry's interpretation of the validity of his powers.[1]

There was no need for haste, since Talleyrand's goal was only to prevent Gerry's departure and "to engage him in a negotiation which we will be able to prolong at will, because there would be grave inconvenience in breaking abruptly with the United States, while our present position, half friendly, half hostile, is profitable to us while our colonies continue to be provisioned by the Americans and while our corsairs are enriching themselves from the prizes they make on them." But ultimately there would have to be a settlement of differences, "and we will take care that it preserves for us all our advantages or that it gains us their equivalents."[2]

Talleyrand was trying with some success to extricate Létombe from his financial difficulties when the brig *Sophia* reached Le Havre on May 11 with Pickering's conditional recall of her envoys, and with orders to carry them home. Gerry received the instructions on the following day and at once wrote to Pickering his intention of availing himself of this "fortunate circumstance" to return home, promising that "the ultimate views of this government . . . shall be obtained if possible." Only the day before he had written that he would not send his secretary back to America alone, because he expected soon to be able to return himself, "with the acquiescence of this government."[3]

Gerry's differences with Marshall and Pinckney amounted, at bottom, to a difference of opinion on whether their instructions allowed them to consider a loan to France to be paid *after* the

[1] AECPE-U, 49, 144–46; *ASP, FR* II, 209.

[2] G. Pallain, *La Ministère de Talleyrand sous le Directoire* (Paris, 1891), 309.

[3] Talleyrand to Minister of Marine, Apr. 7, Minister of Marine to Talleyrand, Apr. 21, Talleyrand to Minister of Finances, May 3, 1798, AECPE-U, 49, 299–300vo, 337–38vo, 345; *ASP, FR* II, 208. Létombe continued in a semiofficial exercise of his office, causing Uriah Tracy, a rabid Connecticut war-hawk, to complain to McHenry one year later: "Why is old Létombe permitted to exercise the functions of his defunct consulship in overt defiance of all the shadow of govt. we have?" Steiner, *McHenry*, 436.

present war, that being the final essence of Talleyrand's proposition for the purchase of Dutch inscriptions. Gerry saw no impediment to an acceptance of the principle, conditioned on the conclusion of a mutually acceptable treaty, but that line of reasoning was destroyed by Pickering's letter. The secretary had missed the nice distinction between loans payable during and after the war and hence had not specifically answered that question, but his tone left no doubt in Gerry's mind about what it would have been. To Jefferson, the proposition sounded reasonable, especially since Talleyrand had agreed in principle to honor claims for illegal spoliations; and he saw no reason why Gerry should not make a treaty with the Directory, "if they can get through it before the brig Sophia takes him off." Unfortunately for his country, which might have been spared the undeclared naval war, and for President Adams, who might have gained control of his party and spared it the odium which its violence soon won for it, Gerry persisted in his refusal to negotiate despite relentless pressures from Talleyrand, who now had personal reasons for wanting a settlement with the United States.[4]

The imputation of personal corruption carried by the published dispatches forced Talleyrand to lay the whole affair before the Directory. On the last day of May he presented a report which sought to prove that the episode was only "the last attempt of the British cabinet and the American government to provoke the Directory's resentment." Because measures proposed by the President which "seem to indicate a certainty of war" were being strongly opposed in the United States, Adams had "unmasked all of his batteries." Submission of the dispatches to Congress was a trap into which the "friends of France" had been led, because they thought that the President had not done all that he should

4James T. Austin, *The Life of Elbridge Gerry* (Boston, 1829) II, 213–19; Pickering to Envoys, Mar. 23, 1798, *ASP, FR* II, 200–201; Ford, *Jefferson's Writings* VII, 266–69, 269–72; Lyon, "Directory and the U. S.," 528. Joel Barlow, "Hartford Wit," speculator in western lands, emissary to the Barbary states and subsequently American minister to the Emperor Napoleon, called Gerry "a little make-weight man, appointed with the intention that he should have no influence." Barlow to Baldwin, Mar. 4, 1798, Jefferson Papers, Library of Congress, No. 17619–17639. See Morison, "Elbridge Gerry," 3–33.

to avert war. The Federalists and the British minister, who were in on the secret, made sure of their publication: "its effect in America can be judged by the indignation it must excite here." Such, continued Talleyrand, was the impudence of a government which wanted war so badly that it stooped to such means to incite the French government to attack it.[5]

Talleyrand devoted thirteen pages to a review of the dispatches themselves. The "shocking propositions" mentioned were not his but came from "subordinate intriguers"; all that came from him and from his department's employees was "simple, all is pure, all is worthy of French loyalty." Even in the dispatches, "Z" (Hauteval, whom he acknowledged) was not tainted, but "X" (Hottinguer, whose identity he claimed not to know) was obviously a speculator trying to win himself a commission and "Y" (Bellamy) had appeared to him as a financial agent appointed by the Americans.[6] And what of the latter? They reflected "the odious intention of Mr. Adams." They were "stiff and cavilling, timid and stubborn, defiant and gullible, holding themselves aloof from the Minister with whom they should have dealt and giving themselves freely to crafty speculators." The result was "a complete misunderstanding," plotted by the American government's hostile envoys.[7]

[5] AECPE-U, 49, 393–404.

[6] Bellamy reacted violently in print to Talleyrand's anonymous defense, claiming that he had done nothing except on orders from the minister, but of course he received no satifaction. Guyot, *Le Directoire et la Paix de l'Europe*, 563.

[7] That Talleyrand's rancor at the envoys was not merely the fruit of his chagrin at being outmaneuvered politically is tistified by Skipwith, whose letter of Mar. 17, 1798, to Jefferson was intercepted by Wolcott. In his edition of Wolcott's papers, Mr. Gibbs printed it as a patent example of Republican treason. "When the news came that Gen. Pinckney was ordered to retake his post at Paris," wrote Skipwith, "and that Gen. Marshall, one of the declaiming apostles of Jay's treaty, was to support him this government, I believe, suspected that their mission was virtually destined for the court of Louis XVIII, and not for the French republic.... Be this as it may, no body expected, from the nomination of those two persons, that concord with the French Republic, was their object, and their deportment since their arrival, added to the President's ill-judged, and ill-timed speech at the opening of your session of Congress, have served powerfully, to confirm that impression. Everybody here remarks, what those two gentlemen do not attempt to conceal, that their doors are open only to the intriguants against, and enemies of the present government; and that they are among the first persons to

But the damage could be repaired. France could catch England and the American government in their own trap, "by secretly proceeding with the negotiation Adams tried to break up." King's and Liston's secretaries had just arrived together in London, Talleyrand reported, so that an immediate decision was necessary. According to Létombe, Jefferson and other Republicans had confided that "the present moment is one of crisis infinitely important to the United States." The parties were united under Tory domination and a French declaration of war would bring about the dreaded English alliance, and make England "triumph forever in the United States." The Directory's answer to the envoy's memorial must already have appeared in America: "It will prove how much the Directory was disposed to treat and discounted the declaration of war that Mr. Adams announced as very probable . . . . It will reassure the people and doubtless stop negotiations with England." If the Directory desired "to perse-

---

hear and buzz about the tales of new coalitions, and counter revolutions. The name of a true supporter of the French revolution is as grating to their ears, as his sight is disgusting to their eyes. From their arrival, their attentions and caresses have been confined to the families of the proscribed and of the transported; and their closest counsellor seems to be Beaumarchais, of whose character you, I know, want no information. When we heard that Mr. Gerry was nominated to the mission, the Directory were pleased, and the patriots in Paris, of both Countries, were delighted in the idea of seeing here one of the tried patriots of '75, and one of the remaining republican chiefs of the American States; but painful it is to me to add, that we beheld him moving here but as the shadow of what we presumed he was; and we much fear, that the longer he stays, the more apt will public opinion be to ascribe the neutrality of his character to the feebleness of his diplomatic talents. We learn in secret whispers from this good old gentlemen, (for I venerate the chastity of his moral character, while I regret he has not courage to shape a political course congenial to the crisis here) that he has a hard and cruel task to think and act with his two associates, and that were he alone, he would be able to stop the frightful breach between the two countries. But I am apprehensive that his paralytic mind would prove too weak to invent, and his arm too feeble to apply the remedy which the disease demands. In fact, no one but a pronounced republican, and friend of the French revolution, and a man unfettered by the forms and schoolreadings of Mr. Adams and Pickering, could stand a chance to heal the wounds which are now bleeding." *Oliver Wolcott* II, 160. Joel Barlow wrote in the same vein to his brother-in-law in the Senate and sent a copy to Jefferson. This letter provoked the Lyon–Griswold fracas on the floor of the House of Representatives and caused the first prosecution under the new Sedition Act. Barlow to Abraham Baldwin, Mar. 4, to Jefferson, Mar. 12, 1798. Jefferson Papers, Library of Congress, 17619–17639, 17640. See James Woodress, *A Yankee's Odyssey* (Philadelphia, 1958), 193–97.

vere in measures of moderation," as he recommended, let Talleyrand make a formal statement on the subject to Gerry, as the envoy of the United States.

The scandal in Paris was so great that Talleyrand thought it advisable to prepare a rebuttal. After several peremptory demands upon Gerry, he succeeded in extracting the names of the pseudonymous intermediaries and then published a pamphlet with that correspondence appended. This defense was itself anonymous and its aim was to distract attention from the French government by excoriating the warmongering of the American government and ridiculing its envoys. For corruption was a sensitive subject, not only to Talleyrand, whose libertine reputation had always included this particular vice, but to the directors themselves. The name of Barras had become almost synonymous with venality; Reubell had recently been accused of connivance with a fraudulent contractor; and Merlin was widely believed to profit from condemnations of American ships by French tribunals. Talleyrand informed Barras of the "reflections" he had produced: "They seem to me to be within the bounds of the moderation we should display; they are not too offensive to Mr. Gerry, of whom we are desirous of making use, but severe against his colleagues; they are very nettling to Mr. Adams, whose liberticide policy they unmask; as a whole encouraging for our friends in America." He had not signed the publication because he did not think it should be "entirely official," though Reubell, relates Barras, objected, as was his custom wherever Talleyrand was concerned.[8]

Talleyrand was now thoroughly alarmed at the unexpected results of the late American mission, and he dedicated all of his energies to abating the storm. By June 9, he was able to inform Létombe that his drafts had been acquitted, thus restoring

[8]Talleyrand to Gerry, May 30, Gerry to Talleyrand, May 31, Talleyrand to Gerry and Gerry to Talleyrand, June 1, Gerry to Talleyrand, June 3, Talleyrand to Gerry, June 4 and June ?, 1798, Talleyrand's pamphlet, undated, *ASP, FR* II, 210–11, 224–27; Guyot, *Le Directoire et la Paix de l'Europe*, 562–63; *Memoirs of Barras* III, 293. Michaud's *Biographie Universelle* XL, 610–11, emphasizes that the corrupt directors imposed the "douceur" system upon their ministers.

France's financial integrity in the United States. He sent Bournonville to Philadelphia with a copy of his March 18 answer to Marshall's memorial, and with "a little publication"—his anonymous defense—which Létombe was to give all possible publicity. The countermemorial expressed the true intentions of the Directory, and the government would soon give further proof of its pacific dispositions. By a decree of May 14, American vessels were excluded from the ports of Brest, Lorient, Rochefort, Toulon, and Dunkerque, and Le Havre was added to the list on June 5, but these measures were not related to "the present situation"; they were merely security precautions. Notwithstanding the attitude of Adams, concluded Talleyrand, "our friends in Congress and Mr. Jefferson in particular" should be assured that the Directory would not fall into the crude trap prepared for it. "We are always ready to discuss in a friendly manner the points in controversy between us."[9]

Ignoring Gerry's request for his passport and for exemption of the *Sophia* from the embargo, Talleyrand wrote to him on June 10 that France "perseveres in the intention of conciliating with sincerity all the differences which have arisen between the two countries," and he concluded by demanding "whether you are at length in a situation to proceed towards this important object." One week later, despite Gerry's reiteration of his inability to negotiate, Talleyrand took the trouble to review the points which a negotiation would comprehend, "as if you were in a situation to receive my overtures." He was confident, "provided your Government is as averse to a rupture as you assure me," that further powers, if needed, were en route. No such powers were on the way, as Talleyrand suspected; but two weeks later, Pickering, in a letter whose insulting malice betrayed a fear that Gerry had accepted Talleyrand's invitation, addressed to the hard-pressed envoy what he was to consider "as a positive letter to recall."[10]

9Talleyrand to Létombe, June 9, Decree of the Directory, May 6, June 5, 1798, AECPE-U, 49, 434–35VO, 364, 433.

10*ASP, FR* II, 211–14, Pickering to Gerry, June 25, 1798, *ibid.* II, 204; Pallain, *Le Ministère de Talleyrand*, 310.

Gerry never received Pickering's letter, but in answer to Talleyrand he repeated his determination to sail on the *Sophia* before the end of the month, adding that he would not remain to treat even if empowered to do so. He had expected to have departed long since with propositions from the French government, which would have sent a minister to Philadelphia "to complete the negotiation." Three days later he sent a more peremptory demand for his papers and received in reply a long lecture concerning his duty to remain, ending with a note which Talleyrand intended to be the first of a mutual exchange upon the treaties of 1778 and 1788. Gerry maintained his ground, but he was still friendly when he complained on July 1 that "my frequent applications for a passport, letter of safe conduct for the vessel, and her exemption from the embargo at Havre, have been altogether unnoticed."[11]

Talleyrand's object in seeking to open a negotiation in writing was to detain Gerry until the increasingly alarming news from America should settle the question of war or peace. He had at hand an intercepted dispatch from Pickering to King which expressed the American government's conviction that "France will continue her actual hostilities . . . without a formal declaration of war," and which concluded: "Addresses are coming in from all quarters, approving the measures of the Government in relation to France, and pledging life and fortune to defend our honor and independence." Another contained a paragraph in cipher, and Talleyrand offered a reward of twenty-five louis to anyone in the postal service who could decipher it, because "it might give us the key to the cipher used by the American government."[12]

On July 10, Talleyrand reported to the Directory that the situation had changed: the hostile measures taken by the American

[11]Gerry to Talleyrand, June 22 and 25, Talleyrand to Gerry, June 27, Gerry to Talleyrand, July 1, Talleyrand to Gerry, July 6, 1798, *ASP, FR* II, 214–16.

[12]Pickering to King, May 3, Talleyrand to Gauvin, postal commissary, Aug. 23, 1798, AECPE-U, 49, 346–46vo, 50, 192. According to Professor Bemis, Grenville, the British foreign minister, had long possessed a copy of the secret cipher of the State Department. *Diplomatic History of U. S.*, 101.

government amounted to "a veritable declaration of war," and the Directory would have to make new dispositions. The embargo already placed upon American ships was a proper response "to the aggressions of the United States" and "all idea of accommodation must be adjourned." The Directory agreed emphatically and decreed a complete embargo on American vessels in all French ports the following day, but Talleyrand only learned of this decree indirectly and had to ask the minister of marine for a copy of it.[13]

Talleyrand also submitted to the Directory on July 10 a project of a letter to Gerry enclosing his passports, "in which he recalls to this envoy the conduct and the loyalty of the Directory towards the Americans." The letter was a lengthy review of his own efforts at conciliation with Gerry, ending with renewed assurances of the pacific intentions of the Directory and of its regret at his departure. Before the letter was sent, however, the Directory's decisions forced new explanations on Talleyrand, which he added in a postscript dated July 15. News received "some days since" gave evidence that, in its provocations against France, "your Government no longer preserves appearances." Nevertheless, the Directory had confined itself to "a measure of security and self-preservation, by laying a temporary embargo on American vessels, with a reserve of indemnities, if there be occasion for them." It was still "as much disposed as ever to terminate, by a candid negotiation the differences which subsist between the two nations." Gerry, since he insisted upon departing, was urged to "hasten, at least to transmit to your Government this solemn declaration."[14]

Gerry replied with a long defense of the conduct of successive American envoys. Admitting that Talleyrand had tried to press seriously a negotiation with him, he could not resist adding that "the merit would have been *greater* had the measure itself been

[13]Minister of Marine to Talleyrand, July 15, Decree of Directory, July 11, 1798, AECPE-U, 50, 58, 59–59vo; Pallain, *Le Ministère de Talleyrand*, 309–10.
[14]Pallain, *Le Ministère de Talleyrand*, 320n.; Gerry to Talleyrand, July 10, Talleyrand to Gerry, July 12, 1798, *ASP, FR* II, 218–20.

*feasible."* He was happy that the Directory desired a speedy reconciliation, but now he thought that "a preliminary measure appears to be requisite." France should curb her privateers, whose unparalleled outrages in the West Indies and on the American coast "have been a great source of irritation in the United States, and a principal cause of the repressive measures adopted by them."[15]

Gerry thus gave Talleyrand, who had no intention of being the goat of a very unpopular war with America caused by the Directory's arrogance, the key to extricating himself from a difficult position and of forcing moderation upon the Directory. He published his own letters to Gerry of July 12 and 15, as well as Gerry's reply. The minister had been genuinely astonished at the extravagance of American war measures, which had made him such a fervent apostle of peace that he even succeeded in converting Admiral Eustache Bruix, now minister of marine and colonies, who at first had advised the Directory to send French warships as well as privateers after American commerce.[16]

The explanation of the unexpected events in Philadelphia having become clearer, Talleyrand had potent arguments to convince the directors of the folly of permitting the two countries to continue the drift toward war. From Holland, dominated by France, and attached to her by an offensive and defensive alliance, he received frantic warnings against involving her with the United States. The Dutch minister presented to him a memorial in English which Talleyrand probably knew was written by William Vans Murray, American minister at The Hague: "Rough Sketches of a few of the reasons why it is not the interest of *France* that Holland should join in the War if the United States and France go to war at present." Several days later Rutger Jan Schimmelpenninck himself drafted a memorial to Talleyrand, presenting the Dutch position even more strongly. Holland's

15July 20, 1798, *ASP, FR* II, 220–21.

16Faÿ, *Revolutionary Spirit in France and America*, 426–27; *ASP, FR* II, 222; Talleyrand to Minister of Marine and Minister of Marine to Secretary General of the Directory, July 25, Minister of Marine to Talleyrand, Aug. 1, 1798, AECPE-U, 50, 30–31vo, 34, 134.

commercial relations with the United States, he wrote, were all that remained of her once vast commerce, and war between France and that country would reduce it to "absolute inactivity." The disadvantage of that to France, which received a large percentage of her imports through Dutch ports, not to mention France's interest in the sources of the wealth from which the Batavian government fulfilled the Directory's demands for financial support, made peace imperative. The United States also had reasons for desiring peace, concluded the minister, and his country was thus in a singularly favorable position to guarantee a reconciliation through its intervention. Schimmelpenninck had offered the mediation of the Batavian Republic to Gerry the previous day—now he offered it officially to France.[17]

France's own commercial interests were deeply concerned as well. An anonymous writer urged the reform of laws concerning neutrals, laws which now hurt only France and "her natural allies," as a means of keeping peace with the United States. America not only consumed much of France's most important export products—wine, vinegar, champagne, table oils, salt, and even manufactured goods—but also carried much more under her flag to many other countries. Perhaps more important was the position of Russia, which was expected to join the new coalition formed by England (she did, in January 1799). When that happened, the Baltic would be closed to France and her allies, whether or not the northern neutrals followed Russia, and thus she would be cut off from her source of naval stores and building materials, particularly wood, leaving the United States as the only possible source of these vital articles.[18]

17 Murray's "Rough Sketches," undated, Schimmelpenninck to Talleyrand, July 26, 1798, AECPE-U, 50, 61–65, 128–30; ASP, FR II, 224; Aug. 3, 1798, "Letters of Murray," 446–47.
18 AECPE-U, 50, 66–67vo. Extracting a Treasury Department report to Congress, Rozier, French consul at New York, showed what was really happening to American commerce with France and Great Britain:

|  | 1793 | 1795 | 1797 | 1798 |
|---|---|---|---|---|
| to France | $7,030,498 | $12,553,635 | $11,664,091 | $ 6,941,416 |
| to Great Britain | 8,431,239 | 9,218,540 | 8,569,748 | 17,086,189 |

Ibid., 50, 390.

Fully aware of the dangers a rupture with the United States held for France's colonies, and no less those of its Spanish ally, Talleyrand ordered Ambassador Guillemardet at Madrid to have Spain's minister at Philadelphia begin at once the stockpiling of provisions for Louisiana, which France had not abandoned hope of regaining from Spain, and for the West Indies. While Talleyrand hoped to supply the French islands from Louisiana, he also engaged his colleague Bruix to work out means of sustaining them from France itself. It was in fact in those islands that the solution of French difficulties lay, and it was with confidence that Talleyrand demanded of Dupont, who had just arrived in Paris from Philadelphia, the information upon which to base a program.[19]

The minister wanted a detailed report on the general unrest in American ports. What were the acts of French cruisers complained of by the Americans? What were the proceedings of colonial tribunals in regard to prizes, and how were the decrees of the Directory, "which authorize, in certain cases, the arrest of neutrals in general, and of Americans in particular," executed on the high seas? Talleyrand wanted precise information to provide the basis for an appeal to the Directory to restrict privateers in the West Indies along the lines suggested by Gerry, and the blistering sixteen-page report that Dupont sent him on July 21 was calculated to arouse even the most cynical and indifferent of the directors.

Dupont began diplomatically: "it appears that our government has never been well instructed on the conduct of our corsairs in American seas"; that conduct was "one of the principal causes of the present coldness and ferment against us" and could lead to the war that the American government desired. The "brigandage" practiced by the corsairs under official encouragement and protection, the piracies and the acts of violence, "would require volumes" to list. Blank commissions were given to un-

---

[19]Talleyrand to Minister of Marine, July 25, Minister of Marine to Talleyrand, July 29, Talleyrand to Létombe, July 26, Talleyrand to Dupont, July 17, 1798, *ibid.*, 50, 31vo, 57–57vo, 127–27vo, 68.

345

THE STRUGGLE FOR NEUTRALITY

bonded ships and were sold in the United States and even coun-
terfeited there, and in both America and in the colonies they
were frequently displayed by adventurers in small boats or
barges who, with only a few rifles, stopped and looted every un-
armed vessel they could waylay. Even in neutral and allied ports,
prizes were adjudged almost without exception by the agents or
the owners of the corsairs, and Commissioner Victor Hugues at
Saint-Domingue not only encouraged the indiscriminate seizure
of American ships, but had their crews thrown into prison and
then exchanged them with the English for French prisoners! The
smallest pretext, real or fabricated, was sufficient to condemn
American ships; and their owners, disgusted with the arbitrari-
ness of the colonial administrations which were ruining them,
now preferred to send their goods to the English islands.[20]

But, "I would abuse your patience . . . by multiplying examples
of these facts." The Directory should disavow all illegal acts, not
only because France's interest required her to respect neutral
rights, but because it would be unwise to throw all of America's
commerce to England simply because the latter's share was nor-
mally a little greater than that of France. For the Americans, war
with France would mean the end of their liberties and of their
independence. It would mean swelling British maritime strength
by twenty thousand expert seamen and the surrender of the
French islands to England. Most important, the Americans needed only such an excuse to invade Louisiana and the Floridas,
which "it will be easy and useful for us to have one day . . . and
that day may be near," provided, meanwhile, France could avoid
giving England the opportunity to use American forces to snatch
them from Spain.[21]

The means of avoiding all these misfortunes were obvious to
Dupont. He proposed a three-point program which he said

20 *Ibid.*, 50, 99–106vo. Samuel E. Morison published this correspondence in "Dupont, Talleyrand and the French Spoliations," *Massachusetts Historical Society
Proceedings* XLIX (1915–16), 63–79.
21 See James A. James, "French Opinion as a Factor in Preventing War between
France and the United States, 1795–1800," *American Historical Review* XXX (Oct.
1924), 49–51.

346

embodied the opinions of the most illustrious men of the Republican party. He proposed that the Directory (1) withdraw provisionally the commissions of all corsairs in the Antilles and disavow the piracies they had committed, (2) announce an intention of revising the laws against neutrals, and in the meantime supervise the judgments of prizes, (3) let the government of the United States know that the Directory would receive and treat with new commissioners. This was the program already being urged by Talleyrand, and it raises a suspicion that he collaborated with Dupont. In any event, the two men were in complete agreement about the nature of the difficulties and their remedy.[22]

With Dupont's report in hand, Talleyrand wrote to Gerry on July 22. Referring to the propositions contained in his letter of June 18, he explicitly renounced any demands for loans or other "reparations," as Gerry had demanded, because "an odious intrigue had got possession of them" which was unworthy of the Directory's dignity. Then, "as to the preliminary measures which you suggest, sir, the Government has already anticipated your desire." It had just learned that his assertions concerning French corsairs were indeed true and "a remedy is preparing for it, and orders will soon reach the West Indies calculated to restore everything within its just limits," pending "an amicable arrangement between France and the United States." Talleyrand regretted that Gerry refused to effect that arrangement himself, but Gerry, about to leave Paris for Le Havre, ignored the hint.[23]

Hauteval now sent a memorial to the Directory blaming the greed of French shipowners, rather than the Directory's policy, for "the hostilities against the American people." French privateersmen, he announced, considered their own interests apart from those of their country, which they would be perfectly content to see ruined, if in the process they could amass personal fortunes. He thought that the Directory should send a well-known and respected minister to the United States to make peace,

22James, "French Opinion," 53–54; Morison, "Dupont, Talleyrand and French Spoliations," 76; Lyon, "Directory and the United States," 529.
23*ASP, FR* II, 222.

fortified by a dramatic move to end depredations and to set up a commission to hear American claims. This memorial was probably written under Talleyrand's inspiration, to prepare an attentive reception of the report enclosing Dupont's memoir, which the minister presented on July 27.[24]

Dupont's report, said Talleyrand, "demands all [the Directory's] attention." It showed "what strange abuse" of the laws regarding neutral commerce had been made without the Directory's knowledge. "The knowledge of these excesses explains at last," he continued, "the ferment that the Britannic cabinet has been able to produce in all the ports of the United States . . . . One can no longer be astonished that the President is reduced to encouraging repressive measures." It was up to the Directory to rise above the provocations of the American government and "open new paths to conciliation." But it was no less important to end "the causes of the ferment introduced among the people of the United States." The laws must be enforced; "but depredations, piracies, violations of territory are illegal acts that the French government cannot condone."[25]

Talleyrand probably shared more than a copy of Dupont's report with Bruix, who a few days later complimented his colleague for "the value of the thought and the skill of expression of all of your productions." "You have indicated to me the course to follow to conform to [the Directory's] liberal and pacific intentions . . . . I should imitate you and I have hastened to do so." Accordingly, the Directory,

> on the report of the Minister of Marine and Colonies, considering that news recently received from the French colonies and from the continent of America leave no doubt that French or so-called French cruisers have not observed the laws of the Republic on privateering and prizes,

decreed as thoroughgoing a reform as Gerry could have wished.

24Extract of a memoir by Citizen Hauteval, and the memoir, both dated July 23, Talleyrand's report to the Directory, July 27, 1798, AECPE-U, 50, 118–19vo, 120–24vo, 131–31vo.
25Ibid., 50, 132, 133.

No letters of marque, or commissions to privateer, were hence-forth to be given in the colonies except by the particular agents of the Directory, and all commissions already given were to ex-pire thirty days after the publication of the present decree. Any agent authorized to judge prizes taken by French cruisers in neu-tral ports, who was suspected of direct or indirect interests in privateering, was to be recalled at once; the Directory's agents in the French colonies were to see that the interests and properties of neutral ships were scrupulously respected. Finally, those agents, as well as the commanders of vessels of the Republic, its consuls and vice-consuls, were all given authority to arrest and punish violators of any of the foregoing provisions.[26]

Talleyrand sent a copy of this decree to Gerry, who was pre-paring to embark at Le Havre, saying that it was "a part of the measures which I announced to you the 4th of this month." The solicitude of the French government, however, would not be con-fined to that.

> Neutrals, in general, will have reason soon to be convinced of its firm attachment to the principles to which it is desirous that all the maritime nations might agree.... It depends upon the United States, in particular, to cause every misunderstanding im-mediately to disappear between them and the French Republic.

Copies of the decree were sent at once to Skipwith, and three days later, on August 6, Talleyrand told the consul general of his hope that "the conduct of the Federal Government may correspond with that of the Directory."[27]

Gerry promised to deliver the decree, with Talleyrand's cov-ering letter, to the President, but there was a delay of several days before the authorities at Le Havre permitted the *Sophia* to de-part. Contrary to Gerry's belief, it was Bruix, not Talleyrand, who was responsible for the delay. Probably because of its posi-tion across the channel from England, Bruix desired that Gerry leave from some other port, but Talleyrand quickly obtained

[26]*Ibid.*, 50, 134, 138–38vo. The decree, dated July 31, 1798, is also in *ASP, FR* II, 222–23.

[27]Talleyrand to Gerry, Aug. 3, 1798, *ASP, FR* II, 222, 227.

from him the necessary release so that, as he explained to his colleague, Gerry could get to the United States promptly with the declarations the Directory had addressed to him for the American government. Talleyrand sent all of his correspondence with Gerry to Létombe, with instructions to have it printed if the government did not, in the hope that "our friends can prevent the President from taking rash steps against France . . . ."[28]

Talleyrand was determined, as he told Bruix regarding war with the United States, "to have neglected nothing to prevent such an unhappy event." By the end of June, he was probably convinced that Gerry would not remain to negotiate a treaty, although early in July he tried to engage him in a written discussion of the points at issue in the treaties. He therefore decided to approach President Adams through Murray, whom he had known at Philadelphia as an orthodox Federalist, and who was a close friend of the President's son, John Quincy Adams, whom Murray had succeeded upon Adams's transfer to Berlin. For this task, Talleyrand chose an able employee of the American section of his department, Louis André Pichon, then twenty-eight years old, who had served previously in America as secretary to Genet and to Fauchet, with whom he had returned to France in the fall of 1796 on the *Medusa*. [29]

Pichon also had known Murray in America, and he lost no time at The Hague in renewing his acquaintance, but his first reports to the minister were not encouraging. He wrote on June 26 that Murray was strongly prejudiced against France and was "convinced that we want no settlement, that the hope of effecting a revolution in the United States directs all our conduct, and that we want furthermore to humiliate America as a nation." He told Talleyrand frankly that Murray seemed familiar with his memorial of March 18, from which the minister had expected so favorable an effect in America, and that Murray was not only uncon-

---

28Gerry to Talleyrand, Aug. 8, 1798, *ASP, FR* II, 222; Minister of Marine to Talleyrand, July 16, Talleyrand to Minister of Marine and Minister of Marine to Talleyrand, July 17, Talleyrand to Létombe, July 26 and 31, 1798, AECPE-U, 50, 78–78vo, 79, 80, 126, 135–35vo.

29Aug. 14, 1798, *ibid.*, 50, 164.

vinced but unimpressed. Pichon had been agreeably surprised, however, at the instructions to the late envoys, a copy of which he obtained from Murray. He recommended that Talleyrand read them and compare "the truly conciliatory principles" they contained with the acts of the American government. The substance of the instructions was substantially "as the vote of the House of Representatives in reply to the address of the President of the United States in May 1797, had enabled us to foresee," but of particular interest was the part authorizing the commissioners to offer an alternative to the mutual guarantees of the treaty of alliance. This deserved "to be looked at as an interesting idea of the policy of the United States in whatever hands is the government."[30]

Talleyrand, seeing the instructions for the first time, was "as surprised as you that the conduct of the envoys followed their spirit so little." Really conciliatory men could easily surmount any difficulties through frank negotiation. Unfortunately, Gerry still insisted upon returning to America, a circumstance which made it more than ever necessary that Murray be convinced "of our sincere intentions of putting an end to a state of affairs so contrary to the interests of the two countries." Pichon's task was to win Murray's cooperation for the sending of a new mission, of "a Plenipotentiary favorably known in France." Perhaps recalling Benjamin Franklin's famous remark to Vergennes after concluding a separate peace with England in 1782, Talleyrand suggested that a new negotiation would find France and the United States more in agreement that "the English party imagines." In conversation with Murray, Pichon used this in its original sense; but its subtlety was lost on Murray, who wrote incredulously to his friend in Berlin that France's language was "that if the United States would but send an envoy soon, things might be better arranged than *Great Britain*!! expects!"[31]

On July 18, Pichon reported that Murray was a "most pro-

[30]*Ibid.*, 49, 455–58.
[31]Talleyrand to Pichon, July 10, 1798, *ibid.*, 50, 24–24vo; July 20, 1798, "Letters of Murray," 437.

nounced Federalist" and very sensitive on the subject of parties in the United States. Pichon did not know that Murray had recently relayed a rumor that two new French agents were to be sent as consuls to America; the appointments of such "incendiary" characters, Murray told Pickering, "indicate probably the last effort at insurrection." To Pichon, Murray stoutly defended his government's policy, but when he insisted that France had refused to treat even with Gerry, Pichon was able to produce evidence to the contrary. Murray was much impressed with that, reported Pichon, and was afterwards more friendly, insisting repeatedly that his country wanted to side with neither France nor England, and that its safety lay in a balance of power between the two. The United States fought not for reparations nor even for principles of neutrality, but for its independence. There, remarked Pichon, is "a confession of faith which is that of Murray's whole party."[32]

As Pichon hoped, Murray had decided to relate the development of these conversations to President Adams. On July 17, he explained their conferences at length and sent to the President a copy of the extract of Talleyrand's letter to Pichon on the instructions to the commissioners. To avoid the imputation of being thought either officious or gullible, however, Murray assured Adams that he had been careful to discourage any expectation that he would communicate any part of the business to his government, a business of which he thought the object was "to amuse America with a new chime of bells." This letter was received at Quincy, where the President had gone because of "the long-continued dangerous sickness" of Mrs. Adams. This cause of anxiety was doubtless compounded by the disloyal intrigue of Hamilton's henchmen in the cabinet—an intrigue which won for their mentor the actual command of the new army. Pickering, to whom Adams had to send Murray's letter for decipherment, described it, sphinxlike, as "in different points of view, very inter-

32AECPE-U, 50, 81–88vo; July 10, 1798, "Letters of Murray," 430, 430n. See *Writings of John Quincy Adams* II, 328.

esting," but Adams answered on October 29 that it was "important" and had "made a great impression on me."[33]

Pichon told Talleyrand that the extract of his letter had produced a great effect on Murray: half of conviction, because of his honesty; half of embarrasment, because of party spirit. Murray, Pichon had decided, was not a blind partisan. Some Federalists wanted war, he admitted, but Murray represented "the influential mass [which] wants only to defend [America's] honor and otherwise avoid at any price the mixing in Europe's quarrels." Pichon thought now (August 1) that he could predict the success of Talleyrand's plan.[34]

Talleyrand expressed much gratification at Pichon's progress, because "it is important to make some impression on men devoted to the Administration of Mr. Adams and to put them in the position at least of doubting the justice of the measures that he continues to have adopted in the legislative body of the United States." Pichon could tell Murray "that the provisory embargo is going to be lifted," and that the government was busy with a revision of the laws concerning neutral nations.[35]

It was at this juncture, when all was going smoothly along the course plotted by Talleyrand, that the Quaker Republican, Dr. George Logan, appeared on the scene, ostensibly to conduct agricultural experiments in France. Murray first heard, late in July, that "a Mr. Droghan" was at Hamburg on his way from America to Paris, with letters from Jefferson and others to Merlin and Talleyrand, "with the hope of averting war between France and the United States!" On August 3, Murray learned Logan's true identity and flew into a panic, prevailing upon the Dutch police to agree to arrest him for interrogation at Rotterdam, where he

[33]*Works of Adams* VIII, 680–84, 677n., 601. Kurtz, *Presidency of Adams,* 330, states that this split over control of the army actually caused the split between Adams and the Hamiltonian wing of the party which later wrecked it.

[34]AECPE-U, 50, 139–42. Murray, complaining to J. Q. Adams on July 20 that "I am almost daily beset by [Pichon]," nevertheless wanted to know: "Is there no mode of stopping things! . . . NONE that I dare to think of . . . . I have no right to judge or go between them now." "Letters of Murray," 438.

[35]Aug. 15, 1798, AECPE-U, 50, 166.

was expected from Amsterdam. Murray himself hastened to Rotterdam with Mountflorence in tow, but Logan, having taken another route from Amsterdam, arrived unmolested in Paris on August 7.[36]

Logan, in fact, had been planning a private peace mission to France for more than one year, as Jefferson told Madison, and as even Pickering had known from a letter written in June 1796, from Monroe to Logan, which the secretary had intercepted and which he had then laid before President Washington as "proof" of Monroe's treachery. When Logan at length accumulated the money for the journey and quietly sailed from Philadelphia on June 13, 1798, Jefferson thought he had been unwise in making a mystery of it. The Federalist extremists, led by Robert Goodloe Harper of South Carolina in the House, shortly demonstrated this truth by raising a ridiculous clamor about Jacobin agents of the French plotting to introduce an army from France into the United States. What constituted the "traitorous correspondence" ominously announced by Harper was a dispatch for Talleyrand entrusted to Logan by Létombe, and letters from Jefferson and Judge Thomas McKean, chief justice of Pennsylvania and likewise a Republican, attesting Logan's citizenship and his good character. Both letters were addressed to Merlin as president of the Directory.[37]

Possibly informed of Murray's exertions, and certainly aware of the danger Logan's mere presence held for the success of Pichon's efforts, Talleyrand received Logan coldly but politely and accepted some works on agriculture and some experiments with plaster of Paris, "which I have sent to the Minister of the Interior." A letter from Mountflorence warning him against "criminal and unaccredited negociation" with an emissary of "the

36 To J. Q. Adams, Aug. 2, 6, 10, 14, to Pickering, Aug. 7 and 13, 1798, "Letters of Murray," 444, 448–49, 450–51, 452, 454–55, 456.

37 June 21, 1798, to Gerry, Jan. 26, 1799, Ford, *Jefferson's Writings* VII, 272–75, 325–36; Monroe to Logan, June 24, 1796, *Writings of Monroe* III, 7; Washington to Secretary of State, July 8, 1796, *Writings of Washington* XXXV, 128, 128n. The Logan mission is discussed in Frederick B. Tolles, "Unofficial Ambassador: George Logan's Mission to France, 1798," *W & M Quarterly* 3d ser., VII (Jan. 1950), 4–25; Frederick B. Tolles, *George Logan of Philadelphia* (New York, 1953), 153–84.

party of the opposition" confirmed Talleyrand's fears, but he could have had nothing but contempt for Mountflorence's demand that he seize and turn over to the American government Logan's "letters, declarations and propositions," or for Mountflorence's sly statement that the leaders of Logan's party hated him and regretted his being in the ministry. It was with Mountflorence in mind that Talleyrand wrote to Pichon: "However, I learn that men always occupied in chicanery insinuate that Dr. Logan is sent to the French government without the knowledge of the American government with private letters and for secret negotiations." The reports that Logan carried letters to Talleyrand or that he pretended to "a political status" were absolutely false, and it was absurd to suppose that the Directory did not know that official relations with a foreign country could only be conducted through the head of the government. Logan had received the same assurances of France's amical dispositions as had been given Gerry: nothing else.[38]

Pichon reported to Talleyrand on August 19 that he was still on terms of "great mutual confidence" with Murray, who now had "a desire that I believe equally sincere . . . to see an end to the existing misunderstanding . . . ." Murray was now convinced, according to Pichon, that France's conduct since 1794 stemmed from "betrayed confidence" and "violated friendship" and not, as he suspected, from designs to agitate and revolutionize the United States. But Murray now pleaded the difficulty of appointing new envoys and suggested that Paris might not be the best place for a fresh negotiation, and three days later he alluded significantly to the proffered mediation of Holland. Pichon thought that Murray's cooling off was attributable to overtures for a new armed neutrality from the Swedish minister at The Hague, and to the influence of Mountflorence, "another who works against me"; but the real reason was information from Swedish Count de Lowenhielm that Spain had at last ceded Louisiana to France. This news was later authoritatively denied by

[38]Talleyrand to Pichon, Aug. 16, Mountflorence to Talleyrand, Aug. 9, 1798. AECPE-U, 50, 169, 159–59vo.

355

the secretary of the Spanish legation. Murray's suspicions concerning Logan were not entirely erased by Pichon's communication of the pertinent paragraphs of Talleyrand's letter of August 16, but nevertheless Pichon felt himself justified in assuring his master that Murray still desired a reconciliation because he feared that a war would ruin his country.[39]

The strategist in Paris had cause to be pleased with Pichon: "I see a gradual development of the opinions of Mr. Murray which make me presume the step that the American government will follow." He enclosed a letter ostensibly to Pichon dated August 28, which Murray was to copy on condition that he keep it a secret between himself and President Adams. This letter was official, and Pichon was now able to confirm what Murray already knew—that he had been sent to Holland solely to make overtures—and also that the Directory had from the middle of June turned over the management of relations with America to Talleyrand and had assigned La Forest to him to assist in preventing a war with the United States. Pichon had left The Hague for a few days in the north of Holland, but Talleyrand's letter was sent after him by a special courier of the Batavian government, and he returned to the capital to see Murray once more.[40]

Murray told John Quincy Adams that Talleyrand's letter was "a sort of assurance on some of the points of our conversation, and pretty explicit and very soothing, with a small spice for M. Murray who was a loyal American, neither F(rench) nor B(ritish)." Pichon reported to Talleyrand that Murray was most impressed with the letter. He had read it on two different occasions before asking permission to copy it, and Pichon discovered that the copy was being sent off at once. Murray had believed the story from Paris that Logan, after being feted by Merlin and others of the Directory, had received the decree raising the embargo on American ships "as a present from a Directorial dinner," but Pichon

39*Ibid.*, 50, 182–85vo, 188–91vo; Murray to Pickering, July 18, Aug. 23, 1798, "Letters of Murray," 435, 459–60.

40Talleyrand to Pichon, Aug. 29, Pichon to Talleyrand, Sept. 1 and 7, 1798, AECPE-U, 50, 200, 201–202VO, 206, 209.

insisted the measure was the product of their own conversations. Murray knew that Logan, whose sojourn in Paris lasted a bare three weeks, had gone to Bordeaux to take ship home immediately after the raising of the embargo, and Pichon, seconded by Schimmelpenninck, convinced him that the mission of the "plaister of Paris philanthropist" had been innocent. Pichon now, on September 7, wanted to return to Paris because, he told Talleyrand, "the thing seems set up here," and his supposed position at The Hague under Champigny, who on Talleyrand's instructions remained completely ignorant of Pichon's real mission, was inferior to his regular one at the Quai d'Orsay.[41]

By September 8, Pichon was sure that his mission had ended successfully. He summarized the points on which he assumed that Murray had been convinced, concluding that if Gerry's letters had not convinced Adams, then those from Talleyrand which Murray had sent certainly should. Talleyrand was of the same opinion and was now willing that Pichon should return to Paris after reinforcing the opinions he had left with Murray.[42]

Murray had become increasingly fearful that he was exposing himself to censure in his talks with Pichon. Despite his frequent reminders that he was unauthorized in the matter, as he repeatedly told his friend in Berlin, ". . . yet things kept working up into 'consistency,' and I am afraid of this business." He had felt the lash of the Pickering pen on a previous occasion, and by September 1 had decided that a full explanation of the whole affair was necessary. To Pichon, he insisted that Talleyrand's letter, while gratifying to the United States, was not the positive and literal assurance required by the President, and he promised to write a short statement to that effect for the minister's benefit.

[41]Sept. 6, Aug. 31, Sept. 11, 1798, "Letters of Murray," 468–69, 462, 470; Pichon to Talleyrand, Sept. 7 and 8, 1798, AECPE-U, 50, 209–10vo, 211–15vo. Nathaniel Cutting wrote to Jefferson from Paris on Aug. 27, 1798, that Logan and another American were returning home with unequivocal proof that the Directory "are emerging from that cloud of error in which some of their artful and interested subalterns have long strove to envelope them." Jefferson Papers, Library of Congress, 17849.

[42]Pichon to Talleyrand, Sept. 8, Talleyrand to Pichon, Sept. 12, Pichon to Talleyrand, Sept. 13, 1798, AECPE-U, 50, 211–16vo, 222–22vo, 223–25vo.

John Quincy Adams thought the leter of Augus 28 sufficient and wrote to Pickering his opinion that Murray should be authorized to discuss the bases of a negotiation with Pichon, with formal assurances that the new envoys would be received as the representatives of a "great, free, powerful, and independent nation," and the repeal of the law of January 18 the *sine qua non* for the negotiation itself.[43]

Pichon thought that Murray was being overly fastidious. He reported Murray's stubborness to Talleyrand on September 13, and again ten days later, enclosing Murray's note in a letter of September 24. His replacement at The Hague had already arrived, but he waited a few days more for an answer before setting out once more for Paris. Murray was sorry that "good Mr. Pichon" had gone, but on October 7 he received from the military French postmaster a letter from the Frenchmen covering one to himself from Talleyrand. This, Pichon explained, had crossed him on the way to Paris, been returned, and then sent back to The Hague under cover to him. It was, he was satisfied, "the assurances" required by Murray.[44]

Talleyrand's letter was dated September 28. After expressing his satisfaction with Pichon's conversations with Murray, "which have taken on an official character by the approval which I transmitted to you," he evinced surprise at Murray's remaining doubts.

What Mr. Murray still doubts has been declared very explicitly even before the message of the President to Congress, of 3 Messidor [21 June] last, was known in France. I had written it to Mr. Gerry, notably the 24 Messidor and 4 Thermidor; I repeated it to him before his departure. An entire paragraph of the letter that you received from me dated 11 Fructidor, and of which a

43To J. Q. Adams, Aug. 31, Oct. 12, Pickering to Murray, Apr. 20, Murray to Pickering, Sept. 1, to J. Q. Adams, Sept. 6 and 28, 1798, "Letters of Murray," 463, 482, 397–99, 465, 467–68, 475–76. John Quincy Adams is given considerable credit for Murray's actions, and for the later determination of the President, in Bemis, *John Quincy Adams and Foundations of American Foreign Policy*, 99–100, and in Kurtz, *Presidency of Adams*, 348–49.

44AECPE-U, 50, 223–24vo, 227–29vo, 230, 231; to J. Q. Adams, Sept. 28, Oct. 5 and 9, 1798, "Letters of Murray," 476, 479, 480.

copy is in the hands of Mr. Murray, is devoted to developing further the fixed determination of the French Government. On these bases, you were right to suggest that any plenipotentiary that the government of the United States will send to France, to terminate the differences which subsist between the two countries, will be incontestably received with the regard due the representative of a free, independent and powerful nation.

I cannot persuade myself, Citizen, that the American Government has need of further declarations on our part to determine it to take, in order to renew the negotiations, the measures which will suggest its desire of forwarding the differences toward a peaceful termination . . . . Take, then, Citizen, these positive expressions to Mr. Murray to convince him of our sincerity and engage him to transmit them to his government.[45]

Talleyrand's letter was forwarded to President Adams on October 7. Murray still was not satisfied, writing to the President's son that "this is not *the declaration* which meets the wrong . . . . It is more an *authorization of Mr. Pichon's several declarations . . .* than *that* explicit declaration which I meant." Nevertheless, despite recurring fears concerning his own censurability, Murray was glad that Pichon had let his secret escape. "In truth all the world chuckles believe me," he exulted to his Berlin confidante, "at what they believe to be the humiliation of *France* respecting the United States."[46] But Talleyrand had found a way to save the peace and the Directory's pride at the same time. He had gauged President Adams correctly. Peace, and the consecration of the new American neutrality, were once again the option of the President.

---

[45]AECPE-U, 50, 223–33vo. Translations are in *ASP, FR* II, 242, and in *Works of Adams* VIII, 688–90.

[46]*Works of Adams* VIII, 688–89; Oct. 9, Nov. 5, 1798, "Letters of Murray," 480, 485.

CHAPTER XV    Obstacles to
Peace, 1798–1799

Columbia rise! be firm, be free!
The friends of *France* are foes to *Thee*.
Detest the tools of Talleyrand,
And spurn each *Traitor* from the land!

SONG FOR THE CELEBRATION OF JULY 4, 1799.

TALLEYRAND's zeal for peace was not reciprocated by the American government, which was busy with the creation of an army and a navy. Dire warnings of an imminent French invasion failed to elicit any general enthusiasm for enlistment, and few besides the authors were convinced. Pickering's frenzy led him to ask Liston whether the United States might *"beg* or *borrow* or *buy"* some cannon captured from the French in the Seven Years' War which were then rusting at Halifax, and the amazed Grenville graciously consented. A few months later, Liston was instructed to inform the American government that "His Majesty has been pleased as a Testimony of Friendship towards the United States" to present the guns as a gift. Retired British officers living in America were granted permission to offer their services to the American government, although President Adams ridiculed such propositions: "At present there is no more prospect of seeing a French army here," he told his secretary of war, "than there is in Heaven."[1]

Adams knew that "regiments are costly articles everywhere, and more so in this country than in any other under the sun." He

[1] Liston to Grenville, June 12, 1798, Grenville to Liston, Jan. 19, 1799, Nov. 13, 1798, I. B. M., 162n., 168, 164; Oct. 22, 1798, *Works of Adams* VIII, 613.

feared that "if this nation sees a great army to maintain, without an enemy to fight, there may arise an enthusiasm that seems to be little foreseen." Still ignorant of the fact that his cabinet was not his own, Adams was unaware that even then Liston was being informed of the administration's chagrin at France's refusal to declare war, and at the political difficulties of bringing about the "natural and reasonable" exchange of American seamen for British ships. Early in December 1798, Grenville irritably summarized not only his own views but those of High Federalist warmongers as well:

> I had entertained Hopes that long before the Date of these Dispatches the Course of the Disputes between America and France would have led to a State of open Hostility between them, and that the People of the United States would have perceived in the temporizing Policy, which has been recently observed toward them by France, nothing more than an Attempt to promote Dissentions between them and their own Government, and a desire to procrastinate a Rupture until France should be relieved from the Apprehension of a Renewal of Hostilities against Her by the Powers on the Continent. It was therefore with much Concern that I learnt from your last Dispatches, that the same doubts and Hesitation, which have existed on this Point, still continue, and that the Members of the American Government have been unable to communicate to their Citizens a due portion of their own Energy and Decision.[2]

Adams, belatedly alarmed at the bellicose militarism which surrounded him, was already pondering a way out of his situation. On October 10, he wrote from Quincy to his secretaries for suggestions concerning his December message to Congress. Wolcott and Benjamin Stoddert, the secretary of the newly created

---

[2]Adams to McHenry, Oct. 22, 1798, *Works of Adams* VIII, 613; Liston to Grenville, Nov. 7, Grenville to Liston, Dec. 8, 1798, I. B. M., 164n., 164. Liston's dispatches accurately reflect the war party's changing moods during 1798: certainty of war with France (Feb. 29, May 2); "Hostilities may be said at last to have started . . . ." (July 10); Federalists planned to declare war but barely lacked a majority (July 14); "protraction of present State of uncertainty has an unavoidable tendency to damp the energy of the warlike preparations . . . ," but war is inevitable (Sept. 27); Federalists lament failure to declare war but hoped France would force it anyway (Nov. 7). F. O. 5, 22. See also Dauer, *Adams Federalists*, 168–72.

Navy Department, urged new vigor in the execution of the measures already taken against France, while McHenry frankly wanted Congress to be invited to declare war. Pickering agreed with the first two and wanted also to review the conduct in France of Gerry, who had reached Boston on October 1 to find himself the object of violent public abuse and private ostracism. Then Adams followed his first request to Pickering with another on October 20, listing three questions for his secretary's consideration. First, should the President recommend a declaration of war? And last, should he not lay all of Gerry's correspondence before Congress? But the second question had obviously claimed more of Adams's thought: "whether any further proposals of negotiation can be made with safety . . . ." This was a logical consideration, assuming a negative answer to the first question, and Adams's attachment to this idea was evidenced by the ten names he suggested for a new mission.[3]

From a variety of sources, Adams was receiving information regarding French intentions. Gerry sat down as soon as he debarked and wrote a lengthy report defending his conduct. Shortly thereafter, Gerry read in a Boston gazette some Pickering aspersions on himself and wrote a sharp refutation to the President which he wanted published in turn. His old friend thought the demand just and requested the secretary "to have it inserted in a public print." Pickering categorically refused to do this, on the grounds that it would force him to "subjoin such remarks" as would display not only Gerry's "pusillanimity, weakness, and meanness alone, but his *duplicity* and *treachery*." Knowing the vitriolic quality of Pickering's tireless pen, Adams then advised Gerry to remain silent, "although I am well satisfied that your conduct was upright and well intended . . . ." Pickering nevertheless did his best to damn Gerry in a report to Congress; Adams, however, after submitting Gerry's entire correspondence to Congress on January 18, 1799, ordered Pickering to delete some of his most objectionable remarks before submitting the report three days

3*Works of Adams* VIII, 604, 609-10; *Oliver Wolcott* II, 169; Morison, "Elbridge Gerry," 28.

later. The High Federalists were delighted, as usual, with Pickering's performance, and even relative moderates like Washington and Marshall approved. But, as Jefferson wrote to Monroe, "Gerry's correspondence and Pickering's report on it [show] the willingness of France to treat with us, and our determination not to believe it, & therefore to go to war with them."[4]

Early in November, Dr. Logan arrived at Philadelphia to run the gauntlet of Federalist ridicule and vilification in his turn. No politician, the gentle Quaker tried to ignore his detractors and hurried immediately to deliver Skipwith's dispatches to Pickering. The rudeness and contempt of the secretary were succeeded by extreme coldness on the part of Washington, whom he called on next. Logan could not have been surprised, therefore, when two weeks later President Adams berated him almost as severely as had Pickering, although ten years later Adams insisted that he had received Logan politely and was then convinced by his "candor and sincerity." The Senate, on December 11, gratuitously hinted at Logan in its reply to the President's Second Annual Message, and Adams took the bait with alacrity. "Although the officious interference" of private citizens deserved no credit, he told the Senate the next day, "yet it deserved to be considered

[4]Gerry to Pickering, Oct. 1, 1798. Pickering's report was dated Jan. 18, but Adams sent it to Congress on Jan. 21, 1799. *ASP, FR* II, 204–27, 229–38. Adams to Gerry, Oct. 20, Pickering to Adams, Nov. 5, Adams to Gerry, Dec. 15, 1798, Adams to Pickering, Jan. 15, 1799, *Works of Adams* VIII, 610–12, 616, 614, 621–23; Upham, *Pickering* III, 388–90; Jefferson to Monroe, Jan. 23, 1799, Ford, *Jefferson's Writings* VII, 320. See Morison, "Elbridge Gerry," 28–29, and Henry J. Ford, "Timothy Pickering," in Samuel F. Bemis, ed., *American Secretaries of State* II, 229–31. Pickering's malice pursued Gerry as it had Randolph and Monroe, through unjust and petty pecuniary claims. Gerry appealed to the President, who upheld him on the evidence, but the account was not closed until after Pickering had left office. Adams to Pickering, Aug. 3, 1799, *Works of Adams* IX, 7–8; Austin, *Gerry* II, 277. Years later, Adams wrote that Gerry had "finally saved the peace of the nation; for he alone discovered and furnished the evidence that X. Y. and Z. were employed by Talleyrand; and he alone brought home the direct, formal, and official assurances upon which the subsequent commission proceeded, and peace was made . . . ." "Letters to the Boston Patriot," 1809, *Works of Adams* IX, 287. Adams was wiser in retrospect than he had been in 1798, and Gerry was vilified for the wrong reason on his return from France. As E. Wilson Lyon comments, "the country might more properly have deplored his failure to go all the way and make a treaty." "Directory and the United States," 528.

whether that temerity and impertinence . . . ought not to be inquired into and corrected."[5]

The Federalists in Congress seized the President's suggestion at once. After a spirited three-week debate, in which Gallatin demonstrated the hypocrisy of Federalists who would apply one standard to themselves and another to their opposition, the House passed triumphantly, on January 17, 1799, the so-called Logan Act, which made any unauthorized correspondence with a foreign government a high misdemeanor. The intelligence that Logan brought from France, combined with Gerry's, caused the Federalists much embarrassment, although it was well known that Gerry had assured them that he would loyally support the measures of the government. It required no very shrewd political eye to see that the Logan Act, which Adams signed on January 30, was intended to discredit the Republicans and was really the repairment of an omission in the Sedition Law.

The Gerry affair figured prominently in the President's Annual Address to Congress of December 8, 1798. After Pickering had received Adams's hint of a new mission to France, there was a hastily assembled meeting of the officials of the administration, presided over by Hamilton but minus the President. This group prepared an address to Congress containing a categorical refusal to consider a new mission. Adams, however, refused to go along with such belligerence, stating instead that "more determinate assurances" than those thus far received would have to be given, it being incumbent upon France "(if she is indeed desirous of accommodation)" to initiate steps toward a reconciliation. Meanwhile, Adams admonished Congress, "whether we negotiate with

[5]Tolles, "Unofficial Ambassador," 20–23; Tolles, *George Logan*, 179; "Memorandum of an Interview," Nov. 13, 1798, *Writings of Washington* XXXVII, 18–20; *Oliver Wolcott* II, 195; Kurtz, *Presidency of Adams*, 346; "Letters to the Boston Patriot," 1809, *Works of Adams* IX, 244; William Shaw to Abigail Adams, Nov. 28, 1798, Adams Papers, "Letters Received and other Loose Papers," reel (microfilm ed.) 392, Massachusetts Historical Society; *Messages and Papers of the Presidents* I, 276, 277. Dupont wrote to Jefferson from Paris on Aug. 27, 1798: "Dr. Logan will tell you that he has found in France good and zealous friends of America...." Dumas Malone, ed., *Correspondence between Thomas Jefferson and Pierre Samuel duPont de Nemours, 1798–1817* (Boston, 1930), 1.

her or not, vigorous preparations for war will be alike indispensable . . . . These alone will give to us an equal treaty and insure its observance."[6]

Jefferson was surprised at the President's speech, "so unlike himself in point of moderation," but Madison thought it was "the old song with no other variation of the tune than the spirit of the moment was thought to exact." Both of them attributed it to "the genius of the subtle partizan of England who has contributed so much to the public misfortunes." The answers of the Senate and House, that of the former in particular being much more belligerent toward France than the President's speech, were "cooked in the same shop," according to Madison, who saw Adams converted into a puppet through the flattery and guile of Hamilton's creatures in his official family. Neither of the Republican leaders knew then of the private shrieks of pain from many High Federalists at the President's "having declared the door to be open for negotiation," which would cause "French agents and French diplomatic intrigues to appear in all the forms and modes their ingenuity can suggest."[7]

Jefferson wrote to Madison on January 3, 1799, that the government had received assurances from Murray of French sincerity in desiring a reconciliation. France had even agreed to accept Dutch mediation in case its overtures were rejected. Adams, meanwhile, ordered Pickering on January 15 to prepare the draft of a treaty and a consular convention "such as in his opinion might at this day be acceded to by the U.S., if proposed by France." This order was ignored by Pickering and by all "the heads of dept." whom he was told to consult. On January 21, the day on which Pickering's animadversions on Gerry were transmitted to Congress, the President received from Murray an authentic copy of a note from Talleyrand to Schimmelpenninck.

[6]*Messages and Papers of the Presidents* I, 272–73; *Works of Adams* IX, 130–31, VIII, 604n.; Wolcott to Adams, Nov. 1798, *Oliver Wolcott* II, 170–73, 186–87.

[7]Jefferson to Madison, Jan. 3, 1799, Ford, *Jefferson's Writings* VII, 313; Madison to Jefferson, Dec. 29, 1798, *Writings of Madison* VI, 326–27; Stephen Higginson to Wolcott, Dec. 13, 1798, *Oliver Wolcott* II, 180; Morison, *Otis* I, 161.

The note contained unmistakable proof of France's "conciliatory dispositions," which France did not believe "would much longer be unrecognized in Phila."[8]

The President still was not convinced. He communicated to Congress on January 28 a French decree announcing that all foreigners of allied or neutral countries captured on enemy vessels would be treated as pirates. This information had come from King, but news of the suspension of the decree, also relayed by King, was not sent until a resolution of the House on February 14 requested it.[9]

On February 18, 1799, President Adams suddenly sent to the Senate the nomination of William Vans Murray to be "minister plenipotentiary of the United States to the French Republic." It is probable that a letter Murray wrote on October 7, 1798, reached Adams between February 15 and 18, since that letter was made the basis for the nomination. With his message to the Senate, Adams enclosed Talleyrand's letter of September 28, 1798, to Pichon, which the latter had forwarded to Murray from Paris. That letter contained the specific assurances which Murray had demanded.[10]

Without consulting his cabinet, which he knew would unanimously oppose the measure, Adams wrote out the message himself and had it delivered to the Senate by his private secretary. "Always disposed and ready to embrace every plausible appearance of probability of preserving or restoring tranquility," he wrote, he was nominating Murray with the reservation that he would not go to France until he had received "direct and unequivocal assurances" from the French government that he would be properly received, and that a minister with equal powers would be appointed to treat with him.[11]

8Ford, *Jefferson's Writings* VII, 313–15; Murray to Adams, Aug. 20, 1798, *Works of Adams* VIII, 621; *Oliver Wolcott* II, 187–88.

9*Messages and Papers of the Presidents* I, 281–82; King to Secretary of State, Nov. 16, 1798, King, *Life and Correspondence* II, 469–71.

10*Messages and Papers of the Presidents* I, 282–83; *Works of Adams* VIII, 688n.; Kurtz, *Presidency of Adams*, 348.

11Pickering to Murray, July 10, 1799, "Letters of Murray," 573–74; *Oliver Wolcott* II, 188–89.

Adams's sudden snatching of the initiative from the Hamiltonian cabal entailed profound consequences—the developing split
among the Federalists yawned wide, and across the gulf the two
factions berated each other with a vituperation each had heretofore reserved for the most extreme Jacobins. Wolcott's biographer has described the effect of the message upon the Senate's
dominant war party:

> Had a thunderbolt fallen upon that body, it could not have
> produced more amazement. Warlike preparations pursuant to
> the recommendations of the speech, had been adopted; up to
> that very hour, every measure had been in reference to prospec-
> tive war, and now the action of the political engine was suddenly
> reversed, at the moment when its every joint was strained to the
> utmost.

"Thunderstruck" was the word used by Pickering, who, in vent-
ing "the bitterness of my indignation, chagrin and distress on the
appointment of new envoys to the execrable government of
France," conveniently forgot presidential orders which he had
deliberately ignored. His feelings, he wrote to Murray, were
shared by all of "the wise and the good" men; "among them I
need mention only General Hamilton, Mr. Cabot and Mr.
Ames."[12]

Pickering might have added the name of the British minister,
Mr. Liston, who perhaps not coincidentally used Pickering's
term to describe the Federalist reaction to the President's coup:
"The federal party were thunderstruck with this step which to
say the least of it appears to have been at the same time precipitate and unreasonable." A little later, Liston reported that some
Federalists claimed Adams was senile, but he added: "of this
however I can discover no marks." On the contrary, he specu-
lated that the President was wary of the French peace campaign
and proposed to call Talleyrand's bluff, hoping thereby to re-

12*Oliver Wolcott* II, 189; Pickering to Murray, July 10, Oct. 25, 1799, "Letters
of Murray," 574, 610–11; Jacob E. Cooke, "Country Above Party: John Adams and
the 1799 Mission to France," in Edmund P. Willis, ed., *Fame and the Founding
Fathers* (Bethlehem, Pa., 1967), 54.

gain for the government the support of the "democratick faction."[13]

It was understandable that many Federalists and perhaps all Republicans should have been thunderstruck, but Pickering had known for four months that Adams was thinking in terms of a fresh attempt at negotiation with France. It is surprising, however, that historians have registered such bemusement at the logical tendency of Adams's policy, which consistently—if such a word can be applied to any program of this proud and headstrong man —pursued the ultimate goal of negotiation, while at the same time pressing hard for building the country's defenses, a naval force in particular. The President had, or almost had, the French assurances he had demanded; naval construction was proceeding, while Hamiltonian demands for pushing the creation of an expensive army pointed to unknown dangers. Most important, to Adams it seemed that battle lines presaging civil war were beginning to form; only by a dramatic move toward peace could domestic tranquillity be preserved and, perhaps, his own candidacy in the next presidential election freed of the warmonger label. Motives of individuals, including Presidents, are varied and also dangerous to speculate upon, but it is probably safe to say that in this case good policy was good politics.[14]

Probably anticipating a storm, Adams wrote immediately to explain his action to Washington, whose influence had so recently been manipulated by his cabinet to his own humiliation in the "affair of the generals."[15] The former President had received on the last day of January a letter from Joel Barlow in Paris, ex-

13Liston to Grenville, Feb. 22, Mar. 4, 1799, F. O. 5, 25.

14Cooke, "Country Above Party," 56–62; Stephen G. Kurtz, "The French Mission of 1799–1800: Concluding Chapter in the Statecraft of John Adams," *Political Science Quarterly* LXXX (Dec. 1965), 549–52; Page Smith, *John Adams* 2 vols. (New York, 1962), II, 999–1002. Relevant here is the remark of Richard Hofstadter, *Idea of a Party System*, 120: "It became clear that while the public could be aroused at insults to American 'honor' such as that involved in the XYZ affair, it was adamantine when it came to bearing the actual burdens of an avoidable war." See also Kurtz, *Presidency of Adams*, 350; Dauer, *Adams Federalists*, 231–32; Beveridge, *Marshall* II, 423–28; Morison, *Otis* I, 161–63; Bemis, *John Quincy Adams and Foundations of American Foreign Policy*, 98–103.

15See Dauer, *Adams Federalists*, 231–32; Channing, *History of U. S.* IV, 190–96.

patiating on the conciliatory desires of the Directory and asking Washington's agency in presenting them to Adams. This letter the general had forwarded to the President, withholding judgment but suggesting that any opportunity for peace deserved looking into. Adams harshly condemned Barlow in his reply—"Tom Paine is not a more worthless fellow"—and asserted that he had nominated Murray on the strength of Talleyrand's letter, assuming that "tranquility upon just and honorable terms, is undoubtedly the ardent desire of the friends of this country." Washington, although he had rejected the idea two months earlier in answer to a plea from the Marquis de Lafayette, supported the President, and the war faction's dream of bringing a more amenable puppet than Adams to the presidency in the next year's elections evaporated.[16]

Adams recalled later that the Senate had postponed consideration of Murray's nomination. Sedgwick wrote at once to Hamilton for instructions, and a committee of five war senators called upon the President to endeavor to change his mind. Adams persisted, whereupon they decided to reject the nomination. Hearing of this decision, Adams decided to change his mode of approach, and one week after the original message he enlarged the mission to three, because

> The proposition of a fresh negotiation with France in consequence of advances made by the French Government has excited so general an attention and so much conversation as to have given occasion to many manifestations of the public opinion, from which it appears to me that a new modification of the embassy will give more general satisfaction to the Legislature and to the nation, and perhaps better answer the purposes we have in view.[17]

The Chief Justice of the United States, Oliver Ellsworth of Connecticut, and the old patriot of the Revolution, Patrick

[16]Adams to Washington, Feb. 19, 1799, *Works of Adams* VIII, 624–26; Washington to Lafayette, Dec. 25, 1798, to the President of the United States, Feb. 1, Mar. 3, 1799, *Writings of Washington* XXXVII, 119–20, 64–70, 143–44; Kurtz, *Presidency of Adams,* 347.

[17]"Letters to the Boston Patriot," 1809, *Works of Adams* IX, 248–51; *Messages and Papers of the Presidents* I, 284. See *Oliver Wolcott* II, 204–205.

Henry of Virginia, were nominated with Murray, but they were not to leave the United States until Murray had received official verification of Talleyrand's "assurances." To this modification the Federalists acceded, Sedgwick having just received from New York the news that "my present impression is that the measure must go into effect with the additional idea of a commission of three." Hamilton had realized that Adams's move was too popular to resist openly. He thought that the departure of additional commissioners could be postponed indefinitely, until either Congress and its spoiling little navy could goad France to a declaration of war in sheer exasperation, or until Louis XVIII was restored to the throne of France. The latter was a fantasy conjured up, as it had often been before, by British naval victories and the probability of the formation of a new coalition against France. As Adams himself later pointed out, had Murray's nomination been approved and a new treaty made in the summer of 1799, when French military fortunes were desperate, the United States would have gained better terms than it was able to get later from the triumphant Bonaparte.[18]

Jefferson jubilantly announced to Madison on February 19 that "the event of events was announced to the Senate yesterday." Because Murray's nomination arrived on the eve of the Senate's rising, he suspected the worst of Adams: "However, it silences all arguments against the sincerity of France, and renders desperate every further effort towards war . . . ." In the meantime, the Federalists "have been permitted to go on with all the measures of war and patronage," though this had its advantages. The "X. Y. Z. delusion" was wearing off, and the people's eyes were being opened to the real intentions of France.

> Besides this several other impressive circumstances will all be bearing on the public mind. The alien & sedition laws as before, the direct tax, the additional army & navy, an usurious loan to set those follies on foot, a prospect of heavy additional taxes on the war, recruiting officers lounging at every court-house and decoying the laborer from his plough. A clause in a bill now under

[18]Feb. 21, 1799, *Works of Hamilton* X, 345–46; "Letters to the Boston Patriot," 1809, *Works of Adams* IX, 256.

debate for opening commerce with Toussaint & his black subjects now in open rebellion against France, will be a circumstance
of high aggravation to that country, and in addition to our
cruising round their islands will put their patience to a great
proof.[19]

Adams's stroke had split the Federalists and they were doomed
anyway, as Jefferson shrewdly reasoned. The saner and wiser
Federalists gradually swung to the support of the President, and
one of Hamilton's erstwhile firebrands in the House, Harrison
Gray Otis, tried to heal the breach without success, while his twin
Federalist star in the congressional firmament, Harper, continued to parrot Pickering. Henry Knox thought Adams's action
"one of the most dignified, decisive, and beneficial ever adopted
by the Chief Magistrate of any nation." Knox, having been
bruised in Hamilton's ruthless rush to military glory, might be
considered prejudiced, but this could not be said of John Marshall. Marshall's letter of approval, written before the enlarge-
ment of the mission, was sent to Adams by Charles Lee, the attorney general, whose agreement with Marshall made him the first
defection from the Hamiltonian cabinet phalanx. In his answer
to Lee, Adams showed his first real awareness of his position: "If
combinations of senators, generals, and heads of dept. shall be
formed, such as I cannot resist, and measures are demanded of
me that I cannot adopt, my remedy is plain and certain . . . . I
will try my own strength at resistance first, however."[20]

As the war hawks had expected, England's attitude toward the
United States turned cold abruptly with news of the designation
of the new mission. The letters from London of Rufus King undoubtedly strengthened Pickering's resistance to what he termed
"the most unfortunate and the most humiliating event to the
United States which has happened since the commencement of

19Jefferson to Madison, Feb. 19, 26, to Monroe, Jan. 23, 1799, Ford, *Jefferson's
Writings* VII, 361–63, 369–72, 319–22.
20Morison, *Otis* I, 163–67; Harper to his Constituents, Mar. 20, 1799, in Elizabeth Donnan, ed., "Papers of James A. Bayard, 1796–1815," *Annual Report of the
American Historical Association, 1913* 2 vols. (1915), II, 89–92; Knox to Adams,
Mar. 5, Lee to Adams, Mar. 14, Adams to Lee, Mar. 29, 1799, *Works of Adams* VIII,
626–27, 628, 629.

the French revolution." Every report from Europe injurious to France, or sanguine about the operations of the coalition, was dispatched at once to the President. Adams, to the great detriment of his policy, spent the period from March to mid-October 1799, in Quincy, tortured with anxiety over the serious illness of his beloved Abigail. The Hamiltonian cabal was thus able to regain dominance quickly after the President's brief display of independence.[21]

By the middle of April, Murray heard of his nomination and innocently told Pickering: "I am profoundly grateful for and justly proud of this mark of his [Adams'] confidence!" He also knew of the nominations of Ellsworth, which gave him "great consolation," and of Henry. It was not until early in May that Murray received official confirmation of the appointments and instructions to obtain the official assurances still required of Talleyrand. This was quickly accomplished and the correspondence forwarded to Pickering, who with a few other bellicose High Federalists now hated Murray as the author of their discomfiture. Pickering had first tried to obtain Murray's cooperation in defeating the mission, but when Murray insisted on its wisdom he could not restrain his fury. For having addressed "that shameless villain" Talleyrand with civility, Murray's conduct was censured as "injurious and degrading," but Pickering betrayed the real source of his anger by telling Murray that he should have dashed Pichon's letter in his face. Pickering succeeded in embroiling Murray with Pichon over the publication of that letter, in violation of their agreement, in the Richmond *Examiner*. But even before the secretary's desperate attempt to poison Murray's mind against the President, Murray had had enough. After defending his conduct and the President's policy, Murray concluded that he was sincerely sorry to lose Pickering's friendship; but "the terms, the harsh and ungenerous terms, on which you have withdrawn it from such a man as I am conscious I am as an American, have

21Grenville to Liston, Oct. 21, 1799, I. B. M., 176–79; King to Pickering, Oct. 11, 1799, King, *Life and Correspondence* III, 122–31; *Writings of John Quincy Adams* II, 466–67; Pickering to Murray, Oct. 4, 1799, "Letters of Murray," 600–601; *Works of Adams* VII, 634–88 *passim*.

helped me to bear it." Murray told the President's son that he had received a "most flogging" letter from Pickering and had "pushed in turn."[22]

But the President was no underling to be tongue-lashed with impunity. Pickering's tactics at home displayed as much guile as that exceedingly blunt man could command; and Adams, thinking he had already squelched the war party's plot, actually gave it a new lease on life. On March 10, Adams agreed in cabinet meeting to certain ultimata in the instructions for the new envoys—indemnification for spoliations, compensation for seizures under the *rôle d'équipage* regulation and exclusion of those claims from the authority of any joint board established to review mutual claims, and a stipulation against any guarantee of French possessions—and the following day he left Philadelphia for Quincy. Further work on the instructions was thereupon suspended, and Pickering's public activities were soon so flagrantly contrary to the President's announced policy that General Uriah Forrest sent Adams an urgent warning to return and check his cabinet officers.[23]

In response to Forrest's reminder that only he had been elected to administer the government, Adams commented: "I do administer it here at Quincy, as really as I could at Philadelphia." His secretaries corresponded with him daily, "and nothing is done without my advice and direction . . . ." Adams mistook the point, despite the simultaneous demonstration of its relevancy

[22]Apr. 13, 1799, Murray to J. Q. Adams, May 7 and 21, Pickering to Murray, July 10, Murray to Pickering, Aug. 28, Pickering to Murray, Oct. 4 and 25, Murray to Pickering, Dec. 1, Murray to J. Q. Adams, Dec. 6, 1799, "Letters of Murray," 538, 549, 553, 573–74, 586–88, 600–602, 612, 623–27, 629–30; Murray to Talleyrand, May 5, Talleyrand to Murray, May 12, 1799, AECPE-U, 51, 146–46vo, 156–56vo. Pickering had earlier rebuked Murray for excessive politeness toward the revolutionary government of the Batavian Republic. In a letter of Oct. 25, 1799, replete with strictures upon President Adams's conduct and even upon his intelligence, Pickering maliciously observed: "I formerly noticed your congratulations to the revolutionary government of Holland; but I did not, I believe, repeat the President's earnest remark upon them: 'that young man will ruin me.'" "Letters of Murray," 397–99, 612. See also Peter P. Hill, *William Vans Murray, Federalist Diplomat* (Syracuse, 1971), 149–52.

[23]*Oliver Wolcott* II, 248; "Points, as *ultimata*," Mar. 11, Forrest to Adams, Apr. 28, 1799, *Works of Adams* VIII, 627–28, 637–38.

in the replacement of Patrick Henry, who, as even the President had foreseen, had declined his appointment. Adams at once ordered Pickering to send Henry's commission to Governor William R. Davie of North Carolina. But Pickering suggested that the business be held up for political reasons, "while it remained uncertain whether he would be ever called on to proceed on his mission to France . . . ." Adams fell in with his secretary's views, with only the reservation that "we ought to be informed that he will accept, when his acceptance shall become indispensable."[24]

Thus encouraged, Pickering missed no opportunity to impress upon the President the impropriety of any further conciliatory gestures toward France. When Talleyrand's formal assurances arrived from Murray, Pickering opined that they were not exactly what was demanded, and he tried to prick Adams's vanity with the insinuation that he personally had been insulted. The President reacted with a denunciation of French diplomacy and a reiteration of his determination that "our operations and preparations by sea and land are not to be relaxed in the smallest degree." But, he continued, Ellsworth and Davie were to prepare for immediate departure and were to command the use of whichever United States frigate was most readily available. Pickering's draft of the instructions should be laid before his colleagues for final corrections and forwarded to Quincy at once for his own final approval.[25]

This apparent inconsistency must have disheartened Pickering, until he bethought himself of the instructions. More than one month later, on September 9, he wrote that he was revising his draft and expected to forward it the following day. Having at last mailed the instructions, Pickering explained that the removal of the government to Trenton, on account of another terrible revisitation of yellow fever at Philadelphia, had occasioned the delay. A few words concerning the instructions gave the impression that the conspirators were now willing to cooperate in fur-

[24]Adams to Forrest, May 13, Pickering to Adams, May 8, Adams to Pickering, May 21, 1799, *ibid.*, VIII, 645–46, 641, 651.
[25]Adams to Pickering, May 25, Aug. 6, 1799, *ibid.*, VIII, 652–53, IX, 10–12.

thering the mission, and this would seem surprising if it were not evident from what followed that a new stratagem had been adopted. A letter from Murray of the previous June reported new internal convulsions preparing in France. Talk of the restoration of the monarchy, commented Pickering, raised doubts about the advisability of sending the mission immediately. Also, news from New York indicated that there had already been a change at Paris which was "purely Jacobinical." Such instability and uncertainty, and the expectation of "further and essential changes," concluded Pickering, led his colleagues to join him in suggesting "a temporary suspension of the mission to that country."[26]

The treachery of Pickering, Wolcott, and McHenry, abetted by Hamilton and uncompromisingly supported by the Essex Junto, finally became too much for Navy Secretary Stoddert. On August 29 he had written to Adams, hinting at a suspension of the mission and suggesting that his presence at Trenton would be useful. Adams did not yet see any necessity for leaving Quincy, so Stoddert addressed him more at length on September 13. He was disturbed at the increasingly hostile demonstrations of Great Britain, both in impressments and spoliations at sea, and in the disruption, to the accompaniment of mutual expressions of acrimony, of the joint claims commission provided by the Jay Treaty. Pickering, continued Stoddert generously, was too busy to understand the latter dispute, and the American commissioners and the attorney general should be called to Trenton to prepare a representation to the British government on the subject. He concluded mysteriously:

As to the considerations which I meant as more immediately relating to yourself, I have been apprehensive that artful designing men might make such use of your absence from the seat of govt. when things so important to restore peace with one country, and to preserve it with another, were transacting, as to make your next election less honorable than it would otherwise be.

26*Ibid.*, IX, 21, 23–25; Pickering to Adams, Sept. 11, 1799, *Oliver Wolcott* II, 263–65. For a discussion attributing the delays to Adams, see Cooke, "Country Above Party," 66–70.

The President read this letter "over and over again" and promptly replied that he would be in Trenton between October 10 and 15. He had "one favor to beg" of Stoddert—that "a certain election" be omitted from all consideration. He knew the American people so well, he said, that he would never have any alternative "but to be a pres. of three votes or no President at all, and the difference, in my estimation, is not worth three farthings."[27]

Meanwhile, Ellsworth, the ranking member of the new commission to France, had been drawn into the plot by Wolcott and Pickering and was prevailed upon to ask the President whether he intended, "as many seem to expect, to postpone the mission." The chief justice was arranging his circuit court itinerary and desired the earliest notice of the President's intention. Adams replied that events necessitated a temporary postponement of the mission, and Ellsworth should therefore "pursue your office of Chief Justice of the United States without interruption, till you are requested to embark." He gave Ellsworth to understand, however, that his departure would not be delayed beyond November 1, at latest.[28]

Adams wrote to Pickering on September 21 of his intention of coming to Trenton, and he used the occasion to remark that the end of October was as good a time to sail for Europe as any part of the year. England, thanks probably to Stoddert's letter, was more on his mind than France, and he complained to Pickering on September 23 of the English commissioners' lack of good faith. He echoed the opinions of most Americans in his warning: "If we believe Britons less hungry for plunder than Frenchmen, we shall be deceived."[29] Indeed, England's bad conduct had so far

27 *Works of Adams* IX, 18–19, 25–27, Adams to Stoddert, Sept. 4, 21, 1799, *ibid.* IX, 19–20, 33–34. Lee, who had differed with his colleagues from the first appointment of Murray, was in Virginia. Cooke, "Country Above Party," 68n., interprets Stoddert's letter differently.

28 Ellsworth to Wolcott, Sept. 23, 1799, *Oliver Wolcott* II, 265; Ellsworth to Adams, Sept. 18, Adams to Ellsworth, Sept. 22, 1799, *Works of Adams* IX, 31, 35.

29 *Works of Adams* IX, 33, 35–36.

surpassed French irritations that the Junto's Chauncey Goodrich was moved to inquire plaintively of his brother-in-law, Wolcott:

> Are the British giving us some side-wind strokes in revenge for the mission? 'Tis bad policy for them. Although the good folks of our country don't love the mission, they will resent any indications of ill humor from the British.[30]

Jefferson, on the other hand, saw some utility in England's conduct:

> The misfortune of the French would probably produce at the next session [of Congress] still greater intolerance than we have hitherto experienced, did not the insolences of the English keep their votaries here in check for us.[31]

But as far as the high priests of Federalism were concerned, England could do her worst with impunity. At Dedham, the brilliant and bilious guardian of "our [New England's] floating capital," Fisher Ames, denounced the mission to France as tending to aggravate the unfriendliness of Great Britain! He admitted that the Order-in-Council authorizing the British navy to stop and search American warships denoted an intention to go to war, an eventuality which he thought would please "the anti-funding party."[32]

The conspiratorial triumvirate (since Stoddert's defection) already knew of the President's determination to come to Trenton and disliked it. Pickering wrote to Adams on September 24 that Davie was expected to arrive shortly and would be better satisfied to return to North Carolina, "if the further suspension of the mission take place." News from Europe warranted a further postponement, Pickering claimed, in which case "the trouble of your journey may be saved." But the President left Quincy at the beginning of October, stopped at Windsor to assure himself of Ellsworth's readiness to depart, and arrived in Trenton on October

[30]Sept. 28, 1799, *Oliver Wolcott* II, 266.
[31]Jefferson to Stevens T. Mason, Oct. 27, 1799, Ford, *Jefferson's Writings* VII, 396–97.
[32]Seth Ames, ed., *Works of Fisher Ames* 2 vols. (Boston, 1854), I, 260–64.

10, a few hours after Hamilton rode in with his military lieutenant, and secret spy for Spain, General James Wilkinson.[33]

Of all the assembled worthies whom Adams met at Trenton, only Davie was anxious for the mission to proceed. Hamilton, the triumvirate, and Ellsworth were all for a further postponement, perhaps wishfully believing that the recent Russian and Austrian victories in Europe, which had dislocated the French government once more, would soon reestablish the Bourbons on the throne of France. But Attorney General Lee wrote from Virginia, where he had heard of the late suspension of the mission, to urge the President to let the envoys proceed. He could see no disadvantage to the United States, even though the envoys should find monarchy restored in France, "which I by no means expect will very soon happen." In conversation with Ellsworth, whom he convinced, Adams was much more emphatic in the same opinion, but Hamilton and his satellites were not to be moved by the man they all despised.[34]

After five days of discussions of Europe and of the envoys' instructions, Adams made up his mind to end the uncertainty by repeating his stroke of eight months earlier. Consulting no one, on October 16 he sent Pickering a letter instructing him to deliver fair copies of the instructions to the envoys "without loss of time," and to request them to sail for France on the *United States*, then lying off Rhode Island, before November 1. The President concluded:

> As their visit to France is at one of the most critical, important, and interesting moments that ever have occurred, it cannot fail to be highly entertaining and instructive to them, and useful to their country, whether it terminates in peace and reconciliation

[33]*Works of Adams* IX, 36–37, "Letters to the Boston Patriot," 1809, *ibid.* IX, 252–53; *Oliver Wolcott* II, 267–68; Steiner, *McHenry*, 417.

[34]Lee to Adams, Oct. 6, 1799, "Letters to the Boston Patriot," 1809, *Works of Adams* IX, 38, 254–55. Ellsworth's conversion ruled out Cabot's plan that he should refuse to embark. Pickering never favored that idea, thinking it would only accomplish the substitution of Madison or Burr. Pickering to Cabot, Oct. 22, 1799 (Private and Confidential), Henry Cabot Lodge, *Life and Letters of George Cabot* (Boston, 1877), 248.

or not. The President sincerely prays God to have them in his holy keeping.[35]

Defeated once again by Adams's stubbornness, the Hamiltonians, as usual, appealed to Washington. Their peerless leader himself, seeing his dreams of military glory dashed, deprecated the President's move restrainedly: "All my calculations lead me to regret the measure . . . . I hope that it may not in its consequences involve the United States in a war on the side of France with her enemies." Pickering could only rail at Adams for his refusal to comprehend the real situation and still hoped "in the interposition of Providence." It was McHenry who remained practical. The President, he informed Washington, was most displeased with Pickering and Wolcott, and slightly less so with himself. He could not tell whether any or all would be dismissed, but he believed that Stoddert and Lee favored the replacement of all three of them and would so advise the President. "The evil does not lie in a change of Secretaries," McHenry continued, but in the French mission, which "put in jeopardy the fruits of all [the Federalists'] past labours . . . ." Adams's policy, he suggested, would lead to the triumph of "French innovations and demoralizing principles . . . . It is this dreaded consequence which afflicts, and calls for all the wisdom of, the federalists." McHenry's unposed question: Would Washington consent to lead the country back to the true faith by offering himself for the presidency in 1800?[36]

Washington answered McHenry less than one month before his death on December 14, 1799. He did not choose to run anyway, and his death finally destroyed the electoral hopes of the war party. Hamilton's fears of war with England on account of the French mission were shared by most of his disciples, who seemed already to have forgotten the appeasement of Britain in the name of peace barely five years before. Having surrendered by negotiation to England once, they proposed now to do the same thing

35 *Works of Adams* IX, 39.
36 Hamilton to Washington, Oct. 21, 1799, *Works of Hamilton* X, 356; Pickering to Washington, Oct. 24, McHenry to Washington, Nov. 10, 1799, *Oliver Wolcott* II, 280, 281–82; Steiner, *McHenry*, 418–20.

in reverse by refusing to negotiate with France and going to war with her to keep peace with England.[37]

While the Federalist party was dashing itself to pieces on the rock of French policy, the principal author of its difficulties continued to pursue conciliation with fervor in Paris. Talleyrand did his best, with the cooperation of Lambrechts, the minister of justice, to obtain justice, and even to induce a prejudice, for American claimants before French prize courts. The most troublesome problem was that of the *rôle d'équipage*, and Talleyrand admitted to Lambrechts that there would be difficulty in negotiating a settlement of it without loading the national treasury with debt. In order to save some defense against a flood of claims based on the illegality of that provision, Talleyrand succeeded in obtaining from the Directory an order "interpreting" the article of the provision decree of March 2, 1797, relating to the *rôle d'équipage*, which seemed at first glance to be a repeal of the provision, but was actually a reenactment of it![38]

Talleyrand did all that was possible in view of the political problems which confronted him. The Council of the Five Hundred, which Murray called that "nest of privateersmen," persistently refused to rectify the injustices of France's maritime laws, and Talleyrand recurred to this problem in a full-dress report which he presented to the Directory on February 14. Beginning with the familiar charges of British intrigues in the United

37Washington to McHenry, Nov. 17, 1799, *Oliver Wolcott* II, 282; Steiner, *McHenry*, 420–21.

38Talleyrand to Minister of Justice, Dec. 19 and 22, Minister of Justice to Talleyrand, Dec. 23, 1798, Talleyrand's report to the Directory, Jan. 1, Extract from the *Redacteur*, No. 1192, Mar. 23, 1799, AECPE-U, 50, 360–60vo, 378, 380–81vo, 51, 3–10vo, 78. See Lyon, "Directory and the United States," 529. Talleyrand's formula on the *rôle d'équipage* was ingenious. It consisted merely of dropping from ART. 4 of the decree the clause which claimed the treaty of 1778 as authority for requiring the paper. Thus by citing in the decree of Mar. 18, 1799, the royal decrees of 1744 and 1778, Talleyrand enabled the Directory to retain its legal defense against the American claims concerning the *rôle d'équipage*. The regulations of Oct. 21, 1744, and July 26, 1778, are practically identical in language: "All foreign ships will be good prize . . . which will not have on board the roster of the crew ordered by the French representatives in the neutral ports from which those ships have sailed." Athanase J. L. Jourdan, Decrusy & François A. Isambert, *Recueil Général des Anciennes Lois Françaises* (Paris, 1822), XXII, 176, XXV, 369.

States, he proceeded to explain his own policy. Because Adams, seconded by the fanatic Pickering, was a party to "the Liston plot," a ferment had been produced in America so serious that for a time none knew where it would end. France had to gain time so that her allies, especially Holland and Spain, whose valuable colonies bordering the United States were most exposed, would be able to take necessary precautions. Moderation was necessary, despite the increasingly aggravating provocations of the federal government, as not only Létombe and Rozier, but Jefferson and also Carlos Martinez de Yrujo advised. Most Americans loved liberty and feared English monarchy. They desired absolute independence for their country and supported Adams only through a chimerical fear of French invasion. This "permanent majority" in America needed only to be reassured regarding French intentions to see that the fictitious danger of attack from France really masked an actual assault on American liberty.[39]

Those considerations, continued Talleyrand, determined his relations with the "irresolute negotiator" Gerry and the "officious missionary" Logan. Pichon's interviews with Murray would result in detaching some very influential men from the President's confidence. The Federalist war engine was stalled, and Adams and his party were doomed to defeat at the next election. But this welcome result could be prevented by French mistakes, and the time was coming when only acts of justice could finish the work so auspiciously begun. The decree of July 31 was not executed at Guadeloupe or at Cayenne and the seizure of American ships continued in European waters. The courts continued to manufacture pretexts for condemnation of American property, and the Council of the Five Hundred repeatedly rejected motions for revision of the maritime regulations whose "unlimited, irregular, depredatory action" aggravated French relations with all allied and neutral countries. The Directory must make good on its promises—to continue to temporize would save Adams and his party, and the position of France would be worse

[39]Murray to J. Q. Adams, Dec. 10, 1799, "Letters of Murray," 630; AECPE-U, 51, 40–50.

than ever, because the "independent mass of friends of liberty" would begin to believe the incessant assertions of French insincerity. The Directory must conquer the privateer interests, who constituted a war party in France whose rapacity would involve their country in ruin. But these pirates were already stronger than the Directory—"perhaps it is too late."

There was as much shrewdness as courage in Talleyrand's indictment of the privateering councils, but his advice on policy toward America displayed genuine statesmanship. American political groupings were breaking up, he said, but whatever new alignments took place France must never again meddle in the domestic affairs of the United States. France should remember that England's hope of dominating America depended on being able to divide it. France's interest, therefore, was to keep it united and to aid its development so that one day its maritime weight would counterbalance that of England. Creation of a French party would inevitably raise one in opposition; better legitimately to win the share of American commerce which "the territorial extent of the Republic and the destruction of the shackles which burden its industry promise it in a few years." In effect, *"il faut les laisser faire."*

While the increasingly impotent Directors were reading—if they ever did—Talleyrand's report, the maritime hostilities between the two nations were settling into a dangerous pattern. The attack of the *Constellation* on the *Insurgente* off the West Indian island of Nevis in February 1799, overturned at once the conciliatory policy of the Directory's new agents in the West Indies. Edme-Étienne-Borne Desfourneaux, who had replaced the hated Victor Hugues at Guadeloupe, had made friendly overtures to President Adams for the restoration of commercial relations between that island and the United States, but within two months of his arrival Captain Thomas Truxtun's victory caused a retaliatory order authorizing the indiscriminate seizure of American ships. The *Insurgente* affair aroused resentment in France—Murray wrote Pickering that it was expressed "more in a complaining than indignant manner"—and jubilation among the Federalists. Commercial intercourse was soon reopened between the United States and Santo Domingo, but only because Toussaint, supported by the British, was in full revolt against French authority. Rozier reported to Talleyrand early in August that Desfourneaux was still seizing American ships, although his conduct aroused little feeling in New York because most of the people believed that his reprisals were justified. More important than that, however, the English continued "their customary piracies": twenty-five American ships had been taken in to Jamaica alone in the past five weeks.[40]

Talleyrand never allowed the informal naval hostilities to divert him from his goal. When he learned of Murray's nomination by Adams, he hurried to inform the Directory. He had the satisfaction, he wrote on April 10, "of announcing to the Executive Directory the entire success of the measures taken against the English faction in the United States." Murray's views had already been the subject of discussion; Patrick Henry, he for once misinformed the Directors, was "a pronounced Republican"; and the naming of the chief justice was doubtless intended as the same compliment for France that the Jay appointment had been for England. But Rozier had told him that Liston had sent off a dispatch boat for London at once; English intrigues could therefore be expected to recommence. With a view to minimizing the effect of those maneuvers, he suggested, the Directory should immediately assure the United States, without waiting for a formal demand, of its determination to receive their envoys suitably, "and of its still unalterable conciliatory dispositions." There would be a delay of about four months before negotiations could begin, but that need present no inconvenience. It might, concluded Talleyrand, even be useful in giving the government time to repeal the law of January 18, 1798, authorizing

[40]*Naval Documents related to the Quasi-War with France* (Washington, D. C., 1935), Operations, Nov. 1798–Mar. 1799, 248–49; AECPE-U, 51, 96, 212–13vo; Apr. 23, 1799, "Letters of Murray," 543; *Oliver Wolcott* II, 237. The *Naval Documents,* published in 7 vols. by the Government Printing Office, contain a mass of information on political as well as maritime affairs in the West Indies. The fullest secondary account is Gardner W. Allen, *Our Naval War with France* (Boston, 1909).

seizures of American vessels, which alone remained a barrier to a resumption of the old relationship.[41]

Talleyrand failed again to stiffen the Directory's collective back against the privateer-owners, and he had to wait for Murray's note requesting the assurances, which he promptly and gladly renewed.[42] For the Directory itself, the handwriting was on the wall. More unpopular than ever, particularly on account of the increasingly heavy conscription for seemingly endless wars, it strove to postpone its fall by throwing out frantic alarms against new royalist and Jacobin plots. The reactivated coalition was preparing to carry the war to France anew in the spring of 1799, while the elections of that year were destroying what little influence the Directory had retained in the councils. Barras, knowing that Reubell was the focus of much of the odium attached to the Directory, offered his colleague the Ministry of Exterior Relations. Reubell, ill and broken, refused: at the annual drawing for the retirement of a director he was not surprised to discover that Barras had arranged for his name to be drawn. The once-mighty dictator of France's foreign policy and "soul of the Directory" retired on May 20 at the end of his power, with a generous farewell bonus from his colleagues to compensate for the irregularity of the proceedings.[43]

The Directory's troubles were just beginning. Emmanuel Joseph Siéyès, former abbott and ambassador to Berlin and contemptuous enemy of the Directory, in which he had previously refused to serve because of his hatred of Reubell, was elected to the latter's place. The war between the councils and the Directory was in the open: "the Trojan horse was in place," no doubt with his pet constitution, rejected in the year III, in his pocket. Barras, this time seeing victory for the antidirectorial forces, al-

41Rozier to Talleyrand, Mar. 2, 1799, AECPE-U, 51, 121–22, 79.

42Murray to Talleyrand, May 5, Talleyrand to Murray, May 12, 1799, *ibid.*, 51, 146–46vo, 156–56vo.

43Lefebvre, *Directory*, 191–92; Guyot, *Le Directoire et la Paix de l'Europe*, 901; Barras, *Memoirs* III, 399; H. M. Stephens, "Recent Memoirs of the French Directory," *American Historical Review* I (Apr. 1896); Duff Cooper, *Talleyrand* (Stockholm, 1946), 105.

lied himself with Siéyès when the councils voted the expulsion of Jean Baptiste Treilhard, and in the so-called coup d'état of 30 Prairial (June 18, 1799), Merlin and La Revellière were forced out in turn. Thus the councils on June 18 gained complete dominance over the Directory, and Murray cheered the downfall of Merlin, "that bloodsucker of our commerce." The chameleon Barras was the only one of the original directors left, the three remaining places being filled by two political ciphers, Louis Antoine Gohier and General Jean François Auguste Moulins, and Roger Ducos, whom Barras expected to use but who became instead the tool of Siéyès.[44]

44Lefebvre, *Directory*, 195–97; Murray to J. Q. Adams, June 25, 1799, "Letters of Murray," 565–66.

## CHAPTER XVI

The Convention of 1800

> You have rendered a real service to the French
> nation . . . in re-establishing between the two peo-
> ples relations of concord and attachment which
> nothing should have altered.
>
> TALLEYRAND TO FRENCH MINISTERS PLENIPOTENTIARY,
> SEPTEMBER 26, 1800.

TALLEYRAND had watched the crumbling of the Directory
without regret—in fact he had contributed importantly to the
result and was looking ahead to the next move. Not wishing to
be caught accidentally in the wreckage, he offered his resignation on July 13, 1799, when it was refused, and again one week
later, when it was accepted. He received a letter of appreciation
for his services and a request to continue in office until the arrival of his successor. Talleyrand was quite content to remain a
few days longer, for he had taken the precaution of securing the
appointment of one of his own disciples. Charles Reinhard, then
at Toulon en route to his new post as minister to the Helvetic
Republic, soon proved to be merely the agent of his predecessor,
and he adopted Talleyrand's policy *in toto*.[1]

One of Reinhard's first acts was to write to Rozier, consul
general at Philadelphia according to Talleyrand's instructions,
that the Directory still persevered in the conciliatory dispositions
repeatedly expressed by Talleyrand. The assurances required by
the President should have reached him already, and the new en-

---

[1]Cooper, *Talleyrand*, 105–107; Masson, *Le Département des Affaires Étrangères*, 430–32; Albert Aulard, *The French Revolution: A Political History* 4 vols.
(London, 1910), IV, 128; Louis Madelin, *Talleyrand* (New York, 1948), 93.

voys should reach Europe soon. Meanwhile, Rozier should lose no occasion to assure the American government that "we will do everything within reason to reestablish the natural bonds between the two countries." Victor Dupont, for whom Reinhard wrote a letter of recommendation, was returning to the United States on private business and would be of considerable help in ascertaining the real views of the American government toward the approaching negotiation.[2]

Reinhard apparently toyed with the idea of sending a minister to the United States to make a treaty. In a note to the Directory he suggested that, since Murray and Ellsworth belonged to the English party (he had not yet learned who Henry's replacement was) the aim of the American government might be to ensure the failure of the negotiations. The possibility would be minimized by treating at Philadelphia, where the American government would be prevented from carrying out any such plot by the vigilance of the vast majority of Americans who desired peace.[3]

The only sign of a possible change in attitude came from the new minister of police. Talleyrand had persistently demanded the release of American prisoners in France right down to his last day in office, and the minister of police asked Reinhard on October 17 if Talleyrand's desires still reflected the views of the Directory. Reinhard promptly replied in the affirmative: "Nothing has been able to cause [the Directory] to lose hope of re-establishing the bonds of amity which should unite the two peoples." That letter was not sent until Talleyrand had reentered the

[2]Reinhard to Rozier, Sept. 9, 1799, enclosing letter of introduction for Dupont, AECPE-U, 51, 232–32vo, 233.

[3]Oct. 1, 1799, *ibid.*, 51, 240–41vo. E. Wilson Lyon, "The Franco-American Convention of 1800," *Journal of Modern History* XII (Sept. 1940), 307, says that Reinhard "took a stiffer tone toward the United States." The basis for this is a "Projet d'Instructions" dated 1797 (erroneously converted to 1799), drafted by Delacroix under very different circumstances. Why it was later misfiled is probably not ascertainable; Reinhard may have pulled it out for study, but there is no reason to believe he intended to develop a policy of his own. AECPE-U, 51, 244–47. See also Cooke, "Country Above Party," 72n., and Hill, *Murray*, 156–57.

ministry, when he merely changed the date and had it delivered to Joseph Fouché, the minister of police who came into office after Bonaparte's overthrow of the Directory.[4]

Siéyès and Talleyrand had meanwhile been busy plotting the final destruction of the directorial government. That helpless and inept body seems to have lost even the ability to protect the homeland, as the loss of Italy to the Austrians and Russians under Aleksandr Suvorov, and of Switzerland to the Archduke Charles, seemed to demonstrate. The Great Nation's greatest soldier was bottled up in Egypt and the victorious coalition had two new heroes—Suvorov and Lord Nelson—and so, incidentally, did the Federalist war-hawks in the United States. Yet, even before Bonaparte landed, unexpected and unannounced, in southern France, the military tide was turning once more in France's favor. Suvorov took over the command in Switzerland, but by September he had lost much of what had been gained; and, two weeks after the future emperor set out to meet his destiny in Paris, Russia withdrew from the coalition.[5]

One month after Bonaparte's inglorious return from Egypt the coup d'état of 18 Brumaire (November 9) abolished the Directory forever and placed "the man of victory" at the head of the state. In the government of the Consulate, Siéyès and Roger Ducos, Napoleon's two directorial coadjutors, were shunted aside and Jean-Jacques Régis de Cambacérès and Charles François Lebrun became second and third consuls, respectively, but the strong-willed Bonaparte kept all real power in his own hands. Barras was bought off for the last time, and supporters of the First Consul succeeded to positions of authority. On November 21, Talleyrand, who had organized the political victory, returned to the office of Exterior Relations, while Reinhard resumed his interrupted journey to the French embassy in Switzerland. One week later, Skipwith enthusiastically congratulated Talleyrand

4Talleyrand to Minister of Marine, Aug. 30, Minister of Police to Reinhard and Reinhard to Minister of Police, Oct. 17, 1799, AECPE-U, 51, 230–31, 250–51, 272–72vo.

5See Lefebvre, *Directory*, 193–94, 206–209; Lefebvre, Guyot, and Sagnac, *La Révolution Française*, 448–60.

on his return, esteeming it a happy omen in view of the imminent arrival of envoys from the United States.[6]

Talleyrand proceeded at once to the business of conciliation with the United States. Before the end of November, he presented a report to the consuls, calling their attention to the impending negotiation. He was surprised that the American envoys had not yet arrived, but he thought that the explanation could be found in the reverses which had recently threatened the existence of the Republic, and in the hostility of Adams and Pickering. Nevertheless, the obstructionist tactics of the latter had been frustrated, their own party divided, and the Republicans were stronger than ever as a result of France's moderation. Despite rumors of a suspension of the mission, the American envoys could be expected momentarily.[7]

But, continued Talleyrand, the nearer a settlement approached, the more necessary it was to guard against new intrigues. The great objects which caused France to support American independence in the first place were still valid. France could no longer prevent the United States from achieving its destiny, and "the nation which keeps their friendship will retain the last colonies in the New World."

According to Talleyrand, the differences between the two countries were really the consequences of sending clumsy agents to America who were "carried away by the effervescence of the time"—there could be no rivalry or conflict of interests. Excessive demands had brought refusals, and the creation of a French party had naturally caused the birth of an English one in opposition. The Directory had retaliated against the Jay Treaty with a system of "depredations and piracy" crowned by the law of January 18, 1798. This law had already cost the Americans losses which they estimated at one hundred millions (livres) and remained an obstacle to friendly relations, although its injurious effects were now being felt less every day. Conciliation could

[6]Skipwith to Talleyrand, Nov. 27, 1799, AECPE-U, 51, 259–59vo. See Lefebvre, *Directory*, 210–22; Madelin, *Talleyrand*, 94–98; Cooper, *Talleyrand*, 107–19.
[7]Nov. 29, 1799, AECPE-U, 51, 260–62vo.

proceed, thought Talleyrand, on four bases: dissipation of mutual suspicions through frank explanations, agreement on the meaning of the treaties, provision for the reciprocal enjoyment of rights, and discovery of means for compensating wrongs.

In the meantime, immediate measures should be taken in the United States. The only agent from whom he could expect intelligent information, reported Talleyrand, was Rozier, and he was dead of yellow fever. Létombe was an incompetent old man whose political reports were useless. A new consul general and a skillful political agent were needed at once at Philadelphia. At first unofficial, the latter could be made chargé d'affaires when the negotiations neared a successful conclusion. Thus the communication broken by Rozier's death could be restored and the affairs of the colonies straightened out. The agreement between the United States and Saint-Domingue reopening trade was mysterious. England seemed to have had a hand in this negotiation and had gained equal commercial privileges; it was essential, therefore, to find out what was actually happening.[8]

Bonaparte, at first in favor of sending a new minister to the United States at once, was dissuaded by Talleyrand.[9] The minister was proved right in expecting the envoys, who had at last sailed from Newport on November 3 in the *United States*. Because Captain John Barry feared risking his ship in the North Sea in winter, Ellsworth and Davie landed at Lisbon on November 27. They remained there, waiting to see what course France's new government would take, until December 7, when they sailed for Lorient. Owing to continuing bad weather they were unable to beat into the Bay of Biscay, landing on January 16, 1800, at Corunna. From there they wrote to Talleyrand of their delays at sea and asked him for passports to enable them to continue their journey by land. The French minister answered at once that they were awaited with impatience; there should be no difficulty about their powers, though addressed to the now defunct Directory. He also forwarded their letter to Murray, with his

8Létombe to Talleyrand, Aug. 21, 1799, *ibid.*, 51, 218–18vo.
9Note for the consul Bonaparte, Dec. 31, 1799, *ibid.*, 51, 291–92.

passports, to Sémonville, French minister at The Hague, who was instructed to deliver them along with Talleyrand's hopes for a speedy reconciliation.[10]

Murray, "freezing in the marshes of Holland, and burning with impatience *to know what may be their intention*," as he told his friend at Berlin, was infinitely relieved to hear from his colleagues. He informed Talleyrand on February 4 that he would prepare to leave The Hague at once, and one month later the three envoys were finally united at Paris. On March 3, they asked for an appointment with the minister, who officially received them the next day. Talleyrand had already informed Bonaparte of the Americans' arrival. He wanted to avoid any recriminations over the "accidental or willful" procrastination on their part because he thought it had actually served the interests of both countries. He wanted authority to receive them and to name three ministers to treat with them. The instructions for the negotiators would present no difficulties: the damages claimed on each side should almost balance each other, and the regulation of consular and political questions should pose no problems either.[11]

Talleyrand suggested that the French commission be composed of La Forest, François La Rochefoucauld-Liancourt, and Joseph Bonaparte, who would act as president. Volney, Adet, and Hauterive were also qualified on American affairs, but there would be inconvenience in taking them away from their present duties. The First Consul, however, was not as interested in American experience as he was in rewarding his political supporters, and he paid little attention to Talleyrand's nominees. His brother Joseph did receive the first place on the commission, but the others, Fleurieu and Roederer, were of Bonaparte's own selection. Pichon was appointed secretary to the commission

10Note contained in report to the Senate transmitting Instructions to the U. S. commissioners, Dec. 22, 1800, *ASP, FR* II, 307; Ellsworth and Davie to Talleyrand, Jan. 10, Talleyrand to Ellsworth and Davie, to Murray, to Sémonville, Jan. 31, 1800, AECPE-U, 51, 296–96vo, 306–306vo, 307, 308.

11Jan. 3, 1800, "Letters of Murray," 635; Talleyrand to First Consul, Mar. 3, 1800, AECPE-U, 51, 309–309vo, 352, 353, 357–57vo.

three weeks later, and he was the only member with any direct knowledge of America. The First Consul himself received the Americans graciously on March 7, and they were officially informed of the appointments of their opposite numbers on the following day. Murray, who had heard that they would be Liancourt and La Forest, whom he called "moderates," nevertheless saw "no insurmountable things" in the appointment of the former admiral and minister of marine under Louis XVI, and the onetime national assemblyman now counsellor of state.[12]

Meanwhile, Talleyrand had learned of the death of Washington, and he perceived a magnificent opportunity to usher in a new era in Franco-American relations with a burst of fraternal feeling for the man who personified American independence to all Europe. He therefore proposed to Bonaparte the erection of a statue to the departed American hero, whose sins since 1793 were to be magically forgotten in France as they already had been in America. There was nothing of the opprobrium which French officials had lately become accustomed to in the eulogy to Washington with which Talleyrand prefaced his suggestion, and the virtues which he lauded in Washington were precisely those which Bonaparte wished to associate with himself. The mighty warrior who brought peace, the upright statesman who turned chaos into order—this was also the fame which would fasten the Corsican's grip on the devotions of an inexpressibly war-weary people.[13]

As Talleyrand had doubtless foreseen, Bonaparte accepted his proposal with enthusiasm and at once ordered the commissioning of Houdon to make a statue which would be placed in the Tuileries. In addition, he ordered ten days of mourning in the army, and flags and uniforms were sprinkled with crêpe. On February 8, a giant ceremony was held in the Temple of Mars, where a public orator eulogized Washington at length, in a

12Talleyrand to First Consul, Mar. 3, Decrees of Mar. 3 and 28, Talleyrand to American envoys, Mar. 4 and 7, 1800, AECPE-U, 51, 358–58vo, 359, 397, 363, 371; Murray to J. Q. Adams, Mar. 7, 1800, "Letters of Murray," 644. See Lyon, "Franco-American Convention of 1800," 310–11.
13Undated, AECPE-U, 51, 311–11vo.

speech full of allusions so subtly contrived that the First Consul actually was extolled more than the ostensible subject. Murray had previously commented on this campaign: "They quote *Washington* as the role for Bonaparte in the committee of 500. Strange how they confound everything! But little Caesar seems resolved to play a game strong as their stomachs will bear." But Murray was flattered when Bonaparte spoke to him in praise of Washington at the reception of the ministers.[14]

Murray's comment on the little Corsican's use of America was appropriate. Bonaparte was now intent upon consolidating his hold on the French imagination, and the leader of American independence was a symbol all Frenchmen would recognize and approve. But Bonaparte was no real friend to the United States, as he was later to prove. Nevertheless, a conciliatory policy toward the United States was an essential part of his program for annihilating England. Dedicated to the advancement of his own fortunes, he would bend toward America whenever European conditions required. To Bonaparte, the United States. like the small neutrals of Europe, was again a pawn in the struggle with Great Britain for European domination. Talleyrand recognized the value of American friendship and a real American neutrality in terms of long-range French policy; the means to its realization coincided with Napoleon's immediate interests, and he would go along with them for that reason.

Bonaparte's identification of himself with America's heritage should have been the prelude to a speedy settlement, but Talleyrand's optimistic forecast was belied from the very beginning of the negotiations. On March 9, the Americans announced their readiness to commence negotiations, but the illness of Joseph Bonaparte prevented an immediate beginning. Two weeks later he had recovered, and the two commissions exchanged their powers at a conference on April 2. Here the American devotion to legal forms asserted itself, and another week was consumed

[14]*Ibid.*, 51, 312, 316, 313–27; to J. Q. Adams, Jan. 7, Mar. 7, 1800, "Letters of Murray," 635, 644. See Faÿ, *Revolutionary Spirit in France and America*, 430–36; *Correspondance de Napoléon I^er* (Paris, 1870), XXX, 467.

in invoking the authority of the First Consul and of Talleyrand for the assurance that powers to negotiate were intended to include powers to conclude a treaty.[15]

The Americans proposed first to discuss the problem of reciprocal indemnities. The French ministers countered with a suggestion that methods of evaluating national as well as individual claims be first established, and that the full execution of the treaties of friendship and commerce between the two nations be ensured. Further to test the powers of their opposite numbers, as they reported to Talleyrand, the Frenchmen added that the communication of orders for the discontinuance of measures hostile to France by the American government would be a favorable preliminary to the negotiation. The Americans were forced to admit that no such orders had been issued and could only offer their mission as pledge that the acts repugnant to France would be rescinded as soon as they were seen to be no longer necessary. To the hint regarding the former treaties, they answered that they had not intended to renew or amend them, but to propose a new treaty.[16] Thus early in the negotiations the two opposing positions were established: the United States demanded indemnities, which France wished to avoid as much as possible; and the Americans wanted to bury the old treaties, while the French sought to revive them.

The demand for a cessation of actual hostilities by the United States was not merely a thrust in a diplomatic fencing match. Talleyrand had achieved considerable success in restraining the depredations of French privateers on American commerce. One of the first acts of the legislative body after the advent to power of Bonaparte had been the abolition of the law of January 18, 1798, which President Adams had stigmatized as "an unequivo-

15 *ASP, FR* II, 310–14.

16 American envoys to Ministers of the French Republic, Apr. 7, 1800, *ibid.* II, 314–15; Ministers of the French Republic to American envoys, Apr. 9, 1800, AECPE-U, 51, 455. Much of the correspondence of the negotiations has been published in A. Du Casse, *Histoire des Négociations Diplomatiques Relatives aux Traités de Mortfontaine, de Lunéville et d'Amiens* 3 vols. (Paris, 1855). The Convention of 1800 (Treaty of Mortfontaine) is treated in vol. I, 175–380.

cal act of war." Thereafter, the First Consul was given the authority to regulate privateering.[17] Talleyrand was still suggesting to Bonaparte, in July 1800, reforms in French commercial regulations which would placate neutral countries.[18]

In mid-April Minister of Marine Pierre-Alexandre-Laurent Forfait assured Talleyrand that French cruisers had never been instructed to attack the armed vessels of the United States, although he complained at the same time of United States frigates taking English prizes by force from legitimate French privateers. By the end of the same month Forfait was angered at news of the *Constellation*'s attack upon the French frigate *La Vengeance*. Despite a sensation in Paris over the episode, Forfait restrained his impulse toward retaliation and plaintively asked Talleyrand whether the American envoys could not stop such aggressions. Talleyrand brushed aside the complaint with the response that the negotiations were even then dealing with the problem, but he felt compelled to add that France could never forbid resistance to attack.[19]

The French commissioners were disappointed at the reply of the Americans, but still they "do not perceive, from the considerations suggested rather than developed by the envoys . . . of the United States, any obstacle to arrangements which it may be proper to make, on the subject of the individual claims of one nation upon the other." Nevertheless, they continued, it would be impossible to estimate those claims except by reference to "the principles of the law of nations and the obligations of treaties." The French representatives once more tacitly agreed to consider claims for indemnities but again firmly attached them

17Copies of these laws were given to the American envoys on May 17, 1800. Envoys to Pickering, same date, *ASP, FR* II, 325.

18Report to the First Consul, July 26, 1800, AECPE-U, 52, 189–91. Arthur A. Richmond has shown that Talleyrand and Napoleon planned to use the Franco-American negotiation as a step toward creating a new armed neutrality. "Napoleon and the Armed Neutrality of 1800," *Journal of the Royal United Service Institution* CIV (May 1959), 186–94.

19Forfait to Talleyrand, Apr. 18 and 30, May 11, Talleyrand to Forfait, May 17, 1800, AECPE-U, 51, 467, 488, 496–96vo, 52, 22–23vo, 26–26vo; *Messages and Papers of the Presidents* I, 272. Descriptive documents relating to the *Vengeance* affair are in *Quasi-War with France* V, 160–76.

to the question of the old treaties. They expressed concern, after the efforts of France to remove obstacles to conciliation, that the Americans were unable to assure their government, as it "has a right to expect," that the armed vessels of the United States "should no longer continue to attack the vessels of the Republic, and that the spilling of human blood should no longer be feared." To this more pointed demand the Americans answered that "they must explicitly declare that they are not authorized to give assurances, otherwise than by incorporating them in a treaty." They then presented for discussion several articles of a proposed treaty, all but the first of which had to do with the subject of reciprocal indemnities.[20]

The negotiations were now seriously under way. The Americans reported to their government on April 18 that "We shall be hard pressed to revive the old treaty, so far, at least, as to save its anteriority." The French answer to the American note of April 17 was an emphatic fulfillment of that expectation:

> In hastening to recognize the principle of compensation, it was the intention of the undersigned to exhibit an unequivocal proof of the fidelity of France to her ancient engagements; all pecuniary stipulations appearing to her proper as results from ancient treaties, not as preliminaries to a new one.

Two days later, with a long letter defending the congressional abrogation of the treaties, the Americans enclosed the second part of their proposed treaty. Most of the month of May was consumed in futile argument over the status of the old treaties, and by May 23 the negotiations were at a standstill.[21]

Now the French ministers informed the Americans that they would be unable to proceed without obtaining new instructions. Bonaparte had left Paris on May 6 to take personal command of the campaign against the Austrians in Italy, but a courier would be sent to him as soon as the commissioners' report was ready.

20Du Casse, *Mortfontaine* I, 243–47; Ministers of France to American envoys, Apr. 14, 1800, *ASP, FR* II, 315–17.

21Ministers of France to American envoys, Apr. 19, American envoys to Ministers of France, Apr. 21, 1800, *ASP, FR* II, 317–18, 319–20, 320–24, 325; Du Casse, *Mortfontaine* I, 256–70.

The report was presented to Talleyrand three days later, while Joseph Bonaparte had already written in the same sense to his brother.[22]

The French plenipotentiaries examined the points in contention exhaustively. According to their instructions, they began, three ultimata were stipulated: reestablishment of the old treaties so as to restore to France all rights not contested before the present war; reclamation of the right of French consular jurisdiction in America; and a revision of the articles of the treaties conferring privileges on the United States, to bring them in line with the American treaty with England. But the Americans refused to consider the old treaties at all, insisting that they were officially dead as the result of an act of Congress. It was impossible to revoke the act abolishing the treaties and they could not be reestablished, at least not so as to retain precedence over later treaties (i.e., the Jay Treaty). The Americans had powers neither to recognize the old treaties, nor to reestablish them with rights of precedence.[23]

The respective powers of the two commissions, continued the French ministers, were in direct contradiction and had led to an impasse in the negotiations. Reconsidering their own position, two questions seemed pertinent: Were the treaties really abolished? Had France any interest in maintaining them? The answer to the first question was no. According to the American constitution, and the practice of every civilized state, foreign relations were a function of the executive, and Congress had no right to invalidate treaties. The Act of July 7, 1798, was therefore "a private, domestic act": it did not make the treaties void, although it did make it impossible for the executive and the American courts to enforce them. In the circumstances, France had three options: (1) to surrender her rights under the treaties in forming new ones, (2) merely to accept the dissolution of the old ones, or (3) to interpret the action of Congress as a declaration of war. France could refute the American assertions and re-

22 *ASP, FR* II, 325; Du Casse, *Mortfontaine* I, 272, 272n.
23 May 25, 1800, AECPE-U, 52, 36–49.

quire the envoys to ask for new powers. But that might eliminate completely the first option, and either of the latter two had many more disadvantages.

The second question involved several considerations. The exclusive advantages of the old treaties, those relating to prizes in particular, had proved to be illusory anyway, and the nonexclusive advantages could probably be restored to France in a new treaty. That was also true of the advantages other nations held by their treaties with the United States. But the recognition, or the reestablishment, of the old treaties would require the payment of indemnities, while accepting abrogation would dispense with them, since indemnities would necessarily depend upon stipulations of the former treaties. Finally, would peace result sooner from accepting the abolition of the old treaties or from insisting upon their restoration? Insistence on restoration might force a rupture; at best it would require the Americans to send for new instructions, involving a delay of at least three months and many attendant risks.

The French commissioners advised acceptance of the treaties' abrogation. Experience had shown that all exorbitant advantages were worthless or actual causes of war, and that unequal treaties could be upheld only by force. Except for France's unwarranted pretensions regarding her treaties with the United States, the latter would not have concluded in 1794 the treaty with England.

As a matter of fact, concluded the French commissioners, echoing their own instructions, France's interest required only that the United States prosper. Its growth could never cause the Republic alarm and would on the contrary be useful to it against England. For the United States was destined "by the nature of things" to appropriate part of Britain's maritime trade and thus would gradually diminish British power. Joseph Bonaparte and his colleagues, therefore, desired new powers which would permit them to drop their demands regarding the treaties.[24]

[24]The instructions to the French negotiators, drafted by Talleyrand's "permanent secretary," Hauterive, are in *ibid.*, 51, 381–95vo, and in Du Casse, *Mortfon-*

On May 17, the Americans had written to Pickering that "our success is yet doubtful," because "the French think it hard to indemnify for violating engagements, unless they can thereby be restored to the benefits of them." They might have said that their instructions, much more than those of the mission of 1797, precluded success. Indemnities to American citizens were declared to be "an indispensable condition of the treaty," while the former treaties were not to be "in whole or in part revived by the new treaty."[25]

Talleyrand put the problem into a concise report which he sent to the First Consul on June 3. The Americans demanded that the principle of indemnities due to private citizens be admitted, and France had complied at once. But the Americans rejected the French demand that the former treaties be recognized as a basis for claims. If France accepted the abolition of the treaties, she would impart a completely hostile character to the "mis-

---

taine I, 186–224. Those of the Americans are in *ASP, FR* II, 301–306. Both sets are summarized in Lyon, "Franco-American Convention of 1800," 312–14.

[25]*ASP, FR* II, 325, 302, 306. The instructions concluded thus: "The following points are to be considered as ultimated:

1. That an article be inserted for establishing a board, with suitable powers, to hear and determine the claims of our citizens, for the causes herein before expressed, and binding France to pay or secure payment of the sums which shall be awarded.

2. That the treaties and consular convention, declared to be no longer obligatory by act of Congress, be not in whole or in part revived by the new treaty; but that all the engagements, to which the United States are to become parties, be specified in the new treaty.

3. That no guaranty of the whole or any part of the dominions of France be stipulated, nor any engagements made, in the nature of an alliance.

4. That no aid or loan be promised in any form whatever.

5. That no engagement be made inconsistent with the obligations of any prior treaty; and, as it may respect our treaty with Great Britain, the instruction herein marked XXI is to be particularly observed.

6. That no stipulation be made granting powers to consuls or others, under color of which tribunals can be established within our jurisdiction, or personal privileges be claimed by Frenchmen, incompatible with the complete sovereignty of the United States in matters of policy, commerce, and Government.

7. That the duration of the proposed treaty be limited to twelve years, at furthest, from the date of the exchange of ratifications, with the exceptions respecting its permanence in certain cases, specified under the instruction marked XXX." *Ibid*. II, 306.

understanding," and any consideration of indemnities would be inappropriate. It would mean that France and the United States were at war, "and we shall certainly not buy peace."[26]

Nevertheless, Talleyrand continued, there would be more dignity in not insisting. France should acquiesce in the abolition of the treaties, and with them would go all claims for indemnities. Liberal commercial provisions could be incorporated in a new treaty—provisions which would benefit France and the United States and, by making American commerce more independent, injure England. As for the old alliance, it would be best to forget it as belonging to another time.

The American plenipotentiaries decided to press for a decision. To their note of June 1, the French commissioners replied that new instructions had not yet been received from the First Consul. The French representatives promised an answer as soon as possible, and Joseph set out to see his brother in person. Talleyrand hoped that Bonaparte would not long postpone his decision.[27]

Napoleon's smashing victory over the coalition at Marengo on June 14, 1800, seemed to presage a general armistice, at least on the continent of Europe. The American envoys, apprehensive lest such an eventuality should find them as far as ever from a solution, waited a bare three days after the First Consul's return to Paris on July 3 to request a conference with the French representatives. Talleyrand was almost as impatient as the Americans, and on July 7 he sent to the First Consul the first of a new series of reports on the American negotiations. His object was to inform Bonaparte about American affairs and also to lead him to a generous and statesmanlike decision.[28]

There had lately been, said Talleyrand, a remarkable change in the government of the United States and in American public

26 AECPE-U, 52, 63.

27 *ASP, FR* II, 326–27; Ministers of France to Talleyrand, Talleyrand to Ministers of France, June 4, 1800, AECPE-U, 52, 64–64vo, 65.

28 *ASP, FR* II, 327; Murray to Samuel Dexter, July 12, 1800, "Letters of Murray," 649; William G. Brown, *The Life of Oliver Ellsworth* (New York, 1905), 294; Talleyrand to First Consul, July 7, 1800, AECPE-U, 52, 130–39.

opinion. Adams had forcibly turned out of office the mad Pickering, and the latter's crony, McHenry, had been forced to resign. The President had pardoned three men condemned to death as rebels, and he was even showing consideration for his political opponents. The fact that he himself had reduced the new army by ten thousand men was belated evidence of a peaceful intention. But none of that could save Adams—the struggle between his adherents and the violent Pickering faction ensured his defeat in the coming elections. The domestic and foreign situation of the United States was so unfavorable that the Federalist party itself was doomed to destruction. "In fact, can one conceive of a situation more embarrassing than that of the United States towards foreign powers?" The Federalists had made themselves hated in America in the interest of harmony with England, which reciprocated by redoubling its depredations on American commerce and threatening war over the squabbles of the claims commissioners.[29]

But all of this had been foreseen and prepared for in the negotiations of the last two years. France's noninterference in America's internal affairs and her perseverance in conciliation "has atoned for the wrongs of our depredations." This policy had shown England to be the real wielder of influence and had forced the renewal of negotiations. These advantages had now to be consolidated, and the certainty that Jefferson would be elected to the presidency promised a true reconciliation.

His accession must end in bringing the United States back to us; but we must not forget that if we have improved our relations by moderation and by a complete renunciation of all influence in the affairs of the United States, we will give strength to the administration of Mr. Jefferson only in proving that we do not

[29]Talleyrand's shrewd estimate of American conditions was corroborated by Liston, who reported sadly to Grenville on Aug. 16, 1800: "In diligence and activity the faction combined in opposition to government seem here, as in other parts of the world, to have the superiority over their Antagonists; and to judge from present appearances their interest is gaining ground ... it is particularly mortifying to find that no degree of fair and friendly conduct towards the United States can prevent Great Britain from becoming the object of the most rancorous obloquy." F. O. 5, 29. See Perkins, *First Rapprochement*, 116–28.

want to abuse his partiality for us, and in renouncing any expectation of sacrifices and condescensions which would give to his policy a character that he will never allow it to assume. Mr. Jefferson surely will make it his duty to unite around himself the true Americans and to resume in all its force the system of perfect equilibrium between France and England, which alone suits the United States. It is that system which best suits our interests: we have nothing to desire of the United States, but to see them grow and prosper; without disturbances, without intrigues, jealousy of England and of her demands will bring them into intimate relationships with us.

All of this, Talleyrand observed sagely, gave France new reason for generosity toward the United States. Conviction of her liberality and desire for conciliation had brought the imminent downfall of England's party; it would be blindness to take advantage of circumstances and thereby unite all Americans against France. New political alignments, hastened by the death of Washington, were taking place in America. England's interest lay in dividing and weakening the United States; but France's was the opposite: "it is to see America united, free and prosperous, thus she is a rival of England . . . . Her accretions of strength are interesting to us as much as her weakness is important to our enemy." England could never offer anything to America but vain threats or empty promises. France could strike hard if provoked, but her true relationship to the United States was that of a useful and protective friend.

Aware of the First Consul's reluctance to yield on the question of the treaties, Talleyrand next proposed that the French plenipotentiaries answer the Americans, discussing in a precise manner the point of law involved to prove that the treaties were not abolished. But France must be fair and generous toward the United States. The Jay Treaty should serve as a warning. The party which had made that unequal compact was dying. If France also forced a hard treaty on America, a party would again spring up against the government that accepted it.[30]

Joseph Bonaparte now returned to Paris and invited the

30 July 12, 1800, AECPE-U, 52, 147–55.

American commissioners to dinner on July 11. He had intended to inform them merely that the First Consul was still considering the problem and would announce his decision in a few days, when formal discussions could recommence. Pressed by the Americans, however, Joseph told them in confidence what had caused the First Consul to hesitate. The former treaties, in Napoleon's opinion, ought to be the basis for the negotiation, and "compensation could only be a consequence of the existence of the treaties, and the re-establishment under them of the former privileges and relations." He could never surrender the exclusive privileges of France to her enemy and would insist upon at least an equal footing with Great Britain. Furthermore, it would reflect discredit upon the present government if it should make a treaty with the United States less honorable than that of the royal government.[31]

Now the Americans receded significantly for the first time from their position of indemnities without the old treaties. They requested an interview for July 15, at which they presented a proposition that the indemnities should be

> ascertained and secured in the manner proposed in our project of a treaty, but not to be paid until the United States shall have offered to France an article, stipulating free admission into the ports of each for the privateers and prizes of the other, and the exclusion of those of their enemies; nor unless the article be offered within seven years: such article to have the same effect, in point of priority, as a similar provision had in the treaty of 1778.[32]

It was clear to the Americans that the Frenchmen were not impressed with this overture, and a conference five days later at Roederer's home failed to elicit anything beyond the fact that Talleyrand had been kept informed and was hopeful. The minister had in fact almost despaired of reaching agreement on the treaties and indemnities. In another report to Bonaparte he again urged a speedy decision. A successful end to the negoti-

31*ASP, FR* II, 327–28.
32*Ibid.* II, 328.

ations, he insisted, became more imperative every day. What could now be arranged would soon become difficult because of France's colonial situation; this would perhaps become impossible if it were known that Spain was about to retrocede New Orleans. To bring the negotiations to a prompt and favorable conclusion, therefore, Talleyrand proposed: (1) that the First Consul send to the Council of State for legislative action a supplementary decree further restricting privateering, (2) that he himself be authorized to propose to the American ministers an adjournment of the discussion regarding the treaties and indemnities, until after a general peace, (3) the restoration of commercial relations on the basis of the treaty of 1778, with the exception of the articles incompatible with neutrality ,and (4) the reestablishment of political relations.[33]

Talleyrand developed these ideas at more length in a supplementary report dated July 24. The recent changes of opinion in the United States, he said, were known to the American envoys. As a result, they were no longer obstinate and demanding but sincere in desiring a mutually satisfactory arrangement. The status of the treaties was nevertheless still the main problem: the Americans, "in whose eyes constitutional ideas are infinitely more important than political ideas," could not admit any discussion of the right of Congress to deprive France of her title to treaty precedence and to transfer it to England. They thought that continued concessions to England were necessary to keep England and America at peace. For the record, Talleyrand proposed to discuss the status of the treaties in an official note: to prove that domestic laws had no application to a nation's foreign policy, and that treaties could only be abrogated by mutual consent or by war. This would also dispel the myth of English intent to wage war on the United States, admitting at the same time that England would always threaten war as a means of keeping the United States subservient. England knew its own interests too well to sacrifice a favorable balance of trade with the United States of one hundred million francs (which was precisely

33*Idem*; undated, AECPE-U, 52, 169–70vo.

the sum of her advantage in wealth over other European peoples) and its monopoly of foreign shipping in the American trade.[34]

But Talleyrand did not expect this to have any effect upon the Americans. In his only recorded expression of irritation with them, he told Bonaparte that the only way to end discussions "with men of more obstinacy than character and more pusillanimity than prudence" was to be adamant. He apparently had no suspicion of the similarities between the present mission and that of 1797, of the internal friction between the narrowly legalistic and prejudiced Ellsworth and the junior member of the commission, Murray, who was patronized by both of his colleagues.[35]

"Declare peremptorily," Talleyrand advised, "that France is resolved to make all the sacrifices that friendship can claim; that the principle of indemnities has been agreed upon and will be respected; that the Government of the Republic does not want to engage the Americans in the wars of Europe; that it has more interest than any other in their prosperity, that there can be no rivalry between them; that its pretends to no unusual rights; that it will freely renounce by interpretative stipuations everything in its old treaties which accords advantages not shared by other nations." But France's honor and obligation to the American people prevented acquiescence in the unilateral abrogation of the treaties.

Before Talleyrand had finished this report, he was handed the American proposition regarding the postponement of the payment of indemnities. While he did not find the proposition acceptable, it nevertheless represented a concession, and he altered his conclusions accordingly. First, he would reject the American view of the treaties, but not decisively enough to end the negotiations. If that had no effect upon the American representatives,

---

[34] AECPE-U, 52, 171–77vo.

[35] See Alexander DeConde, "The Role of William Vans Murray in the Peace Negotiations between France and the United States, 1800," *Huntington Library Quarterly* XV (Feb. 1952), 192; Alexander DeConde, *The Quasi-War: The Politics and Diplomacy of the Undeclared War with France, 1797–1801* (New York, 1966), 184–87.

then he would recur to his former proposal—put off for discussion at the general peace the question of the treaties, proceed to the other points of the negotiation and finish them as soon as possible, and reestablish at once commercial and political relations.

The French ministers reported to Talleyrand on July 22 that Ellsworth had hinted that a way could be found to equalize the positions of France and of England in America without injuring Britain. They thought that a solution would be hastened if they could bring the Americans to make a concrete proposal, and they called the minister's attention to the fact that they had evaded the question of indemnities so as to retain complete freedom in regard to the new hypothesis.[36]

Talleyrand replied that he was glad that his ministers thought that the point would be conceded. The honor of the Republic, he continued, demanded that France be accorded the right to bring prizes into American ports on the same terms as England. This admitted, Talleyrand saw no further serious obstacles to the success of the negotiations, which must now proceed to a consideration of indemnities. The original acknowledgement of that principle would be brought forward by the Americans: it should not be withdrawn, but ignored as much as possible. Payments were to be put off to an unspecified time, and similarly the liquidation of claims, but if stipulated payments had to be agreed to, then the installments were to be as small as possible and designated for as far distant a time as possible. "You will see from this, citizen ministers, that we are moving as much as possible to set aside the indemnities."[37]

Talleyrand had constructed an ingenious set of alternatives with but two carefully disguised ultimata: France was to be placed upon a footing of equality with Great Britain, and the indemnities were to be so hedged with counterclaims, and put off to so distant a time, that there would be little, if anything, that would ever have to be paid. But in the end it was his proposal to make an "abstraction" of the related problems of the

36Du Casse, *Mortfontaine* I, 279–81.
37Undated, AECPE-U, 52, 185–88.

treaties and indemnities which was adopted, and the scurrying about of Pichon and La Forest in the wake of Ellsworth's unguarded remark turned out to be useless.

Bonaparte, in this instance, had no use for Talleyrand's subtleties. His long-awaited decision arrived on August 5, directing the minister to instruct the French plenipotentiaries of the two alternatives that he would offer to the United States: (1) restore the exclusive privileges of France and withdraw those of England, and France would pay indemnities; (2) place France and England upon an equal footing regarding maritime privileges, but in this case renounce indemnities. Both propositions, continued the order of the First Consul, were to be made at the same time in a single note which should establish the following facts:

1. That we have never been at war.
2. That we have never enjoyed the advantages of our treaties.
3. That on the contrary the Americans have denied them to us while granting them to the English.
4. That we can admit that our corsairs have done wrongs to their flag: we will make reparation: but on the same principle the United States must indemnify us for granting the same privileges to England by treaty and for giving the same advantages to England even before that.[38]

Years later, in exile at St. Helena, Bonaparte claimed credit for putting the Americans at one stroke on the defensive, although at the time his brother objected that the First Consul's ultimatum would wreck the negotiations. Replying to Talleyrand's *minute* containing Bonaparte's orders, Joseph suggested a modification: since the Americans would not consent to the outright abolition of the principle of indemnities, let France secure an agreement that the surplus of indemnities due the United States, over those due France, be withheld until the United States could guarantee France the absolute and entire enjoyment of its rights under the treaties. Joseph agreed with his colleagues that a conclusion could speedily be reached on this basis. Since he wanted to avoid useless delays, now that the two

38 *Ibid.*, 52, 207–208

commissions were so near agreement, he had already obtained the approval of the First Consul.[39]

The French ministers sent to the Americans on August 11 the note outlined by the First Consul. The day before this they had received from Talleyrand the *projet* of a new commercial treaty. This *projet* had not been presented before, the minister explained, because the necessity for a new treaty had not been foreseen. Although the result of the First Consul's final offer could not yet be known, Talleyrand wanted the government's views on commercial subjects digested at once, so that no time would be lost after settlement of the question of indemnities. He thought he could predict the Americans' choice: France, he said, was going with its consent from an exclusive status to one of equality with other nations. There were two subjects to be considered: the rights and privileges of persons in the respective states, and commerce and navigation. As far as the first was concerned, the American project had repeated the articles of the treaty of 1776, and that was exactly what France wanted.

In regard to commerce and navigation, however, the United States had surrendered liberal principles in its treaty with England, and it now offered the same restrictive articles to France. But France's interest lay in liberal commercial stipulations, and she would continue to uphold the principle of "free ships, free goods." Those principles accorded American interests better, too, so their representatives should be relieved and grateful for the change.[40]

After the Americans had seen Bonaparte's instructions, they wrote to the secretary of state that

> It has, however, became manifest, that the negotiation must be abandoned, or our instructions deviated from. Should the latter be ventured upon, which, from present appearances is not improbable, the deviation will be no greater than a change of circumstances may be presumed to justify.

[39]*Correspondance de Napoléon I*er XXX, 470–71; Joseph Bonaparte to Talleyrand, Aug. 6, 1800, AECPE-U, 52, 209–10vo, 216–16vo.
[40]AECPE-U, 52, 217–29vo.

They added significantly that the armistice, which followed Bonaparte's defeat of the Austrians at Marengo, had succeeded to peace negotiations whose result was daily expected.[41]

A conference with the French ministers failed to produce a more favorable interpretation of the French note, and the Americans now contended for the renewal of the old treaties without the exclusive privileges, and also for the indemnities. But, "because time has become precious," they made a series of proposals which provided an option of a money payment for the exclusive articles of the commercial treaty and substituted a financial obligation for the mutual guarantees of the treaty of alliance. In reply, the French plenipotentiaries pointed out the inconsistency of mixing the First Consul's propositions, but they were willing to discuss the specific proposals, which promised to lead to the modification of Bonaparte's ultimatum which Joseph had demanded.[42]

For the next three weeks, both sides spent their time fruitlessly searching for a mutually acceptable formula. The successive proposals were compared in the Department of Exterior Relations in an undated paper which illustrated their futility. First, the Americans offered a clause giving the United States the option of restoring to France within seven years the exclusive privileges of the old treaties, or of renouncing the indemnities. The French ministers answered this proposal with a reiteration of Bonaparte's propositions. The Americans then proposed that each nation have the option of paying within seven years eight million francs in lieu of the exclusive privileges of the treaties. This offer was accepted by France with the provision that it be permitted to surrender its privileges within seven years and be thereby absolved from all payment of indemnities, and that the guarantee of the treaty of alliance be valued at ten million francs. This stipulation was unacceptable to the Americans, who countered with an offer to convert the guarantee into a loan of one million francs during each war, and the reservation to the Presi-

41Envoys to Secretary of State, Aug. 15, 1800, *ASP, FR* II, 333.
42Envoys to Secretary of State, Aug. 15 and 20, 1800, *ibid.* II, 333–34.

dent of the option of renouncing mutual indemnities upon ratification of the agreement. France thereupon returned to a variation of the original ultimatum: the United States would pay to their citizens the indemnities due from France, and France would renounce both the privileges and the guarantee of the treaties.[43]

At a conference held at the residence of Ellsworth and Davie, the *Hôtel des Oiseaux,* on September 12, the French ministers avowed that their real aim was to avoid paying any indemnities at all. They gave as their motive the utter impossibility of France to pay in its postwar financial condition. The usually mild Joseph Bonaparte closed the discussion with the assertion that he would resign rather than sign a treaty on the basis of indemnities and a modified renewal of the old treaties. He was convinced that an impartial nation would judge "that the present state of things was *war* on the side of America, and that no indemnities could be claimed."[44]

Murray, like other enlightened Federalists in Europe,[45] appreciated the force of the French position—"No nation ever yet gave compensation on an end of hostilities unless treaties were put *in statu quo;*" he told Adams on August 20, and his colleagues were now obliged to surrender the hope of ensuring the indemnities

---

[43]AECPE-U, 52, 117–18vo; *ASP, FR* II, 328–37.

[44]This could not have been unsuspected by the Americans. Five months earlier Murray doubted that France could continue the war, "such is the want of money and of all things necessary!!" and Ellsworth and Davie must have been acquainted with the chronic financial embarrassment of French affairs in America. To J. Q. Adams, Apr. 19, 1800, "Letters of Murray," 645–46; *ASP, FR* II, 337.

[45]John Trumbull, Jay's secretary during his negotiation at London and later U. S. commissioner on the joint claims commission there, was one. "It is very natural for France to wish to retain an advantage [the privileges regarding privateers] so important to her but I do not know how we are to *remake*, nor do I exactly understand why or how we *unmade* the old Treaty: at least it appears strange that we should have transferred this benefit from the one power to the other in a manner so very gratuitous, and without even asking from G. Britain any sort of compensation for what Events might render very inconvenient to us while it was highly beneficial to her. I should not suppose that it was thought advisable for us to contribute to increase that maritime preponderance which is constantly directed to the aggrandizement of one Nation, and constantly heedless, to say the least, of the Interests of all others . . . ." John Trumbull to James Wadsworth, Aug. 16, 1800, Rufus King Papers, New-York Historical Society. For Trumbull's career, see Theodore Sizer, "John Trumbull," *DAB* XIX, 11–15.

at present. They outlined their position to the secretary of state thus:

> The American ministers being now convinced that the door was perfectly closed against all hope of obtaining indemnities, with any modification of the treaties, it only remained to be determined whether, under all circumstances, it would not be expedient to attempt a temporary arrangement which would extricate the United States from the war, or that peculiar state of hostility in which they are at present involved, save the immense property of our citizens now depending before the council of prizes, and secure, as far as possible, our commerce against the abuses of captures during the present war.

They therefore proposed on September 13 what Talleyrand had suggested to the First Consul in July, on the following bases:

> 1. The ministers plenipotentiary of the respective parties, not being able to agree at present respecting the former treaties and indemnities, the parties will in due and convenient time further treat on these subjects; and, until they shall have agreed respecting the same, the said treaties shall have no operation. In the meantime,
> 2. The parties shall abstain from all unfriendly acts; their commercial intercourse shall be free, and debts shall be recoverable in the same manner as if no misunderstanding had intervened.
> 3. Property captured and not yet definitively condemned, or which may be captured before the exchange of ratification, shall be mutually restored. Proofs of ownership to be specified in the convention.
> 4. Some provisional regulations shall be made to prevent abuses and disputes that may arise out of future cases of capture.[46]

Bonaparte now agreed with Talleyrand that a temporary arrangement with the United States, which would in effect give France an ally and England an enemy at sea, was preferable to dragging out the negotiations any longer. Joseph was ordered to proceed. But the negotiation had already been spun out at such length that President Adams was becoming restive, writing to Secretary of State Marshall that he expected to see the envoys

---

[46]"Letters of Murray," 651; *ASP, FR* II, 339.

soon without a treaty, but "loaded with professions and protestations of love, to serve as a substitute for a treaty." Since Congress had already declared war "within the meaning of the Constitution against that republic," he wondered whether "all restrictions and limitations" ought not to be removed. Fortunately for both countries, Marshall supplied the caution which had so long been lacking in the office of the secretary of state. He thought that France's changed policy toward neutrals would probably make such a step unwise even in the absence of a treaty. Adams, after reading King's evidence that France was "courting or flattering the northern powers into an armed neutrality," was inclined to agree.[47]

The French counterproposals were presented and discussed in a conference on September 19. There were few differences now, "and it was agreed to meet from day to day until the business was finished." On September 25, the French ministers announced the end of the negotiations to Talleyrand, and on the same day September 29 was agreed upon as the day for the signing of the provisional treaty. Talleyrand replied to his ministers on September 26:

> You have rendered a real service to the French nation and to its government in putting an end to the quarrels which deprive France of one of the most important branches of its commercial communications and in re-establishing between the two peoples relations of concord and attachment which nothing should have altered.

In accordance with the desire of the American ministers, he ordered at once the suspension of all American prize cases pending before the Council of Prizes.[48]

The French ministers reported to Talleyrand on September 28 that the treaty was completed. A final obstacle had been encountered in the refusal of the Americans to call the document a "treaty of amity and commerce," as the Frenchmen wished.

---

[47]Du Casse, *Mortfontaine* I, 306–307; Sept. 4 and 27, 1800, *Works of Adams* IX, 80–81, 84–85.

[48]*ASP, FR* II, 339–40; AECPE-U, 52, 320–20vo, 327–27vo, 328–28vo.

Since they had surrendered for the time being the two great *sine qua non* of their instructions, they insisted upon regarding it as temporary and preferred the title of "convention." Rather than imperil the results of their long labor, the French representatives accepted the American offer to call it a "provisional treaty."[49]

Only the signing remained on September 29, when a last dispute arose. The French ministers demanded that the provisional treaty be signed in the French language only, in accordance with the practice of the consular convention of 1788 and the commercial treaty between France and England of 1786. If the Americans objected to this demand, two alternatives were offered: the instrument to be signed in French, but with an additional article stipulating that such a mode of signing was not to constitute a precedent nor operate to the prejudice of either party; or, to sign in both French and English, but with an article declaring that the treaty was originally concluded and written in the French language. This last was the form which had been adopted in the treaties of 1778, and the Americans finally agreed to follow that precedent.[50]

The provisional treaty was thereupon signed at the *Hôtel des Oiseaux*, at two o'clock in the morning of October 1, 1800, but since the copies all bore the date of September 30, that was left as the original date. Joseph Bonaparte invited the Americans to a fête at his country estate to celebrate the restoration of amity between the two countries, and the First Consul let it be known that he would be present to ratify for the French government.[51]

The fête at Joseph Bonaparte's chateau at Mortfontaine was scheduled for October 3, but the French ministers called upon the Americans the day before with some last minute changes of form desired by the First Consul. The most important of these related to the title—Bonaparte, desiring that France's rapprochement with the United States appear in the eyes of Europe as

49AECPE-U, 52, 329–35vo.
50*ASP, FR* II, 340–42.
51AECPE-U, 52, 316–17vo.

nearly permanent as possible, requested that the title of "convention" be restored. As a matter of personal prerogative, he also required that the preamble establish the convention as between the First Consul and the President of the United States, rather than as between the respective governments of the two nations. These changes were quickly agreed to, and the business of the negotiation was finally terminated.[52]

[52]ASP, FR II, 342; AECPE-U, 52, 318–19vo, 308–308vo.

## CHAPTER XVII

Reconciliation and Neutrality

> I shall leave the State with its coffers full, and the
> fair prospects of a peace with all the world smiling
> in its face.
>
> JOHN ADAMS, DECEMBER 28, 1800.

> Mr. Jefferson surely will make it his duty to unite
> around himself the true Americans and to resume
> in all its force the system of perfect equilibrium
> between France and England, which alone suits
> the United States.
>
> TALLEYRAND TO NAPOLEON, JULY 7, 1800.

THE gala celebration staged at Mortfontaine by Joseph Bonaparte was said to have been the most splendid affair of its kind
since the beginning of the Revolution. It was decided that the
convention needed to be signed again, and the ceremony was enacted once more in the presence of the First Consul and all of his
relatives, with most high officials of the French government and
foreign diplomatic corps also in attendance. The decorations, the
entertainment—introduced with a display of fireworks intended
to symbolize the unity of France and the United States—and the
festal dinner were all on a lavish scale. Bonaparte wanted to ensure careful attention both at home and abroad to the first international agreement concluded by the Consular government, and
the toasts offered at the dinner by the three consuls were pointed:

BONAPARTE, FIRST CONSUL:      "To the *manes* of the French and
Americans dead on the field of
battle for the independence of the
new world."

| | |
|---|---|
| CAMBACÉRÈS, SECOND CONSUL: | "To the successor of Washington." |
| LEBRUN, THIRD CONSUL: | "To the union of America with the powers of the north, for the protection of freedom of the seas."[1] |

Ellsworth and Davie remained in France only long enough to attend the fête in their honor and departed for Le Havre on October 4, Davie to sail directly for home, Ellsworth to stop briefly in England. Murray returned from Mortfontaine to Paris, setting out on October 10 for his post at The Hague. The chief justice, who had been in ill health for several months, soon decided to spend the winter in England, and Murray lamented the necessity: "It will be a great loss, if he do [sic] not go on to defend our work!" Murray himself was "extremely rejoiced at" that work, and he confided to Adams that "we have, I dare think, made a better treaty than the last mission might according to their instructions have made . . . ."

> If we have not accomplished every object of the government of the United States, we have done all in our power—all I believe which any others would have done, all that could be expected in the present state of our relations, and of the world's affairs! We, at all events, put an end to the equivocal state of things, draw the government of the United States out of the quarrel with honour, and establish honourable rules for the future.[2]

The American ministers jointly defended their work in a report of October 4 to Secretary of State Marshall. The convention had renewed the favorable features of the old treaties, whereas those that had proved troublesome were suspended. Although the indemnities had not been obtained, all American rights to claim them at a future negotiation had been reserved; France's evident

---

[1]George F. Hoar, "A Famous Fête," *Proceedings of the American Antiquarian Society* XII (1898), 240–59. This includes accounts from the diary of Murray (Murray Papers, Library of Congress) and from the semiofficial *Gazette Nationale ou le Moniteur Universel.* See also Brown, *Ellsworth,* 305–10; Faÿ, *Revolutionary Spirit in France and America,* 437–38.

[2]Murray to J. Q. Adams, Oct. 5, Nov. 18, Oct. 10, Sept. 27, 1800, "Letters of Murray," 645–55, 662, 657, 653–54.

inability to pay would have rendered any promise to do so at present a new source of irritation.

> It accorded as little with their views as with their instructions, to subject their country perpetually to the mischievous effects of those treaties, in order to obtain a promise of indemnity at a remote period—a promise which might as easily prove delusive as it would reluctantly be made; especially, as under the guaranty of the treaty of alliance, the United States might be immediately called upon for succors, which if not furnished, would of itself be a sufficient pretext to render abortive the hope of indemnity . . . . It only remained for the undersigned to quit France, leaving the United States involved in a contest, and, according to appearances, soon alone in a contest, which it might be as difficult for them to relinquish with honor as to pursue with a prospect of advantage; or else to propose a temporary arrangement, reserving for a definitive adjustment points which could not then be satisfactorily settled, and providing in the meantime against a state of things of which neither party could profit. They elected the latter, and the result has been the signature of a convention.[3]

Fear that England might take offense at any arrangement with France had nagged at the envoys throughout the negotiations, but they thought that London could find little pretext for retaliation in the convention itself. The document was immediately published in the *Moniteur*, and its substance was soon widely known in Europe. Talleyrand feared that Murray, back in Holland, would resent this publication of the agreement, and early in November he ordered Sémonville to reassure him. Publication was not for the purpose of influencing the convention's reception in America—Ellsworth and Davie had already sailed with their copies before it appeared—but, "since neutrality everywhere was so openly attacked and compromised," the First Consul wanted to assure "interested nations" that he did not merely promise protection to neutral commerce. The convention with the United States showed "the unequivocal determination of France to resist such conduct and to respect neutral rights."[4]

The United States, therefore, was a means and beneficiary

3 *ASP, FR* II, 342–43.
4 *Ibid.* II, 343–44; AECPE-U, 52, 410–11.

of Bonaparte's already-forming League of Armed Neutrality, and that without incurring the obligations of membership. The Americans had imperfectly understood this important French purpose during the negotiations. Murray was greatly relieved later to learn from King that England found no ground for complaint. Ellsworth, he learned, had been "not only received well but with distinction" at Court, where the British monarch had even congratulated him on his handiwork. The British chargé at Philadelphia wrote that, though the United States had got nothing from the convention except freedom of the treaties of 1778, ". . . thinking men may allow this advantage to have been cheaply purchased . . . ."[5]

President Adams's Annual Address, delivered on November 22, 1800, a few days before news of the convention was confirmed officially, "contained merely brief notices of the principal topics of public interest," but the expiring House made a final, forlorn plea for the retention of "that system of maritime defence" in its Reply. Already, as Létombe wrote to Talleyrand, Hamilton's diatribe against Adams, which the vigilance of Aaron Burr had made public property, had administered the *coup de grâce* to the Federalists.[6]

The President sent the convention to the Senate, "for their consideration and decision," on December 15; and at the news, the irreconcilable Ames moaned: "We are, by treaty, to embrace France, and Frenchmen will swarm in our porridge-pots." Jefferson's election was already, although prematurely, as it turned out, a foregone conclusion: "Jefferson will say he only supports the friendly system of his predecessor." Cabot told Wolcott that

[5]Murray to J. Q. Adams, Nov. 18, 1800, "Letters of Murray," 661–62; Edward Thornton to Grenville, Jan. 16, 1801, F. O. 5, 32. Having rejected Bonaparte's first peace overtures one year earlier, England now had no desire to impede the approaching general pacification. Joseph Bonaparte was already engaged in the negotiations with the Emperor at Lunéville which resulted in a continental peace, and Otto was conducting in London the preliminary talks which resulted in the peace of Amiens one and one-half years later. AECPE-U, 52, 391. The British Foreign Office kept King informed of the talks' progress. Hammond to King, Nov. 4, 1800, King Papers, New-York Historical Society.

[6]*Oliver Wolcott* II, 450; *Messages and Papers of the Presidents* I, 305–308; Oct. 31, 1800, AECPE-U, 52, 401–402.

"the affairs of our country are in the worst possible situation, in regard to foreign nations." Wolcott warned Hamilton of the blow which was to fall: "You will be afflicted on reading the treaty with France." Since even Wolcott could not accuse Ellsworth of treachery, his explanation to both Hamilton and Pickering was that the illness of the chief justice had deranged his mind![7]

The derangement, however, was in the minds of the dwindling Massachusetts-Connecticut junto. As he had found it necessary to do before, Hamilton attempted to administer a check to the New Englanders, writing to Senator Sedgwick that "The convention with France is just such an issue as was to have been expected. It plays into the hands of France . . . [but] I am of opinion the treaty must be ratified." Analyzing the convention more at length for the benefit of Gouverneur Morris, now senator from New York, Hamilton concluded that "there is nothing in it contrary to our treaty with Great Britain." He confessed that he had lately been charged with "being fond of giving advice," but he could not forbear urging Morris to help overcome the "hesitation in the Senate" to its ratification. To Sedgwick, Hamilton spoke plainly: to reject the convention with France "would, I think, utterly ruin the federal party and endanger our internal tranquillity." But the convention was by now a secondary matter. As if to repair the damage done by his effort to undercut Adams, Hamilton was now exerting himself to prevent the Federalist-dominated House of Representatives from choosing Aaron Burr over Jefferson as president of the United States.[8]

President Adams was content, and he faced retirement with

7 To Gore, Dec. 29, 1800, *Works of Ames* I, 289; Wolcott to Hamilton, Dec. 25, to Pickering, Dec. 28, 1800, *Oliver Wolcott* II, 460, 461.

8 Hamilton to Sedgwick, Dec. 22, to Morris, Dec. 24, 1800, *Works of Hamilton* X, 397–401, 408–11. According to Jacob Cooke: "That many New England Federalists should have viewed the Convention of 1800 as a betrayal of the interests of their section is understandable." The convention failed to provide indemnities for French spoliations, reserving under ART. II that question and others for renewed negotiation "at a convenient time." Thus, says Cooke, the convention "was more a French than an American diplomatic triumph." But Cooke himself explains that it was a Federalist-controlled Senate which required the expunging of ART. II as a condition of ratification. "Country Above Party," 74–75, 75n.

pride in his accomplishments: "I shall leave the State with its coffers full, and the fair prospects of a peace with all the world smiling in its face . . . ." He thought that the Convention should be ratified unconditionally and regretted the advice of the Senate on February 3, requiring him to ratify on condition that the second article, representing the agreement to disagree on the indemnities and old treaties, be expunged and that the convention be limited to eight years' duration. He decided to ratify according to the Senate's advice but, because Senator Bayard of Delaware refused the appointment as minister to France, he left the whole business to his successor.[9]

President Jefferson ratified the convention upon assuming office on March 4. He sent his copy to France on a sloop of war with instructions to Ellsworth and Murray, or either one of them, to negotiate the exchange of ratifications.[10]

By the time the convention returned to Murray's care, Talleyrand had long since done all that depended upon France. On October 7, 1800, he sent orders to the Council of Prizes for the restoration to their owners of all American ships involved in cases pending before it, in accordance with the convention's provisions. On the same day he wrote to the minister of marine, asking him to dispatch orders to the colonies putting the convention into effect there. Two weeks later he reported to the First Consul that the convention was finished and the orders necessary to put it in force already sent. It was important, he continued, to send a new commissioner (formerly consul) general to America at once. Létombe was not adequate, and he would have been replaced earlier but for circumstances. He nominated Pichon, back at his post of assistant chief of the second (American) division of the department. Pichon, who knew America well, could also fill the place of chargé d'affaires until a minister should be sent.

9Adams to F. A. Vanderkemp, Dec. 28, 1800, *Works of Adams* IX, 577; *ASP, FR* II, 344.
10Murray to J. Q. Adams, May 16, 1801, "Letters of Murray," 697–98; Jefferson to Monroe, Mar. 7, 1801, L & B, *Writings of Jefferson* X, 220–21.

Bonaparte confirmed Pichon's appointment by a decree of October 25.[11]

Three weeks earlier, Talleyrand had sent a copy of the convention to Létombe, who was to reactivate France's commercial operations in the United States. Létombe was instructed not to publish the convention, and Talleyrand assured Ellsworth and Davie, to whom he entrusted the dispatch, that it was for his agent's information only. Létombe was also ordered to busy himself securing American ratification of the convention and compliance with its provisions. Talleyrand thought that normal relations could be resumed even if the ratification did not take place, but he naturally preferred to leave nothing to chance.[12]

From the convention, Talleyrand turned to the problem of Louisiana. On August 1, 1800, General Louis Alexandre Berthier had taken over the negotiations with Spain for the retrocession of what was envisioned as the cornerstone of a new French colonial empire in America. His efforts resulted in the secret treaty signed at San Ildefonso on October 1, actually the same day as the signing of the convention with the United States. Under provisions of this new treaty, Louisiana was to be returned to France "with the same extent that it actually has in the hands of Spain, that it had when France previously possessed it and such as it ought to be according to the treaties passed subsequently between Spain and other states." The retrocession was to take place six months after the fulfillment of France's engagement to create a kingdom in Italy for the Duke of Parma. Bonaparte never did discharge his obligation to the duke, but he and Talleyrand began at once the preparations necessary for a French return to Louisiana. General Collot, whom Adet had commissioned to make a military survey of the area five years earlier, finally was exchanged with England through the long and tireless efforts of Talleyrand and arrived in Paris early in October 1800. He hardly had time to find lodgings before the First Consul commissioned him to draw up an exhaus-

11AECPE-U, 52, 369–70, 371–74vo, 390–90vo, 393–93vo.
12Ibid., 52, 364–65vo, 366–67.

tive report on Louisiana, for which he was given the freedom of the archives of Talleyrand's department.[13]

Although the United States could have no legal objection, Talleyrand was sure that Louisiana would cause future misunderstanding. He nominated Bournonville as commissioner at Charleston on November 4, for the primary mission of keeping a watch over England's intrigues with the Indians for the wresting of the Floridas from Spain. Reconciliation with the United States, he told the First Consul, would stop most of those plots, but they would be revived, "and who knows whether the United States will not connive in them at the first suspicion of our reintegration in Louisiana?"[14]

To postpone those suspicions as long as possible, Pichon was instructed to avoid any discussion of France's future colonization plans. If vague rumors concerning the retrocession produced a hostile attitude, then he could assure the American government that the only aim of France in her possessions was the maintenance of order, which the distance of her colonies required for their preservation. Talleyrand thought that the convention would be ratified by the time Pichon reached America; if not, he was to work for its ratification through the secretary of state. Pichon would inform the American government of France's haste in fulfilling the convention, and he was made responsible for preventing any threat to Franco-American harmony from the West Indian colonies. He was empowered to require of the

---

[13]*Ibid.*, 52, 205–206vo, 341, 211, 392. See Echeverria, "General Collot's Plan," 512–20. In his instructions to General Berthier, Talleyrand reviewed French efforts to regain Louisiana. Emphasizing Spain's decrepitude, Talleyrand insisted that Louisiana was in greater danger than ever; England's loss in 1783 of her colonies, "whose commerce is still in her hands and whose government is consistently directed by her influence," had cost her nothing, and only American neutrality had thus far spared Louisiana from Anglo-American conquest. Instructions on the retrocession of Louisiana, Aug. 1, 1800, AECPE-U, 52, 198–204vo. Talleyrand had repeatedly warned Spanish ministers of an Anglo-American alliance, effected by "Pitt's gold and intrigues," to attack Louisiana. Arthur P. Whitaker, "Spain and the Retrocession of Louisiana," *American Historical Review* XXXIX (Apr. 1934), 467. See the same author's *The Mississippi Question, 1793–1803* (New York, 1934), 176–86.

[14]AECPE-U, 52, 408–409.

colonial agents both respect for American neutrality and good treatment of American commerce. He must attach himself to no political party and maintain a strict neutrality between them.[15]

Talleyrand wanted Pichon to reach the United States as quickly as possible, and he asked Minister of Marine Forfait for a frigate to transport him. Forfait agreed to lend Pichon the *Sémillante,* waiting at Lorient with materials necessary for the reequipment of the *Insurgente,* which was to be returned to France under the convention's terms. Pichon reached Norfolk on March 10, and one week later he reported from the new federal city of Washington that the convention had been conditionally ratified. He thought that France should accept the Senate's reservations rather than return matters to their former confusion. A little later Pichon told Talleyrand that the reoccupation of Louisiana would be an extremely delicate matter, and his words were echoed from Holland by Murray: "I fear that we have another iron in the fire—that France is to have the Floridas and Louisiana!!!"[16]

The secret treaty of San Ildefonso might have undone the Franco-American reconciliation, but its terms were not known officially for many months. When President Jefferson took office in March 1801, it was British maritime aggressions which again disturbed him, rather than the appearance of an aggressive French empire on the Mississippi. French acquisition of Louisiana, in fact, permitted Jefferson eventually to achieve his greatest diplomatic scuccess and provided the classic example of the Jeffersonian policy of using the distresses of Europe for the advantage of the United States.

Three months after assuming office, President Jefferson relayed the rumor of the transfer of Louisiana to Monroe: "There is considerable reason to apprehend that Spain ceded Louisiana and the Floridas to France. It is a policy very unwise in both, and very ominous to us." Three days later he repeated this warn-

15*Ibid.,* 52, 417–18vo.
16*Ibid.,* 52, 412–12vo, 427–27vo, 53, 50, 115–18; Murray to J. Q. Adams, Mar. 30, 1801, "Letters of Murray," 693.

ing: "we have great reason to fear that Spain is to cede Louisiana and the Floridas to France."[17]

By late July, James Madison, now secretary of state, was sufficiently certain of the report to explain the administration's position to King, who had been retained as minister to London. The United States preferred Spain in Louisiana, and Robert R. Livingston, going to Paris as minister, would be instructed to work against the actual transfer taking place. He and Charles Pinckney at Madrid would both use proper means—"that is to say the means of peace and persuasion"—to accomplish this end. But Madison was more concerned about the possibility of England acquiring Louisiana, since "she is the last of Neighbors that would be agreeable to the U.S."![18]

Livingston reached Paris early in December 1801 and set to work on Talleyrand at once, but it was almost six months before the French officially acknowledged Louisiana. Jefferson and Madison then worked out a diplomatic campaign against Bonaparte, a campaign reminiscent of the diplomatic bluster in which Jefferson had indulged during the affair of Nootka Sound a dozen years earlier. On April 18, 1802, Jefferson wrote to Livingston the famous letter threatening a marriage of the United States with "the British fleet and nation." Jefferson entrusted this letter to Dupont de Nemours, about to return to France from America, and he asked Dupont to read it before delivering it to Livingston. To Dupont himself, Jefferson wrote of the Louisiana cession: "—this speck which now appears as an almost invisible point in the horizon, is the embryo of a tornado which will burst on the countries on both sides of the Atlantic and involve in its effects their highest destinies."[19]

Jefferson and Madison probably expected that the speck would never assume dangerous proportions. In the early months of his administration, however, Jefferson could not have fore-

17Jefferson to Monroe, May 26 and 29, 1801, Ford, *Jefferson's Writings* VIII, 58, 62.
18July 24, 1801, *Writings of Madison* VI, 426–35.
19Apr. 25, 1802, L & B, *Writings of Jefferson* X, 311–16, 316–19.

seen that the French acquisition of Louisiana would have such a fortunate denouement. But there never was any doubt in his mind that events would one day peacefully deliver Louisiana into the American Union. This, however, was in a future which Jefferson contemplated with confidence when he ushered in the Republican era.

The advent of the Republicans to power consummated the Franco-American reconciliation which John Adams's courageous initiative had begun. It confirmed that equilibrium between France and England which, as only the High Federalists had forgot, was America's true interest. France and the United States resumed their true relationship, which had a greater significance than what one writer wittily calls "a friendship based on mutual misunderstanding."[20]

Proving the accuracy of Talleyrand's prediction, Jefferson accepted the decision of the expiring Federalist Senate. Murray acknowledged receipt of his instructions for the exchange of ratifications at Paris on May 20, and nine days later he had returned to begin negotiations once more, this time alone, as Ellsworth had already sailed from England for home. Murray was received by Talleyrand on June 1 and delivered his credentials to the First Consul at a public audience on June 6. Bonaparte, he reported, did not seem pleased with the conditional ratification but intimated that the exchange would not encounter insurmountable difficulties. Joseph Bonaparte, Roederer, and Fleurieu were immediately appointed to treat with Murray, and the negotiations began on June 14.[21]

The French ministers would agree to the suppression of ARTICLE II only on the understanding that all the claims under it be considered renounced. This renunciation would have ended forever the possibility of obtaining indemnities from France, and Murray countered with a proposal to reinstate the article, reserv-

20Crane Brinton, *The Lives of Talleyrand*, 109–10. Edward Channing, *History of U. S.* IV, 208, calls the Convention of 1800 "one of the most fortunate bits of negotiation that ever took place."

21*ASP, FR* VI, 137–40.

ing to the Senate the right to agree or not. The French ministers objected that this would prove a source of future discord and proposed that on the exchange of ratifications both sides agree to interpret the suppression of ARTICLE II as ending its respective pretensions. Murray replied that he had no powers to enter into explanations of the convention as approved by the Senate, and the negotiations came to a halt while Talleyrand sought a way out of the difficulty.[22]

On June 19, Talleyrand suggested to Bonaparte that the best solution would be his pure and simple ratification, prefaced by a statement that he interpreted the abolition of ARTICLE II as a reciprocal relinquishment of its reservations. Two days later he explained the problem again. The eight-year limit imposed by the Senate, he thought, was useful to both countries in permitting an automatic review of their relations. Agreeing to the outright abolition of ARTICLE II, however, would mean acquiescing in the abrogation of the treaties, while the United States could renew her claims for indemnities at any time. The only alternatives were to demand a new negotiation or to ratify conditionally, as the United States had. The first course would take a long time and would return relations with America to a status of uncertainty. Furthermore, France had an important interest in preserving the first treaty made by the Republic on liberal principles respecting the rights of neutrals. This treaty had already influenced "the freeing of the northern neutrals from the English yoke," and it alone assured the convention an honorable place in the history of public law. A conditional ratification, therefore, was the best solution—the First Consul could ratify the convention "Provided that: within a year the two nations have agreed never to raise the claims of Article 2."[23]

<hr/>

[22]AECPE-U, 52, 70–71; *ASP, FR* VI, 141–45.

[23]AECPE-U, 52, 71vo, 110–12. The question of the validity of the unilateral abrogation of American treaties with France by the U. S. Congress has never been satisfactorily resolved, nor is it ever likely to be. Despite the legal arguments on both sides, the question remained a political rather than a legal one. The U. S. did not deny that unilateral abrogation was a *casus belli*, if not tantamount to a declaration of war. It became essentially a matter of expedience for France, and since she emphatically did not desire war, her only alternative was acquiescence. The U. S.

By July 23, Murray was convinced that nothing better than a conditional French ratification could be obtained, and he agreed to exchange ratifications on that basis. The formalities took place on July 31, 1801, France adding to the Senate's reservations a clause providing that "the two States renounce the respective pretensions which are the object of" the excepted ARTICLE II.[24] Bonaparte proclaimed the convention on December 15, 1801, but President Jefferson held the French ratification for one month before concluding that he would have to resubmit the instrument to the Senate. This was done on December 11; and the Senate resolved, on December 19, 1801, to "consider the convention between the United States and the French republic as fully ratified."[25]

For all practical purposes it had been so for almost one year before it was proclaimed by President Jefferson on December 21, 1801. The Republicans had recognized their debt to Talleyrand for preserving American independence. A year and a half earlier, Létombe had reported that Republican leaders referred to the minister as "their savior," adding that, "except for your prudence, your calmness, your wise and farseeing policy the United States would have been English two years ago."[26]

The United States was able at last to adopt a neutrality which was neither French nor English, but American. President Adams, blamed by High Federalists for destroying his party by insisting on peace, emphatically asserted years later that he wanted no

Court of Claims decided for the American contention in a series of French Spoliation cases, notably *William R. Hooper, Administrator*, v. *United States*, in 1886 and 1887, but the court's decision can be supported only by acceptance of its premises. It should also be noted that the court had no international jurisdiction, and that France had admitted the legality of congressional abrogation so far as domestic law was concerned. See U. S., *Court of Claims Reports* XXII, 408ff. These decisions are collected in *The Controversy over Neutral Rights*. The cases are discussed in George A. King, "The French Spoliation Claims," *American Journal of International Law* VI, (1912), 359–80, 629–49. The convention is printed in *ASP, FR* II, 295–301, *Treaties and Other International Acts of the United States* II, 457–87, and elsewhere.

24*ASP, FR* VI, 146–49, II, 344.
25AECPE-U, 52, 428–35vo; *ASP, FR* II, 345.
26AECPE-U, 52, 156–60vo.

epitaph save: "Here lies John Adams, who took upon himself the responsibility of the peace with France in the year 1800."[27] Adams had made a significant, however erratic and truculent, contribution to American independence, as much from England as from France. Precious time had been gained so that thereafter the natural development of America, especially after what Edward Channing called the "procurement" of Louisiana, gave to the United States the strength to protect its own interests. The Convention of 1800 contributed to more than one century of growth which was uniquely American.

The first decade of the American Federal Union coincided exactly with the French Revolution, frequently described as the culminating act of the "Age of the Democratic Revolution."[28] As the initial protagonist of the democratic revolution, the United States could not stand aloof; its sympathies and its interests were both involved. Britain in the 1790s, as in the 1770s, was cast in the role of freedom's enemy, while France now fought for her own liberty, equality, and fraternity. The French Revolution therefore revived old enthusiasms, as the renewal of war between Britain and France in 1793 awakened old hatreds. But the United States, having passed through its revolution, had entered a postrevolutionary phase of national consolidation and development. Needing peace at home and abroad, America's struggle for neutrality was hindered by both the partisans of the French Rights of Man and the admirers of Britain's ordered business

[27]Adams to James Lloyd, Jan. 1815, *Works of Adams* X, 113. To his correspondent's censure of his missions to France as "the greatest shade in my Presidential escutcheon," Adams replied with a rejoinder almost Jeffersonian: "I agree, Sir, that they did with that third of the people, who had been averse to the revolution, and who were then, and always, before and since, governed by English prejudices; and who then, and always, before and since, constantly sighed for a war with France and an alliance with Great Britain; but with none others. The house would have fallen with a much more violent explosion, if those missions to France had not been instituted .... I will defend my missions to France, as long as I have an eye to direct my hand, or a finger to hold my pen. They were the most disinterested and meritorious actions of my life." *Id.*

[28]See George Rudé, *Revolutionary Europe, 1783–1815* (New York, 1964), 7; Godechot, *France and the Atlantic Revolution*; Palmer, *Age of the Democratic Revolution: The Challenge*, and *The Age of the Democratic Revolution: The Struggle* (Princeton, 1964).

civilization, and it was compromised by the efforts of both of the European giants to force the weight of the United States into the scales against its enemy.

Neutrality, moreover, was not a policy which Americans accepted without reservations. A majority of Americans, led by Jefferson and Madison, wanted a neutrality which was not only uncompromising in its defense of American interests but also faithful to American treaty commitments to France. The Federalists wanted neutrality too, but their conception of American interests was restricted to the preservation of economic stability, the integrity of Hamilton's fiscal programs and the safety of their commercial operations. Since these interests depended on undisturbed commercial intercourse with Great Britain, they were willing to limit the advantages to France of her treaties with the United States in order to avoid giving offense to the former enemy. Because British naval power controlled the seas, a strict American neutrality inevitably meant Anglo-American disputes, but a neutrality acceptable to Britain entailed a departure from American engagements to France which was itself a breach of neutrality. Secretary of State Jefferson restricted the treaty privileges of France as much as he reasonably could in order to give Britain no pretext for hostility; successive French ministers and their governments complained repeatedly in vain. Although Girondist schemes involved the manipulation of American neutrality to belligerent French purposes, they were nullified. France retaliated only after the United States compromised its neutrality in the British treaty of 1794. Because foreign commerce was an essential branch of its economy, the United States could not escape embroilment in the Anglo-French war.

At bottom, the kind of neutrality Americans wanted depended on their conceptions of the American future and on the inherent power of the United States to fashion it. Madison and Jefferson, and the party which gradually formed around them in the struggles of the 1790s, saw an egalitarian "empire for liberty" dedicated to individual freedom and unfettered opportunity for all. Federalists assumed a continuance of the upper-class domination of the state of colonial times—the "politics of deference" with its social stratification, and leadership dependent on family, status, and wealth—for the protection and advancement of the interests of the privileged class and the maintenance of public order. It was consistent with their assumed right to a monopoly of government offices that they described themselves as "the wise, the rich, and the good."[29]

Madison and Jefferson acted from the first on the assumption that American independence was established and that it could be maintained. The means, they thought, were obvious: America's distance from Europe, and the actual importance to Britain and the potential importance to France of American commerce. In the First Congress, Madison tried to establish American economic independence of Britain through commercial discrimination; soon after, in the Nootka Sound crisis, Jefferson was prepared to use America's geographical position to force concessions from Europe. Both reflected a self-confident optimism that has been characteristically American. Federalists, on the other hand, were pessimistic about America's ability to act independently and preferred the safety of the traditional economic dependence on England. It is ironic that Republicans who looked to a future of peace and contentment, undisturbed by Europe's quarrels, thought the United States strong enough to force respect for its interests, while even those Federalists who shared Hamilton's vision of a powerful, heroic state doubted American power in their time.[30]

It was inevitable that contrasting views of America's future—of the kind of society America should become—and of America's power should produce conflicts over policies. Madison and his supporters in Congress upheld American independence in oppo-

29See J. R. Pole, "Historians and the Problem of Early American Democracy," *American Historical Review* LXVII (Apr. 1962), 626–46; David H. Fischer, *The Revolution of American Conservatism* (New York, 1965), 1–28, 201–26; Sidney H. Aronson, *Status and Kinship in the Higher Civil Service* (Cambridge, England, 1964), 1–2.
30See Combs, *Jay Treaty*, ix–x.

sition to Hamilton's economic measures, but they were unable to arouse popular interest until the Anglo-French struggle beginning early in 1793 clarified the issues in terms of political principles. Almost from the outbreak of war, and certainly from the arrival of the minister of Republican France, Citizen Genet, Americans were ideologically and emotionally involved in the contest. Widespread and deep-seated partisan passions were awakened, if not created, and local and national issues were simplified and dramatized in the context of the assumed European death struggle between despotism and liberty, as many put it, or between order and anarchy, as it seemed to others. If it is true that ideological passions have only rarely disrupted the normal calm of the American political process, this crisis, coming to a head in the uproar over the Jay Treaty, was certainly a first, and decided, exception. As one historian has suggested, the political battles of the mid-1790s were all the more bitter because the legitimacy of political parties themselves was not yet recognized; both Federalists and Republicans assumed that they represented the tradition and the will of the nation; and each side believed the other was disloyal to the national heritage, especially to the heritage of the American Revolution.[31]

Federalist leaders used every means at their disposal to win their battles over foreign policy. In the struggle over the Jay Treaty, they managed to purge their last opponents from the government. Their use of the failing Washington illustrated their cynical ruthlessness. Repeatedly, they pressed the prestige

31 Paul Goodman, "The First American Party System," in William N. Chambers and Walter D. Burnham, eds., The American Party Systems: Stages of Political Development (New York, 1967), 75, 57; William N. Chambers, "Party Development and the American Mainstream," in ibid., 28; Hofstadter, Idea of a Party System, 124–25; James M. Banner, To the Hartford Convention (New York, 1970), 122–67. See also William N. Chambers, Political Parties in a New Nation (New York, 1963); Morton Grodzins, "Political Parties and the Crisis of Succession in the United States: the Case of 1800," in Joseph LaPalombara and Myron Weiner, eds., Political Parties and Political Development (Princeton, 1966), 303–27; Marshall J. Smelser, "The Federalist Period as an Age of Passion," American Quarterly X (Winter 1958), 391–419; and John R. Howe, Jr., "Republican Thought and the Political Violence of the 1790's," American Quarterly XIX (Summer 1967), 147–65.

of the old hero into their service and wrung from him support of measures he disliked or did not fully understand.[32] It was natural that on Washington's death the British minister should particularly praise "... the part he had taken during the last years of his life in opposition to the system of the present rulers of France...." But Washington dead was of no further use to the Hamiltonians. Liston's report of the first Washington birthday celebration explained the real feeling of those who owed to him most of their successes: "Notwithstanding this ostentatious display of regret and veneration, I find a great proportion of his apparent friends and intimate acquaintances more inclined to depreciate his merits than to exalt his fame, and he seems already to be in a great measure forgotten by the multitude." Washington had carried the flame of independence through the Revolution and had become its personification; in his last years he became a figurehead and a tool of Hamilton. His greatness comes from his earlier career, and it was that which "the multitude" continued to honor. In his second term as President, Washington belonged only to the Federalists, and after their final failure even gratitude was absent.[33]

Following their successful drive toward an accommodation with England, the High Federalists of the Pickering persuasion[34] worked steadily for an active role in Britain's conflict with France, in defiance even of their erstwhile mentor, Hamilton. They had converted an ally into an enemy by Jay's treaty; now they tried to convert the former enemy into an ally. A series of insults to France—the recall of Monroe, the appointment of the

[32]Richard B. Morris, in his edition of Hamilton's writings, *Alexander Hamilton and the Founding of the Nation* (New York, 1957), vii, describes the old commander's role: Washington was "perhaps Hamilton's greatest admirer, and certainly his chief disciple."

[33]Liston to Grenville, Dec. 21, 1799, Feb. 2, 1800, F. O. 5, 25, 29. See Charles, *Origins of American Party System*, 52; DeConde, *Entangling Alliance*, 509–11.

[34]Gerald H. Clarfield, *Timothy Pickering and American Diplomacy* (Columbia, Mo., 1969), vii–ix, says that Pickering's objectives from 1795 on were to: "... end the threat of British harassment of American commerce, throw the weight of the United States into the scales against the French Revolution, afford British naval protection for American shipping threatened by French cruisers, and lastly, disarm the opponents of government at home."

432

Federalist, C. C. Pinckney, and the composition of the first mission of President Adams—was followed by the "XYZ frenzy." Both American and French historians have been surprisingly unanimous in accepting the version of the XYZ affair related by John Marshall, who was hardly an objective reporter.[35] The record shows that the truth was much more complicated and that heaping the entire blame on Talleyrand is mistaken. The circumstances under which the mission was sent, the instructions of the commissioners, and the personalities of the commissioners were together enough to make its outcome precarious. Of those involved in this episode, only Talleyrand and Gerry were clearly working for peace, and Gerry was betrayed at the crucial moment by his own indecision. Considering the state of French fortunes in Europe at this time, its seems likely that the United States missed an opportunity in the spring and summer of 1798 to negotiate a better settlement with France than was obtainable in 1800. Federalist ideologues were not interested in neutrality in 1795, when they championed the Jay Treaty in the name of peace, or in 1798, when they used the XYZ affair to provoke war. Pickering, Wolcott, McHenry, and their senatorial collaborators paraded the nation's wounded honor as a cloak for their frantic efforts to obtain a declaration of war, which they coveted to strike at the French Revolution and to crush their opposition at home and hold on to their offices and power. Had John Adams been blessed with a quicker sense of irony, he might have appreciated Dr. Johnson's remark, as reported by Boswell, that patriotism is the last refuge of a scoundrel.

35This applies not only to the tireless, Napoleon-worshipping school of French historians which consistently condemns Talleyrand for his "treason" against their hero, but also to others of entirely different persuasions. See, for example, Guyot, *Le Directoire et la Paix de l'Europe*, 559ff. This subject is treated incidentally in the brilliant book of Pieter Geyl, *Napoleon, For and Against* (New Haven, 1949). John Marshall, besides maintaining the Supreme Court of the U. S. as a citadel of federalism for thirty-four years, led the parade of Federalist historians with his *Life of George Washington* 5 vols. (Philadelphia, 1804–1807). Probably no group of political leaders comparable in size has been so prolific, nor had descendants so loyally industrious, as that which presided over the American government from 1789 to 1801. The wealth of easily accessible Federalist materials must have influenced historical writing, if only through the sheer weight of repetition.

433

The High Federalists were cheated of their French war by Talleyrand, and by Adams—perhaps one should say, Adams and son. At the eleventh hour the moderate Federalists drew back, thanks largely to the prodding of Talleyrand, and federalism collapsed. Adams had saved the peace and prevented his country's falling into the hands of a militaristic oligarchy; Hamiltonian intrigues with Britain and the South American revolutionist Miranda suggest the United States may even have been spared a Bonaparte.[36] Hamilton himself, who, as one historian has noted, had "swung like a pendulum" between war and accommodation, was closer to political realities than his irreconcilable followers. Almost as the convention was being signed he wrote: "Of one thing I am sure, if France will slide into a state of Peace *de facto*, we must meet her on that ground. The actual posture of European affairs and the opinions of our people demand an accommodating course."[37]

Of the amazing occurrences of the election campaign of 1800, one of the strangest was the effort of the High Federalists to avert the defeat their divisions invited by claiming credit for peace with France. Assertions that the Convention of 1800 was a diplomatic triumph for Napoleon and, by implication, a defeat for the United States, came later.[38]

In fact, the convention is rivaled only by the peace treaty with England of 1783 as the most fortunate peace settlement ever ne-

[36]See Dauer, *Adams Federalists*, 172–90; Kurtz, *Presidency of Adams*, 353; Marshall J. Smelser, "George Washington Declines the Part of El Libertador," *W & M Quarterly* 3d ser., XI (Jan. 1954), 42–51. Merrill Peterson is doubtless correct in his judgment that "Hamilton's commitment was not to America, but to his own glorious image of a great nation." Review of Clinton Rossiter, *Alexander Hamilton and the Constitution* (New York, 1964), in *W & M Quarterly*, 3d ser. XXII (Jan. 1966), 142. John Adams related the story of the South American chimera to James Lloyd in a series of letters in Feb., Mar., and Apr. 1815. *Works of Adams* X, 126–31, 134–58.

[37]DeConde, *Quasi-War*, 332; Hamilton to Secretary of State John Marshall, Oct. 2, 1800, quoted in Rossiter, *Hamilton and Constitution*, 313, from letter in private collection.

[38]Elbridge Gerry told Jefferson that Federalist insistence that the government's "martial attitude" in the spring of 1798 had prevented war was ridiculous because such an attitude was not then known in Paris and would have been laughed at anyway. Jan. 29, 1801, Gerry Papers, Massachusetts Historical Society.

gotiated by the United States.[39] Like any durable international agreement, it was mutually beneficial; if Napoleon could claim a diplomatic victory, so could the United States. The public avowal of a common Franco-American interest in freedom of the seas for neutral trade was useful in furthering Napoleon's scheme for the organization of a new League of Armed Neutrality of the Baltic Powers; and it reiterated the traditional American commitment to "free ships, free goods" which the Jay Treaty had put in question. Ending the limited hostilities with the United States gave Napoleon an initial success in his effort to bring about a general pacification; and the abrogation of the Franco-American treaties of 1778 formally released the United States from an entanglement which had become inconvenient, if not onerous. The mutual relinquishment of the alliance enabled President Jefferson to pursue neutrality without troublesome legal connections with any of the hostile powers.[40]

Of the "causes of the approaching triumph of the Democratick interest" which Liston enumerated to Grenville on October 8, 1800, the "most efficient of all" was continuing British depredations on American commerce.[41] Federalist foreign policy had brought the United States full circle, and Jefferson as President had to start again where he had begun as secretary of state eight years before. The French Revolution and the Federalist struggle against it both were over, and neutrality would at last become feasible.

---

[39]It is worth noting that peace commissioners in every instance since American Independence had succeeded by violating their instructions: Franklin, Adams, and Jay in 1782; Jay in 1794; Ellsworth, Davie, and Murray in 1800; and Murray in 1801. The notable failure was the Pinckney–Marshall–Gerry mission of 1797, and it might have succeeded had the commissioners together, and later Gerry alone, done likewise. DeConde, *Quasi-War*, 332–33.

[40]*Ibid.*, 338. DeConde notes also that "isolationism, in the sense of the American government seeking to sever political, and even diplomatic, connections in Europe," was Jeffersonian, not Federalist, policy. *Ibid.*, 335.

[41]F. O. 5, 29.

# French and American Foreign Ministers and Ministers Plenipotentiary

(All dates refer to time entered upon service.)

| French Foreign Ministers | U. S. Secretaries of State | French Ministers to U. S. | U. S. Ministers to France |
|---|---|---|---|
| Montmorin Feb. 1787 | Jefferson Mar. 21, 1790 | Otto (Chargé) Oct. 1789 | Short (Chargé) Sept. 1789 |
| DeLessart Nov. 28, 1791 | | Ternant Aug. 10, 1791 | |
| Dumouriez Mar. 17, 1792 | | | Morris May 8, 1792 |
| Faillac June 14, 1792 | | | |
| Chambonas June 17, 1792 | | | |
| Sainte-Croix Aug. 1, 1792 | | | |
| Lebrun Aug. 12, 1792 | | | |
| Deforgues June 14, 1793 | | Genet May 18, 1793 | |
| Buchot April, 1794 | Randolph Jan. 2, 1794 | Fauchet Feb. 20, 1794 | Monroe Aug. 2, 1794 |
| Miot Nov. 1794 | | | |
| Colchen Feb. 1795 | | | |
| Delacroix Nov. 1795 | Pickering Aug. 20, 1795 | Adet June 19, 1795 | Pinckney Dec. 1796 |
| Talleyrand July 18, 1797 | | Létombe (Con. Gen.) Nov. 7, 1796 | Marshall; Pinckney; Gerry Oct. 4, 1797 |
| Reinhard July 20, 1799 | | | |
| Talleyrand Nov. 21, 1799 | Marshall June 6, 1800 | Pichon (Chargé) Mar. 17, 1801 | Ellsworth; Davie; Murray Mar. 3, 1800 |

Chronology

*1790*

March 21      Thomas Jefferson takes office as first American secretary of state

*1791*

August 10      Ternant arrives at Philadelphia
October 1      Legislative Assembly

*1792*

January      Morris confirmed by U. S. Senate as minister to France
April 20      France declares war on Austria
September 21      Abolition of the Monarchy: France proclaimed a Republic
     National Convention
September 22      First day of the year I of French Republic
November 19      Convention offers aid to republicans under monarchial governments

*1793*

January 21      Execution of Louis XVI
February 1      England, Holland, Spain and the Holy Roman Empire form coalition against Republican France
April 6      Mountain (Jacobins) wins control of committees (General Security and Public Safety)
April 8      Genet lands at Charleston
April 22      Washington's Neutrality Proclamation
July      Robespierre appointed to Committee of Public Safety
August 22      Thomas Jefferson's indictment of Genet sent to Morris
1793–1794      Reign of Terror under Committee of Public Safety, dominated by Robespierre
November 17      Robespierre announces his American policy
December 15      Thomas Jefferson's Report on Commerce
December 31      Thomas Jefferson's retirement

### *1794*

| | |
|---|---|
| January–April | Congressional debate over Madison's Resolutions |
| March 6 | Fauchet's proclamation ordering Frenchmen to respect American neutrality |
| March 24 | Robespierre destroys Hébertists |
| March 26 | Thirty-day embargo voted by Congress |
| April 6 | Robespierre destroys Dantonists |
| April 18 | Jay confirmed as envoy to London |
| May 28 | Monroe confirmed as envoy to Paris |
| July 27 | Nine Thermidor—Fall of Robespierre |
| July 1794– May 1795 | Thermidoreans liquidate Terror, Robespierre's economic system, and remnants of Mountain |
| August 15 | Monroe received by National Convention |
| November 24 | Jay signs treaty with England |

### *1795*

| | |
|---|---|
| March 5 | Treaty of Basel—Prussia withdraws from coalition, followed by lesser German principalities |
| June 22 | Spain withdraws from coalition in a second treaty of Basel |
| June 24 | Senate approves Jay Treaty |
| August 14 | Washington ratifies Jay Treaty |
| August 22 | French Constitution of 1795 |
| October 26 | The Directory. New Government takes office under Constitution of 1795 |
| October 27 | Pinckney signs treaty with Spain |

### *1796*

| | |
|---|---|
| January 16 | Delacroix's Report on United States |
| April– July 1797 | Bonaparte's Italian campaign—Austria defeated, creation of satellite republics in Italy |
| July 2 | Directory decrees that U. S. commerce will be treated by France as by England |
| September 17 | Washington's Farewell Address |
| November 15 | Adet's manifesto to Pickering |

### *1797*

| | |
|---|---|
| January 19 | Pickering's report on France in reply to Adet's manifesto |
| January 23 | C. C. Pinckney ordered out of France |
| March 2 | Decree of Directory abandoning "free ships, free goods" in regard to U. S. commerce |

439

| | |
|---|---|
| May 31 | Adams nominates mission to France |
| June 1 | Otto's memoir on U. S. |
| June 20 | Pastoret's attack on Directory's American policy |
| September 4 | Eighteen Fructidor. Coup d'état of Jacobin Directors against moderate peace party |
| October 8 | Marshall, Pinckney, and Gerry received by Talleyrand |
| October 17 | Bonaparte's Treaty of Campo Formio. Peace with Austria, England isolated |

### 1798

| | |
|---|---|
| January 18 | Decree of Directory subjecting American cargoes with any article of English produce to confiscation |
| April 3 | Adams sends XYZ dispatches to Congress |
| July 7 | Congress abrogates treaties with France |
| May, June, July | Congress passes war measures directed against France |
| July 27 | Talleyrand presents Dupont's report on French depredations to Directory |
| June–September | Murray–Pichon conversations |
| October 1 | Gerry lands at Boston with Talleyrand correspondence |
| December 24 | Great Britain raises Second Coalition against France |

### 1799

| | |
|---|---|
| February 18 | Adams nominates Murray as minister to France |
| October 16 | Adams orders Ellsworth and Davie to depart for France |
| October 22 | Russia withdraws from coalition |
| November 9 | Eighteen Brumaire. Bonaparte overthrows Directory, establishes Consulate |
| December 14 | Washington's death |
| December 24 | Constitution of year VIII. Consulate adopted by people. Bonaparte becomes First Consul and virtual dictator. |

### 1800

| | |
|---|---|
| November 1799–April 1800 | England and Austria reject Bonaparte's peace overtures |
| March 7 | Bonaparte receives Ellsworth, Davie, and Murray |

| | |
|---|---|
| June 14 | Bonaparte's victory at Marengo |
| September 30, October 3 | Convention of 1800 signed between France and United States |
| October 1 | Spain retrocedes Louisiana to France |
| October– December | Formation of League of Armed Neutrality of Northern Neutrals |

### *1801*

| | |
|---|---|
| February 9 | Treaty of Lunéville. Peace with Austria |
| March 4 | Jefferson assumes presidency |
| December 19 | Senate resolution considering convention fully ratified |
| December 21 | Convention proclaimed by President Jefferson |

### *1802*

| | |
|---|---|
| March 27 | Treaty of Amiens. Peace between France and Great Britain |

# Note on Sources

The truly formidable amount of material relating to the diplomacy of the Federalist era would require a small volume simply to list. What follows is intended to identify the principal primary sources, both manuscript and printed, which I have used. Numerous secondary works are cited in the footnotes, and many others can be found in the bibliographical apparatuses of the standard diplomatic history textbooks, such as Samuel Flagg Bemis, *A Diplomatic History of the United States* 5th ed. (New York, 1965), Thomas A. Bailey, *A Diplomatic History of the American People* 7th ed. (New York, 1964), Julius W. Pratt, *A History of American Foreign Policy* 2d ed. (Englewood Cliffs, N. J., 1965), Robert H. Ferrell, *American Diplomacy* 2d ed. (New York, 1969), and Daniel M. Smith, *The American Diplomatic Experience* (Boston, 1972). The best of the texts, in my opinion, is Alexander DeConde, *History of American Foreign Policy* 2d ed. (New York, 1971), which brings up to date the standard guides: Samuel Flagg Bemis and Grace Gardner Griffin, *Guide to the Diplomatic History of the United States, 1775–1921* (Washington, D. C., 1935); Oscar Handlin *et al.*, *Harvard Guide to American History* (Cambridge, Mass., 1954); the Library of Congress' *A Guide to the Study of the United States of America* (Washington, D. C., 1960); and the American Historical Association's *Guide to Historical Literature* (New York, 1961). Useful, too, are Alexander DeConde, *New Interpretations in American Foreign Policy* 2d ed. (Washington, D. C., 1961), and Keith B. Berwick, *The Federal Age, 1789–1829* (Washington, D. C., 1961), both pamphlets in the "Service Center for Teachers of History" series of the American Historical Association.

I. General works dealing with Federalist foreign policy include Arthur B. Darling, *Our Rising Empire* (New Haven, 1940); A. L. Burt, *The United States, Great Britain, and British North America from the Revolution to the Establishment of Peace after the War of 1812* (New Haven, 1940); Felix Gilbert, *To the Farewell Address: Ideas of Early American Foreign Policy* (Princeton, 1961), and Paul A. Varg, *Foreign Policies of the Founding Fathers* (East Lansing, Mich.,

1963; Penguin Books, 1970). A fine synthesis which incorporates the most recent scholarship is Lawrence S. Kaplan, *Colonies into Nation: American Diplomacy, 1763–1801* (New York, 1972). Kaplan calls his book an "interpretive history"; it is perforce a historiographical essay and contains, in addition, an excellent bibliographical essay on "Further Reading." Old, but still helpful, is Samuel Flagg Bemis, ed., *The American Secretaries of State and Their Diplomacy* 10 vols. (New York, 1927–29); vol. I covers the Washington and Adams administrations. Ruhl J. Bartlett, ed., *The Record of American Diplomacy* (New York, 1947, and later editions), is a convenient collection of pertinent documents.

II. The principal manuscript source for this volume is the Archives des Affaires Étrangères, Correspondance Politique, États-Unis, especially vols. 34–52, and the Supplément, États-Unis. These items are housed in the Ministry of Foreign Affairs in Paris, but photocopies are also available in the Manuscripts Division of the Library of Congress, Washington, D. C. An annotated listing of the collection is in Waldo G. Leland, John J. Meng, and Abel Doysié, eds., *Guide to Materials for American History in the Libraries and Archives of Paris, Vol. II: Archives of the Ministry of Foreign Affairs* (Washington, D. C., 1943). A summary of French manuscript material in the Library of Congress is James E. O'Neill, "Copies of French Manuscripts for American History in the Library of Congress," *Journal of American History* LI (Mar. 1965), 674–91. Much material from the French archives has been printed, particularly in *Annual Reports of the American Historical Association.* The Hauterive Journal kept by the French consul at New York for a few months in 1793 is in the New-York Historical Society in New York City. It is discussed in Frances S. Childs, "The Hauterive Journal," *The New-York Historical Society Quarterly* XXXIII (Apr. 1949), 69–86.

British Foreign Office manuscripts are maintained in the Public Records Office in London, but transcripts are in the Library of Congress. The Instructions to and Dispatches from ministers to the United States were most useful, and some material from these has likewise been printed. Vols. 4–29 are pertinent to this study.

While the records of the Department of State are maintained in the National Archives in Washington, D. C., the establishment of regional depositories is gradually making microfilm copies more widely accessible on a selective basis. The well-organized series of Instructions and Dispatches to and from United States representatives in France during the period of this study, however, remain in

444

Washington. Most of the important communications have been printed, although not always with complete accuracy.

Major collections of the papers of George Washington, Thomas Jefferson, Alexander Hamilton, James Madison, James Monroe, and William Short are in the Library of Congress, while the great collections of papers of the Adams family, as well as those of Timothy Pickering and Elbridge Gerry, are in the Massachusetts Historical Society in Boston. The papers of Rufus King and Albert Gallatin are in the New-York Historical Society. As the footnotes indicate, however, the great number of printed collections of the writings of early American public figures has generally been sufficient.

III. Printed general collections of official documents useful to this study include James D. Richardson, ed., *Messages and Papers of the Presidents* 10 vols. (Washington, D. C., 1896); Hunter Miller, ed., *Treaties and Other International Acts of the United States of America, 1776–1863* 8 vols. (Washington, D. C., 1931–48); Athanase J. L. Jourdan, Decrusy, & Francois A. Isambert, eds., *Receuil Général des Anciennes Lois Françaises* 29 vols. (Paris, 1822–33); *Annals of the Congress of the United States, 1789–1824* 42 vols. (Washington, D. C., 1834–56); Walter Lowrie and Matthew St. Clair Clarke, eds., *American State Papers. Class I. Foreign Relations* 6 vols. (Washington, D. C., 1832–59); and *American State Papers. Class IV. Commerce and Navigation* 2 vols. (Washington, D. C., 1832–34).

Specialized collections of official documents include Douglas Brymner, *Report on Canadian Archives, 1890* (Ottawa, 1891); A. DuCasse, *Histoire des Négociations Diplomatiques Relatives aux Traités de Mortfontaine, de Lunéville et d'Amiens* 3 vols. (Paris, 1855); Great Britain, Historical Manuscripts Commission, *The Manuscripts of J. B. Fortescue, Esq., preserved at Dropmore* [papers of Lord Grenville], 3 vols. (London, 1897–1927); J. Franklin Jameson, ed., "Letters of Phineas Bond, British Consul at Philadelphia, to the Foreign Office of Great Britain, 1790–1794," in *Annual Report of the American Historical Association, 1897* (1898); Joseph Fauchet, "Mémoire sur les États-Unis d'Amérique," ed. by Carl Lokke, in *Annual Report of the American Historical Association, 1936* I (1938); Bernard Mayo, ed., "Instructions to the British Ministers to the United States, 1791–1812," in *Annual Report of the American Historical Association, 1936* III (1941); *Correspondence de Napoleon I$^{er}$, publié par ordre de l'empéreur Napoléon III* 32 vols. (Paris, 1858–70); *Naval Documents related to the Quasi-War with France* 7 vols. (Washington, D. C., 1935); Louis-Guillaume Otto, "Considérations sur la conduite

du gouvernement Américain envers la France, depuis le commencement de la Révolution jusqu'en 1797," ed. by Gilbert Chinard, in
*Bulletin de l'Institut Française de Washington*, No. XVI (Dec. 1943);
James B. Scott, ed., *The Controversy over Neutral Rights between
the United States and France 1797–1800* (New York, 1917); the sev-
eral magnificent collections edited by Frederick Jackson Turner:
"Correspondence of the French Ministers to the United States, 1791–
1797," in *Annual Report of the American Historical Association,
1903* (1904); "Documents on the Blount Conspiracy, 1795–1797," in
*American Historical Review* X (Apr. 1905); "Documents on the
Relations of France to Louisiana, 1792–95," in *American Historical
Review* III (1898); "Mangourit Correspondence in Respect to Genet's
Projected Attack upon the Floridas, 1793–94," in *Annual Report of
the American Historical Association for 1897* (1898); and "Selections
from the Draper Collection in the possession of the State Historical
Society of Wisconsin, to elucidate the proposed French expedition
under George Rogers Clark against Louisiana, in the years 1793–94,"
in *Annual Report of the American Historical Association, 1896* I
(1897). Finally, the U. S. Treasury Department issued a pamphlet on
November 8, 1923: "Loans and Subsidies Granted by France to the
United States during and immediately following the Revolutionary
War."

IV. Published collections of the writings of many of the founding
fathers are numerous. Of the several editions of the Federalist Papers,
perhaps the best is Jacob E. Cooke, ed., *The Federalist* (Middletown,
Conn., 1961). *The Adams Papers* currently in process by Harvard
University Press, under the editorship of Lyman H. Butterfield, do
not yet cover the period of this study, but the entire collection of the
Massachusetts Historical Society has been microfilmed and copies
are in several regional depositories, notably for my purposes the
Library of the University of Tennessee at Knoxville. For some time
to come, however, a principal source concerning John Adams will
remain Charles Francis Adams, ed., *The Works of John Adams* 10
vols. (Boston, 1856); and for his son, Worthington C. Ford, ed., *The
Writings of John Quincy Adams* 7 vols. (New York, 1913–17), and
Allan Nevins, ed., *The Diary of John Quincy Adams* (New York,
1951). A convenient collection of writings of the first two Adamses is
Adrienne Koch and William Peden, eds., *The Selected Writings of
John and John Quincy Adams* (New York, 1946). Collections of the
writings of other Federalist leaders include: Seth Ames, ed., *The
Works of Fisher Ames* 2 vols. (Boston, 1854); Elizabeth Donnan, ed.,

"Papers of James A. Bayard, 1796–1815," in *Annual Report of the American Historical Association, 1913* (1915), including some of Robert Goodloe Harper's letters to his constituents; Henry Cabot Lodge, *The Life and Letters of George Cabot* (Boston, 1877); J. Franklin Jameson, ed., "Letters of Stephen Higginson," in *Annual Report of the American Historical Association, 1896* I (1897); Charles R. King, ed., *The Life and Correspondence of Rufus King* 6 vols. (New York, 1894–1900); Henry P. Johnston, ed., *The Correspondence and Public Papers of John Jay* 4 vols. (New York, 1890–93); and George Gibbs, ed., *Memoirs of the Administrations of Washington and John Adams, edited from the Papers of Oliver Wolcott, Secretary of the Treasury* 2 vols. (New York, 1846).

In a different category are the two collections of Gouverneur Morris' writings, chiefly from Revolutionary France: Anne Cary Morris, ed., *The Diary and Letters of Gouverneur Morris* 2 vols. (New York, 1888); and the less inhibited Beatrix C. Davenport, ed., *A Diary of the French Revolution* 2 vols. (Boston, 1939). Although decidedly a Federalist by his second term, George Washington is of course in a special class: John C. Fitzpatrick, ed., *The Writings of George Washington* 39 vols. (Washington, D. C., 1931–41). Noteworthy for Washington's distillation of his presidential experience is Victor H. Paltsits, ed., *Washington's Farewell Address* (New York, 1935).

The chief printed source for Alexander Hamilton, from my point of view the central figure of the era, is rapidly becoming Harold C. Syrett and Jacob E. Cooke, eds., *The Papers of Alexander Hamilton*, which began appearing (Columbia University Press, New York) in 1961. Fifteen volumes have thus far been published, bringing the work up to the second half of 1793. For the period following, the only comprehensive sources are the very partisan Henry Cabot Lodge, ed., *The Works of Alexander Hamilton* 12 vols. (New York, 1904), which superseded Lodge's earlier edition, 9 vols. (New York, 1885–86), and John C. Hamilton, ed., *The Works of Alexander Hamilton* 7 vols. (New York, 1850–51). A very selective bicentennial collection is Richard B. Morris, ed., *Alexander Hamilton and the Founding of the Nation* (New York, 1957). Hamilton's great reports are conveniently collected in Jacob E. Cooke, ed., *The Reports of Alexander Hamilton* (New York, 1964).

The sources for Thomas Jefferson are numerous. The monumental Princeton University project, Julian P. Boyd, ed., *The Papers of Thomas Jefferson* (Princeton, 1950– ), extends down to March 1791 with vol. XVIII and thus was of limited use in this study. I have used, in addition, Paul L. Ford, ed., *The Writings of Thomas Jeffer-*

*son* 10 vols. (New York, 1892–99), and the less accurate but more extensive Andrew A. Lipscomb and Albert E. Bergh, eds., *The Writings of Thomas Jefferson* 20 vols. (Washington, D. C., 1903). Letters not found in either of these are included in Dumas Malone, ed., *Correspondence between Thomas Jefferson and Pierre Samuel duPont de Nemours, 1798–1817* (Boston, 1930). A convenient collection is Adrienne Koch and William Peden, eds., *The Life and Selected Writings of Thomas Jefferson* (New York, 1944).

Another major editorial undertaking is under way at the University of Chicago: *The Papers of James Madison*. The first five volumes, edited by William T. Hutchinson and William M. E. Rachal, carry the work only to the end of 1782. The standard collection therefore is still Gaillard Hunt, ed., *The Writings of James Madison* 9 vols. (New York, 1900–10), but there is material omitted by Hunt in *Letters and Other Writings of James Madison, published under the direction of the Congress of the United States* 4 vols. (Philadelphia, 1865). The only collection of Monroe's writings is Stanislaus M. Hamilton, ed., *The Writings of James Monroe* 7 vols. (New York, 1898–1903), although Monroe's notoriously indecipherable handwritings did not prevent the publication of Stuart Gerry Brown, ed., *The Autobiography of James Monroe* (Syracuse, 1959). To these works should be added James Monroe's own account of his mission to France: *A View of the Conduct of the Executive in the Foreign Affairs of the United States, Connected with the Mission to the French Republic During the Years 1794, 5, 6. By James Monroe Late Minister Plenipotentiary to the Said Republic Illustrated by His Instruction and Other Authentic Documents* (Philadelphia, 1798).

William Maclay, The Journal of William Maclay (New York, 1927), is useful for the beginnings of political conflict in the first Congress of the United States. Edmund Randolph, *A Vindication of Mr. Randolph's Resignation* (Philadelphia, 1795), is his own explanation of his resignation as secretary of state. A good deal of useful material is contained in Lyman H. Butterfield, ed., *Letters of Benjamin Rush* 2 vols. (Princeton, 1951).

Writings of non-Americans cited in the text include George Duruy, ed., *Memoirs of Barras* 3 vols. (London, 1895); Hans Huth and Wilma J. Pugh, trans. and eds., "Talleyrand in America as a Financial Promoter, 1794–96," in *Annual Report of the American Historical Association, 1941* II (1942); and Bradford Perkins, ed., "Lord Hawkesbury and the Jay-Grenville Negotiations," *Mississippi Valley Historical Review* XL (1953–54).

V. The vitality of American scholarship is nowhere better illustrated than in work on the early national period of our history. The stream of books and articles on the origins of American foreign policy and the men who made it of a generation or two ago has become a flood in this one. Too numerous to list here, those which I have specifically used are cited in the footnotes. New studies on the origins of political parties, on the intellectual foundations of foreign policy, and on the crosscurrents of revolutionary activity in the international relations of the eighteenth century abound, and biographies of important figures have now reached down to the third level of Federalist and Republican leaders.

It is perhaps worth remarking, however, that where biographies of Americans are concerned the dichotomous Jefferson-Hamilton framework still prevails. The magisterial multivolume studies of Thomas Jefferson by Dumas Malone and of James Madison by Irving Brant command the Republican scene. The more modest works on Alexander Hamilton by Broadus Mitchell and John C. Miller provide the fulcra for a host of specialized studies of Hamilton and of biographies of lesser Federalist lights, some of which border on the extravagant. The reader may conclude that my work falls within the same perhaps inescapable dichotomy.

# Index

Fenwick, Joseph, 116
Fleurieu, Charles Pierre Claret, 391,
425. *See also* commissioners, French
Forfait, Pierre-Alexandre-Laurent, 395,
423
Forrest, General Uriah, 373
Fouché, Joseph, 388
France, 4; U. S. attachment to, 5, 7, 9;
and U. S. commerce, 13, 16, 25, 28–29,
51, 107; policies toward U. S. of, 150;
Adams's first mission to, 279–87; and
"XYZ" affair, 311–24. *See also*
commerce, U. S., with France;
Directory; Gironde; Jacobins;
Thermidoreans
Franco-American alliance, cornerstone
of U. S. foreign policy, 4; U. S.
guarantee of West Indies of, 5, 44;
Gironde and, 44–45, 48; Hamilton
and, 52–53, 58, 83; Directory considers
terminated, 238, 241; and Washington's Farewell Address, 268; Congress
abrogates, 331, 351; in Mortfontaine
negotiations, 394–98, 403, 405–406;
and unilateral abrogation of, 426–27n
Franco-American consular convention,
29, 203–204
Franco-American Treaty of Commerce
(1778); enemy privateers in, 5, 8, 29,
31, 43–44; Genet on, 53, 58, 69; Morris
and, 102, 108–12, 114, 125, 173; French
violations of, 179–82, 193, 200, 203–204,
248; Congress abrogates, 331; in
Mortfontaine negotiations, 394–98,
403; Talleyrand on, 405–406, 408;
426–27n
Franklin, Benjamin, 6, 29, 30, 118
"free ships, free goods," 5–6, 6n;
Jefferson and, 7, 62; Grenville and, 63,
108; Hamilton and, 137, 184, 185;
Directory and, 246, 264; Delacroix and,
304; in Convention of 1800, 408
French Revolution, American
enthusiasm for, 4, 41, 48–49, 127, 428

Gadsden, Christopher, 3–4
Galbaud, General T. F., 84, 85
Gallatin, Albert, 364
Gates, General Horatio, 271
Genet, Edmond Charles: instructions
to, 42–46, 56–57, 58–59; and U. S. debt
to France, 65–66; and U. S. neutrality,
69–70; on Washington, 73; on Jefferson,
73, 88; and Louisiana project, 81–83;
effect on Republican party of, 76, 89;
U. S. demands recall of, 78–80; charges
of Jay and King against, 79–80; and
Canada project, 82–84, 86–87; estimate
of, 95–96, 123; publishes instructions,
156
Gerry, Elbridge, 268, 274n, 280;
nominated to French mission, 284, 314;
and Marshall, 320, 330; Barlow on,
336n; Skipwith on, 337–38n; and
Talleyrand, 340–43, 347, 349; and
quarrel with Pickering, 362; defended
by Adams, 362, 363n, 381
Gironde, 39–59; and U. S. parties, 40;
and U. S. neutrality, 59, 63, 67, 97;
downfall of, 89, 95, 122, 125, 150
Godoy, Manuel de (the Prince of the
Peace), 250
Gohier, Louis Antoine, 385
Goodrich, Chauncey, 377
Gore, Christopher, 224
*Grange* (British ship), 61, 64
Great Britain, 4, 5; and foreign trade,
7–9, 11, 13; policy toward U. S. of, 63,
143–48; and war crisis with U. S.,
150–51, 152. *See also* commerce, U. S.,
with Great Britain
Grenville, William Wyndam, Lord, 34,
46, 47, 136; smoothes Jay negotiations,
182; and armed neutrality, 183–84,
184–85n; on Randolph, 206–208; on
Franco-American war, 361
Guillemardet, Ferdinand-Pierre, 345

Hamilton, Alexander: and U. S.
commercial policy, 13–14, 15, 17;
career, political philosophy of, 18–25,
32; and Nootka Sound dispute, 35–36,
36–38; interference of, 54, 62–63, 71,
74; and Genet's recall, 79; and
Hammond, 81, 143n; and British
commerce, 129, 132, 144–45, 148; and
Jay mission, 151, 152; and U. S. debt to
France, 157, 164; and Jay negotiations,
183–84, 198–99, 204–206; on Randolph,
214–15; defends Jay Treaty, 222–25;
and Monroe, 257; and Washington's
Farewell Address, 267–68, 269; and
election of 1796, 270, 273; outlines
policy toward France, 273–75; and